Peaceland

Conflict Resolution and the Everyday Politics of International Intervention

This book suggests a new explanation for why international peace interventions often fail to reach their full potential. Based on several years of ethnographic research in conflict zones around the world, it demonstrates that everyday elements – such as the expatriates' social habits and usual approaches to understanding their areas of operation – strongly influence peacebuilding effectiveness. Individuals from all over the world and all walks of life share numerous practices, habits, and narratives when they serve as interveners in conflict zones. These common attitudes and actions enable foreign peacebuilders to function in the field, but they also result in unintended consequences that thwart international efforts. Certain expatriates follow alternative modes of thinking and acting, often with notable results, but they remain in the minority. Through an in-depth analysis of the interveners' everyday life and work, this book proposes innovative ways to better help host populations build a sustainable peace.

Séverine Autesserre is Assistant Professor of Political Science, specializing in International Relations and African Studies, at Barnard College, Columbia University. Autesserre's work has appeared in such publications as *Foreign Affairs, International Organization, African Affairs*, the *New York Times*, the *International Herald Tribune, Critique Internationale*, the *Review of African Political Economy*, the *African Studies Review*, the *African Security Review*, and the *Journal of Humanitarian Affairs*. Her previous book, *The Trouble with the Congo: Local Violence and the Failure of International Peacebuilding* (Cambridge University Press, 2010), won the 2012 Grawemeyer Award for Ideas Improving World Order and the 2011 Chadwick Alger Prize presented by the International Studies Association to the best book on international organizations and multilateralism. Autesserre has won several prestigious fellowships for her work, notably research grants from the Harry Frank Guggenheim Foundation and the United States Institute of Peace.

Advance Praise for *Peaceland*

"In this groundbreaking inquest, Autesserre builds on her previous work on the Congo to show the vital significance of 'doing' peacebuilding from the ground up, with sustained attention to the local dynamics of conflict. The number of case studies investigated, the originality of her methodology, the breadth of supporting evidence, and the range of arresting insights are among the principal merits of this outstanding contribution. One can only hope that it will be widely read by peacebuilders everywhere, but also by scholars, journalists, and policy wonks in search of a new angle of vision for making 'Peaceland' a reality."

> – René Lemarchand, Emeritus Professor, University of Florida

"Essential reading for practitioners, policy makers, and donors involved in international interventions in conflict areas. Drawing on her world-wide field experience, Professor Autesserre's comprehensive research offers new perspectives on how and why interveners should develop a thorough understanding of the local history, culture, and customs of populations in conflict zones. Much can be learned from her critical insights as we endeavor to assist those populations in danger."

> – Catherine Dumait-Harper, Former MSF Médecins Sans Frontières/Doctors Without Borders Representative to the United Nations

"In recent years peacebuilding has become something of a vogue in international circles. So Séverine Autesserre's book is a timely and well-reasoned reminder for all would-be peacebuilders and the organizations that stand behind them that they need to be prudent and patient in both their prescriptions for peace and the way they go about trying to achieve them. Good intentions are not enough."

> – Alan Doss, Senior Political Advisor, Kofi Annan Foundation

Problems of International Politics

Series Editors:

KEITH DARDEN, American University
IAN SHAPIRO, Yale University

The series seeks manuscripts central to the understanding of international politics that are empirically rich and conceptually innovative. It is interested in works that illuminate the evolving character of nation-states within the international system. It sets out three broad areas for investigation: 1. identity, security, and conflict; 2. democracy; and 3. justice and distribution.

Titles in the Series:
Şener Aktürk, *Regimes of Ethnicity and Nationhood in Germany, Russia, and Turkey*
Séverine Autesserre, *Peaceland: Conflict Resolution and the Everyday Politics of International Intervention*
Donald Horowitz, *Constitutional Change and Democracy in Indonesia*
Adria Lawrence, *Imperial Rule and the Politics of Nationalism: Anti-Colonial Protest in the French Empire*
Steven Levitsky and Lucan A. Way, *Competitive Authoritarianism: Hybrid Regimes After the Cold War*
Tarek Masoud, *Counting Islam: Religion, Class, and Elections in Egypt*
Harris Mylonas, *The Politics of Nation-Building: Making Co-Nationals, Refugees, and Minorities*

To the victims of violence and those who try to help them
And among the latter, of course, to Philippe

Peaceland

Conflict Resolution and the Everyday Politics of International Intervention

SÉVERINE AUTESSERRE

Barnard College, Columbia University

CAMBRIDGE
UNIVERSITY PRESS

CAMBRIDGE
UNIVERSITY PRESS

32 Avenue of the Americas, New York, NY 10013-2473, USA

Cambridge University Press is part of the University of Cambridge.

It furthers the University's mission by disseminating knowledge in the pursuit of education, learning, and research at the highest international levels of excellence.

www.cambridge.org
Information on this title: www.cambridge.org/9781107632042

First published 2014

Printed in the United States of America

A catalog record for this publication is available from the British Library.

Library of Congress Cataloging in Publication Data
Autesserre, Séverine, 1976–
Peaceland : conflict resolution and the everyday politics of international intervention / Séverine Autesserre.
    pages   cm
ISBN 978-1-107-05210-9 (hardback)
1. Peace-building – International cooperation.   2. Intercultural communication.   3. Peaceful change (International relations)   I. Title.
JZ5538.A87   2014
327.1–dc23   2013044465

ISBN 978-1-107-05210-9 Hardback
ISBN 978-1-107-63204-2 Paperback

Cover image: An Indian UN peacekeeper stands guard as hundreds of displaced civilians seek shelter near the UN base in Kiwanja, in eastern Democratic Republic of Congo, January 21, 2006. Copyright © David Lewis / Reuters / Corbis.

Contents

Figure and Tables

Figure

Tables

Acknowledgments

The individuals who have made this book possible span many countries and continents. Numerous international interveners and local people went out of their way, sometimes at great personal or professional risk, to facilitate my research. They provided opportunities for participant observations where I thought none were possible and put me in contact with interviewees who would never otherwise have come forward. Most of them had never met me and had no reason to confide in me in the first place. Still, they suffered my endless questions and trusted my promise to keep their answers confidential. I have cited some of these generous individuals in the book. Unfortunately, I would place many others – their lives or their careers – in jeopardy if I were to acknowledge them by name. To them, I can only extend my profound and heartfelt thanks. They shared their valuable time with me, invited me to become part of their worlds, and welcomed me when I did. It is because of them that my initial research project has developed into the book it is today.

Although it is customary to thank one's spouse at the end of the acknowledgements, mine deserves a place of honor, along with my interviewees and the contacts who facilitated my research. Philippe Rosen was with me throughout virtually all of my fieldwork. He dealt with the innumerable administrative, financial, logistical, and security challenges inherent to conducting research in conflict zones, allowing me to focus exclusively on collecting data. He was always there when I needed a sounding board for new ideas. Above all, he remained supportive even at the worst moments of my fieldwork, when I was certain that my efforts had all been for naught and that the project was going nowhere. He commented on multiple versions of this manuscript, from draft research proposals to proofs of the book. Thanks to his background as an intervener, he was able to help me put things into perspective and better understand issues that puzzled me. He was an integral part of the project, and he is the reason why I kept going when I otherwise would have quit.

I also owe special thanks to the colleagues who critiqued the entire manuscript, providing invaluable feedback on it. Michael Barnett and Elisabeth King read several versions of the book, and their contributions to my project were invaluable. Alexander Cooley, Kate Cronin-Furman, Michael Doyle, Joshua Goldstein, Robert Jervis, Jessica Luffman Anderson, Mahmood Mamdani, Kimberly Marten, Stephanie Schwartz, Jack Snyder, and Susan Woodward participated in my book incubation workshop in September 2012, offering crucial suggestions, criticisms, and advice. Catherine Dumait-Harper, Nimmi Gowrinathan, Sara Hellmueller, Timothy Longman, Roland Paris, and Laura Seay read a later version of the full manuscript, and their recommendations were critical in helping me finalize the book for publication. Other friends and colleagues also commented on various versions of what would eventually become the book, providing many insights, saving me from numerous errors, and suggesting a number of points that I develop in different chapters. They include: Nida Alahmad, Deborah Avant, Eyal Ben-Ari, Jonathan Blake, Christopher Blattman, Susanna Campbell, Jeffrey Checkel, Christine Cheng, Fletcher Cox, Alan Doss, Nathalie Duclos, Pierre Englebert, Michelle Farley, Catherine Goetze, Reyko Huang, Peter Katzenstein, Adam Kochanski, David Lanz, René Lemarchand, Sarah Lischer, Zachariah Mampilly, Reo Matzuzaki, Audra Mitchell, Adam Moore, Nadège Ragaru, Stephen Rock, Jessica Piombo, Vincent Pouliot, Ingrid Samset, Scott Straus, Fubing Su, and the participants of the numerous workshops, seminars, and conferences where I presented my research.

Brian Abelson, Danielle Boyda, Anneke Dunbar-Gronke, Jennifer Fearon, Allison Grossman, Lauren Hirsch, Katherine Cheasty Kornman, Caitlin Mollica, Alexandra Russo, Sarah Shore, and Kiran Stallone provided superb research and editing assistance. I am also grateful to the editors and anonymous reviewers of the journals that published early versions of sections of the book, notably *Critique Internationale* and *African Affairs*. I appreciate having been authorized to reproduce parts of these articles, namely "Dangerous Tales: Dominant Narratives on the Congo and Their Unintended Consequences" (*African Affairs*, 2012, volume 111, issue 443, pages 202–222, by permission of Oxford University Press) and "Construire la Paix: Conceptions Collectives de son Etablissement, de son Maintien et de sa Consolidation" (*Critique Internationale*, 2011, issue 51, pages 153–167). Finally, I am thankful to the editorial and production teams at Cambridge University Press, and especially to my editor Lew Bateman. Their hard work and undying belief in me and my project helped transform a raw manuscript into this real book.

The United States Institute of Peace and the Harry Frank Guggenheim Foundation provided the bulk of the funds I needed to conduct my fieldwork, and I am deeply appreciative of their generosity. Barnard College and Columbia University were wonderful environments for my research. My colleagues in the political science department went out of their way to ensure that I could take a leave long enough to conduct my fieldwork, gave me a home when I was back in New York, and provided much-needed moral support throughout the project. Many other Barnard faculty and students were similarly helpful, including our president, Debora Spar, who awarded me the additional financial resources necessary to complete my research. Colleagues across the street on Columbia University's main campus also offered invaluable support and advice – and, in the case of the Earth Institute, the Saltzman Institute for War and Peace Studies, and the Institute for Social and Economic Research and Policy, provided much-appreciated grants.

The friends, contacts, relatives, and colleagues with whom I informally brainstormed the topics of this book are too numerous to cite. I am deeply grateful to all of them, not only for their ideas, but also for the laughs we shared and the good moments we spent together. They gave me the energy to continue working on the manuscript when I felt like scrapping it and moving on.

Of course, the views expressed in this book do not necessarily reflect the views of my donors or contacts, and any errors in the text are mine alone. At the same time, the book is as much the child of my mind as it is a product of my environment – my interviewees, other research participants, husband, friends, colleagues, college, university – and I hope that the outcome is worth the efforts we have all put into it.

Introduction

I made a number of faux pas during my first day as an international intervener in a conflict zone. In July 2000, I arrived in Kosovo for a six-month mission and was preparing to attend my first coordination meeting with representatives of the United Nations, non-governmental organizations, donors, and military contingents of the North Atlantic Treaty Organization. My colleagues had told me that these meetings always began with some significant delay, so I decided to postpone my departure and finish some office work in the meantime. When I finally got there, however, I discovered that this particular gathering was under the supervision of a few military actors who, as it turned out, were invariably punctual. To make matters worse, the room's creaking door and regrettable arrangement eliminated any chance for stragglers to enter discretely. Not that I would have been inconspicuous anyway: I was visibly out of place from the moment I stepped inside. In the hope of being easily recognizable to my new colleagues, I had proudly put on a vest emblazoned with my employer's logo, but, to my dismay, the peacekeeping soldiers were the only people displaying their organizational affiliation. Eyes turned from the speaker to me and, for a few interminable moments, I became the center of attention. Mortified, I scurried to the back of the room to find a seat (and hide).

As my first month progressed, I made fewer missteps. Still, I was puzzled. I had two graduate degrees in international affairs and a year of experience as an intern with various humanitarian and peacebuilding agencies in New York. I had even worked as a volunteer for grassroots organizations in India, Nicaragua, and South Africa. By industry standards, I was perfectly qualified for my entry-level role in Kosovo, yet I felt utterly lost.

I ultimately realized that all of this theoretical knowledge and technical experience was not enough to ensure my success. The community of international interveners that I had joined in Kosovo had a culture of their own. I had naively expected my colleagues' attitudes and behaviors to be as varied as the countries they came from and the organizations they represented. In fact they shared a common collection of practices, habits, and narratives that shaped their every attitude and action. If I wanted to fit in, I had to learn the quotidian elements that veteran interveners saw as obvious, or even took for granted.

During my time in Kosovo, I did my best to assimilate into my new community and adapt to the international interveners' way of life. I followed my colleagues' standard practices, like attending coordination meetings, throwing going-away parties, and documenting every professional action in an endless stream of reports. I acquired their shared habits, such as following standard security procedures and socializing primarily with other expatriates. I became fluent in their language, with its technical vocabulary and alphabet soup of acronyms. I also learned their dominant narratives, notably those on our roles as foreign actors, our views of local counterparts, and our reasons for acting as we did. All in all, over the course of six months, I familiarized myself with the subtle hierarchy and the ritualized patterns of interaction that exist not only among interveners themselves but also between them and local populations. Plus, I figured out which meetings started on time and what I was supposed to wear to them.

These newly acquired competencies helped me successfully approach my later missions in Afghanistan and the Democratic Republic of Congo. Despite the staggering differences between each of these countries – in terms of geographies, cultures, people, languages, dynamics of violence, and conflict histories – the interveners who worked in them shared the same daily modes of operation. After learning the ropes in Kosovo, I never again felt out of place when I arrived to work in a new conflict zone, because the characteristics of the international approach – the identities of the participants, the relationships among them and with local populations, and the other everyday elements – were all familiar to me. As I moved from one place to another and found the same kind of environments, the same types of actors, and sometimes even the same individuals, I started to feel part of a transnational community, a community of expatriates who devote their lives to working in conflict zones. I felt that I had become part of a new world: Peaceland.[1]

Peaceland and Its Puzzles

For close to fifteen years, I have been attached to this world. My husband and most of our friends inhabit Peaceland, and I return to it frequently. As I traveled from one conflict zone to another, I became increasingly obsessed with the issue of efficacy. When in the field, during formal meetings or around drinks in the evening, my fellow Peacelanders and I regularly deliberated the same questions: Why do peace interventions regularly fail to reach their full potential? What can account for the effectiveness or ineffectiveness of international peacebuilding efforts? How can interveners be more successful when they are already effective and avoid failure otherwise? These subjects were and still are at the center of

[1] The neologism "Peaceland" is a paraphrase of the word "Aidland" coined in Apthorpe 2005.

policy and scholarly debates on intervention efforts. They are also the concerns that lie at the heart of this book.

For years, my friends and I returned to the same answers. To be more effective, we required more financial, logistical, and human resources. We also needed powerful states and organizations to stop ignoring or encouraging violence and, instead, start actively supporting peace. As I continued to live and work in intervention areas, I began to consider another explanation for ineffective peacebuilding: Many of the practices, habits, and narratives that shape international efforts on the ground – everyday elements that I had come to take for granted as an intervener – are, in fact, counterproductive.

This realization hit me ten years after my embarrassing first day in Kosovo, during one of my many sojourns in the Democratic Republic of Congo (henceforth, Congo), home to a conflict that ranks among the deadliest since World War II.[2] In an attempt to reconstruct state authority in the eastern part of the country, various international peacebuilding agencies had decided to assist the Congolese police in deploying officers to some of the most unstable areas. The implementation of the project began in May 2010, when the United Nations Office for Project Services (UNOPS) constructed police stations and helped transport Congolese police units to selected volatile villages. Upon completing this initiative, officials at the United Nations (UN) headquarters in New York claimed that they had successfully accomplished an essential step in their mandate to stabilize Congo. In theory, mobilizing a greater law enforcement presence in an unstable area would secure it, allowing for the deployment of other state representatives and eventually contributing to the reestablishment of state authority and the return to peace.

In reality, the program made a bad situation worse. The newly deployed police were untrained, and they had to compete for control of the area with both local militias and remnants of rebel groups. As a result, they could not make even a modest contribution to the reestablishment of law and order. Not only did they fail to improve the stability of the region, but they also became one more factor of insecurity. The new officers came from faraway provinces and had no ethnic or family links with surrounding groups. While this strategy was supposed to prevent corruption and collusion, it also produced a new force with no support among local populations, no deep-rooted personal stakes in bettering security in the area, and little knowledge of the specific local history and customs of the villagers. Even more problematic, the authorities in Kinshasa refused to support any units they considered "UNOPS police" and not state police, while the UN maintained that it was the Congolese government's responsibility to pay, feed, and house its own officers. Eventually, nobody took care of these

---

[2] This book deliberately forgoes the use of the article "the" in front of Congo or Sudan, to avoid the colonialist overtones of this grammatical convention.

On mortality in Congo, see the statistics in International Rescue Committee 2008 and the discussion of these figures in Goldstein 2011, pp. 260–264.

obligations. Lacking basic necessities, the police officers ended up preying on the very population they were tasked to protect. The Congolese authorities, the deployed police, and the affected communities all blamed the UN for the decline in the situation.

The initiative had followed a standard pattern for international interventions. Expatriate peacebuilders conceptualized the project with minimal local input. Then, they secured external resources to finance it. Finally, they tasked international agencies with implementing the project, and they involved local counterparts only in the final stages, as assistants, subcontractors, or mere recipients. Throughout this process, the foreign actors in charge relied on their own views of how best to rebuild a state, their own beliefs about what responsibilities a government should meet, and their own notions of what ordinary citizens would want. They worked hard, endured many deprivations, occasionally risked their lives, and became frustrated when – to their surprise – the situation worsened.

In fact, the UN actors could have easily predicted the police initiative's difficulties, as the program contained several elements that interveners commonly acknowledge to be problematic. It is conventional wisdom that local ownership is essential for successful peacebuilding, but local stakeholders rarely feel included in the design of international programs.[3] Practitioners and researchers have written countless books, articles, and reports to explain that approaches based on ready-to-use, universalized templates usually fail and context sensitivity is crucial, and yet interveners often use models that have worked in other conflict zones but are not appropriate for specific local conditions, just as the UN did in Congo.[4] Field-based international peacebuilders regularly emphasize the importance of good relationships between interveners and local actors; however, interactions between the two groups often remain

---

[3] For a review of the main scholarly arguments emphasizing the importance of local ownership, see Sending 2009, p. 4. For the policy perspective, see Anderson and Olson 2003, pp. 32–33; the Organisation for Economic Co-operation and Development's *Paris Declaration* (2005) and *Accra Agenda for Action* (2008) (available at www.oecd.org/dac/effectiveness/parisdeclarationandac craagendaforaction.htm); and the *Principles and Good Practice of Humanitarian Donorship* (Stockholm, 2003), point 7 (available at www.goodhumanitariandonorship.org/Libraries/ Ireland_Doc_Manager/EN-23-Principles-and-Good-Practice-of-Humanitarian-Donorship.sflb. ashx). For analyses of the current implementation of the local ownership idea, see Campbell 2010 (notably pp. 9, 10, and 52–59); Donais 2009; Joseph 2007; Martin and Moser 2012; Richmond 2012; Sending 2010b; and Wilén 2009.

[4] Among many others: Andersen 2005; Anderson, Brown, et al. 2012, pp. 24–25 and chapter 5; Campbell 2012; Chandler 2005, p. 308; Chopra and Hohe 2004; Cousens, Kumar, et al. 2001, notably p. 15; Coyne and Pellillo 2012; Duffey 2000, notably p. 144; Ellis 2005; Escobar 1995; FEWER, International Alert, et al. 2004, chapter 3, module 1; Gilbert 2008, pp. 21–26; Hohe 2002; Lange 2004, notably pp. 12–13; Mac Ginty 2006 and 2008; Ottaway 2003; Paris 2004 and 2010; Peacekeeping Best Practices Section 2008, p. 39; Pouligny 2004, especially pp. 133–136 and 293; Salem 1997, chapter 2; Smith 2004, notably p. 10; Verma 2011, pp. 64–67; and Woodward 2007, pp. 160–161. For a discussion of this literature, see Moore 2013, pp. 29–30.

conflictual.[5] Evaluations of peacebuilding programs consistently underscore the need for interveners to speak at least one of the local languages of their area of deployment, but many interveners in the field lack such linguistic capabilities.[6] Local people and interveners themselves deplore the latter's tendency to live in a bubble, where they interact mostly with other expatriates and lack contact with host populations, and yet this phenomenon still occurs throughout zones of intervention.[7]

The persistence of these inefficient modes of operation is all the more perplexing because in many cases we cannot attribute it to callousness, stupidity, or lack of self-awareness on the part of the international peacebuilders. While not all interveners deployed in the field lie awake at night worrying about the effectiveness of their efforts, most of them genuinely try to end violence and work hard to improve local situations. Far from being callous, they are usually well-meaning individuals who have devoted their lives to combating injustice, violence, and poverty. Moreover, on average, they are intelligent, well-read, and well-educated people. Some of them even realize the consequences of their standard practices and feel very uncomfortable with the way international peacebuilding operates on the ground. Why, then, do certain ways of working persist although they are clearly ineffective? Moreover, why do interveners perpetuate even those modes of operation they know to be counterproductive?

Recent advances in the anthropology of aid provide a useful starting point for approaching these puzzles and the broader question of effectiveness. Raymond Apthorpe coined the term "Aidland" to describe how "aid workers inhabit a separate world with its own time, space, and economics."[8] Apthorpe's insight has inspired a new body of research on development and humanitarian aid, and I propose that it is fruitful to approach peacebuilding similarly.[9] International peacebuilders also inhabit a separate world with its own time, space, and economics – and, even more importantly, its own system of meaning.

---

[5] Among others: Anderson 1999, pp. 62–63; Anderson and Olson 2003, chapters 4 and 5; Duffey 2000, p. 151; Heiberg and Holst 1986, pp. 410–411; Holohan 2005, pp. 74–85; Huang and Harris 2006, pp. 86 and 88–90; McWha 2011; and UN Department of Peacekeeping Operations – Department of Field Support 2012, p. 4.

[6] Public sources include CDA Collaborative Learning Projects 2010b, pp. 3–4; Coles 2007, pp. 28–29; Last 2000, especially p. 87; Lehmann 1999, p. 74; Pouligny 1999 (pp. 416–417) and 2004 (p. 194); and Toshiya and Konishi 2012, pp. 56 and 70.

[7] Among many others: Eyben 2011; Harper 2011; Johnston 2005; McWha 2011, pp. 33–35; Mitchell 2011a, pp. 12–15; Mosse 2008, p. 122; Rajak and Stirrat 2011; and Verma 2011, pp. 67–74.

[8] Apthorpe 2005; and Fechter and Hindman 2011a, p. 13.

[9] For the research on development and humanitarian aid, see notably the various contributions to Fechter and Hindman 2011a and Mosse 2011. As will become clear throughout the book, earlier studies of development – notably Anderson 1999; Ferguson 1990; Mitchell 2002; and Scott 1998 – were also influential in shaping my research.

This metaphorical world, inhabited by the transnational community of interveners for whom peace is either the primary objective (such as peacekeepers) or part of a broader set of goals (such as certain diplomats and development workers), I name Peaceland. In order to understand how and why this world gets created and maintained, and how this process influences peacebuilding effectiveness, I develop an ethnography of its inhabitants, meaning that I paint a portrait of the interveners and their customs, rituals, cultures, structures, beliefs, and behaviors.[10] My study focuses on the everyday elements that characterize life and work in Peaceland: its standard practices (routine activities that are socially meaningful and have an un-thought character[11]), shared habits (automatic responses to the world[12]), and dominant narratives (stories that people create to make sense of their lives and environments[13]). In documenting the dynamics resulting from these elements, I provide a fresh answer to the question of why strong boundaries exist between interveners and host populations. I also explain why dominant modes of operation (actions, behaviors, and discourses based on prevailing practices, habits, and narratives) that most interveners view as inefficient or even detrimental to their efforts nevertheless persist. Finally, I offer a novel perspective from which to consider why international interventions regularly fail to reach their full potential – and sometimes fall flat altogether.

Although they are pervasive, there is nothing innate or unchangeable about these everyday modes of operation. James Scambary, for instance, lived and worked in Peaceland in a markedly different way than I and most of my other contacts did.[14] James recalled that, during his deployment to Timor-Leste in the early 2000s, he "did not have a car, so [he] could not go away to the countryside to a nice guest house or to the beach for the day like all the others were doing" during weekends. Instead of socializing with other foreign peacebuilders, he "spent [his] time in [his] neighbors' backyards talking." Time passed, and James became part of the local fabric. His Timorese friends spoke in his presence in a way that they never did in front of other interveners. They mentioned hopes and fears that they usually hid from expatriates, and they talked about incidents that usually went unreported. The riots that erupted in 2006 in Timor-Leste, which almost collapsed the peace process, took virtually all interveners by surprise, but James Scambary was one of the few foreigners who had predicted a deterioration of the situation and had tried to convince his colleagues to help

---

[10] This sentence builds on the definition of "ethnography" in Harris and Johnson 2000, p. 4.

[11] Swidler 2001, pp. 74–75; Pouliot 2008 and 2010; and Pouliot and Adler 2011b. See Chapter 1 in this book for a more thorough definition and a discussion of this concept.

[12] Swidler 2001, p. 75; and Hopf 2010. See Chapter 1 for more details.

[13] Abbott 2008; De Fina and Georgakopoulou 2008; and Patterson and Monroe 1998. See also Chapter 1 in this book.

[14] The rest of this paragraph is based on the author's on-record interview with James Scambary, independent researcher, Australian National University, Dili, Timor-Leste, February 2012.

prevent the looming crisis.[15] Again, this was not necessarily because Scambary was smarter or better trained than other interveners. He had, however, a comparative advantage: in-depth personal relationships with his neighbors. The backyard discussions had provided him with a different, and much more accurate, perception of the challenges to the ongoing peace process.

This book is not just about the effectiveness or ineffectiveness of the interveners' dominant modes of operation. It is also about the individuals and organizations who, like James, evade, ignore, or even actively challenge the international peacebuilders' dominant practices and suggest alternative modes of operation. It is by looking at these exceptional cases that we can begin to understand how to reform the way peacebuilding works on the ground, so that interveners stop perpetuating ineffective modes of action and instead help construct a better system.

Everyday Dimensions of Peacebuilding Effectiveness

International peace interventions have multiplied since the end of the Cold War, with UN operations, non-governmental agencies, donors, diplomatic missions, and regional organizations becoming increasingly numerous and influential.[16] Identifying the factors that influence the effectiveness of these initiatives is of critical importance to scholars, practitioners, and people living in post-war states.

Admittedly, peacebuilding efficacy relies primarily on the actions, interests, and strategies of national and local actors and of potential outside spoilers.[17] Wars can end only when hostile parties at the local, national, and international levels agree to stop using violence to resolve their differences, and when their fellow citizens concurrently strive to establish and maintain lasting solutions to the conflict. Foreign interveners can, at best, support peace initiatives and undermine efforts to resume violence.

That being said, external contributions, however limited, can mean the difference between war and peace. Regardless of local conditions, foreign peace interventions increase the chances of establishing a durable peace.[18] Recent quantitative analyses show that international interventions have significantly

---

[15] Several other interviewees confirmed the fact that Scambary had been one of the very few foreigners to predict the 2006 riots.

[16] On UN and non-UN peace operations: Daniel and Taft 2008, p. 11; and Duffey 2000, p. 142. On non-governmental organizations: Barnett 2011, pp. 3–5; and Werker and Ahmed 2008, p. 75. On donors: Barnett 2011, p. 4. On international actors in general: Anderson and Olson 2003, p. 8; Barnett 2006, pp. 87–88; Cousens, Kumar, et al. 2001, p. 1; and Garb and Allen Nan 2009, p. xiv.

[17] Sending 2010b and 2011.

[18] Doyle and Sambanis 2000; Fortna 2004 and 2008; Gilligan and Sergenti 2008; Goldstein 2011; Hampson 1996; Howard 2008; and Walter 2002 demonstrate this point based on macro-level data (statistics for national and international conflicts), and Barron and Burke 2008 on micro-level analyses. For a similar claim by local people in countries of intervention, see CDA Collaborative Learning Projects 2011b, p. 1.

improved security conditions in many places where they have been deployed, even if other measures of peacebuilding success are less optimistic.[19] The international efforts in Congo, which most scholars and policy analysts view as failing, also aptly illustrate the value of peacebuilders. Despite their poor overall performance, interveners achieved a number of positive results. Reestablishing even a precarious peace over most of the Congolese territory would not have been possible without the presence of the UN peacekeeping mission and the work of African and Western diplomats. Likewise, it is mostly thanks to these international actors that Congo managed to organize its first democratic elections in 2006. At the time of this writing in 2013, the UN mission remains the only military force capable of protecting the population from abuses by the Congolese army and various other armed groups, even if they do so imperfectly. Foreign humanitarian agencies are similarly the only ones able to respond to epidemics and, in the eastern provinces, to provide access to clean drinking water and basic health care. In sum, improving the effectiveness of external efforts can significantly increase the prospects for peace.

This book uses a situation-specific definition of effectiveness, as it is the most appropriate for studying intervention efforts on the ground (see Chapter 1). A peacebuilding project, program, or intervention is effective when a large majority of the people involved in it – including both implementers (international interveners and local peacebuilders) and intended beneficiaries (including local elite and ordinary citizens) – view it as having promoted peace in the area of intervention.

Ascertaining the reasons for international intervention efficacy and inefficacy, and explaining why international peace efforts regularly fail to reach their full potential, requires a variety of approaches and analyses. The prevailing scholarship on this topic focuses on the impact of vested interests, material constraints, and the imposition of liberal values. These analyses tell us a great deal about how policies, institutions, ideologies, and discourses affect interventions.[20] However, while there are some exceptions, the vast majority of scholars and practitioners consider the everyday dimensions of peacebuilding efforts on the ground unimportant. As a result, we do not know much about the "nuts and bolts" of peacebuilding: the banal, everyday activities that actually make up the bulk of the work.

---

[19] The quantitative studies include: Doyle and Sambanis 2006; Fortna 2008; Gilligan and Sergenti 2008; and Goldstein 2011. For less optimistic evaluations, see Heathershaw 2008; Licklider 1993; Lund 2003; Mac Ginty 2006; Neumann 2011; and Stedman 1991. Paris 2011, pp. 351–353 develops a nuanced discussion of the record of peace interventions. See also Chapter 1 in this book, section "Peacebuilding Effectiveness: Definitions and Contestation," for a more thorough presentation of the debate on the rate of success and failure in international peacebuilding.

[20] The rest of this paragraph builds on the insights presented in Fechter and Hindman 2011a, introduction; and Verma 2011, notably pp. 62–63; as well as on personal communications with Dr. Audra Mitchell (lecturer in international relations, University of York, August and September 2011). See also Sending 2010b, p. 1 for a similar claim.

Scholars such as Oliver Richmond and Shahrbanou Tadjbakhsh have already called for a renewed attention to "the everyday" in the study of international interventions, but the everyday experience in question is usually that of local actors.[21] While we have extensive ethnographic data on host populations and many insightful analyses of how their cultures and practices can promote or impair effective conflict resolution, the ethnographic gaze has rarely focused on those performing the intervention.[22] Several social scientists have recently produced fascinating studies that begin to fill this gap, but these authors focus on the impact of the everyday on development, humanitarian aid, or democratization.[23] Only a few anthropologists (Paul Higate, Marsha Henry, and Robert Rubinstein) and political scientists (Audra Mitchell, Béatrice Pouligny, and Ole-Jacob Sending) have researched the influence of the everyday on peacekeeping and peacebuilding efforts.[24] Building off this diverse array of insights, this book examines the everyday implementation of international initiatives on the ground to develop a complementary explanation for peacebuilding effectiveness, and thus paint a more complete picture of how interventions operate.

My central argument is as follows. I demonstrate that mundane elements – such as the expatriates' social habits, standard security procedures, and habitual approaches to collecting information on violence – strongly impact the effectiveness of intervention efforts. I also emphasize the influence of the informal and the personal on formal professional initiatives. Everyday practices shape overall interventions from the bottom up. They enable, constitute, and help reproduce the strategies, policies, institutions, and discourses that political scientists usually study. They also explain the existence and continued use of ways of working that interveners view as inefficient, ineffective, or even counterproductive.

I am not suggesting that daily habits and practices explain everything about the effectiveness of international peace interventions. I simply argue that an investigation of such everyday elements sheds light on several unexplored facets of this topic. It enables us to grasp why certain modes of action may persist even when interveners know that they are detrimental to their efforts. It also elucidates how the constraints, interests, and liberal values that other scholars study are created, sustained, and reinforced – or challenged – on the ground. As a whole, this book demonstrates that the process of international efforts (the "how") is just as important to examine as their substance (the "what"). The way in which interveners interact with local stakeholders or construct

---

[21] Richmond 2011; Richmond and Mitchell 2011; and Tadjbakhsh 2011. For a related approach, see Mac Ginty 2008 and 2011. For an analysis, see Higate and Henry 2009, pp. 1–2 and 16; and Mitchell 2011b.

[22] On the cultures of host populations and peacebuilding, see, among many others studies: Avruch 1998; Duffey 2000; Mac Ginty 2008; Richmond 2009; Schirch 2005; and Shaw, Waldorf, et al. 2010.

[23] On development: Fechter and Hindman 2011a; and Mosse 2011. On humanitarian aid: Duffield 2010; and Smirl 2008. On democratization: Coles 2007; and Holohan 2005.

[24] Higate and Henry 2009; Mitchell 2011b; Rubinstein 2008; Pouligny 2004; and Sending 2010b.

knowledge of their areas of deployment deserves the same critical attention as the actual objectives that peacebuilders pursue, such as reintegrating militias or promoting geostrategic interests. For this reason, analyses of international interventions which fail to consider everyday elements – for instance, studies based exclusively on instrumental or normative rationality – are necessarily incomplete.[25] In other words, my approach and existing explanations are not mutually exclusive. Rather, they are complementary.

I develop this argument based on a year of ethnographic study in Congo, enriched with material from brief research trips in Burundi, Cyprus, Israel and the Palestinian Territories, South Sudan, and Timor-Leste (see the map of fieldwork sites in Figure 1). The material collected specifically for this project includes 15 months of field observations, 295 in-depth interviews, 124 discrete participant observation events lasting more than 330 hours in total, and hundreds of key documents (see the Appendix for more details). In addition to analyzing this new data, I draw extensively on both the material I collected for a previous project on Congo, which includes more than 330 interviews and another 1.5 years of field observations, and my 2 years of work experience as an intervener in Afghanistan, Congo, Kosovo, Nicaragua, and in the New York headquarters of various organizations. Altogether, I rely on several years of ethnographic inquiry in conflict zones around the world. I spent these years embedded in the communities I was studying, observing them sometimes from the inside, as a fellow intervener, and other times from the outside, as a researcher.

My interpretation of the concept of intervention overlaps with its standard definition in international relations scholarship, which focuses on the use of military force by states.[26] But like most researchers who focus specifically on peacebuilding, I define interveners to include not only states but also inter-governmental and nonstate actors, and their actions to encompass not only use of military force but also a range of other military and civilian undertakings aimed at ending existing violence and preventing its recurrence.[27]

I examine all of the foreign entities – people, countries, and organizations – whose official goal is to help build peace in their countries of deployment, regardless of whether or not they have other objectives alongside that goal. These international peacebuilders may be diplomats, other government officials (such as defense officers), personnel of non-governmental agencies, academic experts serving as advisors or consultants, employees of private subcontractors or for-profit development firms, and staff of international organizations – both military and civilian. The interveners I study are thus a diverse group. They

---

[25] Based on Hopf 2010, p. 540. See also Chapter 1 in this book.

[26] For instance, Chesterman 2001; Walzer 1977; and Wheeler 2000. For a compelling critique of these standard definitions, see Mitchell 2014, pp. 3–9.

[27] Authors using a similar definition include, among many others: Brown 2006; Chopra and Hohe 2004; Coles 2007; Fassin and Pandolfi 2010; Mitchell 2014; Rubinstein 2008; and Sørbø 2010.

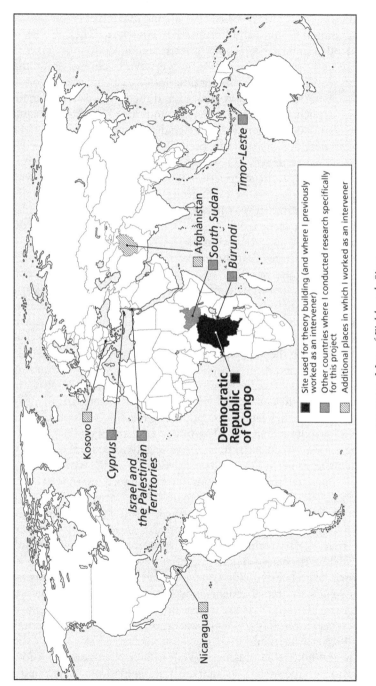

FIGURE 1 Map of Fieldwork Sites

Site used for theory building (and where I previously worked as an intervener)

Other countries where I conducted research specifically for this project

Additional places in which I worked as an intervener

include the staff of peacekeeping missions (notably UN operations) and of non-governmental organizations (NGOs) specializing in conflict resolution, such as Search for Common Ground and Life and Peace Institute. They also encompass members of other international, non-governmental, donor, or governmental agencies who had "peacebuilding," "peacekeeping," "conflict resolution" (or an equivalent word) in their job titles or descriptions, or who worked on projects with an explicit conflict-resolution goal, even if their organizations' main mandate was not explicitly related to peace. In addition, I analyze humanitarian, human rights, and development actors when doing so can help me better understand peacebuilding dynamics. In the book, I focus on the interveners deployed on the ground: the people who actually carry out the interventions on an everyday basis. (That said, I did interview their colleagues based in headquarters, to compare the perspectives of each group on relevant field dynamics.) As Chapter 5 and the introduction to Part I further detail, the individuals at the center of my analysis come from a wide range of geographic, organizational, professional, religious, and personal backgrounds.

This book demonstrates that the interveners' everyday practices and habits influence the effectiveness of international peace efforts in many different ways. To begin with, the manner in which foreign peacebuilders construct knowledge of the countries in which they work often prompts them to rely on narratives that are misleading or incomplete. Since interveners usually value technical proficiency over country-specific expertise, the vast majority arrive with little to no understanding of their locale of deployment. In the field, they regularly use inefficient data collection techniques and rely on biased samples of informants. These standard modes of action limit the extent to which international peacebuilders comprehend the contexts in which they work. Therefore, to make sense of their environments, they tend to use prevailing but overly simplified narratives as substitutes for more nuanced explanations of dynamics on the ground. In the case of Congo, for instance, narratives portraying illegal natural resource exploitation as the main cause of violence, sexual violence as the worst consequence, and statebuilding as the primary solution directly shaped international response to the conflict. The African-versus-Arab narrative carried similar weight in Darfur, as did the emphasis on the East-West divide in Timor-Leste. Because interveners depend on these dominant narratives instead of on in-depth analyses of the local contexts, they regularly misunderstand the phenomena they are trying to address, such as the causes of and potential solutions to violence. As a result, although some projects eventually better the lives of local people, others fail to bring about significant improvements, and some even compound the problems that the interveners originally sought to address.

The interveners' everyday modes of operation also create and maintain firm boundaries between them and their local counterparts. The shared experience of foreign peacebuilders as outsiders living in a conflict zone, in addition to their perception of themselves as markedly different from host populations, creates a distance between the two groups. The international peacebuilders' daily routines, including their security procedures and their insistence on advertising their actions as well as the way that they value external expertise over local knowledge, further widen the split between them and local people. These practices also reinforce a pervasive power disparity between the interveners and their intended beneficiaries. The ostensible goal of the expatriates – to help the host country and its citizens – already enables them to claim the moral high ground. Foreign peacebuilders deployed in conflict zones also enjoy enormous material, symbolic, social, and cultural resources. The expatriates' daily routines publicize, perpetuate, and reinforce awareness of these advantages and construct an image of foreign peacebuilders as superior to local people. The divide between interveners and host populations, and the constant emphasis on the eminence of the former, regularly sour the indispensable relationships between interveners and their local counterparts. These tensions habitually prevent local ownership and authorship, and they marginalize and antagonize host populations. As a result, local people frequently evade, contest, resist, or reject the international initiatives designed to help them.

Ultimately, these everyday elements can perpetuate even the standard modes of operation that interveners acknowledge to be counterproductive. The expatriates' deficient understanding of local contexts prompts them to employ ready-to-use templates of conflict resolution, even when these universal models are ill-suited to local conditions. The routine absence of close relationships between interveners and their local counterparts reinforces the foreigners' tendency to create parallel systems of governance. Their frequent disregard of local knowledge legitimizes their rapid turnover from country to country, as acquiring thematic experience in a variety of conflict settings takes precedence over developing an in-depth understanding of a specific situation. Moreover, their lack of local knowledge enables many of the peacebuilders to view as acceptable short-term and top-down approaches to complex political, economic, and social problems. Their search for neutrality and their obsession with quantifiable outcomes also orient their efforts toward certain strategies and away from others that are just as necessary.

These various dynamics have four distinct, cumulative impacts on peace and conflict. The first set of effects is positive. The dominant modes of operation enable interveners to function in the difficult environments of conflict zones, from getting a handle on complex situations to raising resources and remaining safe and sane. The prevailing practices, habits, and narratives therefore facilitate an international involvement that can, and sometimes does, help build a sustainable peace. At the same time, though, the prevailing modes of operation have unintended consequences that produce three kinds of negative outcomes in peacebuilding efforts: the counterproductive, the ineffective, and the inefficient. The biased information and analysis, frequent misunderstandings, and the focus on top-down causes and solutions (and on other dominant narratives) regularly prevent interveners from recognizing existing signs of violence or indications that conflict might escalate. In the worst-case scenarios, international peacebuilders end up fueling violence, as they did in Congo when their focus on sexual abuse and statebuilding led to more human rights atrocities (see Chapter 4). In most cases, however, the consequences of the dominant practices, habits, and narratives are less severe, though still undesirable. Interveners adopt strategies and policies that are ineffective or inefficient, thus missing opportunities to alleviate conflict.[28]

The existence of these general trends does not mean that all interveners are identical. There are variations in their modes of operation and the extent to which those modes display the precise array of characteristics I detail in this book. Furthermore, many individuals – notably newcomers to Peaceland, interveners from neighboring countries, and people with especially strong personal ties to their areas of deployment – actively contest the dominant practices, habits, and narratives and try to bring to light their detrimental effects. A number of individuals and organizations even constitute exceptions to the dominant modes of acting and thinking, as they embody entirely different approaches. I pay particular attention to these contestations and exceptions throughout the book, as they allow me to specify the conditions under which peace interventions can be more successful. Peacebuilding initiatives are much more effective, for instance, when interveners value local expertise on par with thematic knowledge (Part I), develop personal and social relationships with their local counterparts (Chapter 5), and forgo standard security routines and the requirement to advertise their actions (Chapter 7).

This research objective faces one inherent dilemma, which Peter Uvin perfectly expressed in the introduction to his well-known study of development aid in Rwanda before the 1994 genocide.[29] My analysis focuses on the peacebuilding world at large and is therefore bound to generalize and simplify. No matter how much I tried to delve into the variations that exist within each group and identify exceptions to each trend, it is likely that, for any statement I make, there have been individuals who acted or thought differently. My goal is not to provide a comprehensive list of every variation and exception, but instead to focus on those that offer enhanced theoretical and policy insights.

The culture of secrecy of the organizations I study, together with the sensitivity of the data I collected, raises an additional challenge. Virtually all of my interviewees and contacts asked to remain anonymous due to the personal and professional risks involved in providing information for this book. They also requested that I maintain the same level of confidentiality for all the material gathered through field and participant observations. For this reason, I cite in full only the data I obtained through on-record interviews and from public sources. All of the information and quotations for which I do not provide complete references come from confidential interviews, participant observations, and

---

[28] Table 2 in Chapter 1 clarifies which of the dominant practices, habits, and narratives on which this book focuses are particularly inefficient, ineffective, or counterproductive.

[29] The next two sentences paraphrase Uvin 1998, p. 9.

field observations. To ensure their reliability, I have triangulated all the statements that I make in this book, including those that I could not fully reference: For each, I build on at least three different sources, and usually many more.

In choosing evidence from my many discussions to illustrate my argument, I have selected quotations that express opinions or examples illustrating experiences shared with me by a large number of people (except of course when I analyze exceptions).[30] In some cases, I quote individuals who stated a widely held viewpoint with particular clarity; when relevant, I provide information about this individual to help the reader better contextualize the quote. In other cases, I heard a comment so frequently that I use language such as "according to many interviewees" or "a number of people mentioned." In these situations where many contacts used the same or similar language, I do not try to identify the characteristics of all the people who made the point. Instead, I mention the shared characteristics of the speakers in order to help the reader contextualize my claims.

Why Read This Book?

There are a number of ways to read this book. For the scholar of war and peace, this book suggests a new explanation for the varying effectiveness of international efforts. It also elucidates why certain modes of action may persist even when people are aware that they are ineffective. For other political scientists, I show the influence of the everyday elements of international action that our discipline usually regards as unimportant or irrelevant to understanding macro-level issues. For the student of international organizations and global governance, I demonstrate that peacebuilding actors of all kinds occupy a collective normative and sociological space and that it is fruitful to treat these actors, in aggregate, as a unit of analysis. For the reader interested in social science theories, I contribute to three related topics at the cutting edge of research: the increased attention to practice and ethnography in political science, the focus on micro-level dynamics in peace and conflict research, and the attention to the everyday in the anthropology of aid. For the researcher looking for historical or anthropological data, I present a wealth of unique ethnographic material on how international peace interventions operate in the field, especially in Congo.

Lastly, for policy-makers and practitioners, this book suggests tools and ideas with which to improve their peacebuilding efforts. Would-be interveners can also read this work as part of their predeparture preparations so that they know what to expect when they arrive in the field and how to avoid the pitfalls inherent to their colleagues' everyday practices, habits, and narratives. Additionally, this book may help local peacebuilders to better understand their international

---

[30] This writing approach was inspired by – and the entire paragraph paraphrases – Anderson, Brown, et al. 2012, p. 4.

partners and to find ways to develop more productive relationships between the two groups.

It is also important to keep in mind that the peace interveners I study are an example of a much broader group. As will become clear in the course of the book, and as I further elucidate in the Conclusion, the theoretical and empirical insights that I offer can help scholars and policy-makers better understand other domains of international relations from a range of historical contexts – including development and humanitarian aid, diplomatic engagement, business, counter-insurgency, and colonialism. My approach and findings offer a way to illuminate the everyday habits, practices, and narratives that influence the effectiveness of these various kinds of international efforts and yet remain insufficiently studied.

There is one way not to read this book, however. My argument is not that support for international peacebuilders should be eliminated altogether, letting people who live in conflict zones resolve problems on their own. Relying exclusively on local actors and local expertise is not the answer. Such a tactic would create a number of problems, which other scholars have extensively studied, and which I note throughout the book.[31] Foreign interveners can make a number of distinct contributions, as I discuss in the introduction to Part I. There is therefore a wide consensus among scholars and host populations that outside expertise and outside actors are often indispensible for effective peacebuilding.[32]

As the book details, however, international peacebuilding never reaches its full potential, and it regularly has negative, unintended consequences. It is imperative that we end the dirtiest and nastiest aspects of interventions, such as the human trafficking and the abuses of beneficiaries that other scholars have documented – and that, thankfully, remain the exception rather than the norm.[33] But it is also vital that we take steps to mitigate the unintentional harm that interveners regularly do. We need not stop international peacebuilding activities altogether, but rather end (or at least compensate for) their negative impacts while preserving their positive outcomes.

This book aims to assist this reform process by developing a nuanced and constructive analysis that will enable practitioners and policy-makers to identify the areas most in need of change. Policy-makers and practitioners often blame problems with interventions on the way policies are formulated, the resulting constraints on the international peacebuilders' work, and the populations' high expectations and lack of understanding of the interveners' roles. There is thus far too little acknowledgement that practitioners should also revise their everyday practices and habits, and even less reflection on how to do so. Given all the

---

[31] For references to other studies that develop this point, see the introduction to Part I in this book, section "Outsiders' and Insiders' Roles in Peacebuilding."

[32] Anderson, Brown, et al. 2012, notably chapter 1, and CDA Collaborative Learning Projects 2008a provide a good overview of local perspectives on this question.

[33] Simm 2013 develops a fascinating analysis of these problems and their potential solutions. Earlier useful studies focusing on peacekeeping missions include Higate and Henry 2009, pp. 145–150; Martin 2005; Rehn and Johnson Sirleaf 2002, chapter 5; and UN General Assembly 2005.

constraints and challenges on-the-ground peacebuilders face in their daily work, those who do realize how much damage their routine modes of action can cause often lack ideas on how to change their practices for the better. It is my hope that this book will help bring to light both these flaws and the existing attempts to overcome these shortcomings. The Conclusion also offers ideas about the types of reforms necessary and potential ways to execute them.

Overview

I develop my argument through seven further chapters. Chapter 1 illuminates the theoretical stakes of my analysis and presents my conceptual tools and research approach in more detail. I first discuss the difficulties in defining intervention "successes" and "failures" and emphasize that the attempts to delineate these concepts are part of the very power struggles studied in this book. I then demonstrate that field-based interveners enjoy substantial leeway in implementing instructions from headquarters and national capitals, and thus that consideration of the specific dynamics of on-the-ground peacebuilding is indispensable. The next section develops the main concepts that I use, including practices, habits, and narratives, and clarifies how these concepts help explain the constitution, change, and perpetuation of the status quo. I also elucidate how my analysis complements existing explanations of peacebuilding effectiveness – notably those based on constraints, vested interests, liberal values, and cultural differences among interveners. The last section of this chapter clarifies the scope of my argument. Readers who wish to know more about the methodological aspects of my research can find additional details in the Appendix.

The rest of the book is divided into two parts. Part I (Chapters 2, 3, and 4) examines the process through which interveners construct knowledge on their countries of deployment and the impact of this process on intervention effectiveness. As a prelude to this analysis, I briefly present the international interveners on whom this book focuses and clarify insiders' and outsiders' respective roles in peacebuilding.

Chapter 2 documents the struggle among the inhabitants of Peaceland to determine what constitutes relevant expertise in the field of peacebuilding. I demonstrate that intervening agencies value thematic expertise over local knowledge, and I trace the sources of this preference. I then show how this bias underlies many problems that commonly mar peace interventions on the ground: the excessive reliance on external knowledge and actors, the devaluation of local populations' and local staff's expertise, the deployment of interveners who do not speak any of the local languages, the high turnover rate of expatriate peacebuilders, the use of models and templates unsuited to local conditions, and the compartmentalization of intertwined aspects of the intervention.

Chapter 3 focuses on the reactions of host populations to the patterns documented in Chapter 2. I show that valuing external expertise over local knowledge antagonizes local stakeholders and impedes both their ownership and authorship. These dynamics create a widespread perception that interveners impose their ideas and programs on host populations. The ensuing resentment ultimately encourages local stakeholders to contest, adapt, or resist international efforts. These responses may, at times, improve living conditions for the intended beneficiaries, but their overall impact on the international programs is clear: They generate multiple obstacles to the international efforts, thus decreasing their eventual efficiency and effectiveness.

Chapter 4 examines the manner in which on-the-ground peacebuilders make sense of their environments in the face of these circumstances. I identify the various obstacles that they face when collecting and analyzing data on their locale of deployment, including their tendency to rely on a biased sample of sources. The rest of the chapter emphasizes the harmful consequences of these information-gathering and analytical shortcomings. Lack of in-depth local knowledge regularly entices international peacebuilders to rely on simple (and often overly simplistic) narratives to design their intervention strategies. I develop an in-depth case study of the impact of dominant narratives on the conflict in Congo to illuminate the unintended consequences of this practice. I then flag other detrimental misunderstandings that recur throughout conflict zones, such as the interveners' regular misinterpretations of key dynamics of war and peace, and their recurring failure to appreciate the difference between their conceptions and the local views of peace and peacebuilding. Finally, I explain that the shortage of accurate information reinforces the interveners' tendency to adopt a top-down approach to peacebuilding, thus overlooking critical bottom-up dynamics.

Part II (Chapters 5, 6, and 7) documents the everyday practices and habits – both social and professional – that make the dynamics I study in Part I possible. These dominant modes of operation have a number of positive, intended effects: They enable interveners and their organizations to function in conflict zones and to help the host country build peace. However, they also have a number of negative, unintended consequences.

Chapter 5 studies the bottom-up, everyday personal, social, and professional processes that create boundaries between interveners and local people. Expatriate peacebuilders have a common official goal and dense professional and social interactions. Even more importantly, they share a common experience of life in conflict zones. Although there are many tensions and rivalries between the different types of interveners, a key element preserves the cohesion of the group despite its internal rifts: the presence of "others" (local populations), against whom interveners construct their group identity. I trace the source of the separation between the two groups and identify the factors that lead to variations in these patterned relationships. I then explore the role, presence, and development of exceptions to these dominant trends. The final section highlights the main inadvertent effects of these boundaries.

The next two chapters identify the top-down and bottom-up elements that perpetuate the boundaries and enable them to persist despite the fact that numerous interveners recognize their counterproductive nature and, in some cases, actively challenge them. Chapter 6 focuses on the structure of inequality that permeates relationships between international peacebuilders and local stakeholders. The mission that interveners share – to help the country of intervention and its people – enables them to claim a moral high ground, a process that often antagonizes local people. The enormous material, social, and symbolic resources that foreign peacebuilders enjoy and the fact that interveners are usually accountable to their donors and headquarters, not their intended beneficiaries, further reinforce the boundaries. They also decrease the incentives for expatriates to challenge the structure of inequality and promote change on the ground.

Chapter 7 examines the daily work routines that international peacebuilders follow across areas of deployment and that they usually view as commonsensical. The first section focuses on standard security procedures. I demonstrate that field-based interveners share a culture of insecurity, and I trace the consequences of the common security practices. The second section examines three widespread intervention rituals – the interveners' need to advertise their actions, their obligation to report those activities regularly, and their emphasis on maintaining impartiality. The last section examines the quantifiable and short-term nature of the results that interveners strive to attain. In each of the three sections, I trace the source of these practices, and I illuminate how these habitual ways of working further separate local populations and international peacebuilders into two distinct and unequal groups. I also show how these practices and habits together compound many of the problems analyzed throughout the book, notably the lack of understanding of local contexts and the interveners' beliefs that their narratives are apt and their social and professional routines appropriate.

The Conclusion elucidates the implications of my analysis for researchers and policy-makers. I first summarize the argument of the book and note the topics in need of further research. I end by offering suggestions to improve the effectiveness of international peace efforts. I advise on how to initiate the battle over ideas, and I develop a series of concrete recommendations to rebalance the value of local and thematic knowledge and to break the boundaries between interveners and local people.

I

Studying the Everyday

At first glance, one might assume that a peacekeeping soldier from Pakistan, a diplomat from the United States, and a human rights advocate from Senegal would approach their jobs quite differently. Yet, while in Congo for a previous research project, I observed striking similarities in the ways that international interveners understand the situations they face and in the strategies they adopt, despite their otherwise extremely different national, professional, social, and economic backgrounds.[1] This observation prompted a new research project that confirmed my original insight, highlighted the importance of the interveners' everyday life and work in accounting for these commonalities, and eventually resulted in this book.

In this chapter, I present the theoretical and methodological framework that I use to analyze the everyday dimension of international interventions. The first two sections describe my overall approach: In the first, I discuss the contested notions of intervention success and failure, and in the second, I demonstrate that considering the specific dynamics of on-the-ground peacebuilding is essential. The next section of the chapter presents the three most helpful concepts for analyzing everyday peacebuilding, namely practices, habits, and narratives. In the fourth section, I outline my explanation of the dynamics of intervention in the field and of the processes of change. The fifth and final section elucidates how my analysis complements the existing literature on peacebuilding effectiveness, drawing attention to gaps in those explanations that emphasize constraints, vested interests, liberal values, or the marked differences among interveners.

Peacebuilding and Its Effectiveness

Like all studies of this kind, mine must begin by answering a few fundamental questions: What is peacebuilding, what constitutes its successes and failures, and by what standards do we assess its effectiveness?

---

[1] Autesserre 2010.

Peacebuilding refers to actions aimed at creating, strengthening, and solidifying peace.[2] At a minimum, it involves reestablishing a measure of security. Peacebuilding can therefore include peacemaking – the process of bringing parties in conflict to an agreement through peaceful means – and peacekeeping, which denotes the "deployment of international personnel to help maintain peace and security" after a war.[3] Most scholars and policy-makers add several other elements to this security dimension. A broad consensus has emerged on the need for socioeconomic recovery, which in turn calls for humanitarian and development aid.[4] A fierce debate also exists over what types of political institutions and processes are necessary – most thinkers include statebuilding, justice, and reconciliation, and numerous authors also add democracy.[5] In this book, I define peacebuilding to include any and all elements identified by local and international stakeholders as attempts to create, strengthen, and solidify peace. This definition thus encompasses the various elements of the security, socioeconomic, and political dimensions that scholars study.

Just as scholars of peace and conflict employ multiple definitions of peacebuilding, they use many standards to evaluate intervention success and failure. Criteria vary from the establishment of a negative peace – the absence of large-scale violence – to the promotion of positive peace, in other words, the creation of the deeper conditions that make a peaceful society work.[6] In their analyses of peacekeeping missions, Page Fortna defines success as how long peace lasts after an intervention, Roland Paris as the prospects for sustainable peace after the departure of peacekeepers, Lise Howard as fulfillment of mandates tailored to local circumstances, and Michael Doyle and Nicholas Sambanis as an absence of violence combined with progress toward democratic governance.[7] Academics who evaluate other actors in addition to peacekeeping missions similarly use a variety of criteria: war recurrence, redress of the root causes of the conflict, establishment of a legitimate regime or an effective state, or emergence of economic recovery.[8] Moreover, no consensus exists on what

---

[2] This definition was inspired by Boutros-Ghali 1992, but I diverge from Boutros-Ghali by including peacekeeping and peacemaking in the scope of peacebuilding.

[3] The definition of peacekeeping comes from Fortna 2008, p. 5.

[4] For the flagship argument, see Collier, Elliott, et al. 2003. For a policy perspective: UN Security Council 2001, para. 18–20; and the list of projects selected by the UN Peacebuilding Fund in Burundi (in Campbell 2010, notably pp. 44–45). For a discussion: Call 2008, pp. 186–187; and Samset 2011, pp. 266–267.

[5] Call 2008, pp. 183–186; and Samset 2011, pp. 266–267 present very useful reviews of this literature. For a policy perspective, see UN Security Council 2001, paras. 10–20; and the list of projects selected by the UN Peacebuilding Fund in Burundi (in Campbell 2010, notably pp. 43–44 and 47–48).

[6] On the distinction between positive and negative peace, see Galtung 1969.

[7] Doyle and Sambanis 2006, p. 73; Fortna 2008, pp. 16–17; Howard 2008, pp. 7–8; and Paris 2004, p. 6.

[8] Call 2008.

threshold of violence researchers should use to determine whether war has resumed.[9]

These divergent definitions lead to heated debates over the exact rates of peace-building successes and failures. Although there is a relative consensus that external interventions tend to increase the chances of establishing a durable peace, research-ers disagree about which interventions achieve this goal.[10] Consequently, the rate of success in international peacebuilding varies by source from 31 percent to 85 percent.[11] Estimates for war recurrence similarly oscillate between 20 percent and 56 percent of all civil conflicts.[12] Furthermore, some critics argue that, even in the cases of "successful" interventions, peace is in fact tenuous, and instability and violence persist on the ground.[13] Cambodia and Tajikistan are two countries that scholars and policy-makers hold up as exemplars of international peacebuilding success.[14] However, Oliver Richmond argues that Cambodia enjoys no more than a "virtual peace."[15] Likewise, John Heathershaw demonstrates that Tajikistan has serious underlying antagonisms that remain unresolved, and a governance structure whose legitimacy remains highly disputed.[16] Policy-makers and practitioners often present Burundi as yet another recent case of peacebuilding success, but violence, instability, and dictatorship have marred its post-war years.[17]

The lack of consensus is not confined to scholarly debate: External definitions of success are also frequently at odds with local ones. Richmond has demon-strated that peace (and therefore peacebuilding success) means different things to different people and organizations at different places and times.[18] Interviews I conducted in places like Congo and Timor-Leste reveal how wide the diver-gence can be. While an Indian peacekeeper defined peace as the absence of violence in the area under his purview, a Congolese child argued that it was the possibility to eat to his heart's content. Interveners working in Timor-Leste

---

[9] Among others, see the discussion in ibid., pp. 176–181.

[10] On the relative consensus: Fortna and Howard 2008. For specific studies, see, among others: Doyle and Sambanis 2000; Fortna 2004; Goldstein 2011; Hampson 1996; Howard 2008; Licklider 1993; Stedman 1991; and Walter 2002.

[11] Call 2008, pp. 173–183; Doyle and Sambanis 2006, pp. 74–75; Fortna 2008, pp. 104–116 and 125; Gilligan and Sergenti 2008; and Weinstein 2005, pp. 11 and 33.

[12] Call 2008, pp. 8–16; Doyle and Sambanis 2006, pp. 74–75; Fortna 2008, pp. 104–116 and 125; Gilligan and Sergenti 2008, p. 104; Human Security Report Project 2010, p. 170; Walter 2002, p. 6; and Weinstein 2005, pp. 11 and 33. For useful discussions of these estimates, see Call 2007, pp. 173–183; Goldstein 2011, pp. 303–304; and Suhrke and Samset 2007.

[13] Lund 2003; and Mac Ginty 2006.

[14] Call 2008, p. 179; Doyle and Sambanis 2006, p. 199; and Fortna 2008, p. 113.

[15] Richmond 2011, p. 71. Also Peou 2012.

[16] Heathershaw 2008 (pp. 337–339) and 2009. Also CDA Collaborative Learning Projects 2011b, p. 3.

[17] On Burundi as a success case: Boshoff, Vrey, et al. 2010; Call 2008; Hanson 2009; Peen Rodt 2011; and Elizabeth Dickinson, "Burundi: An Unlikely International Success Story," *The Interdependent*, December 20, 2011. On persisting violence, instability, and dictatorship: Amnesty International 2012, pp. 92–94; Human Rights Watch 2012; International Crisis Group 2012a; and United States Department of State 2012.

[18] Richmond 2005. Also CDA Collaborative Learning Projects 2011b, p. 3.

also defined peace as the absence of violence, but Timorese parents claimed that it meant the possibility to send their children to school. Often, I would travel to countries or districts that scholars or international interveners had characterized as peaceful, such as Burundi in 2010 or Shabunda and Baraka (Congo) in 2004, and local elites and ordinary citizens would repeat the same message during interviews. They did not view on-the-ground conditions as peaceful. They instead emphasized that many causes of instability persisted and that organized violence continued.[19]

My fieldwork in Timor-Leste was particularly striking in this regard. Policy-makers, practitioners, and scholars regularly cite the peace intervention there as some of the best evidence that external efforts can succeed.[20] However, the Timorese I interviewed in 2012 claimed that their country was in no way an example of effective international peacebuilding. They agreed that the situation had improved markedly since the heights of the crises in 1999 and 2006, but they emphasized that violence could erupt at any time because so many sources of conflict were unresolved.[21] Furthermore, virtually all my interviewees, including interveners themselves, credited the Timorese elite and the general population for any progress that had been made. Many local contacts actually viewed the international efforts as irrelevant, and several contacts even went so far as to deem them harmful.

The extent of all these disparities points to a gap in peacebuilding scholarship that I attribute to a widespread neglect of on-the-ground dynamics. For this reason, my analysis does not, unlike most existing literature, seek to account for intervention successes or failures at the aggregate (national or international) level. Instead, it considers the relative effectiveness of specific international projects and programs. I look at what these various efforts accomplish, examining whether they achieve some or all of their intended effects, whether they have unintended consequences, and how these intended and unintended results contribute to promoting peace or perpetuating violence. My goal is to explain why certain initiatives work better than others and why many fail to reach their full potential.

To that end, I use a situation-specific definition of effectiveness that reflects the contested understandings of success and failure. I consider a peacebuilding project, program, or intervention to be effective when a large majority of the people involved in it views it as such. The initiatives I present as effective are programs or projects that, during interviews or informal discussions, both implementers (international interveners and local peacebuilders) and intended beneficiaries (including local elite and ordinary citizens) presented as having promoted peace in the area of intervention. My definition does not require

---

[19] Richmond 2011, p. 4 makes a similar claim.
[20] Dobbins 2005; Doyle and Sambanis 2006; Fortna 2008; Howard 2008; and Zürcher 2011. For a critical discussion, see Bowles and Chopra 2008.
[21] See Babo-Soares 2012 for a similar analysis.

that a program or project garner universal praise – some individuals will always be dissatisfied. Nor does it demand that an initiative's contributions to the establishment of peace take one specific form over another. Some efforts have directly reduced or prevented violence. Others have done so indirectly by creating the broader conditions that facilitate peace – by building relationships among opponents, establishing or strengthening institutions that address conflict, and so on.[22] My definition simply reflects a general consensus among the people involved in or affected by a given initiative that it has advanced, in one way or another, the establishment of peace.

Because it incorporates the perception of both international interveners and local stakeholders, and because it focuses on micro-level dynamics, my definition of effectiveness enables me to consider two important phenomena throughout my analysis. The first is that the disparities in how external and local stakeholders assess peacebuilding effectiveness stem partly from the widespread dispute over which and whose knowledge matters in Peaceland (see Chapter 2). Determining what success means, whose peace should be realized, and on whose terms, are all facets of the struggle for power among foreign interveners and their local counterparts.[23]

The second phenomenon is that countries usually labeled as cases of peacebuilding success are in fact the theaters of many ineffective efforts.[24] Likewise, in all of the interventions I studied – even those labeled as failures, such as that in Congo – I saw a number of isolated initiatives that were effective.[25] Other researchers have made the same observation regarding Georgia and Abkhazia.[26] In other words, "success" or "failure" at the national and international levels mask a lot of variation at the subnational level. My definition of effectiveness not only allows me to study this variation, but also requires me to conduct an in-depth examination of intervention processes at the local level, where one can best appreciate the various realities often obscured by macro-level definitions. This empirical shift carries an added benefit: It enables me to challenge a questionable assumption upon which much existing research is predicated.

An Empirical Shift: Studying On-the-Ground Peacebuilding

Many scholars researching international interventions focus on headquarters, capital cities, and the dynamics of peacebuilding at the national and international

---

[22] See Garb and Allen Nan 2009, pp. 5–6 for a very useful presentation of these distinct contributions to peacebuilding.

[23] For a related understanding of "success" and "failure" in democratization and development, see respectively: Guilhot 2005, pp. 19–20 and throughout the book; and Mosse 2005, pp. 8–10, 17–20, and chapters 7 and 8.

[24] For a similar claim on Burundi, see Campbell 2010, pp. 8 and 41–59.

[25] On Congo as a case of intervention failure, among many others: Autesserre 2010; Kreps 2010; International Crisis Group 2012b; and Trefon 2011.

[26] Garb and Allen Nan 2009, p. 5.

levels.[27] A number of field-based interveners whom I interviewed viewed this emphasis as perfectly appropriate. They insisted that their role was merely to execute orders from the capital and that, compared to their superiors, their ideas and actions had little influence on eventual outcomes.

The researchers who examine grassroots dynamics usually focus on how intended beneficiaries react to interventions. They demonstrate that local authorities and populations regularly contest, adapt, and transform international programs, and thus that the results of foreign efforts are a hybrid between the intentions of the expatriates and the interests of the local stakeholders.[28] I agree with these findings and, based on my research, add to them the contention that field-based interveners engage in similar behavior. As regularly occurs when one party acts on behalf of another in any kind of organization or social situation, peace interveners regularly adapt, transform, and alter top-down instructions.[29] My analysis therefore questions the dominant macro-level approach, challenging its assumption that instructions from capitals and headquarters automatically translate into corresponding action in the field, and complements the micro-level approach that typically focuses on host populations.[30]

On-the-ground peacebuilders are much more than implementers. Instructions from the top must always be interpreted and translated into action, which provides field-based interveners with substantial leeway in conducting their operations. Consider peacekeeping missions. Mandates coming from the United Nations (UN) Security Council are always vague, as they are the product of negotiations among countries with divergent values and interests, and representatives can reach a consensus only when using language open to multiple interpretations. As a result, mandates provide the broad guidelines for a given mission, but offer little detail. The local leaders of peacekeeping operations must translate any new mandate they receive into a series of concrete tasks for implementation; military officers have to translate civilian directives into mission objectives, and then peacekeepers stationed in the field must take their version of their instructions from the capital city and adapt them to specific situations in each part of the country.[31]

---

[27] Studies that, though fascinating, exhibit this bias, include, among many others: Barnett 2002; Chandler 2004; Doyle and Sambanis 2006; Fortna 2008; Howard 2008; Paris 2004; Richmond 2005; and Walter 2002.

[28] Among others: Acharya 2009; Barnett and Zürcher 2009; Mac Ginty 2010 and 2011; Richmond and Mitchell 2011; and Tadjbakhsh 2011.

[29] For theoretical background on this issue, see the enormous body of literature on the principal-agent problem, such as Downs and Rocke 1994; Eisenhardt 1989; Fama and Jensen 1983; Miller 2005; and Sappington 1991, as well as the body of research inspired by Lipsky 1980's insight on "street-level bureaucrats."

[30] For a criticism similar to mine toward the research on humanitarian aid, see Fechter and Hindman 2011a, pp. 4–5, and toward the research on development see Mosse 2005, notably pp. 16–17 and 103.

[31] For detailed examples of this process, see Holt and Berkman 2006; Neumann and Schia 2012, pp. 36–37; Pouligny 2004, pp. 159–164; UN Security Council 2004b, paras. 58 and 59; and MONUSCO news, "MONUSCO Heads of Offices Debate Resolution 1991," July 8, 2011.

A number of peacebuilding institutions actually build autonomy of field offices into their organizational structures. Certain UN peacekeeping operations give staff on the ground the latitude to adjust to local situations.[32] Likewise, according to my interviews, embassy personnel enjoy a certain degree of freedom from their foreign ministries, especially when the ambassadors are seasoned diplomats whose superiors trust them enough to let them take the lead. Consular personnel deployed in the field have a similar degree of independence from their embassies in the capital. Even military personnel do more than just execute orders: Many armies around the world, such as those of the United States, Canada, Holland, Israel, and the United Kingdom, have implemented the concept of "mission command" (otherwise known as "decentralized decision-making"), which promotes increased freedom of action and encourages independent thinking in lower-level officers.[33]

The wide divide between capitals and field offices further reinforces the tendency of on-the-ground peacebuilders to adapt the instructions they receive. Interveners working for international, non-governmental, and diplomatic organizations in a diverse array of countries, from Afghanistan to El Salvador to Timor-Leste, regularly complained about the schism between the capital city – or, even worse, foreign capitals or the headquarters of international organizations – and the provinces where they were based.[34] In Bosnia-Herzegovina, the split became so pronounced that a high-ranking official deployed in the Brčko district in the late 2000s complained of spending "almost 80 percent of [his] energy and time" fighting with his superiors based in Sarajevo.[35]

Interestingly, a number of contacts asserted, in accordance with what I observed on several occasions, that the split between field offices and capital cities regularly proved more significant than any organizational, professional, or national divide among foreign peacebuilders. International interveners stationed in Brčko "tended to view themselves" and act "as part of a coherent 'Brčko team'" despite their differing organizational affiliations.[36] In many of my field sites, peacebuilders representing different agencies or countries on the ground had more in common with each other than with their colleagues in domestic and foreign capitals when it came to understanding the situation and potential solutions to problems. In Congo in late 2010 and early 2011, for instance, interviewees working for all kinds of organizations in South Kivu complained that their Kinshasa-based supervisors had a profoundly biased view of the situation in their province. For the latter, political and security conditions were

---

[32] Howard 2008, notably pp. 68 and 193 (on the UN missions in Namibia and Mozambique); and Moore 2013's analysis of the Brčko district in Bosnia.

[33] Storr 2003, notably pp. 119–120 and 122–125. For an analysis of the obstacles to mission command: Vogelaar and Kramer 2004. For a defense of this approach: Stewart 2006.

[34] On El Salvador (and other countries): Pouligny 2004, pp. 176–184. The other examples are based on my own interviews.

[35] Moore 2013, p. 127.

[36] Ibid., p. 120.

improving and on the way to stabilization, while for the former, they were deteriorating and on the way to extensive renewed violence.

There are two main reasons for this divide: different information and different priorities. Due to their proximity to the places where violence happens, field-based peacebuilders have more details on human rights violations and causes of tensions, and thus they often understand the risks facing peace efforts more intimately. As my interviewees explained, this information is regularly filtered out or censored during communications between the field, capitals, and headquarters.[37] Intermediaries at each level have to synthesize enormous amounts of information into a few pages and present their work in the best possible light, losing content and nuances at each step. In contrast, interveners based in capitals and headquarters tend to have a broader view of the situation and of the pros and cons of each action. In addition, they are often more attuned to strategic questions.

Priorities also differ. As I observed in Burundi, Congo, Israel, and South Sudan, diplomats and international organization staff members based in capital cities often see maintaining good relationships with the host governments as a paramount goal, while a number of their on-the-ground colleagues would prefer to confront those that impede their work. Diplomats involved in peace processes also explained that they tended to feel sympathy for the local counterparts with whom they interacted on a daily basis. This created tensions, for instance, between Kigali- and Kinshasa-based diplomats working on the negotiations between Congo and Rwanda; between Tel Aviv- and West Bank- or Jerusalem-based interveners working on the Israeli-Palestinian conflict; and between the Khartoum- and Juba-based facilitators working on the peace talks between what were then the Northern and Southern parts of Sudan (which resulted in the 2011 referendum).

Due to these various divisions, capital-based interveners often view their field-based colleagues as absorbed in unimportant local matters and unable to see the bigger picture, a perception that was clearly expressed during my interviews. Conversely, field-based peacebuilders frequently present their superiors in capital cities and headquarters as having only a theoretical and superficial knowledge of their areas of deployment.[38] They also regularly complain that their supervisors perceive local situations much more optimistically, and consequently minimize the significance of continuing violence, the many obstacles to peacebuilding, and the needs of interveners on the ground. Numerous field-based peacebuilders lamented that, as a result, the instructions they received were out of touch with local situations and therefore inadequate or irrelevant. Others deplored a lack of clear instructions from superiors, which left them without a concrete sense of how they were supposed to carry out their duties on the ground.

---

[37] For a public source on this topic, see Neumann and Schia 2012, p. 36.
[38] For a public source, see Pouligny 2004, p. 181.

Field-based interviewees therefore routinely view it as their role to adapt instructions to realities on the ground – especially logistical and security constraints, human resources limitations, and requests from local partners – a perception that widens the gap between macro-level intentions and micro-level practice. Several interviewees even believed that their programs could succeed only if they bent the rules and regretted not being able to do so in many cases. For instance, the UN headquarters in Congo insists on using merit as the primary criterion for recruitment, while field-based interveners believe that ethnicity should be even more important: Local populations will never accept well-qualified staff members of the "wrong" ethnic group, and, consequently, peacebuilding programs are condemned from the start. Other UN interviewees based in various countries complained about lengthy and cumbersome procurement procedures, which forced them to choose between respecting the regulations and failing to respond to emergencies, or ignoring the rules and fulfilling their responsibilities. They also abhorred the impossibly strict guidelines for selecting local subcontractors, supporting local authorities, and utilizing their logistical assets. A group of UN officers working in the Palestinian Territories encapsulated the resulting sentiment among field-based interveners when they boasted that they were "very dynamic because [they] bent many rules."

Altogether, these observations expose a crucial implication for the study of peace interventions. The significant influence that decentralized interveners have over what actually happens in the field makes considering the specific dynamics of on-the-ground peacebuilding indispensable. Admittedly, some of these dynamics are the products of top-down instructions, such as the strict guidelines from donors and headquarters concerning issues like security, recruitment, and visibility. These generate on-the-ground practices that prevent peacebuilding initiatives from reaching their full potential (see Chapter 7). However, orders from above do not fully determine behavior in the field. Instructions are usually broad, so there is wide variation in how expatriates implement them. A number of interveners go so far as to circumvent, vocally challenge, or reject the rules and offer alternate ways to operate in conflict zones. Additionally, many of their shared practices – such as the expatriates' tendency to live and work mostly with one another and the specific way they collect and analyze data on their areas of deployment – are unrelated to top-down directives. They result purely from bottom-up dynamics.

Focusing on field-based interveners is also all the more important because their actions shape the way host populations view international peacebuilding.[39] Virtually no local people will ever read the mandate of the UN peacekeeping mission deployed in their village or the country strategy of the non-governmental organization (NGO) helping their families. Those who live in rural parts of war-torn countries most likely have little or no access to media reports on these topics. Instead, their main sources of information on international programs,

[39] Based on Lipsky 1980.

policies, and strategies are their day-to-day impressions of how neighboring interveners live and work and their evaluation of the services they deliver.[40] In this book, I therefore pay particular attention to international peacebuilders deployed in provinces and rural areas away from their organizations' headquarters and away from their host nation's capital cities (locations to which I refer as "in the field" or "on the ground").

The Concepts

The fact that local populations comprehend intervention at least partly through the daily activities of field-based interveners reinforces one of the major contentions of this book: The social lives of international peacebuilders, their personal relationships, and their informal actions carry enormous significance in conflict and post-conflict zones. As Chapter 5 explains, interveners rarely blend in with local populations; instead, they form a visible, closed group whose members are easily identifiable. There is no clear separation between their private and professional lives. It makes no difference if they are on duty or relaxing after work. Whether they want to or not, foreign peacebuilders represent their organizations and the broader intervention community at all times.

Three concepts – practices, habits, and narratives – are particularly useful for analyzing this everyday dimension of the lives and work of interveners. This section presents each of these concepts in turn. For added clarity, Table 1 summarizes the key practices, habits, and narratives that are most central to my argument – the list being selective rather than exhaustive. Readers less interested in theoretical debates can skip the rest of this chapter (with the possible exception of Table 2) and go straight to the substantive portions of my analysis, which start in Part I.

Practices

Pierre Bourdieu's concept of "practical sense" has inspired an enormous body of research in the social sciences.[41] Practices are "routine activities (rather than consciously chosen actions) notable for their unconscious, automatic, un-thought character."[42] They can be individual – inscribed in habits and usual ways of using one's body – or transpersonal, embedded in organizational processes.[43]

---

[40] Also Pouligny 2004, p. 195.
[41] Bourdieu 1972 and 1979. Schatzki, Knorr-Cetina, et al. 2001 provides an overview of the use of this concept in social sciences.
[42] Swidler 2001, p. 74.
[43] Ibid., p. 75.

TABLE 1. *International Interveners' Dominant Practices, Habits, and Narratives*

Practices	• Helping host countries and populations
	• Valuing thematic expertise over local knowledge
	   ○ Placing expatriates in management positions and local staff in subordinate ones
	   ○ Deploying interveners who are not familiar with local contexts and do not speak local languages
	   ○ Rotating interveners every couple of years
	   ○ Relying on universal templates and "lessons learned"
	   ○ Overlooking local input in project design
	   ○ Compartmentalizing the international system into several distinct components (development, humanitarian, and peace programs)
	• Collecting information on violence mainly from other interveners and local elites
	• Using simplified narratives on the causes, consequences, and solutions to violence in host countries
	• Resolving conflicts from the top down
	• Holding security and coordination meetings
	• Being accountable to donors and not to intended beneficiaries
	• Striving to remain neutral or impartial
	• Perpetually writing reports
	• Quantifying the results of actions
	• Adopting a short-term outlook

Habits	• Socializing primarily with other expatriates • Following security procedures (carrying a handheld radio, informing the base of all movements, not walking around at night, driving with doors locked and windows closed, etc.) • Advertising actions

Narratives	• Technical expertise trumps local knowledge
	• Violence in the host country has a primary cause, consequence, and solution
	• Interveners are deployed to help host populations and governments
	   ○ Host populations need help
	   ○ Local elite lack knowledge and capacity
	• Interveners are distinct from local populations

Vincent Pouliot and Emmanuel Adler have best explained how one may recognize practices in international relations.[44] A practice has five core characteristics.[45] It is (1) "a process of doing something" that is (2) patterned and thus "generally exhibits certain regularities over time and space."[46] Importantly,

---

[44] Pouliot 2008 and 2010; and Pouliot and Adler 2011b.
[45] Pouliot and Adler 2011b.
[46] Ibid., p. 7.

it is (3) "competent in a socially meaningful and recognizable way," meaning that "groups of individuals tend to interpret its performance along similar standards."[47] It (4) "rests on [people's] background knowledge," and it is (5) both ideational and material: It represents preferences and policies and, in doing so, makes use of a variety of materials.[48] For instance, as I explain in the course of this book, the practice of helping a host country build peace consists of a number of actions and processes (such as providing advice or participating in meetings) that are patterned: They recur in a recognizable way across theaters of interventions. Groups of individuals, such as interveners, tend to interpret the performance of these actions and processes along similar lines because this practice rests on shared background knowledge, such as the difference between those who provide aid and their beneficiaries. This practice is also both ideational (enacting a moral claim) and material (embodied in banners and logos).

The aforementioned fourth and fifth essential features enable us to locate the sources of practices. They tell us that a practice is the product of "background dispositions," which "every social being carries and uses constantly, if unconsciously," in everyday life.[49] It results from tacit, "inarticulate know-how that makes what is to be done appear 'self-evident' or commonsensical."[50] As individuals perform practices "more or less competently," these practices "simultaneously embody, act out, and possibly reify background knowledge and discourse in and on the material world."[51] The practice of helping, for example, rests on the tacit understanding that international interveners are somehow different from host populations. When, as routinely happens in Peaceland, expatriates take the lead in designing and implementing conflict-resolution programs, they substantiate this notion that they have capacities which local people lack.

These two traits also illuminate the relationships between practices and other concepts used in this book. Practices are "sustained by a repertoire of ideational and material communal resources," such as "routines, words, tools, ways of doing things, stories, symbols, and discourse" – including narratives.[52] To continue with the example of the practice of helping, it relies on narratives such as "host populations need help," words like "peacekeepers" and "beneficiaries," tools like evaluation surveys, and symbols like logos and banners.

One last related concept, Ann Swidler's concept of "anchoring practice," is particularly useful for analyzing international peacebuilding.[53] An anchoring practice is a "bundle of interwoven practices" that makes "possible other, more

[47] Ibid., p. 7.
[48] Ibid., p. 8.
[49] Pouliot 2008, pp. 258 and 269.
[50] Ibid., p. 257. See also Pouliot 2010, p. 12
[51] Pouliot and Adler 2011a, p. 4.
[52] Adler 2005, pp. 15 and 17.
[53] Swidler, 2001. See also Neumann and Sending 2011.

specific practices" by providing "a common reference-point, an infrastructure for interaction that allows actors to engage in other, non-anchoring practices."[54] The practice of helping a host country or population, for instance, includes and makes possible numerous other practices that characterize international intervention in the early twenty-first century. These more specific practices, which I document in this book, comprise actions as varied as reporting, collecting data on violence, following security routines, promoting visibility, valuing thematic expertise over local knowledge, attending periodic meetings among peacebuilders, fighting or cooperating with other interveners, interacting with local populations, and developing "best practices" – a buzzword in intervention circles, applied to tasks as varied as protection of populations, food distribution, and community reconciliation.

Habits

A habit is simply a term that refers to a specific kind of practice:[55] an automatic response to the world.[56] Habits share many of the same characteristics as practices – they are actions that are patterned, competent, socially meaningful, and so on. However, I distinguish these two by using the term "habits" to refer to certain everyday elements when I want specifically to emphasize the profoundly unthought and automatic nature of those particular practices. The security routines that peacebuilders follow when deployed in conflict zones, such as not walking around at night, driving with doors locked, and – for interveners in many organizations – using codenames on the radio and informing the base of all movements, are all examples of such elements. As I experienced, these routines are among the first things that newcomers to Peaceland learn. Within a few weeks, they become habitual ways of acting that expatriates then use whenever they are deployed in unstable settings. Interveners do not even need to think about them; they become such automatic responses to perceptions of danger.

Other examples of interveners' habits include "sustained and patterned relationships between and among" groups.[57] These relationships can be conflictual (as is often the case with humanitarian NGOs and military peacekeepers), cooperative (like among many of the NGO actors deployed in the same remote field location), or mixed (like between expatriates and local populations). As the following chapters demonstrate, such patterned relationships "yield systematically biased perceptions, attitudes, and practices toward these automatically categorized" groups.[58]

---

[54] Ibid., pp. 232 and 236.
[55] Swidler 2001, p. 75.
[56] Hopf 2010. This section presents the main ideas of Hopf 2010 that help develop this book's analysis.
[57] Ibid., p. 549.
[58] Ibid., p. 549.

Habits are commonplace in social life. According to numerous social theorists and neuroscientists, they "account for what most of us do most of the time."[59] They especially prevail under two conditions that occur very frequently for peacebuilders: situations of "cognitive overload" – having to think about more than one task at once – and those with "severe time constraints," in which people lack the time necessary for conscious deliberation.[60] Circumstances like these are partially responsible for the persistence of the "expatriate bubble." International interveners have so many priorities to address in so little time that they do not have the opportunity to question their usual patterns of after-work socialization, let alone consider whether interacting mostly with other expatriates – rather than local people – may diminish the effectiveness of their efforts.

Even more importantly, habits help account not only "for what we perceive and do, but also for what we do not perceive or do."[61] They shape what is thinkable and what is not. As Ted Hopf explains, habits provide "ready-made responses to the world that we execute without thinking. They prevent other behaviors by short-circuiting any need to decide what we are doing. So an infinite array of behaviors is effectively deleted from the available repertoire of possible actions."[62] For instance, international peacebuilders do not prioritize intimate understanding of local histories, cultures, or languages, except in rare cases. They do not recruit or give promotions based upon knowledge of local contexts. Likewise, they do not make a point of developing personal and social relationships with host populations. This is simply not done. It was clear during my fieldwork that many interveners do not even consider that alternative ways of living and working are possible. Thus, as I will explain in the next section, the fact that habits eliminate many possible actions from an otherwise broad catalogue helps explain why interveners may reproduce counterproductive modes of operation instead of challenging them.

Narratives

The last concept central to my analysis, that of narratives, is especially helpful for studying the politics of knowledge in Peaceland. Narratives are stories that people create to make sense of their lives and environments.[63] Some examples of narratives dominant in Peaceland include views about the primary causes, consequences, and solutions to violence in the country of intervention (see Chapter 4), or the idea that foreign peacebuilders come to help host populations and governments (see Chapter 6).

---

[59] Ibid., p. 547.
[60] Ibid., pp. 542–543 and 547.
[61] Ibid., p. 542.
[62] Ibid., p. 541.
[63] This sentence and the next one are based on Abbott 2008; De Fina and Georgakopoulou 2008; and Patterson and Monroe 1998.

Narratives usually include a central frame or combination of frames. Frames are social objects.[64] They exist not only inside individuals' minds (as psychological approaches would emphasize[65]), but they are also embedded in social routines, practices, discourses, technologies, and institutions. They can consist of ideologies (such as liberalism), "assumptions and definitions that are taken as given" (for example, host populations lack capacity), and paradigms (like the liberal peace paradigm that I discuss below) – which include standard operating procedures (such as election organization) and "shared definitions of the environment" (for instance, Timor-Leste is a post-conflict situation).[66]

Narratives and frames are socially constructed over long periods of time.[67] Consider for instance the dominant collective understanding that interveners should approach their roles in a top-down manner through regular interactions with national and international elites. This understanding originated in the practice of diplomacy in classical antiquity, and each critical historical juncture – such as the 1648 treaty of Westphalia and the rise of international organizations in the twentieth century – has reinforced it.[68]

Organizational theorists and international sociologists disagree on where to locate the sources of dominant collective understandings.[69] For the purpose of this book, it suffices to remember that narratives can originate at the level of international organizations (such as the idea that interveners should be impartial), the peacebuilding field (the view that interveners are distinct from local people), or the global international stage (the consensus that statebuilding is an appropriate answer to war and violence).[70] My case study of dominant narratives concerning the Congolese conflict highlights the varied origins of several specific narratives and explains of how and why some of them became dominant instead of others.

Narratives constantly interact with practices.[71] To begin with, some narratives emerge from practices.[72] For example, the idea that international peacebuilders

---

[64] The rest of this paragraph builds on Barnett and Finnemore 2004; Eden 2004; Finnemore 1996; Klotz and Lynch 2007; and Weick 1995. The rest of this section also draws on Autesserre 2009, pp. 252–256.

[65] For a political science application, see Jervis 2006.

[66] Based on Weick 1995, chapter 5, citations from pp. 113 and 118.

[67] Based on Berger and Luckmann 1967.

[68] Autesserre 2010, pp. 94–97 sketches the history of this conception.

[69] For more on this debate, see Ibid., pp. 25–27.

[70] On organizations as the source of frames, see Barnett 2002; and Barnett and Finnemore 2004. On the field as the source of dominant collective understandings: Autesserre 2010, notably p. 26. On the global international scene: Finnemore 1996; Paris 2003, p. 442; and Richmond 2002 and 2005.

[71] Mosse 2005 provides a very useful discussion of the anthropological literature on the complex relationship between ideas and practice on pp. 10 and 16–17 and a fascinating application of this literature's main insights in chapters 4 to 7.

[72] See Weick 1995 for an overview of the sociological literature on the topic; and Autesserre 2010, pp. 24–28 for a summary of political science debates.

are distinct from local populations derives from the very experience of living and working in conflict zones. Furthermore, practices make possible and sustain dominant narratives already in existence, as occurs when subpar data collection practices lead peacebuilders to rely on dominant narratives to interpret their environments. Conversely, existing dominant narratives also enable and justify specific practices. For instance, the prevailing narrative that host populations and their elites lack capacity legitimizes the practice of sending foreigners to help build peace in conflict zones and of putting these foreigners in leadership positions.

The interveners' reliance on a dominant narrative or a dominant frame generates a preferred vantage point from which to analyze the situations they face. Various individuals and organizations use this perspective in different ways, and there are many exceptions to the dominant view. These variations and exceptions notwithstanding, the existence of dominant narratives and frames helps account for some of the striking similarities between interveners that one can observe when studying on-the-ground peacebuilding.

The Explanation

These three concepts – practices, habits, and narratives – allow me to analyze the set of tools that interveners use in their everyday professional and personal lives.[73] These tools are varied. They include techniques (like mediation), best practices (like promoting local ownership), models (like power-sharing), and protocols for measuring the world (like evaluation surveys). They also consist of rules (like living in a secured compound), rituals (like goodbye parties), taken-for-granted behaviors (like security routines), accepted skills (like theoretical knowledge of conflict resolution), and established approaches (like top-down peacebuilding). Finally, they comprise ways of seeing things (like deeming people in conflict zones lacking in knowledge and capacity) and a general understanding of the way situations are (like believing that interveners know better than local populations). This book studies how these tools are developed, shared, and, at times, contested. It also examines how interveners build expertise and the strategies they use to make that expertise relevant.

In this section, I discuss how I weave these various ideas and concepts together into an explanation of intervention effectiveness.[74] I first elucidate how practice, habits, and narratives shape outcomes and how they diffuse to various actors in Peaceland. I then emphasize the presence and importance of exceptional individuals and organizations who suggest alternative modes of operations. Lastly, I describe how dominant ways of thinking and acting usually evolve over time, and I show how practices and habits may obstruct this process of change, instead

---

[73] This paragraph builds on Bourdieu 1972; Chabal and Daloz 2011; Mitchell 2002; Pouliot 2010; and Swidler 1986.

[74] Along with the books and articles cited in the footnotes of the following subsections, Chabal and Daloz 2011; and Geertz 1973 were among the main sources of inspiration for my analysis.

enabling inefficient, ineffective, and counterproductive elements to persist. For added clarity, Table 2 summarizes which of the interveners' key practices, habits, and narratives are particularly inefficient, ineffective, or even counterproductive for peacebuilding, thus making it especially important for us to understand the reasons behind their persistence.

TABLE 2. *Main Negative Impacts of the International Interveners' Dominant Practices, Habits, and Narratives*

Inefficient	• Placing expatriates in management positions and local staff in subordinate ones • Rotating interveners every couple of years • Deploying interveners who are not familiar with local contexts and do not speak local languages • Compartmentalizing the international system into several distinct components • Following "bunkerization" security procedures • Perpetually writing reports • Adopting a short-term outlook <div align="center">***Mixed (partly efficient and partly inefficient)***</div>• Overlooking local input in project design • Quantifying the results of actions
Ineffective	• Placing expatriates in management positions and local staff in subordinate ones • Deploying interveners who are not familiar with local contexts and do not speak local languages • Relying on universal templates and "lessons learned" • Overlooking local input in project design • Compartmentalizing the international system into several distinct components • Collecting information on violence mainly from other interveners and local elites • Using simplified narratives on the causes, consequences, and solutions to violence in host countries • Narrative that violence in the host country has a primary cause, consequence, and solution • Resolving conflicts exclusively from the top down • Being accountable to donors and not to intended beneficiaries • Adopting a short-term outlook <div align="center">***Construct boundaries***</div>• Holding exclusive security and coordination meetings • Socializing primarily with other expatriates • Narrative that host populations need help • Narrative that local elite lack knowledge and capacity

- Following security procedures
- Perpetually writing reports
- Adopting a short term outlook

	• Deploying interveners who are not familiar with local contexts and do not speak local languages
	Occasionally fuel violence
	• Relying on universal templates and "lessons learned"
	• Collecting information on violence mainly from other interveners and local elites (because leads to reliance on simplistic narratives)
	• Using simplified narratives on the causes, consequences, and solutions to violence in host countries
	• Narrative that violence in the host country has a primary cause, consequence, and solution
	• Resolving conflicts exclusively from the top down
Counterproductive	*Fuel local resentment*
	• Valuing thematic expertise over local knowledge (overall)
	• Placing expatriates in management positions and local staff in subordinate ones
	• Overlooking local input in project design
	• Narrative that host populations need help
	• Narrative that local elite lack knowledge and capacity
	• Being accountable to donors and not to intended beneficiaries
	Decrease local ownership
	• Placing expatriates in management positions and local staff in subordinate ones
	• Overlooking local input for project design
	• Being accountable to donors and not to intended beneficiaries
	• Advertising actions

Overall Process

Practices, habits, and narratives enable human beings to function in the social world. Dominant narratives help us sift through and interpret the massive amount of information we perpetually receive, sparing us the need to analyze each occurrence anew. Dominant practices and habits suggest routine ways to respond to new events, circumventing choosing every time between an infinite number of possible reactions.

Practices, habits, and narratives do not cause or determine action.[75] Instead, they orient action. They are "dispositional: [Each] inclines or disposes actors to

---

[75] This paragraph builds on an analysis I developed in Autesserre 2010, pp. 23–30. It draws extensively on Barnett and Finnemore 2004; Berger and Luckmann 1967; Eden 2004; Fearon

do certain things. [Each] generates propensities and tendencies."[76] Practices, habits, and narratives shape people's understandings of the world and its meanings. They make the choice of certain actors or strategies seem natural, appropriate, and effective, while others appear inappropriate, illegitimate, or even unthinkable. For instance, Chapter 2 documents how the knowledge politics in Peaceland makes it seem appropriate and legitimate for interveners to rely on external expertise, material, and structures instead of using, developing, and reinforcing those available locally.

Another important function of shared understandings and practices is that they shape peoples' views on what counts as a problem and what does not.[77] They affect which events will be noticed and which will not, as well as how these events will be interpreted. In Congo, for example, various narratives have constructed both the illegal exploitation of natural resources and sexual violence as problems that international actors should address. This precipitated not only an increase in attention to events connected with these topics, but also a proliferation of actions aimed at solving these problems. By contrast, other narratives framed micro-level community conflict and nonsexual torture as domestic issues unworthy of international attention, and, as a result, international interveners habitually disregarded them (see Chapter 4).

Ultimately, practices, habits, and narratives authorize, enable, and justify specific actions while precluding others. These actions in turn reproduce and reinforce existing practices, habits, and narratives. Over time, as various modes of operation spread through Peaceland and as they are reproduced and perpetuated, interveners progressively come to take them for granted, seeing them as natural and as the only conceivable modes of thinking and acting.[78]

Diffusion

Numerous formal and informal mechanisms help spread and perpetuate the ways of understanding and acting in Peaceland. These mechanisms include professional trainings and formal education – numerous interveners have attended graduate programs in international affairs, aid, or conflict studies. These various courses encourage a common mindset, which takes for granted, for instance, the possibility to solve problems in the developing world using universalist, technical solutions. They also teach students tools to employ in the field, like monitoring and evaluation techniques. Participants then bring this common perspective and training to various organizations.

---

and Wendt 2002, notably p. 58; Finnemore 1996; Hopf 2010; Klotz and Lynch 2007; Pouliot 2010; Swidler 1986; Weick 1995; and Wendt 1999, pp. 83–88.

[76] Based on Pouliot 2010, p. 33.

[77] This sentence and the next one are based on Barnett and Finnemore 2004; Eden 2004; Goldstein and Keohane 1993 (notably p. 12); Neumann 2008; and Weick 1995.

[78] Based on Berger and Luckmann 1967.

Another key mechanism for the diffusion of practices, habits, and narratives is professional turnover. Many expatriates change organizations over the course of their careers. International organizations such as the World Bank or the UN regularly "borrow" diplomats from member states as personnel, while other peacebuilders move from one NGO to the next, or alternate between NGOs and UN agencies. Certain seasoned interveners also carry multiple affiliations at the same time: Senior academic scholars of peace and conflict may act as consultants for governmental or international agencies, while also serving as board members for NGOs.[79] Moreover, foreign peacebuilders usually change countries of deployment every few years. Each time expatriates change place or organization, they carry over the mindset, tools, and ways of understanding the world acquired from their previous postings to their new positions.

In the field, the personal and professional gatherings of expatriates from various organizational, national, or professional groups form one last key mechanism of diffusion of everyday modes of operation. Such events can be as formal as the management meetings that each organization arranges regularly, or the coordination meetings periodically held in each field location; or as informal as getting together for happy hour at popular bars, living in a common residence, and going to parties with colleagues. These various settings provide forums for interveners to share information and reiterate narratives. They also allow veterans to introduce dominant practices to newcomers, who thereby learn to mimic prevailing habits. Novices adopt leading ways of thinking and acting through "instrumental cost–benefit calculations," "socialization to some normative standard," or "mere imitation of what does, and does not, go on in the world around" them.[80] The tendency toward imitation is important to note, as it demonstrates that actual socialization does not necessarily need to take place: Mere "repeated exposure to how things are, and are not, done" may be sufficient.[81]

Exceptions and Contestation

Despite these various mechanisms of diffusion, there are exceptions to all the dominant modes of operation that I analyze in this book. Dissenters regularly challenge the prevailing practices, habits, and narratives.[82] As explained in the first section of this chapter, exceptions do not take place at the level of an entire country or province but at that of an organization, initiative, or individual. Across all the conflict zones in which I researched, regardless of whether policy-makers and academics consider the interventions there to have been successful or not, most interveners I met constantly reproduced dominant modes of

---

[79] Guilhot 2005, p. 12.
[80] Based on the analysis of habits in Hopf 2010, p. 542.
[81] Ibid., p. 542.
[82] For more on dissenters in general, see Dunn 2003; and Klotz and Lynch 2007, notably pp. 8–9.

operation. In all of my field sites, however, I encountered individuals and organizations who rejected the prevailing modes of acting and thinking and promoted alternative ones. None of these actors were immune to all of the dynamics I describe in the following chapters, but each of them successfully challenged at least one or more of the dominant practices, habits, or narratives. My aim in this book is not to provide an exhaustive list of such organizations and individuals, but rather to analyze a few representative examples of exceptional actors for each of the dominant modes of operation I examine in order to draw lessons from their experiences. These actors were often more effective in achieving their goals, revealing both specific ways to improve peace interventions and the extent to which the dominant practices are inefficient. Furthermore, as the rest of this section explains, the actions of such exceptional individuals and organizations drive contestation of dominant practices, habits, and narratives, and ultimately help account for change in Peaceland.

Following Alexander Wendt, I view agents and structures as mutually constitutive – meaning that they shape each other.[83] Structures can be institutions, systems of incentives and disincentives, or, more broadly, any "set of relatively unchangeable constraints" on the conduct of individuals and organizations.[84] As such, structures shape people's beliefs and behaviors. However, through their practices, individuals are able to create, instantiate, and maintain specific structures over others. By doing so, actors can challenge, undermine, and even alter the dominant structures.

This book examines "how an action does or does not reproduce both the actor[s] and the structure[s]" in Peaceland.[85] My analysis of the structure of inequality in the international peacebuilding system illustrates this process. The very idea of sending foreign peacebuilders into conflict zones is predicated on the idea that outsiders have something to contribute that local people lack. Chapter 2 traces the process through which various groups of individuals constructed and promoted this narrative. As I show throughout the book, this structure now generates power asymmetries between external interveners and local stakeholders, and it shapes both the perceptions of local people and the interveners' everyday actions on the ground. The fact that even expatriates who are competent, hardworking, and altruistic nevertheless follow the harmful practices that perpetuate these inequalities demonstrates how powerful the structure of the intervention system can be and how difficult it is to escape. Beyond the impact of the structure of inequality, the book shows that many of the interveners' practices, habits, and narratives are understandable responses to the structures of the situations that they face.

Despite their strength, however, structures do not fully determine the actions of the inhabitants of Peaceland. Different actors respond differently to the same

---

[83] Wendt 1987. This paragraph builds notably on pp. 394–395. See also Onuf 1998.
[84] Hopf 1998, p. 172.
[85] Based on ibid., p. 172.

set of constraints, and as a result their habits and practices may vary even when the structure remains similar. For instance, although most interveners engage in everyday practices that reproduce and perpetuate the structure of inequality – such as disregarding local input while designing initiatives and following different security procedures for expatriates and for local staff – a few individuals and agencies adopt alternative modes of operation. They base their programs on local demands and ideas, put local staff in management positions, strive to be accountable to intended beneficiaries, rely on neighboring citizens to ensure their security; in brief, they escape the dominant modes of operation, suggest alternate ones, and in doing so undermine Peaceland's structure of inequality.

Two groups lead the process of contestation in Peaceland. The first consists of those excluded from access to power, including ordinary citizens in conflict zones and, to a lesser extent, the international interveners' local counterparts. These people regularly challenge the interveners' dominant modes of operation and highlight their detrimental impacts. In particular, the widespread phenomena of contestation, resistance, distortion, or rejection of a given international program are ways for local actors to provide feedback in situations where few other critiques are forthcoming (see Chapter 3).[86] The second group includes expatriates who find themselves at the margin of the interveners' club. They may be individuals who have not yet been socialized to Peaceland (the newcomers), interveners from the same region as the host country (for example, Kenyans and Ugandans in South Sudan), and those with particularly strong ties to the host countries due to personal or family history (members of the diaspora, spouses of citizens, individuals whose parents or family are nationals of the host country, or researchers who focus on a particular conflict zone). As the subsequent chapters highlight, the foreign peacebuilders at the margin of the interveners' club are the most likely to promote competing practices, habits, and narratives, and they routinely do so.

Identifying the sociological and psychological roots of exceptional behavior among interveners is not the primary goal of this book. However, I have developed a tentative argument based again on the work of Alexander Wendt and the application of his analysis to my field material.[87] Wendt draws a distinction between the "social determination of the self" and "the personal determination of choice." The former is the "me," produced by "effects of socialization to structures of identity and interests"; it is the "part of subjectivity" that is "defined in terms of others" and assumes roles that are "socially constituted." The latter is the "I," which appropriates and reacts to these social roles, adapting them "in idiosyncratic ways." It is the ability of the "I" to choose whether and how to perform the social roles of the "me" that provides

---

[86] See also Richmond and Mitchell 2011 for more on this topic.

[87] This paragraph quotes and paraphrases Wendt 1992, p. 419. Wendt builds on Mead 1934; and Turner 1962.

individuals with the freedom they need to contest, challenge, and try to change social structures. The "I" is the seat of the agency that enables people to destabilize even deeply institutionalized meanings, to challenge even the most pervasive narratives, and to reject even widely accepted roles.[88]

Wendt identifies "two preconditions" for an individual to consciously choose "to transform or transcend roles" (and thus evade and challenge the existing structure).[89] "First, there must be a reason to think of oneself in novel terms."[90] In Peaceland, this occasion may arise when interveners from the same region as the host country, or with particularly strong ties to it, experience a dissonance between the modes of operation to which they might personally be inclined and those dominant in the intervention world. A related case is when organizations with strong preexisting values or bylaws that demand relations with local partners (such as faith-based NGOs whose primary entry point in the field is a network of local religious groups) find that the practices prevalent among other intervening agencies conflict with their own. This reevaluation of the self can also occur when newcomers arrive in the field, or when a person from an entirely different social setting sets up a new intervening organization, as was the case when a Hollywood star founded the Eastern Congo Initiative. In all of these scenarios, the individuals face new social situations that they cannot handle simply by taking on established roles and scripts, and they therefore create alternative modes of thinking and doing.

The second precondition that Wendt identifies is that "the expected costs of intentional role change – the sanctions imposed by others with whom one interacted in previous roles – [do not exceed] its rewards."[91] This cost-benefit ratio differs with each situation and individual, but several variables are consistent. To start, expatriates benefit personally from some of the prevailing modes of operation. Various dynamics in Peaceland, such as the structure of inequality and the emphasis on thematic expertise over local knowledge, work to the advantage of foreign peacebuilders. Furthermore, interveners rarely suffer from the consequences of their ineffective practices, and they are barely accountable to their beneficiaries. The benefits of the status quo and the insulation from its harmful effects diminish potential incentives for expatriates to challenge the prevailing modes of operation. To make matters worse, as explained in the following section, the costs of role-breaking in Peaceland are often steep. As a result, exceptions remain relatively rare in the current intervention world.

It is out of the scope of this book to explore the many other factors that affect the cost-benefit ratio and the perceived usefulness of established roles and scripts. My anecdotal evidence provides a few indications of the role of personal characteristics and emotions, which other researchers may want to investigate.

---

[88] This sentence builds on Klotz and Lynch 2007, p. 67 and chapter 4.
[89] Wendt 1992, p. 419.
[90] Ibid., p. 419.
[91] Ibid., p. 419.

For instance, the expatriates who challenged the usual patterns of interactions between interveners and local actors were often people who showed significant empathy and respect for the downtrodden. Desire to fit in and respect for rules seemed to have the opposite effect. My interviews and personal experience also suggest that emotions like frustration, disillusionment, and anger increase the rewards expected from intentional role-change, while fear and stress instead heighten the costs of role-breaking. Careful investigation would probably uncover a number of other individual-level elements. Even without the results of this further research, however, one thing is already clear. No matter how ad-hoc or personal the reasons for which a specific person challenges prevailing modes of operation, the eventual outcome is that exceptional individuals do exist, and they drive the process of change in Peaceland.

Change and Perpetuation of the Status Quo

While dominant modes of thinking and acting are resilient and often persistent, they are not immutable. Instead, they are inherently unstable: Their content and relative importance changes over time, primarily because of the process of contestation.[92]

Other scholars have thoroughly demonstrated that shocks from the outside are the most effective trigger of widespread change because they boost the effectiveness of existing contestation and make the replacement of dominant modes of operation both possible and easier.[93] Shocks can enable otherwise silenced voices to be heard. They can also offer marginalized groups an opportunity to destabilize meanings by offering new, more persuasive narratives (or more effective practices and habits) during a time of crisis. When this happens, change can occur rapidly. New dominant modes of operation emerge and hold currency for a time – only to be replaced again later. The Rwandan genocide and its aftermath, for instance, instigated an important evolution in the aid system. It spurred a large debate on the political dimensions of relief initiatives and on aid's potential to fuel violence, and, in response, many humanitarians turned to conflict-sensitive programming.[94] Another example (which I further detail in Chapter 7) is the increased number of attacks on interveners that took place in the late 1990s and early 2000s, and notably the 2003 bombing of the UN and ICRC headquarters in Iraq. These shocks prompted a change in everyday security practices, encouraging foreign peacebuilders to rely increasingly on bunkerization rather than on acceptance to ensure their safety.

---

[92] Dunn 2003; Eden 2004; and Klotz and Lynch 2007, pp. 13 and 44.

[93] The rest of this paragraph is based on Dunn 2003; Eden 2004; Hopf 2010, p. 543; Klotz and Lynch 2007, p. 44; and Lantis 2002, p. 111. See also an earlier analysis of the process of change, along with detailed examples, in Autesserre 2010, pp. 30–31 and chapter 5.

[94] On aid and violence in Rwanda: Rieff 1995 and 2002 (chapter 5); Terry 2002, chapter 5; and Uvin 1998. On the debate around aid and politics that ensued: De Waal 1997; Macrae and Zwi 1994; and Prendergast 1996.

However, such shocks are rare in Peaceland. Normally, three mechanisms counteract the effects of contestation and perpetuate the status quo. First, people tend to interpret new information in ways that confirm their existing beliefs.[95] Chapter 6, for instance, shows how interveners often view local elites' resistance as evidence of their lack of capacity or lack of interest in the public good, instead of understanding it as an indication that the intervention programs might be flawed and thus perceiving it as a critique of the prevailing international practices.

Second, individuals and organizations need at least some measure of consistency and continuity to function. Psychological research has shown that individuals regularly maintain taken-for-granted beliefs "even in the face of contradictory evidence" because these schemas provide "cognitive consistency," meaning "a measure of predictability for understanding the world."[96] Large-scale bureaucracies, including most international organizations and foreign ministries, rely on routines and stability to function, so they are similarly resistant to change – especially when, as often happens, change "threatens entrenched organizational culture and interests."[97] Several interviewees in fact emphasized how their organizations (notably the UN and the European Union) encouraged conformity and condemned dissent. According to these contacts, a candidate's ability to "fit the mold" was a central criterion for hiring and promotion.

Third and finally, the presence of habits helps explain the perpetuation of the status quo even when individuals voice a different discourse. Incorporating the findings of cognitive neuroscience into his study of habits, Ted Hopf explains that habits are "physiological features of the brain"; they "remain neural pathways until they erode with time, through disuse." While "reflection may override" those pathways, it "may not destroy them," because the neural structure remains in the brain. Consequently, "Habits may continue to control what we do even while we explicitly express a contrary attitude."[98] It is true that habits can change. Change happens when individuals discover that their habits are "no longer working, instrumentally, normatively, or functionally,"[99] and that "the costs of following them become too high and are recognized as such."[100] However, such realizations are rare, especially when habits are dominant and

[95] Jervis 1976, chapter 4 (notably pp. 143–202); and Weick 1995, chapters 4 and 6.
[96] Paris in progress, p. 7, building on Padesky 1994, p. 268; and Rafaeli, Bernstein, et al. 2011, p. 15.
[97] Barnett and Finnemore 2004, p. 2. Also Campbell 2012; Eden 2004; Hopf 2010, p. 547; and Weaver 2008. For a case study of resistance to change on the ground, see Autesserre 2010, chapter 5.
[98] Hopf 2010, p. 543 (my emphasis) drawing on Burton 2008, pp. 43–54; Ledoux 2002; and Wilson et al. 2000.
[99] Ibid., p. 544.
[100] Ibid., p. 543.

are widely and deeply shared within a group.[101] As a result, most interveners do not even consider that their habitual modes of action may be detrimental to the effectiveness of their peacebuilding efforts.

It is due to these three mechanisms that dominant modes of operation persist, even those widely acknowledged by interveners as ineffective or counterproductive. These mechanisms also hinder changes in the prevailing ways of thinking and acting, usually rendering most evolutions slow and incremental.[102] The many actors who enact particular habits and practices, or who reproduce certain narratives, often do so with some degree of variation. Over time, this leads to a gradual evolution. (This is how, for instance, recruitment practices progressively changed from a focus on the would-be interveners' motivations and ideals to an evaluation of their thematic and technical expertise – see Chapter 2.)

The Other Explanations

The reader may wonder how this analysis fits with existing explanations of peacebuilding effectiveness and ineffectiveness. On a basic level, this book contributes to the emerging literature on the influence of the everyday in international interventions. Political scientists such as Oliver Richmond and Shahrbanou Tadjbakhsh have demonstrated the importance of examining the everyday in international peacebuilding. They have produced fascinating analyses – on which I draw heavily in Chapter 3 – but they mostly focus on the "everyday" of local actors, not of international interveners.[103] The way my interviewees reacted to presentations of my work indicates the extent to which studying the expatriates' cultures remains an unfamiliar idea. My contacts often thought that I was researching the impact of local cultures, and it took several attempts before they understood that I was more interested in international narratives and practices.

The anthropologists David Mosse, Anne-Meike Fechter, and Heather Hindman and the political scientists Mark Duffield and Lisa Smirl have demonstrated the importance of studying the interveners' everyday lives and work in accounting for the effectiveness of development and humanitarian programs.[104] The sociologist Anne Holohan and the anthropologist Kimberley Coles have done the same with regard to democratization efforts.[105] Paul Higate and Marsha Henry, also in anthropology, have turned the focus toward peace-keepers, examining the influence of their everyday practices on perceptions of

---

[101] Ibid., p. 555.

[102] Barnett and Finnemore 2004; Hopf 2010, pp. 543–544; and Weaver 2008, chapter 2.

[103] Richmond 2011; Richmond and Mitchell 2011; and Tadjbakhsh 2011. For an analysis, see Mitchell 2011b. Higate and Henry 2009, pp. 1–2 and 16 develop an evaluation of the literature on international interventions that is similar to mine.

[104] Duffield 2010; Fechter and Hindman 2011a; Mosse 2005 and 2011; and Smirl 2008 and 2012.

[105] Coles 2007; and Holohan 2005.

security in conflict zones.[106] Recently, three political scientists have further illustrated the value of this approach to studying peacebuilding initiatives. Audra Mitchell has emphasized the importance of the everyday in explaining the development of "affective" peacebuilding in Bosnia-Herzegovina and "threatworks" in Northern Ireland; Ole-Jacob Sending has analyzed the everyday implementation of the "local ownership" principle in Afghanistan, Haiti, Liberia, and Sudan, and Béatrice Pouligny has investigated how local people perceive peacekeepers.[107] Building off the insights of all of these authors, this book demonstrates the importance of studying the everyday of international interveners when approaching the question of peacebuilding effectiveness. This focus helps resolve the puzzle of why certain dominant practices may persist even when interveners know that these modes of operation are inefficient and at times harmful.

I anticipate two sets of objections to the argument that I develop in this book. The first regards my claim that interveners from various backgrounds share important similarities and that these similarities influence the effectiveness of intervention efforts. Some critics would instead emphasize the impact of differences between interveners on peacebuilding effectiveness. They would argue that the cultures of different countries, organizations, or professional groups all orient intervention strategies in dissimilar ways. This precludes the kind of coordination that could achieve coherent strategies and thus decreases the effectiveness of international efforts. The second set of objections would be raised by critics who assert that constraints, vested interests, or the imposition of liberal values are the main elements that shape peacebuilding strategies and influence their effectiveness. In the next two subsections, I address each of these concerns in turn, demonstrating that their proponents offer explanations for peacebuilding effectiveness that are valid but incomplete. In doing so, I clarify that my argument actually enhances such explanations. The additional elements that I consider enable me to provide a more comprehensive and accurate account of how international interventions operate on the ground and why ineffective ways of working persist.

Similarities and Differences

A major trend in existing research is to emphasize the divergences between the national, regional, professional, organizational, and gender groups to which peacebuilders belong.[108] The argument is that each of these groups has a specific

---

[106] Higate and Henry 2009.
[107] Mitchell 2011b; Pouligny 2004; and Sending 2010b.
[108] Duffey 2000; Fetherston and Nordstrom 1995; and Rubinstein 2008. On national and regional differences: Avruch 1998; Ben-Ari and Elron 2001; Faure and Rubin 1993; Fowler 2009; Heiberg 1990; Lederach 1995; and Tomforde 2005 – for a critical evaluation see Higate and Henry 2009, chapter 7. On professional divergences: Ferguson 1990; Uvin 1998; and Winslow 1998. On organizational cultures: Barnett 2002; Barnett and Finnemore 2004; and Campbell

cultural framework that disposes its members to act in different ways. The coexistence of these cultures and subcultures generates tensions and misunderstandings, precludes coordination, and thus decreases the effectiveness of international efforts.

I agree that these divergences exist. The misunderstandings, competition, antagonisms, and differences in approaches, values, and strategies that other scholars have documented are real and often persist without resolution (see Chapter 5). However, I demonstrate that it is the underlying similarities among interveners, rather than their differences, that are more striking in the field.

This claim is similar to one of the central contentions of those who focus on the topic of the "liberal peace," and whose research I discuss in greater depth in the next section. Like my own work, scholarship on the liberal peace emphasizes that differences among interveners coexist with an array of deeper commonalities. While I agree with this assessment, I contend that these commonalities are not necessarily based on shared representations and ideas, like shared liberal values. They can also be rooted in everyday practices and habits that have no connections to liberal values.

The insights of the sociological research on practice, and the political science inquiries that this research has inspired, are particularly useful to explain how the similarities I study interact with the differences among interveners. Jean Lave and Etienne Wenger demonstrate that practices "are the property of a kind of community created over time by the sustained pursuit of a shared enterprise."[109] These "communities of practice" are often informal and invisible to their participants. They have certain core characteristics.[110] Members share (1) a domain of interest, (2) a community, and (3) common practices. Examples vary tremendously and include (in Lave and Wenger's research) meat cutters, insurance claims processors, and (in subsequent works) "most of the transnational communities described in the [international relations] literature," such as transnational advocacy networks and epistemic communities.[111] In this book, I show that, in war and post-war environments, employees of international agencies, non-governmental organizations, donor structures, and diplomatic missions, each hailing from different personal and professional backgrounds, form a transnational community of practice. Their common domain is their official goal: to help the host country and its people reach a sustainable peace. Their community encompasses other interveners based in conflict zones. Their specific practices include ritualized patterns of relationships, a particular approach to helping local populations, established views on which and whose knowledge matters, and common professional and security routines.

2012. On gender groups: Enloe 1993, notably chapter 1; Sanghera, Henry, et al. 2008; Sion 2008; and Whitworth 2004. For a review of this literature, see Autesserre 2011.

[109] Lave and Wenger 1991, p. 45.

[110] Ibid.; and Wenger 1998.

[111] Adler 2005, pp. 15–19 (quotation from p. 15; see also the rest of the article for additional examples in international relations); Lave and Wenger 1991; and Wenger 1998.

Identifying this community of practice is essential for analyzing international interventions because it "allows us to see past more obvious formal structures such as organizations [...] and nations and perceive the structures defined by engagement in practice and the informal learning that comes with it."[112] By participating in the community, members knowingly or unknowingly establish norms (for instance, standard ways of interacting with host populations), create shared understandings (for example, particular views on causes of violence in a given conflict), and produce a set of resources (such as best-practices guidelines) that they can draw on to pursue their common goal.[113]

One of the central insights of the sociological literature on the subject is that everyone belongs to several overlapping communities of practice.[114] In my research, these include a global community of interveners that encompasses all of the international peacebuilders around the world, as well as field-specific communities of interveners deployed in particular locales – such as in Kosovo, in the Congolese province of North Kivu, or in the Timorese city of Baucau. These groups coexist and overlap with other professional communities of practice, such as those of diplomats, war reporters, soldiers, academics, humanitarian aid workers, development specialists, and human rights professionals. The broader community of interveners is thus a meeting place of these various smaller communities; it transcends organizational, professional, national, and religious boundaries.

Another key insight of the sociological literature is that the presence of a community and of shared practices does not preclude the existence of internal divisions.[115] The complex relationships among communities of interveners that I document in this book are comparable to those found in other professions and organizations, such as the military. Each branch of a national military, such as the navy or air force, has its own culture that includes specific rituals, hierarchies, myths, practices, and standard operating procedures. Each body also hosts a bewildering variety of subcultures and subunits. For instance, South African soldiers belong to eleven different linguistic and cultural groups, like the Xhosa and Zulu, that are further subdivided by tribal affiliations. The Belgian, Indian, and U.S. forces similarly include soldiers from very different regional backgrounds. Entrenched rivalries therefore exist within the various military branches as well as between them. Yet, all of these bodies share common characteristics (for example, a given vision of the place of the armed services within society), which unite them as part of the Belgian, Indian, or U.S. forces, and distinguish them from other national militaries. Furthermore, there are

---

[112] Etienne Wenger, "Communities of Practice – a Brief Introduction," June 2006 (http://wenger-trayner.com/theory/, last accessed in December 2013).

[113] Based on Wenger 1998, pp. 72–73.

[114] Lave and Wenger 1991, p. 98; and Wenger 1998, chapter 4. See also Adler 2005, pp. 5, 23, and 142–176.

[115] Lave and Wenger 1991, pp. 103–104 and 107; and Wenger 1998, p. 77.

obvious competitions and occasional animosities between national forces of different countries, but these tensions and differences also coexist with broader underlying similarities. Officers from various countries explained to me that shared norms, such as the importance of hierarchy and obedience or the honored tradition of leaving no soldier behind, unite all members of the military world-wide and differentiate them from civilians.

Likewise, the broad interveners' group includes a number of distinct and competing subgroups. There are clear differences between civilians and soldiers or between international agencies and NGOs. Within an international organization such as the UN, members of specific subunits – such as UN Habitat, the UN Development Program, and various peacekeeping missions – compete with one another. Each of these subunits is also internally divided. In other words, there are worlds within worlds, and each one has its distinct goals, interests, cultures, actors, and ritualized patterns of conflict and cooperation. However, these differences and rivalries do not prevent each participant from belonging to a broader group and sharing practices and understandings with members of that group.

The presence of underlying commonalities (based on practices, habits, and narratives) elucidates how people who disagree about values, norms, fundamental beliefs, and political ends "can do so within a shared perspective."[116] At the same time, the fact that interveners belong to different professional, national, and organizational groups helps us understand the contradictions and tensions among them – for instance the rivalries between military peace-keepers and aid workers. Interveners belong to a shared community on the ground, but conflicts often arise within that community due to divergent professional, organizational, and national subgroup affiliations. Thus, interveners who belong to the same community of practice can often, despite their clear similarities, fail to coordinate.

Constraints, Interests, and Liberal Values

To any analyst of peacebuilding, the influences of constraints, vested interests, and liberal values in shaping international efforts and promoting effective or ineffective modes of operation are just as evident as differences among interveners.

Material, logistical, and political constraints clearly impact what field-based interveners believe they can or cannot do in a given situation.[117] To begin with, peacebuilders often complain that they lack the financial, logistical, and human

---

[116] Based on Chabal and Daloz 2011, p. 22.

[117] Among many others: Downs and Stedman 2002; Doyle, Johnstone, et al. 1997; Doyle and Sambanis 2000 and 2006; Howard 2008, notably pp. 8–10; Kim and Metrikas 1997; Marchal and Messiant 2002; Stedman 2002; Touval and Zartman 1985; Zartman 1989; and Zartman and Rasmussen 1997.

resources to implement all the projects needed.[118] They also lament the absence of infrastructure in most post-war states, which significantly impedes their peace efforts.[119] As practitioners, policy-makers, and scholars regularly emphasize, international efforts are likely to be much more effective when interveners enjoy sufficient resources and face few material and logistical constraints.[120]

The related research on political constraints emphasizes two issues. First is the importance of "local capacities for peace."[121] International efforts can succeed only when warring parties are ready to stop using violence, when spoilers (leaders and factions who use violence to undermine the implementation of peace agreements) are absent or controllable, and when local, national, and regional peacebuilding capacities are strong enough to make peace sustainable.[122] The second issue is the question of whether local authorities and populations view international efforts as legitimate.[123] Foreign peacebuilders deployed in places where interventions were imposed on unwilling host authorities, like in Iraq and Darfur, face many more obstacles than their colleagues working in contexts where the state owes its very existence to the work of international interveners, like in Kosovo and South Sudan.

All of these constraints are certainly important in explaining the relative efficacy of international efforts. In line with this body of research, Chapter 3 emphasizes that international initiatives are much less effective when they face significant local resistance. Moreover, the extent of an intervention's perceived legitimacy (or lack thereof) influences the number and stringency of the security routines that expatriates must follow, which in turn create boundaries between them and local populations (see Chapter 7). However, constraints do not appear out of nowhere; they must be accounted for. Furthermore, recent inquiries have demonstrated that constraints alone do not determine the success or failure of peacebuilding initiatives.[124] Researchers therefore need to supplement analyses of constraints with an inquiry into their sources and to consider additional explanations for the relative effectiveness of international efforts.

---

[118] For scholarly analyses of this issue, see Autesserre 2010, pp. 86–91; Chesterman 2005, pp. 161–164; Doyle and Sambanis 2006; Stedman 2002; and Walter 2002.

[119] Howard 2008, notably p. 9.

[120] Chesterman 2005, p. 167; Cousens, Kumar, et al. 2001, p. 194; Doyle and Sambanis 2006, chapter 5; Hampson 1996, pp. 208–210; Howard 2008, pp. 6–8; Stedman 2002; and Zartman and Rasmussen 1997, pp. 180–185.

[121] Doyle and Sambanis 2006.

[122] Barnett and Zürcher 2009; Barron and Burke 2008, notably pp. xii-xiii and 53; Doyle and Sambanis 2006; Howard 2008, notably pp. 8–10; Touval and Zartman 1985; Zartman 1989; and Zartman and Rasmussen 1997. On spoilers: Stedman 1997 (the definition comes from pp. 5 and 7).

[123] For instance Berdal 2009; Howard 2008; and Talentino 2007, especially pp. 156–157. See also Howard 2008's demonstration of the importance of consent from the warring parties to ensure peacekeeping success.

[124] Howard 2008, pp. 8–11 and throughout the book; Manning and Zürcher 2013, notably p. 34; and Moore 2013, introduction.

Many scholars who attempt to look beyond constraints underscore the influence of vested interests.[125] In this analysis, interveners perform cost-benefit calculations when they design and implement programs. Due to international political disputes, the domestic situations of their respective countries and agencies, or internal developments in the theater of deployment, interveners develop vested economic, political, security, or institutional interests in whether and how peacebuilding initiatives are implemented. As a result of these interests, various actors may prioritize certain strategies or tasks over others. This process may ensure adequate resources for international efforts, thus promoting effective peacebuilding, or it may generate constraints, including lack of funding, local legitimacy, and international support.

The vested interests explanation has contributed significantly to our understanding of which factors determine international involvement in peace processes, whether such engagement makes a difference, and which types of interventions succeed or fail. Like those of constraints, though, the origins of vested interests are not immediately apparent; researchers must study how these interests are constructed. Furthermore, the deliberate cost-benefit calculations implicit in the vested interests argument account for only part of the story. Many cases of social and individual actions are the product of automatic and unreflective dynamics.[126] For instance, peace interveners strategically promoted the narrative of sexual violence as the worst form of abuse in Congo, but nobody strategically designed the interveners' habits of interacting mostly with each other. Another weakness of the research on vested interests and constraints is that it looks at intervention failure as a "problem for which technical solutions," such as additional resource provision or more robust involvement, "could be worked out."[127] Unfortunately, technical solutions alone cannot ensure peace.[128]

A final explanation of peacebuilding effectiveness helps address these concerns (as do the analyses of different national, organizational, and professional cultures that I considered in the previous section). The scholars who develop this last line of analysis have different theoretical positions, but they share the same focus: the imposition of liberal values and templates on host populations.[129] Their research demonstrates the prevalence of a "liberal peace" agenda not only in the policies of numerous countries, including the United States and South

---

[125] Among many others: Adebajo 2011; Alao, Mackinlay, et al. 1999; Chesterman 2005, pp. 161–164; De Waal 1997; Downs and Stedman 2002; Doyle and Sambanis 2006; Fortna 2008; Howard 2008, pp. 11–13 and throughout the book; Ottaway 2002; Rajasingham 2005; Stedman, Rothchild, et al. 2002; and Zartman and Touval 1996.

[126] Based on Hopf 2010, pp. 539–544. Also Pouliot 2010.

[127] Rubinstein 2008, pp. 8–9.

[128] Moore 2013, p. 4. For a similar argument on democracy: Manning and Zürcher 2013, introduction.

[129] Among others: Campbell, Chandler, et al. 2011; Heathershaw 2009; Mac Ginty 2006; Paris 2004; Pugh 2005; Richmond 2005; and Tadjbakhsh 2011.

Africa, but also in the strategies of institutions as diverse as the African Union, the UN, the World Bank, and various NGOs.[130] This agenda promotes a Western conception of political and economic liberalization. It typically emphasizes the organization of free and fair elections; the creation of a market economy; the separation of powers; the reform of the security sector; the rule of law; and the advancement of human rights and civil society.

Building on this common starting point, researchers focusing on the liberal peace identify a number of reasons why international interventions might be ineffective or even counterproductive.[131] Foreign peacebuilders foster the wrong type and pace of reforms.[132] They overlook the local specificities of the host countries; consequently, their strategies are ill adapted to local conditions.[133] (In contrast, international efforts that refrain from imposing Western or liberal models and tailor their initiatives to local cultures and values are much more effective at promoting a sustainable peace.[134]) The promotion of market liberalization aggravates socioeconomic problems in war-torn societies.[135] Worse, for the most radical critics, current peace interventions are "neoimperial" or even "neocolonial" endeavors that enable major powers to perpetuate their hegemony without accepting accountability for their exercise of power.[136]

Although most of these arguments are compelling, the research on the liberal peace provides an incomplete account of how peacebuilding operates. The stated aims and justifications that interveners articulate in official reports, interviews with media, and other public documents often differ strikingly from the debates, interests, practices, and habits that shape policy initiatives and outcomes on the ground.[137] Furthermore, as mentioned in the second section of this chapter, peacebuilders in the field enjoy much more agency than the research on the liberal peace implies.[138] Finally, as I demonstrate both in previous work and in this book, many of the shared understandings and practices that shape

---

[130] Barnett 2006; Chandler 2004; Hohe 2002; Mac Ginty 2008; Newman, Paris, et al. 2009; Paris 2002 and 2004; Pugh 2005; Richmond 2005, notably chapter 5; Richmond and Franks 2009; Richmond and Mitchell 2011; and Tadjbakhsh 2011.

[131] For a defense of the liberal peace agenda, see Fukuyama 2004 and Paris 2010.

[132] Paris 2004.

[133] Hohe 2002; Mac Ginty 2008; Richmond 2011; and Richmond and Mitchell 2011. A number of publications also develop this explanation without linking it to the liberal peace agenda: Chopra and Hohe 2004; Duffey 2000; Fetherston and Nordstrom 1995; Heiberg 1990; Rubinstein 2008, chapter 7; Pouligny 2004, pp. 133–136; Salem 1997; and Winslow 1997. See also Peterson 2011 for a related analysis focused on the interveners' ignorance of the role of emotion in generating or perpetuating violence.

[134] Fetherston and Nordstrom 1995, p. 113; Mac Ginty 2008, notably pp. 140–154; Paris 2004, p. 180; Richmond 2011, p. 110; Richmond and Mitchell 2011, notably on pp. 8–13; and Tadjbakhsh 2011, pp. 3–5, 38–42, and 122–124.

[135] Pugh 2005.

[136] Chandler 2006; Debrix 1999; Duffield 2007; Orford 2003, notably chapter 4; and Pugh 2004.

[137] Mosse 2005 offers a book-length demonstration of this point.

[138] Newman 2009, p. 46 emphasizes a similar point.

intervention strategies on the ground are unrelated to the liberal peace paradigm.[139] Security routines, reporting techniques, patterns of social relationships, and standard modes of collecting information fall outside the purview of the research on the liberal peace, yet they are all instrumental in shaping intervention outcomes.

My foregoing the usual focus on liberalism sets my analysis apart from those of liberal peace and postcolonial scholars. The latter attribute the recurrent problems of international interventions – such as lack of local ownership, dearth of local knowledge, use of universal models, and conflictual relationships between interveners and local stakeholders – to the essential characteristics of liberalism as a political system.[140] I identify the same problems, but I contend that they are not primarily due to the liberal content of intervention programs. Instead, I locate their source at the very act of imposition, regardless of the liberal or nonliberal character of the model or program being imposed, and I trace the roots of this imposition to the everyday practice of peacebuilding on the ground.

For the domains in which liberal values are indeed influential (such as the focus on statebuilding), this book takes the existing analysis one step further. I show *how* liberal conceptions of peace and stability are put into practice and reproduced on a daily basis through the actions of the interveners. Conceptions of liberalism are based on the understanding that liberal programs can be implemented anywhere, an assumption that fits with the technical and universalist biases of the community I study.

Overall, this book offers a different way to think about the roles of the constraints, interests, institutions, policies, discourses, and norms that are at the center of most research on international peace interventions.[141] Existing research ascribes the interveners' lack of contextual knowledge – a well-known obstacle to successful peacebuilding – to material, logistic, or human resources constraints, or to the essential characteristics of liberalism as an ideological and political project.[142] This book instead emphasizes the everyday practices and habits that create, sustain, and reinforce the international peacebuilders' ignorance of local conditions. In doing so, my argument builds on Lise Howard's pioneering analysis of the role of learning in peacekeeping, which demonstrates that UN missions can successfully fulfill their mandates only when they learn from local populations.[143] Howard identifies the state interests and organizational preconditions that make such learning possible, and

---

[139] Autesserre 2010.

[140] Richmond 2011 provides a representative example of the liberal peace approach. For postcolonial analysis, see the fascinating work of Mehta 1999; and Orford 2003.

[141] This paragraph is based on a personal communication from Dr. Eyal Ben-Ari, Hebrew University of Jerusalem, September 2011.

[142] For instance, among others: Duffey 2000, notably p. 156; Escobar 1995, p. 108; and Mosse 2005, pp. 82–84. The criticism in the next sentence builds on Chandler 2010, p. 14; Richmond 2011; and Sending 2009, pp. 16–20.

[143] Howard 2008.

I complement her analysis by pointing to everyday modes of operation that further promote or hinder on-the-ground learning by peacekeepers.

This book enhances the findings of existing research on constraints, interests, and the liberal peace in three more ways. To begin with, most analyses of international interventions focus on the "what" of peacebuilding – the programs and priorities that interveners pursue, such as constructing a liberal state, reintegrating militias, or promoting geostrategic interests (see the Introduction). I demonstrate that it is just as important to examine the "how" of their actions, such as the way interveners interact with local stakeholders, construct knowledge on their areas of deployment, ensure their safety, and go about their jobs on a daily basis. The objectives of the interveners may differ widely across organizations and contexts, but the processes of intervention are often remarkably similar.

Second, my work presents an alternative to studying one type of intervention in isolation and ignoring its interactions with other, concurrent types of peacemaking, peacekeeping, and peacebuilding work. Many researchers focus on a specific organization (like a UN peacekeeping mission), a specific category of actors (like humanitarian aid workers), or relationships between two of these groups (like that between humanitarian aid workers and military peacekeepers).[144] They rarely consider all of the peacebuilders deployed in a conflict zone simultaneously.[145] This narrower focus often causes analysts to attribute all of the improvements or deteriorations in conflict situations to one kind of organization, even though these developments usually result from the combined work of different local and external actors.[146] This approach also prevents researchers from analyzing the interactions of the assorted national, professional, and organizational cultures, and of the various actors and functions of peace interventions. This book offers a theoretical framework and a methodological approach for overcoming these shortcomings.

Finally, as mentioned in the second section of this chapter, this book shifts the empirical focus of research on peacebuilding from macro-level politics – such as resources, vested interests, liberal values, and the politics of UN peacekeeping mandates – to what those who work in conflict zones actually do. It studies events and actions unfolding on the ground and thus brings the actual practice of intervention back into the debate, instead of simply analyzing the stated

---

[144] On specific organizations: Barnett 2002; Barnett and Finnemore 2004; Doyle and Sambanis 2006; Fortna 2008; Higate and Henry 2009; Howard 2008; Jones 2001; Paris 2004; and Pouligny 2004. On humanitarian and development aid workers: Ferguson 1990; and Uvin 1998. On military peacekeepers versus aid workers: Rubinstein 2008, chapter 7; Slim 1996; and Winslow 2002.

[145] Exceptions include, among others: Autesserre 2010; Barron and Burke 2008; Branch 2011; Campbell 2012; Coles 2007; Fassin and Pandolfi 2010; Lefranc 2008; Manning and Malbrough 2010; Mitchell 2014; Peterson 2011; and Sending 2010b.

[146] Fortna 2008; and Doyle and Sambanis 2006 provide the clearest examples of such inference. Lederach 1997, p. 67 develops the most convincing demonstration that peacebuilding cannot be sustained by only one category of actor.

aims and goals of peacebuilders and their ability to achieve them.[147] The contents and the ideological dimensions of the programs are not the only elements that increase or decrease peacebuilding effectiveness; the everyday practices and habits of interveners on the ground also matter. All in all, Fechter and Hindman's insights are as relevant for peacebuilding as they are for development aid: Successes and failures "not only occur at the level of theory, history, and hegemony but also emanate from the daily tasks undertaken by [. . .] practitioners."[148]

A concrete example will clarify how my approach complements other explanations and accounts for dynamics that the latter leave unexplained. Consider the infamous "bubble," where interveners live and interact with one another, separate from host populations. This arrangement isolates international peacebuilders, severely diminishing the effectiveness of international efforts.[149] Vested interests cannot account for this phenomenon, as no intervening country or organization has an interest in preventing its staff from interacting with local people. On the contrary, scholars and practitioners constantly emphasize that, whatever the goal of a given intervention – whether it is a military invasion or peacebuilding initiative – expatriates need to create good relationships with their local counterparts in order to be effective. The liberal peace paradigm cannot explain the "bubble" either. There is nothing specifically liberal in failing to interact with one's counterparts, and it is rather the opposite: Liberal values would actually encourage interactions between interveners and local populations. Postcolonial and critical international relations scholars would argue that certain liberal discourses at the macro level necessarily entail a code of conduct wrought with prejudice and violence on the ground.[150] However, there is no a priori reason why prejudice and violence would take the form of lack of relationships rather than that of constant interactions.

Constraints – whether they involve logistics, economics, language, or security – can partially explain the constitution and perpetuation of the "bubble" in which interveners live. Take one such constraint: security procedures. Security procedures compel interveners to respect curfews and no-go areas. These restrictions prevent after-work socialization between expatriates and their local colleagues and counterparts, as the former are forbidden to go at night to the "unsafe" neighborhoods where the latter live. However, security routines do not just come into use naturally or organically; we must account for their origins. To do so, we must turn to an explanation focused on everyday life

---

[147] On the need to bring the actual practice of intervention back into the debate, see Campbell, Chandler, et al. 2011, pp. 2–3.

[148] Fechter and Hindman 2011a, p. 2.

[149] Among many other sources: Eyben 2011; Harper 2011; Johnston 2005; McWha 2011, pp. 33–35; Mitchell 2011a, pp. 12–15; Rajak and Stirrat 2011; and Verma 2011, pp. 67–74. See Part II (Chapters 5, 6, and 7) in this book for more on this phenomenon and for an in-depth analysis of the dynamics I mention in the rest of this paragraph.

[150] This interpretation builds on Mehta 1999; and Orford 2003.

and work in conflict zones, and on the shared practices and narratives that develop in Peaceland.

Chapter 7 traces the sources of such security routines to a widespread perception that peacebuilding work is a dangerous business. Risks do exist, but because of the interveners' daily experience of living and working in a conflict zone, and because of the narratives of international aid that dominate the global scene, expatriates who serve as interveners perceive danger in a much more acute way than those who do not. This perception initiates a vicious cycle. Strict security procedures isolate interveners from any real or perceived dangers, preventing expatriates from realizing that local conditions are often less perilous than they appear. This process legitimizes stricter security procedures and leads to an even greater divide between interveners and local people, and so on. Eventually, security routines become ingrained habits for most field interveners, erasing other potential security practices from the realm of possible action. Nevertheless, a few expatriates and international agencies reject these dominant modes of operation and ensure their safety through close contact with local inhabitants. In doing so, these exceptional interveners show that there are alternate ways to manage the security challenges inherent to working in conflict zones. Their actions demonstrate that the structure of the international aid system could perfectly well generate different practices, habits, and narratives in the field.

This book develops a related analysis of these and other "constraints" that decrease the possibility of socialization between international peacebuilders and their local counterparts. In all of these cases, I demonstrate that interveners perpetuate shared, dominant understandings through their everyday life and work on the ground, thereby generating or reinforcing these constraints. By drawing attention to the exceptional expatriates who refuse or vocally challenge these dominant practices, I also show that these shared understandings and the broader structure of the international system could accommodate alternative ways of thinking and acting on the ground. These different everyday practices, which a few foreign peacebuilders already follow, would enable interveners to step outside of their bubbles and engage in more productive interactions with local people.

Conclusion

The theoretical purpose of this book is to offer a framework to study the impact of the interveners' everyday lives and work on peacebuilding effectiveness and to address the question of why ineffective modes of action may persist unchallenged. This framework includes an approach that acknowledges the specificity of on-the-ground dynamics and views definitions of success and failure as integral to the power struggles in Peaceland. It revolves around practices, habits, and narratives, which shape and orient international action. It relies on ethnographic methods of data collection, which I discuss in the Appendix.

The resulting explanation does not illuminate everything about the processes or outcomes of international peace interventions. Instead, it accounts for a dimension that existing explanations overlook. As such, it allows us to have a more complete and, thereby, more accurate understanding of international peacebuilding. Researchers need to move beyond their usual focus on macro-level dynamics to study the daily practice of intervention on the ground. Without attention to these micro-level dynamics, any account of peacebuilding is incomplete.

In the analysis that follows, I build upon the theoretical framework I have presented in this chapter to illuminate the dynamics of ongoing and recent (post-Cold War) international peace interventions in conflict and post-conflict zones around the world. I restrict my focus to places where the reestablishment of peace is the official goal of some or all of the interveners – keeping in mind that interveners may simultaneously try to fulfill a number of other national, institutional, or personal interests even in these places. My study focuses on expatriates deployed in countries that host a UN or African Union peacekeeping mission (seventeen countries as of December 2013, including Congo, Haiti, Ivory Coast, Timor-Leste, Somalia, and South Sudan). The evidence I present should also help analyze peacebuilding efforts in war and post-war zones that have a comparable level of international engagement, even in the absence of peacekeeping operations – such as Sri Lanka and Burundi. Finally, my analysis sheds light on the actions of peacebuilders working in countries where the primary objectives of most other interveners are not peace. This category includes UN and NGO personnel deployed in Iraq and Afghanistan, as the primary goal of these actors is to reestablish peace, despite the fact that broader international efforts are mostly concerned with protecting the safety and interests of the United States and its allies.[151] Although I thus limit the scope of my argument in this book specifically to peacebuilding initiatives, my theoretical and empirical insights have, as I explain in the Conclusion, much broader implications.

---

[151] Paris 2010, pp. 347–348 develops an excellent analysis of the differences between the interventions that are the focus of this book and those in Iraq and Afghanistan.

Part I

Constructing Knowledge of the Host Country

Michel Losembe, a Congolese businessman, was shocked by the way interveners treated him and other Congolese elites. To him, foreign peacebuilders communicated condescendingly, as though they were saying, "Here is how things work in the rest of the world; don't you realize how far you deviate from that?!" He felt that the expatriates did not listen to the ideas of the Congolese, and they regularly made their Congolese counterparts feel unqualified. Frustrated by this attitude, Michel decided to conduct an experiment. He was from a mixed background, American-born, with Belgian, Portuguese, and Congolese ancestors, and he could pass for someone of another nationality with relative ease. One day, instead of introducing himself as Congolese, he told the group that he came from Puerto Rico. The result was clear: "The attitude in the meeting" was "completely different." The interveners listened to his ideas with respect and interest. He found he had much more credibility and influence when he passed as an outsider.[1]

Losembe's experience illustrates one of the many consequences of the politics of knowledge in Peaceland, where foreign experts have a lot more clout than local ones. Successful peacebuilding requires a nuanced understanding of the intervention area and of the specific dynamics of peace and conflict on the ground. Too often, though, such knowledge is absent because international interveners rely upon thematic rather than country expertise and regularly ignore insights from local stakeholders. In Part I of this book, I study the process of knowledge construction that produces this pattern, and I examine how it has both positive (usually intentional) and negative (unintentional) consequences for peacebuilding effectiveness.

As with any process of knowledge construction, this one is fraught with struggles, contestations, and dissensions. Chapters 2 and 3 present an overview of the politics of knowledge in Peaceland: I examine the power struggles that establish whose and which knowledge matters, focusing first on international modes of operations (Chapter 2) and then on local reactions (Chapter 3).

[1] Author's on-record interview with Michel Losembe, vice president of the Fédération des Entreprises du Congo, June 2011, Kinshasa.

Chapter 4 subsequently analyzes the everyday manner through which peace-builders on the ground make sense of their environments. Before delving into these topics, however, a brief presentation of the main actors at the center of this book and their respective roles in peacebuilding is in order, as it will help clarify the dynamics analyzed in subsequent chapters.

The Inhabitants of Peaceland

International Interveners

International peace interveners come from all over the world and represent a wide variety of professional, religious, and organizational backgrounds.[2] During my fieldwork in the Congolese province of North Kivu, for instance, the intervening institutions included the second largest and second most expensive peacekeeping mission in the world, the International Criminal Court, European and American diplomatic delegations, regional organizations such as the African Union and the European Union, virtually all existing United Nations (UN) agencies, and many non-governmental organizations (NGOs) that specialized in relief, development, human rights, environmental protection, and conflict resolution. Their staff members – the interveners – encompassed military personnel, police officers, and a wide array of civilian professions, such as lawyers, doctors, diplomats, engineers, auto mechanics, accountants, social workers, academics, nurses, pilots, human resources specialists, secretaries, journalists, and professional managers of aid projects. These people professed all kinds of religious beliefs, including various forms of Christianity, Judaism, Buddhism, Hinduism, Confucianism, and Islam, not to mention atheism and agnosticism. Among the religious affiliates, some were devout; others never practiced. The group also comprised people of all genders and sexual orientations. Although it was impossible to obtain statistics on the social status of these individuals, anecdotal evidence indicates that it, too, was varied. Most interveners seemed to come from the middle class and hold university degrees, but I met people whose families belonged to the highest intellectual or economic strata of their countries and others who came from a working-class or impoverished background (especially among rank-and-file soldiers).

The quota systems used by intergovernmental organizations like the UN and the World Bank also guarantee the geographic diversity of the expatriate community in any given theater of intervention. In North Kivu in 2010–2011, peacekeeping staff came from states as varied as Egypt, India, Niger, South Africa, the United Kingdom, Uruguay, and Yemen. Other UN agencies exhibited a similar diversity. By way of illustration, Table 3 summarizes the regional origin of expatriate staff members working for the UN peacekeeping mission in Congo as of May 2011:

[2] As discussed in the Introduction, I define peace interveners as foreign actors whose official, stated goal is to help build peace in their country of deployment, regardless of whether or not they also have other objectives.

TABLE 3. *Geographic Origin of Staff Members, United Nations Organization Stabilization Mission in the Democratic Republic of Congo, May 2011*[3]

	Civilians staff (980)	Military contingents (16,908)	Military observers (737)	UN volunteers (588)	Police (1,248)
Africa	49.2%	16%	33.4%	60.7%	42.5%
Asia and Pacific	12.2%	66.2%	31.5%	20.2%	51.4%
Europe	21.2%	0.2%	15.2%	10.2%	2.5 %
Middle East	3.3%	8.1%	6.4%	1.9%	3%
North America	6.3%	–	1.9%	1.7%	0.4%
South America and the Caribbean	7.8%	9.5%	11.7%	5.3%	0.2%

While the Congo mission did have a relatively high proportion of Asian and African peacekeepers, it still drew interveners from every major region. Furthermore, other UN agencies or peacekeeping operations include a larger number of staff from the Middle East (as the UN Mission in Darfur) or South America and the Caribbean (like the UN Mission in Haiti), thereby adding to the overall diversity of the intervention community.[4] Admittedly, not all UN field representations present a geographic diversity on par with that of the missions in Congo, Darfur, and Haiti. For historical and geopolitical reasons, peacekeepers, police officers, diplomats, and NGO staff members in Cyprus and Kosovo came overwhelmingly from areas that the people I interviewed labeled as "Western," including both regions like Europe and North America and countries like Australia.[5] In the rest of my field sites, however, even though my interviewees regularly complained that the leaders of their organizations were "too Western," I observed this bias only in headquarters and capitals, if at all.[6]

The high proportion of employees from non-European or North American continents in intergovernmental organizations such as the UN and the World

[3] Statistics calculated from the figures available on the official Web site of the UN mission (www. monusco.unmissions.org, section "Mission Staff," last accessed in June 2013).

[4] See the monthly reports "UN Mission's Contribution by Countries" available on the official Web site of the UN peacekeeping department, www.un.org/en/peacekeeping/resources/statistics/con tributors.shtml (last accessed in December 2013).

[5] Ibid. On Kosovo, see also Goetze and Bliesemann de Guevara 2012, p. 209.

[6] It is impossible to find figures for civilian staff and UN volunteers within UN peace operations apart from the mission in Congo. However, the UN monthly factsheets of Military and Police Contributions to Peacekeeping Operations (available at www.un.org/ en/peacekeeping/resources/statistics/contributors.shtml) provides data for military and police officers, and it evidences a national diversity of staff on par with that found in the Congo mission.

Bank is especially noteworthy in view of the overrepresentation of European and North American staff within NGOs, diplomatic delegations, and donor agencies. It has been impossible to obtain statistical data on this topic (though I made repeated requests for it), but interviewees confirmed my general observations. Although there is now more diversity than in the 1980s – a significant minority of NGO officials now come from Africa or Asia – NGO staff members are mostly European or North American.[7] This geographic disparity is exacerbated by the fact that only wealthy countries or regions have the means to establish a diplomatic or donor presence on the ground in conflict areas. Affluent, non-Western countries – such as Brazil, China, India, Japan, Russia, Saudi Arabia, South Africa, and South Korea – have become "new" donors in recent years, but they tend to prioritize conflicts within their respective regions, leading to a disproportionate number of delegations from "Western" states in most conflict zones.[8] On the whole, however, the fact that the vast majority of employees deployed by international organizations in the field come from non-Western countries helps mitigate the overrepresentation of Western individuals among diplomatic missions, donor agencies, and NGOs, and results in a fairly diverse group of interveners in most intervention sites.

In terms of the gender balance, it is true that the staff of peacekeeping missions is overwhelmingly male. In June 2012, for instance, men made up 96.34 percent of all military and police officers working in UN peacekeeping missions around the world.[9] However, NGO and diplomatic personnel, as well as the civilian staff of international agencies, include many women. At times, women even dominate certain spheres of peacebuilding, such as education in emergencies.[10] Examined as a whole, the gender distribution at any given intervention site is, generally speaking, fairly balanced.

One last notable characteristic of the interveners' group helps explain the local reactions I detail in Chapters 3, 5, and 6. International NGOs and military corps tend to deploy a relatively young expatriate staff. In most countries, members of the military retire earlier than do other professionals, comparatively

[7] Fechter and Hindman 2011a, p. 10 corroborates this analysis.

[8] For more details on each of these donors, see "In-Depth: The Rise of the 'New' Donors," IRIN, October 19, 2011 (www.irinnews.org/IndepthMain.aspx?reportid=94004&indepthid=91, last accessed in December 2013).

[9] Statistics calculated from the figures available in the June 2012 factsheet Military and Police Contributions to Peacekeeping Operations posted on the UN Web site (www.un.org/en/peace keeping/contributors/2012/june12_2.pdf, accessed in December 2013). The figures for other months in 2012 and for 2001–2011 are available at www.un.org/en/peacekeeping/resources/statistics/contributors_archive.shtml (last accessed in December 2013). All these documents show a similar prevalence of male peacekeepers.

[10] Personal communication from Dr. Elisabeth King (Balsillie School of International Affairs, Canada), February 2013.

skewing the age distribution of the troops. There is also a higher portion of young adults (in their 20s or early 30s) in international NGOs compared to the general population for three main reasons. To begin with, the employment conditions for NGO staff on the ground – short-term contracts and lower salaries than they would earn at home – are not very attractive. Thus, young people, rather than mid-career professionals, embrace NGO work. Furthermore, since conditions on the ground are often grueling (see Chapter 5) and since leadership positions are usually located in headquarters or, at least, in capital cities, older employees tend to leave the field, only to be replaced by younger, more junior colleagues. When experienced people stay in the field, they often move from NGOs to other, better-paying organizations like the UN or donor agencies. Finally, conflict zones are too dangerous to raise children in, so many people leave Peaceland when they want to start a family.

As I show in the following chapters, interveners, diverse in their geographic origins, religious backgrounds, genders, professional training, organizational affiliations, and areas of deployment form a transnational group with a transnational culture. While the interveners' narratives can be context-specific, their shared practices and habits often transcend national and regional boundaries. These everyday elements are not tied to the geographic origin of the interveners, and the cultures of the host countries influence them only marginally. The everyday approach to intervention is part of a "'free-floating,' transportable, mobile, and transient culture," and thus it may be readily "transplanted in any [conflict and post-conflict] context."[11] It remains similar whether one is in Afghanistan, Congo, Cyprus, or Kosovo. When adaptation occurs, it is usually the product of local populations who learn the language and techniques of international interveners and assume their ways of working rather than the opposite.[12]

Local Counterparts

The definition of "local," like that of "peace," is constructed rather than given. In Peaceland, the word "local" usually refers to a given host population.

The opposition between expatriates and local people is central to the interveners' way of seeing the world (see Chapter 5). It is important to note, however, that this opposition relies on two unsubstantiated assumptions that this book eschews and, at times, deconstructs. The first equates being "local" with being insular or provincial. This ignores the fact that many residents of the host countries have international knowledge and experience, ranging from dual citizenship, to time spent abroad as students or refugees, to work done in

---

[11] This sentence paraphrases the analysis of development practitioners in Verma 2011, p. 59.

[12] The body of research on the liberal peace corroborates this finding. See notably: Chopra and Hohe 2004; Duffey 2000; Fetherston and Nordstrom 1995; Hohe 2002; Paris 2004; and Tadjbakhsh 2011.

partnership with foreign organizations.[13] The phrase "local people" also implies that the residents of the host country form a homogenous community when, as with any population, they in fact comprise an infinitude of political, economic, social, and religious groups (see Chapter 3).

"Local" in this book means "from the area targeted by a peacebuilding initiative." This area can be as large as an entire country or as small as a hamlet. Given that my analysis focuses on interveners deployed in provinces and rural areas, "local" usually refers to the inhabitants of a specific province or village, and "national" refers to citizens who live in the same country but not in the same specific locale. As the next section demonstrates, whether they are local participants, national actors, or international interveners, all stakeholders of international intervention have crucial roles to play in conflict resolution.

Outsiders' and Insiders' Roles in Peacebuilding

It is a truism that local people are essential to peacebuilding, as no solution can be sustainable if it fails to involve host populations. Genuine reconciliation, just like societal and governance reforms, requires the involvement of local stakeholders – it cannot merely be dictated from the outside.[14] Solutions rooted in domestic realities are much more likely to be sustainable than arrangements that are externally imposed, since local people can more easily maintain the former kinds of initiatives even after foreign peacebuilders have left.[15] Peace efforts are also more likely to be effective when they build on existing institutions, structures, or practices.[16] Outsiders may not know of or recognize these existing elements – for instance, when they are informal (such as neighborhood solidarity associations) or when they do not conform to international standards (such as traditional, community-based justice mechanisms in places like Bangladesh, Sierra Leone, and Timor-Leste) – but local inhabitants can easily identify them.[17]

Insiders also have a number of advantages compared to outsiders. Local elites command networks, reputations, legitimacy, and credibility that are impossible for foreigners to develop.[18] Insiders also have an intimate understanding of the country of intervention – its customs, taboos, history, and politics – that would take outsiders years to acquire. Involving local people in the design and implementation of peacebuilding initiatives thus ensures that the strategies reflect the actual experience and desires of insiders rather than the outsiders' perceptions of

---

[13] Simons and Zanker 2012 (throughout the article, and notably on pp. 11–14) and Mac Ginty 2010 (throughout the book and most clearly on p. 208) develop excellent critiques of the simplified definition of the word "local."

[14] For an overview of this argument, see Donais 2009, pp. 9–10.

[15] Ibid., pp. 10–11; and Hayman 2012, pp. 23–25. For concrete illustrations, see the case studies on Congo and Burundi in McGuinness 2012 (respectively pp. 44–64 and 65–84).

[16] Hayman 2012, pp. 22–24, 27, and 32–34.

[17] Ibid., pp. 22–24.

[18] For detailed examples, see Anderson and Olson 2003, p. 38.

what local communities need.[19] Furthermore, conditions in conflict zones are extremely fluid; they evolve constantly. Involving members of the local communities enables peacebuilders to adapt their initiatives to these changing conditions instead of using static approaches that quickly become irrelevant.[20] Lastly, relying on local people rather than on expatriates is more cost-effective because the latter command salaries, per diems, and benefits that are much higher than those of their local counterparts (see Chapters 5 and 6).

However, people living in conflict zones regularly emphasize the particular challenges of undertaking comprehensive peacebuilding efforts without outside assistance. Certain local elites favor upholding the violent status quo that enabled their rise to power.[21] Governments and civil society organizations do not necessarily promote the welfare of ordinary citizens. Instead, in many war and post-war contexts, they engage in corruption, malversation, and favoritism to advance their own agendas or those of their kin.[22] While some governments and civil society representatives contribute positively to reconciliation, others instead promote violence by fueling ethnic hatred, propagating nationalistic discourses, and spreading prejudices and discrimination.[23] The severity of this malfeasance is often such that citizens profoundly distrust sitting authorities and community leaders.[24]

Local practices and structures can be similarly detrimental to peacebuilding. Take traditional and indigenous practices, institutions, and actors, which most peacebuilding scholars view as a crucial dimension of the "local."[25] They are often complicit in local power struggles and therefore contribute to exclusionary or even oppressive conditions.[26] They may serve to perpetuate the authority of existing elite, stifle criticism, deepen divisions, reinforce exclusion, and prevent change, as various authors observed in Burundi, Congo, Kenya, and Sierra Leone.[27]

Furthermore, insiders face a number of distinct challenges. People from the country of intervention are vulnerable to blackmail from armed groups and political leaders, who can easily threaten them and their families.[28] They are

---

[19] Based on Lambourne 2009, pp. 28–30.

[20] Pouligny 1999, p. 412.

[21] Barnett and Zürcher 2009, pp. 24 and 31.

[22] Anderson, Brown, et al. 2012, chapter 6.

[23] Among others: Donais 2009, p. 14; Richmond and Franks 2009, pp. 95–96; Paris 2004, pp. 159–169; and Prendergast and Plumb 2002, pp. 328 and 334.

[24] Anderson, Brown, et al. 2012, pp. 84–87; and author's confidential interviews with ordinary citizens in Afghanistan, Burundi, Congo, Israel and the Palestinian Territories, Kosovo, South Sudan, and Timor-Leste.

[25] Simons and Zanker 2012, pp. 6–7.

[26] Schaefer 2010; and Simons and Zanker 2012.

[27] On Burundi: Simons and Zanker 2012, pp. 8–10. On Congo: Autesserre 2010, chapter 4; and Simons and Zanker 2012, pp. 7–8. On Kenya: Chopra 2009. On Sierra Leone: Fanthorpe 2006; Millar 2011; Richards 2005; and Sawyer 2008. See also Donais 2009; Hayman 2012, p. 22; and Mac Ginty 2011, pp. 51–53.

[28] For public sources, see Anderson 2008, p. 101; and CDA Collaborative Learning Projects 2008a, pp. 3–4 and 6–7.

under constant pressure from their kin, who demand jobs, money, or other services – a type of stress that is especially strong in war and post-war environments, where unemployment rates typically run very high. Violence and instability also impact local inhabitants and their loved ones more acutely, making it more difficult for insiders to remain objective (and, even when they manage to, the parties in conflict will rarely believe them impartial and will thus refuse to work with them).

By dint of having few to no preexisting links to their areas of intervention, expatriate interveners avert most of these challenges and can thus assume several critical peacebuilding tasks. Outsiders usually have no local relatives who can exploit their sense of family obligation. They are therefore in a comparatively better position to ensure that jobs go to the most qualified candidates and that benefits and services reach their intended beneficiaries. Since foreigners are less susceptible to local political pressure, they are also better placed to make sensitive and unpopular decisions. For instance, they can act as counterweights to local power brokers who may try to shape peace and reconstruction processes to suit their interests. Foreigners can put pressure on powerful elites who fuel violence, or they can leverage outside constituencies to do so. To a certain extent, expatriates also avoid the perception of ethnic, religious, or political bias, so it is easier for them to serve as impartial mediators. Consequently, they are often in the best position to initiate peacebuilding processes in cases of highly escalated or frozen conflicts, or to maintain communication with all parties during those setbacks or crises that often affect peace implementation.[29] Finally, outsiders can provide a fresh look at problems and think of solutions that those immersed in the issue for too long may have overlooked.

Another advantage of international agencies – notably peacekeeping military forces – is that they are frequently the only actors capable of protecting populations (even if imperfectly) from abuses by various armed groups, or of protecting local activists from the worse forms of repression by their governments.[30] Foreign peacebuilders can therefore provide safe spaces for interaction and communication between various conflicting parties.[31] The military forces can also supply a modicum of security, which is indispensable for public service delivery and for reconstruction of peaceful government institutions.[32]

Lastly, international interveners enjoy assets, networks, and leverage that local peacebuilders lack. Material support from outsiders can provide local actors the funds and logistical assets that they need to realize their initiatives.[33]

---

[29] Zelizer and Rubinstein 2009, pp. 12–13 and chapters 2 and 13.

[30] For local views on this issue, see CDA Collaborative Learning Projects 2008a, p. 6. On local activists, see Doyle 2001, p. 108.

[31] CDA Collaborative Learning Projects 2012, p. 5; and Hayman 2012, p. 19.

[32] Cousens, Kumar, et al. 2001, p. 14; and Sherman 2008, p. 304.

[33] Anderson and Olson 2003, p. 40; CDA Collaborative Learning Projects 2010b (pp. 7–8) and 2012 (p. 4); and Pouligny 2004, pp. 245–251. For more details, see Chapter 6 in this book, section "The Interveners' Resources."

Networks and leverage also make it possible for foreign peacebuilders to address the potential international dimensions of domestic or local conflicts, and thereby ensure that tensions at the macro level will not jeopardize progress at the micro level.[34] Furthermore, networks help international interveners publicize the stories of local communities in the outside world, hence contributing to raising material and political support for those in need.[35]

For all of these reasons, outsiders can help level the playing field between the groups in conflict. They can create conditions that facilitate the inclusion of marginalized groups and the emergence of new leaders, instead of letting the national and local power brokers involved in the conflict maintain control in the post-war period.

Ultimately, inside and outside actors make the greatest contributions to peace when they work together, each challenging the biases of the other.[36] After interviewing more than 6,000 people in 26 different conflict zones, Mary Anderson and her coauthors concluded that what citizens of conflict zones desire "is an international assistance system that integrates the resources and experiences of outsiders with the assets and capacities of insiders to develop contextually appropriate strategies for pursuing positive change."[37] They want a middle ground, where both outsiders and insiders use their specific skills, expertise, and experience to analyze the context, generate options, and determine the best strategy for achieving their objectives.[38] Unfortunately, as the following chapters demonstrate, this is far from being the way things work on the ground, largely due to the politics of knowledge that pervades Peaceland.

[34] Anderson and Olson 2003, p. 37; and Reychler 2006, p. 7.

[35] Keck and Sikkink 1998 provide one of the best analyses of this phenomenon.

[36] Anderson and Olson 2003, p. 42. See also Mac Ginty 2008, pp. 141–142; and McGuinness 2012, pp. 182–183 and throughout the book.

[37] Anderson, Brown, et al. 2012, p. 137.

[38] Ibid., p. 137.

2

The Politics of Knowledge

In mid-2011, the United Nations (UN) Integrated Office tried to recruit an international consultant to conduct an analysis of conflict dynamics in Congo. The study would serve as a basis for the new UN five-year plan to fight poverty in the country, so it was a high-stakes exercise. The job description for the consultancy enumerated the desired technical skills: a master's degree in conflict studies or political science, ten years of experience managing peacebuilding programs, knowledge of French, and analytical and synthesis skills. Country expertise was not required. The listing simply stated that "knowledge of the DRC and/or of countries in transition would be a plus."[1] Needless to say, with only six weeks to complete on-the-ground research and write a fifty-page report on the complex conflict dynamics of a country the size of Western Europe, it would be impossible for someone without preexisting knowledge of the situation to develop an accurate and useful analysis.

Unfortunately, job posts like these are not unique to the UN Integrated Office. They exemplify a pervasive trend in Peaceland. That same year, the European Commission sent out a request for applications to its upcoming election observation mission in Congo. Positions available included "political/country analyst," "legal analyst," and "human rights/gender analyst." The document enumerated a series of criteria for choosing applicants. Candidates did not need specific knowledge of Congo to secure a place on the short list. Country expertise was included in the criteria for final selection, but it was last on the list.[2]

[1] Bureau Intégré des Nations Unies, "Termes de Référence: Mission d'Analyse des Conflits," internal document, United Nations, Kinshasa.
[2] European Commission, Request for candidatures – European Union Election Observation Mission Democratic Republic of Congo 2011, Brussels, August 24, 2011, FPI4/ON/XF D (2011), available at http://ec.europa.eu/europeaid/what/human-rights/election_observation_missions/documents/2011/core_team_notice_drc_en.pdf, last accessed in December 2013.

Even more puzzling, when intervention structures do hire staff with knowledge of local conditions, they routinely send these employees outside their area of expertise. In 2010, the UN peacekeeping mission in Congo recruited a historian who specialized in the politics of the Katanga province. Despite his attempts to ensure his deployment there, where he would be most effective, he found himself sent to Oriental Province, 1,000 miles away, where he had no contacts and little knowledge of the local situation.

These baffling practices reflect the politics of knowledge at work in Peaceland: They are by-products of an ongoing dispute over which (and whose) knowledge matters most for effective peacebuilding.[3] There are two principal contenders for this title. The first, which I refer to as either "local knowledge" or "country expertise," is based on a strong familiarity with specific places, whether countries, like Sudan, or subnational areas, like districts or villages. Such knowledge or expertise (I use the terms interchangeably) entails an intimate understanding of the place's history, key actors, and political, social, cultural, and economic dynamics. One can acquire this expertise in various ways: growing up in the country or village, living there for a significant period of time, studying it extensively, or conducting long-term ethnographic research or demographic surveys there. The second contender is a category that I call "thematic knowledge" or "technical expertise," and it relies on an in-depth understanding of particular aspects of intervention work. These may be general aspects, as in conflict-resolution, development, or humanitarian aid, or they may be specialized ones, as in project management, public finance, or agricultural engineering. Usually, individuals acquire this expertise through formal education and develop it further through practice, but some obtain it through experience alone.

The tensions between these two competencies, both of which are necessary for effective peacebuilding, are part of a broader competition for authority in Peaceland. Both expatriate and local actors possess each type of knowledge to varying degrees, and they employ various strategies to demonstrate the importance of their particular expertise. Each argues that he or she has the most appropriate training, the most relevant skills, and the best experience. In this struggle to assert whose knowledge matters, each actor brings to bear the material, moral, social, and symbolic resources that I analyze in Chapter 6. Of course, the outcome of this contest influences how these resources are distributed in the first place: It determines who will be hired as management and who as staff; who will design intervention strategies and who will merely execute them; and who will have financial, logistical, and human resources at their disposal and who will not.

In this chapter, I document the course of this struggle and explain how the politics of knowledge operates on the ground. I begin by demonstrating that

---

[3] This chapter stems from a discussion with Dr. Vincent Pouliot (McGill University, March 2011). This paragraph builds on Pouliot's ideas and suggestions, and loosely draws on Bourdieu 1979's insights about cultural capital.

thematic knowledge currently overshadows country expertise throughout Peaceland. Next, I locate the sources of this hierarchy. I then dedicate the rest of the chapter to illuminating its impacts on peacebuilding effectiveness. One section emphasizes its positive effects, linked to the professionalization of peacebuilding. The subsequent sections detail its negative consequences: deploying expatriates who lack sufficient understanding of local contexts to achieve their objectives, encouraging a rapid turnover among international interveners, marginalizing local partners, legitimizing the use of templates and models that are often not adapted to local realities, and compartmentalizing different aspects of the international efforts.

Thematic Expertise Over Local Knowledge

Two Necessary Competencies

Peace interventions must draw on both local and thematic knowledge to be effective.[4] Familiarity with the local contexts is crucial for various reasons.[5] First, peacebuilding is an attempt to change the conditions that sustain and promote violence; therefore, understanding the roots of these conditions is an indispensable prerequisite of any successful initiative.[6] Furthermore, the dynamics of violent conflicts are usually localized; they often vary tremendously from place to place.[7] A nuanced understanding of the specific conditions in each theater of intervention – the motivations of each party, the patterns of alliance and conflict at play, the history of antagonisms – is essential for peacebuilders to determine whom to approach, which arguments to use, and, ultimately, what strategies to adopt. In-depth knowledge of local histories, cultures, traditions, attitudes, and worldviews also enables peacebuilders to adapt foreign ideas to on-the-ground conditions during project design.[8] That expertise remains critical throughout project implementation given that conflict and post-conflict settings are extremely volatile, so plans must be continually updated.[9] Finally, cultural understanding helps promote effective communication between peacebuilders and target populations. People in conflict zones all over the world thus emphasize the importance of local knowledge (for national and international staff) in

---

[4] For a similar claim, and ideas related to those I develop in this section, see Anderson and Olson 2003, chapter 5; Campbell 2010, notably pp. 11, 14, 16, 25, 52–59, and 69; CDA Collaborative Learning Projects 2010b, pp. 2–5; and Mac Ginty 2008, notably pp. 141–143.

[5] For a high-level policy statement on this topic, see UN Security Council 2004a, para. 15.

[6] Based on Campbell 2010, p. 25. See also Call and Cousens 2008, pp. 14 and 15.

[7] For the landmark book on this issue, see Kalyvas 2006. For in-depth illustrations on various conflicts, see (among many others): Autesserre 2010; Coyne and Pellillo 2012; Dennys and Zaman 2009; Fujii 2008; Leonard 2013; Straus 2006; and Sørbø 2010.

[8] Mac Ginty 2008; and Richmond 2005, introduction.

[9] Also Campbell 2010, p. 40; and Huang and Harris 2006, notably pp. 86–87.

designing and implementing "appropriate and relevant projects," "communicating effectively," and, as I discuss later in the book, ensuring that project staff do not divert aid to their friends and relatives.[10]

At the same time, technical knowledge is just as necessary. Thematic experts bring ideas, techniques, and approaches that research and experience have identified as the most useful and efficient in conflict resolution. These skills can range from the most basic, such as filing and use of computers, to the most sophisticated, such as project evaluation and conflict analysis.[11] This technical expertise provides peacebuilders with an overview of the available tools for any given situation.[12] Thematic experts play another key role: They drive organizational learning, notably by developing best practices to follow, documenting errors to avoid, and creating codes of conduct.[13] As I develop later in this chapter, this process helps peacebuilding organizations become more effective.

While both insiders and outsiders may possess thematic knowledge, a number of local interviewees emphasized that the insights of foreign interveners provided an essential source of inspiration.[14] International peacebuilders can provide local stakeholders with an understanding of how individuals in other countries at other times have responded to similar situations. Expatriates with thematic expertise can also contribute different perspectives on the situation and help insiders gain critical distance while analyzing problems and developing solutions.

Foreign interveners are not only useful for their thematic expertise: Outsiders with local knowledge are equally indispensable to effective peacebuilding, since relying solely on insiders as the source of such knowledge poses several problems. To begin with, there is never one unified body of local expertise. Instead, there is a dizzying array of competing views, advanced by various local experts who disagree about matters big and small.[15] As in any society, politicians, peacebuilders, and other stakeholders in post-war zones believe in a variety of ideological, political, or economic ideas, and they pursue different interests. Local actors also come from diverse backgrounds, and there is often an enormous distinction between elite and nonelite knowledge.[16] And of course, there is no inherent way to determine whose version of the truth is the truest, or the most likely to help achieve sustainable peace. Having outsiders who are familiar with the country, province, or village in question is therefore essential to navigating the varying bodies of local knowledge in competition. Finally, the presence of foreign peacebuilders is important because wars usually destroy the mechanisms, institutions, and traditions that enable the peaceful competition of rival

---

[10] CDA Collaborative Learning Projects 2010b, p. 2, additional details on pp. 2–5.
[11] For example, Bowles and Chopra 2008, p. 284.
[12] Reychler 2006, p. 5.
[13] Benner, Mergenthaler, et al. 2011; Campbell 2008; and UN General Assembly 2007.
[14] Also Barron and Burke 2008, p. 57; and CDA Collaborative Learning Projects 2010b, p. 3.
[15] Anderson, Brown, et al. 2012, p. 84; and Donais 2009, p. 12. See also Barnett and Zürcher 2009, p. 29.
[16] Barnett and Zürcher 2009, p. 29

interests and ideas. As Roland Paris has demonstrated, external actors can help prevent the potentially healthy competition of ideas from escalating into violence.[17]

Like inside and outside actors, country and thematic expertise work best in combination. Whether they are local stakeholders with thematic knowledge, expatriates with country knowledge, or vice versa, peacebuilders with various competencies each contribute different "perspectives, networks, assets, and leverage with particular constituencies," all of which are essential to effective peacebuilding.[18]

Knowledge Hierarchies

Unfortunately, a clear imbalance exists in the current international system. The most valued expertise is that of foreign interveners who are trained in peacebuilding, humanitarian, or development techniques and who have extensive experience in a variety of conflict zones. By contrast, local knowledge is much less valued.[19]

The structure of the current intervention system is predicated upon this hierarchy. The idea of sending foreigners to a country they have never visited or studied so they can help people they know nothing about makes sense only to individuals and institutions who place the highest value on thematic competency and who deem local expertise unnecessary. Without such knowledge hierarchy to justify it, the very notion would seem absurd. Nobody would ever think to put a public health expert from Kenya in charge of promoting primary care access in the Appalachian counties of eastern Kentucky (United States) without ensuring that this expert – or one of her bosses – understood what existing health services were like in the region, what obstacles to development the mountainous terrain might present, what the community wanted most out of its health-care system, what cultural issues might arise during implementation (such as debates over providing abortions), and so on. These local dynamics are so obviously fundamental that no one would think it remotely reasonable to put someone in charge who lacked familiarity with them. And yet, as one non-governmental organization (NGO) recruiter explained to me, such familiarity is "neither a prerequisite nor a necessity" for interveners in Peaceland.

Recruitment and promotion practices embody the valorization of thematic expertise over local knowledge. The introduction for this chapter already offered some anecdotal evidence. The "career" pages of non-governmental and international organizations' Web sites provide a more thorough illustration.[20] These

---

[17] Paris 2004, chapters 9 and 10.

[18] Anderson and Olson 2003, pp. 35 and 38–39.

[19] See Apthorpe 2011, pp. 200 and 202; Englebert and Tull 2008, pp. 134–135; Ferguson 1990; and Sending 2009, pp. 8–14 for a similar claim and for additional examples.

[20] Representative examples from NGOs include, among many others: www.rescue.org/careers (International Rescue Committee); www.opensocietyfoundations.org/about/jobs (Open Society Foundations); and http://employment.sfcg.org (Search for Common Ground). Representative

sources show that peacebuilding organizations recruit operational experts, such as "political affairs officer," "police commissioner," "country director," or "media coordinator." They rarely hire anthropologists, historians, or other kinds of country specialists who can help interveners gain an in-depth understanding of their work environment, and they virtually never ask for a specialist on, for example, Cyprus, the Kivus, or the Nuba Mountains.

Foreign ministries and diplomatic missions similarly privilege thematic expertise over local knowledge.[21] Competitive exams to select career diplomats test analytical skills, foreign languages, and understandings of economics and geopolitics. None focus on a specific country or context. At best, they have specific recruitment tracks for experts on broad regions, such as Africa or Asia, even though political and socioeconomic situations, languages, and cultures vary widely within these areas. Furthermore, most diplomats hired for their knowledge of a specific area will spend a large part of their careers outside of the bureaus or departmental units that focus on their regions of expertise. Overall, as one U.S. diplomat explained, foreign service officers "are not held to know what the country is like" prior to their deployment there because foreign ministries and donor agencies hire them as experts in domains such as health or negotiations. Moreover, "It is not typical to go to the same country more than once." In the words of this interviewee, "We are not specialists in the countries. We are supposed to know themes and apply our knowledge."

The consequence of these various recruitment processes is that, of the hundreds of expatriate peacebuilders I have met during my career – and of the thousands of interveners that the Listening Project teams encountered in other conflict zones or that Kimberly Coles worked with in Bosnia-Herzegovina – very few had preexisting knowledge of their countries of deployment.[22] All others had been hired based on their substantive and technical capacities. Meanwhile, during interviews, experts on Burundian, Congolese, Timorese, and Somali politics regularly complained of tremendous difficulties in obtaining jobs in their countries of specialization because recruiters usually preferred experts who focused on conflict resolution or gender issues, for example.

Recruiters disregard not only country knowledge gained through formal education but also local expertise gained through years of on-the-ground experience. When violence started during the 2006 riots in Timor-Leste, intervening

examples from international organizations include www.aucareers.org/vacancies.aspx (African Union), www.un.org/Depts/OHRM/examin/exam.htm (UN recruitment exam), https://jobs.un. org/Galaxy/Release3/vacancy/vacancy.aspx (UN Secretariat), www.un.org/Depts/OHRM/ indexpo.htm (UN specialized agencies), and http://web.worldbank.org/external/default/ main?contentMDK=23158967&hlPK=8470978&menuPK=8453611&pagePK=8453982& piPK=8453986&theSitePK=8453353 (World Bank).

[21] Most foreign ministries present their recruitment process online. See, for instance, www.diplo matie.gouv.fr/fr/ministere_817/emplois-stages-concours_825/index.html (for France) and www. state.gov/careers (for the United States). For assignment-specific recruitment, see, for example, www.btcctb.org/en/jobs (Coopération Technique Belge).

[22] Coles 2007, pp. 27–28 and 42; and CDA Collaborative Learning Projects 2010b, p. 2.

organizations evacuated large numbers of their staff (who were working on development issues at the time) and flew in consultants with peacebuilding expertise. Essentially, as soon as these organizations recategorized Timor-Leste as a conflict zone, they replaced actors who had already become conversant in local politics, language, and customs with individuals who were ignorant in these matters, because their thematic expertise was deemed more relevant. In fact, familiarity with conditions on the ground counts for so little that an unsettling experience befell a number of NGO employees, myself included: We applied for a specific position (such as logistician, head of mission, or context analyst), were hired, and told that we would work in a specific town. Then, we learned a few days before our departure to the field that our country of deployment had changed. I thus ended up as a context analyst in Afghanistan instead of returning to Congo; my husband became country director in Kosovo instead of going back to Burundi. Just like our other colleagues, at the time we both found these changes perfectly acceptable: We wanted to work in a specific position for our NGO and, as our recruiters had noted during hiring, we prided ourselves on being flexible enough to perform our job well anywhere in the world.

In terms of promotion and status, intervening entities and their staff members value the number of missions in different countries rather than the amount of time spent in a particular locale. Anybody who has spent time in Peaceland can recall discussions with interveners who boasted of all of the countries in which they had worked, listing them like badges of honor they had collected. (Admittedly, I did the same when I worked as an intervener.) In a statement representative of what I heard throughout my interviews, a UN official asserted that "you are treated with more respect within the UN world if you hop from one country to the next." In contrast, she explained, the expatriates who stay "too long" in a specific place – usually, more than three to five years – are discredited:

> You are dismissed by the international community if you are considered one of these people who have gone native; you have lots of knowledge, but what do you know about international affairs and policy and [the UN] Secretariat? In Nepal, I was able to very quickly understand – I had great contacts, I knew the context very well, but it took me some time to shade the perception that [I was too close to the population] and be treated like an international diplomat.

The section on rotation in the second half of this chapter clarifies the reasons for the expatriates' rapid turnover and elucidates why interveners are so concerned by the risk of "going native," but one point is already clear – and sufficient for the purpose of this section. That is, the current promotion and retention practices in Peaceland create an incentive system in which interveners are encouraged to develop their thematic skills through experience in various countries rather than to acquire an in-depth knowledge of a specific place.

As always, there are variations and exceptions to this trend. Some recruiters value local expertise more than others. In contexts like Afghanistan and the Palestinian Territories, country specialists seem to have had more success in demonstrating the relevance of their knowledge to the overall intervention. This adjustment to knowledge hierarchies was evident in the comparatively larger proportion of expatriates I met who had been hired based on their preexisting familiarity with the area. However, even in such theaters of intervention, my contacts confirmed that peacebuilding agencies still prioritized thematic expertise over local knowledge in the recruitment and promotion of their staff.

Sources of the Imbalance

Since interveners take the valorization of thematic knowledge over local expertise for granted, my interviews generated little material on the roots of this phenomenon. Questions about its causes usually elicited two responses: confirmation from my contacts that they did value technical over country expertise (and a litany of examples to prove it), or interest in discovering the sources of this pattern, followed by a disclaimer that they could not help me to do so. Upon further inspection, it seems that three elements are at play.

The first element is the global scope of most international, diplomatic, and non-governmental organizations active in peacebuilding. Thematic experts have one important advantage over area specialists: They can work anywhere in the world. Why should the UN hire and train a Congo expert when nobody knows where the UN will next intervene? That Congo expert will not be very helpful when trouble suddenly crops up in Haiti or Yemen, but a generalist may be useful in any of those situations. Having thematic experts on staff facilitates rapid deployment regardless of where the next crisis breaks out. And, in conflict situations, quick deployment is of crucial importance, because loss of time often means loss of lives.

The second element is the creation of the figure of "the expert" in recent history.[23] Several authors have traced in depth how this sociological category emerged in the late nineteenth century due to "the expansion of capitalism, the growth of a more specialized division of labor, the heightened importance of services in the modern economy, and, ultimately, the emphasis of modernity on knowledge gained by formal training and education."[24] Two findings from this body of research are particularly important for my argument regarding the politics of knowledge in Peaceland. The first is that "in modern society, credentialed knowledge" (skills acquired through formal education) "trumps local and practical knowledge."[25] The second finding is that the status of "expert" embodies a claim to authority due to the perception that experts "are committed to scientific inquiry and act in the public interest."[26] As a result,

---

[23] This paragraph draws on Mitchell 2002; and on the summary of Brint 1994; Goldman 2001, pp. 191–217; and Sunstein 1997, pp. 128–150 in Barnett 2012, p. 30.
[24] Barnett 2012, p. 508.
[25] Ibid., p. 508.
[26] Ibid., p. 508.

expertise often creates a distance and power differential between those who hold it and those who do not.[27]

The last element is the historical construction of peace and aid work as a technical endeavor for which thematic experts (and not country experts) are needed. Until the 1990s, agencies usually recruited newcomers for their motivations and values. Expatriates who entered the industry as field-based workers recalled how they needed little more than a university degree, a driver's license, and, above all, an ability to convince the recruiter that they believed in peace and humanitarian ideals.[28] However, just like the democratization organizations studied by Nicolas Guilhot, peacebuilding agencies quickly faced "the need to build up expertise, to deal with complex scientific or legal arguments, [and] to do public relations" in order to reach their goal more effectively.[29] To meet these demands, peace institutions underwent a process of professionalization: They tried to develop "a real technical skill" that "produces demonstrable results," is "difficult enough to require training," and can be validated by scientific credentials (such as diplomas, peer-reviewed publications, and academic affiliations).[30]

The need for training and scientific credentials meant that peacebuilders had to mobilize scholarly communities.[31] At that time, paradigms that favored "universalist, structuralist, and rationalist explanations" dominated the research on peace and security.[32] It had not always been so. The agenda of the late 1950s had placed "the comparative study of systems of meaning at the center of peacebuilding efforts," but new "explanatory frames" on "cognition and social action" had emerged in the 1960s and progressively became dominant.[33] The new research focus emphasized technical and universal approaches at the expense of context-specific ones.[34] In the subsequent decades – when the professionalization of peacebuilding took place – the rise of quantitative and formal model approaches in the social sciences solidified the dominance of thematic and technical knowledge and deemphasized the importance of area studies.[35] As a result, peacebuilding organizations experienced a "technocratic turn" in the 1990s and early 2000s, one which has yet to be reversed.[36]

This professionalization process made getting a job in aid and peacebuilding increasingly competitive. Specific training programs in conflict resolution,

---

[27] On this topic, see also May 1990; and Porter 1994, especially pp. 270–271.
[28] For a public source on this period, see Cain, Postlewait, et al. 2004 (a novel retracing the three authors' personal experiences as international peacebuilders in the 1990s), pp. 2–25.
[29] Guilhot 2005, pp. 8–9 and throughout the book.
[30] Based on ibid., p. 93, citing Collins 1979, p. 132.
[31] Based on Guilhot 2005, p. 93.
[32] Miller and Rudnick 2010, p. 64.
[33] Ibid., p. 64.
[34] Ibid., p. 64. For a historical study of this process, see Guilhot 2005, chapter 3, notably pp. 108–111 and 119–120.
[35] On social sciences: Amadae 2003. On economics: Mitchell 2002.
[36] Mac Ginty 2012, pp. 293–294.

War = technical prob

development, and humanitarian aid emerged in the 1990s to help would-be interveners acquire the skill sets that peace and aid agencies now required.[37] The emphasis on technical and universal approaches in the broad intellectual environment shaped these preparation programs. They were premised on two assumptions: that expertise is somehow fungible – meaning that what works in one context will function just as well in another – and that one can solve problems in any part of the developing world using technical solutions. The training that the new generation of aid professionals received thus included universal tools, such as mediation, conflict assessment, or evaluation techniques, to use in any war or post-war situation.[38] In turn, the new professionals produced an enormous literature aimed at facilitating program design and implementation in any country, for initiatives as varied as using power-sharing to end a civil war or employing the best approach to operating water sources.[39] This literature reinforced the view of peace and aid work as universal and technical. Eventually, interveners came to view issues of war and poverty as "a set of technical problems to be solved by experts."[40]

The influence of this viewpoint is evident on the ground, and it was a recurring theme in my interviews. The vast majority of interveners I met presented their jobs as a series of technical tasks. A human resources director at a large NGO explained that he and his colleagues view "technicity" as "a universal value that has no borders" and believe that "there is one proper way of doing things, not two." The organization thus needs "technical experts" who can implement "guidelines, rules, books, and frameworks of intervention" and "adapt [them] a little bit but not too much." To do so, he concluded, "You do not need to know the context in which you work."[41] A seasoned peacebuilder concurred: "Every conflict is different, but there are also similarities in human beings. There are certain ways of doing things: processes and tools that you can use [across conflicts]" and that are the "skills" necessary to "be able to do the job" of peacebuilding. Another agreed: "The international community puts a premium on experience in other countries because of the idea that one can transfer models. A smart person who works in the Congo can work in another country and transfer what has worked there." Even the experience of violence is seen as transferable to other contexts. Based on in-depth interviews in various theaters of intervention, Audra Mitchell has demonstrated that there is an "assumption that 'violence' is a constant or generic variable that manifests itself

---

[37] See also Mitchell 2011a, p. 26.
[38] For fascinating statistics on the type of competencies taught in conflict resolution programs, see Polkinghorn, La Chance, et al. 2008; and Warters 2008.
[39] See for instance, among many others: Caritas 2002; Lederach 2002; The Sphere Project 2011 (first edition released in 1998); UN Department of Peacekeeping Operations – Peacekeeping Best Practices Unit 2003; and UN Department of Peacekeeping Operations – Department of Field Support 2012.
[40] Fechter and Hindman 2011b, p. 5 (see also p. 8 and throughout the book).
[41] Author's on-record interview with Philippe Rosen, Goma, July 2011.

in distinctive settings [. . .] – and that one can become 'experienced in' violence by encountering it in any of its manifestations."[42]

This view of intervention work as technical has an important corollary: Acquiring sufficient familiarity with local history, structures, and cultures is much easier and much quicker than gaining technical skills. Many expatriate interviewees espoused this view, claiming that newcomers only needed "a week" to "a couple of months" to gain an understanding of their theaters of deployment that was sufficient to perform their job. (Country experts vehemently rejected this claim, but it makes sense when one believes that implementing universal ideas requires only limited local knowledge.) Interveners usually contrasted this short time frame with the "several years" necessary to acquire technical skills. From this point of view, hiring technical specialists is logical.

The various dynamics described in this section create a vicious cycle. Valuing thematic knowledge over local expertise encourages would-be interveners to acquire technical skills rather than in-depth country knowledge. It also entices universities and other training organizations to offer thematic classes (on conflict, peacebuilding, or aid in general) rather than courses focused on specific countries. Consequently, as the recruiters I interviewed mentioned, it is now very difficult to find a candidate for an intervening position who possesses relevant local knowledge, and it is virtually impossible to find people who have both thematic and local expertise – and yet do not have overly close links to the countries on which they are experts. Because agencies can rarely, if ever, find someone who fulfills all the requirements, they devalue the criterion that is the most difficult to find and that they believe to be least important: local knowledge. (At best, they favor familiarity with the region – understood as Africa or Asia – and knowledge of one of the official languages.) This order of priority further disincentivizes the acquisition of in-depth country knowledge by would-be peacebuilders, which in turn makes local experts more rare and prevents intervening agencies from restoring the balance of thematic and local expertise in their recruitments.

Admittedly, scholars and high-level managers stationed in headquarters and capitals still consider alternative visions of peacebuilding.[43] Moreover, several organizations such as the Life and Peace Institute and the Eastern Congo Initiative actually implement these visions in the field. Their employees base their actions on in-depth local knowledge and reject universal approaches to peacebuilding.[44] They rely on local employees supervised by a few expatriates (who have extensive preexisting country knowledge). The staff members venture suggestions or start designing projects only after having learned about the local dynamics in their

---

[42] Mitchell 2011c.

[43] Fechter and Hindman 2011b, p. 5. For representative scholarly examples of such alternative visions, see among others Autesserre 2010, conclusion; and Moore 2013, conclusion.

[44] For more details, see the mission statements of the Life and Peace Institute (www.life-peace.org/what-we-do/guiding-principles/) and the Eastern Congo Initiative (www.easterncongo.org/about).

target areas. However, this alternative approach remains marginal since, as interveners working for other organizations in the field explained to me, the labor required to design, implement, and coordinate technical programs is too demanding; it does not leave them the leisure to consider reforming their standard mode of operation.

Intended and Unintended Effects

Professionalization and Increased Effectiveness

As intended, the professionalization of peacebuilding and the attendant concentration on thematic expertise have increased the effectiveness of intervention programs on the ground in various ways. To begin with, this process has initiated the development of best-practices units, monitoring and evaluation sections, professional standards, and codes of conducts.[45] These advances have enabled organizations to learn from prior experiences and to try to ensure that new initiatives do not reproduce past errors.[46] As mentioned above, they have also facilitated the creation of training programs aimed at increasing the peacebuilders' skills and knowledge, and they have led to the creation of uniform practices and procedures.[47]

This new body of knowledge has equipped peacebuilders with a variety of tools and strategies for use in their efforts to stop violence. Furthermore, unified practices and procedures offer guidance to interveners in the form of policy directives, manuals, and indications of which issues to prioritize.[48] This provides a common approach to peacebuilders coming from a multitude of organizational, national, and professional backgrounds.[49] It also reduces the need for interveners to "reinvent the wheel" when facing a crisis and makes the planning and start-up phases of a mission more straightforward, thus facilitating rapid response to emergencies.[50] Lastly, it promotes continuity in a context of high staff turnover, and facilitates accountability through the articulation of standards and expectations.[51]

Best-practices units and monitoring and evaluation departments have made two additional contributions. They have drawn attention to crosscutting issues,

---

[45] Benner, Mergenthaler, et al. 2011, pp. 215–217; Paffenholz 2010; pp. 48–49; Sending 2010a, p. 10; and UN General Assembly 2007.

[46] Benner, Mergenthaler, et al. 2011, pp. 216–217; Campbell 2008, p. 21; and UN General Assembly 2007, para. 9.

[47] Benner, Mergenthaler, et al. 2011, pp. 217–218; Sending 2010a, p. 20; and UN General Assembly 2007, para. 1.

[48] UN General Assembly 2007, paras. 1 through 10, 22, and 31.

[49] Ibid., para. 1.

[50] Benner, Mergenthaler, et al. 2011, pp. 116–117; and UN General Assembly 2007, paras. 1, 36, 38, and 40–43 (citation from para. 2).

[51] UN General Assembly 2007, para. 1.

such as gender, which were often neglected due to the lack of a dedicated institutional home.[52] Their work has also increased the legitimacy and credibility of their organizations in the eyes of the general public. This in turn has helped peacebuilding agencies secure funding for their efforts, in a context where donors were hesitant to finance missions without adequate data demonstrating the effectiveness of the programs.[53] The greater capacity to secure funding has increased the capacity of organizations to provide training for their staff and to finance monitoring and evaluation sections, thus generating a virtuous cycle.

The positive, intended effects of professionalization (and its attendant focus on thematic and technical knowledge) are clear and largely present on the ground, but they are not sufficient for successful peacebuilding. International efforts can reach their full potential only when intervening structures rely on in-depth local expertise to complement thematic competencies. However, due to the politics of knowledge that pervades Peaceland, most intervening agencies lack such an evenhanded approach. The rest of this chapter analyzes the main detrimental impacts of the resulting imbalance on the effectiveness of international efforts.

Ill-Equipped Interveners

The unyielding emphasis on thematic expertise in Peaceland is so strong that it regularly leads to comparative neglect of even the most essential local knowledge when assigning responsibilities. The person the UN tasked with drawing up an approach to the 2009 peace negotiations in Madagascar had no country expertise or experience. He did not even speak French. (Thankfully, he and his colleagues ultimately recognized the problem with this arrangement and secured the help of advisors with in-depth local knowledge.) Likewise, when Doctors Without Borders sent me, first, to Congo and, later, to Afghanistan to work as a context analyst – the person in charge of analyzing political, military, social, and humanitarian conditions on the ground – I had no preexisting knowledge of either country, and I learned personally how frustrating it was to feel that I was not properly equipped to provide the kinds of analyses that were key to helping beneficiaries. My colleagues deployed as context analysts in other missions and organizations were in the same situation.

Even worse, valuing technical expertise over contextual knowledge legitimizes the deployment of people who do not speak any of the local languages – even though, as Chapter 4 details, interveners and local people alike continually identify the lack of linguistic ability of on-the-ground interveners as one of the main impediments to effective peacebuilding. It takes only a few striking examples to illustrate the widespread neglect of linguistic skills. Out of the 140 diplomats working for the United Kingdom embassy in Kabul in 2010, only

---

[52] Benner, Mergenthaler, et al. 2011, p. 216.
[53] Paffenholz and Spurk 2006, p. 16.

three "spoke an Afghan language."[54] Out of the 1,700 UN police deployed in Haiti in 2005, only 100 spoke French or Creole.[55] In Afghanistan, Cyprus, and Sudan, the working language of virtually all interveners is English; I met only a handful of peacebuilders who had a command of Pashtu, Greek or Turkish, or Arabic or Nuer. Kimberley Coles similarly reports that only a few interveners spoke Serbo-Croatian in Bosnia-Herzegovina.[56] In eastern Congo, interveners master at best French – the official, administrative language of the country – but very few speak Swahili, the vehicular language of the area. The UN mission in Congo waited ten years (until 2009) to start assigning local translators to its peacekeeping contingents. When it finally sent translators, it found it necessary to allocate only a few of them to each peacekeeping contingent – which numbers between 200 and 500 soldiers.

Short Deployments and Rapid Turnover

Another noteworthy consequence of the politics of knowledge is that, as international peacebuilders devalue local expertise, and as experience in numerous countries becomes highly prized, intervening organizations actively cultivate a high turnover rate among interveners. Interviewees working for NGOs, international agencies, and diplomatic missions stated that their organizations "encouraged and almost imposed mobility." A variety of contacts expressed a common sentiment: "You need to change missions otherwise it creates problems for your career." In practice, diplomats usually move every two to three years; NGO staff stay six months to three years (with an average of a year in a mission); peacekeeping contingents rotate every six months to a year, EU military staff every four months, and UN civilian employees have six-month contracts that they usually renew a couple of times.[57] Even development practitioners, who pride themselves on working for the long term, change countries on average every two years.[58]

Relying on outsiders for at least some tasks, and rotating them regularly, is a classic organizational and governmental technique. The Ottoman Empire used this strategy as early as the sixteenth century, in part to prevent its representatives from developing local allegiances.[59] In modern times, NGOs, states, donors, and organizations similarly rotate their staff to prevent the development of detrimental alliances and biases on the ground. Diplomats are expected to remain loyal to and represent the national interests of their countries of origin, so regularly changing their theaters of deployment ensures that they do not develop

---

[54] Mac Ginty 2011, p. 112.
[55] Meharg 2009, p. 136.
[56] Coles 2007, pp. 28–29.
[57] Smirl 2008, p. 243 reports similar estimates.
[58] Verma 2011, p. 60.
[59] Barkey 2008, pp. 17–18 and 93–94.

links to the host countries that might compromise their allegiances. A representative of the International Committee of the Red Cross explained that his organization compels its delegates to rotate every year or two, and to stay for a maximum of three years in a single place, "mostly so that they can keep their neutrality." Many interviewees deployed on the ground, from Burma to Congo to Cyprus, stated that the more one knows about the context, and the more one has personal ties among the population, the more likely one is to become biased in favor of a specific group of local people, thereby abandoning one's objectivity.[60] Some of them further emphasized that having relatives or in-laws among the host population compounds the suspicion that one might become biased. A peacekeeper best captured the logic that results: "The more [local] expertise you have in a domain, the more suspect you are."

International organizations, as well as foreign and defense ministries, also use the rotation system to create a fair playing field among their staff. That way, everybody alternates hardship, nonfamily postings with postings where life is easier and where they can bring their spouses and children.

While outsiders and newcomers do help redress biases, and while they provide a fresh perspective on problems, numerous interviewees emphasized that the turnover in Peaceland is so rapid and systematic that the negative impacts outweigh the positive.[61] To begin with, it leads to a loss of institutional memory. As contacts at all of my field sites deplored, and as I observed firsthand, many interveners repeat previous mistakes (not knowing that their strategies were already tried unsuccessfully in the past), and are unaware of potentially useful research, assessments, and reports produced before their arrival. Rapid and high turnover also impedes the development of trusting relationships between expatriates and their local counterparts, which takes years.[62] In addition, because local staff has to adapt to new management styles and new ways of working every time their expatriate colleagues change, rotation creates disruptions within the intervening organizations, thereby decreasing productivity. Furthermore, it reinforces the lack of accountability for expatriates, since foreign interveners rarely stay long enough in the country to suffer the consequences of their mistakes. At worst, they must deal with them for a couple of months, only until they move on to a new theater of deployment.

Finally, the turnover makes it impossible for interveners to attain deeper understandings of the theaters of deployment. My contacts regularly told me that they spent half of their time in the field getting oriented and thus were effective for only a few months over the course of their stay. As a result, few of the peacebuilders I met had a good sense of the host country's history, even when that history was relevant to the problems they were trying to address. A discussion I had in 2010 with a high-ranking staff member of the UN peacekeeping

---

[60] For public sources, see Verma 2011, p. 72; and Pouligny 2004, p. 187.

[61] For a public source on this topic, see CDA Collaborative Learning Projects 2012, p. 9.

[62] Also Coburn 2011, p. 87 (on Afghanistan); and Moore 2013, p. 134 (on Bosnia-Herzegovina).

mission in Congo provides a striking example. To brief me on the situation in the area before her arrival, she explained: "Even in 2006, before the elections, when the FDLR [Rwandan Hutu militia] issue had not popped up, we assessed the security situation; it was calm. The FDLR were merry and calm." This statement was highly inaccurate. I was in eastern Congo in 2006 and saw firsthand that the FDLR were neither "merry" nor "calm." They were instead responsible for numerous incidents of both small and large-scale fighting, and they frequently committed horrific human rights violations against local populations.[63] I heard countless other examples of such deficient historical understanding from all kinds of interveners. An NGO colleague talked about the conflict between "the Tutus and the Hutsis" in Rwanda (instead of Hutus and Tutsis). Another contact failed to realize that she was about to hire the previous personal assistant to a former (and much abhorred) rebel leader to lead her NGO's operations in Congo. The last section of Chapter 4 recounts a number of other such misunderstandings.

In fact, even peacebuilders who fully believe in the supremacy of thematic expertise sometimes recognize that expatriates who have spent several years in the same country are a good source of information and contacts. This was evident in the recommendations I received on whom to meet when I first arrived as an intervener in a new country, and then when I asked for suggestions of potential interviewees once I returned as a researcher.

The differing degrees of effectiveness of the international agencies that worked in Aceh (Indonesia) in 2005 and 2006 further illuminate the benefit of limiting the number of short-term rotations. Barron and Burke's thorough evaluation of intervention efforts there found that one of the "key practical attributes" shared by the international agencies that did usefully contribute to the peace process was "long-term commitment of staff on the ground, including field managers and people working in more analytical functions."[64] (Others included prior experience in Aceh and in other Indonesian conflict zones, as well as shaping assistance based on in-depth understanding of the local context rather than on technical and institutional priorities alone.[65])

These findings reinforce those drawn from the study of interventions in other very different parts of the world. A multi-donor evaluation of conflict prevention and peacebuilding activities in South Sudan found that one of the reasons why USAID was among the most effective bilateral donors between 2005 and 2010 was that it retained "a number of key staff [. . .] with extensive experience and knowledge of Southern Sudan."[66] The combination of continuity of staff, local

---

[63] On Rwandan Hutu militias in Congo before 2006, see among many others Autesserre 2010, pp. 59–62, 141–151, and 156–158.
[64] Barron and Burke 2008, p. xiii and throughout the book.
[65] Ibid., pp. xiii, 56–58, and throughout the book.
[66] Bennett, Pantuliano, et al. 2010, pp. 132–133.

knowledge, and in-depth conflict analysis proved in fact so successful that other donors requested USAID to manage their funds.[67]

This conclusion echoes the findings of a study of international peace efforts in support of the Abkhaz–Georgian peace process from 1996 to 2008.[68] According to local participants, one of the central reasons for the success of the University of California, Irvine's Citizen Peacebuilding Project in a situation where most other international efforts remained ineffective was that the expatriates working on this project "remained consistent and demonstrate[d] long-term commitment" to the initiatives.[69] One of the interveners actually brought to her post fifteen years of experience in Abkhazia, which proved crucial: "The trust Abkhaz felt for her [helped] them remain engaged in a project that involved working bilaterally with Georgians, even at a time when all other such projects were politically impossible."[70] Just like the effective international peacebuilders in Aceh and South Sudan, those who productively contributed to the reconciliation process in Georgia and Abkhazia possessed in-depth language and local knowledge that enabled them to "shape a culturally relevant" initiative.[71] Sadly, the politics of knowledge in Peaceland means that such local competencies are often cast aside.

Marginalization of Local Counterparts

Another problem with the preference for thematic expertise is that it further asserts the superiority of expatriate peacebuilders over local stakeholders, whose knowledge interveners consider less sophisticated and more parochial. In the eyes of expatriates, the predominance of thematic expertise helps legitimize the practice of giving themselves much higher salaries and much better benefits than local staff receives in comparable positions, as I will discuss in Chapter 5. In the eyes of host populations, these inequalities send a strong implicit message that local expertise is of less value.[72]

Even more strikingly, in virtually all aid and peacebuilding agencies, whether diplomatic, international, or non-governmental, expatriates hold the management positions, while local employees make up the staff. There are rare exceptions, such as organizations like Peace Direct and the Eastern Congo Initiative, which consciously try to fight the trend.[73] Otherwise, very few local people make it into leadership positions in their countries of origin. To move up in the hierarchy, they have to go abroad and become expatriates.

---

[67] Ibid., pp. 132–133.
[68] Garb and Allen Nan 2009.
[69] Ibid., p. 285 and throughout the chapter.
[70] Ibid., p. 284.
[71] Ibid., p. 284 and throughout the chapter. On South Sudan: Cousens, Kumar, et al. 2001, p. 133
[72] CDA Collaborative Learning Projects 2010b, p. 5.
[73] On Peace Direct, see McGuinness 2012. For additional examples, see Juma and Suhrke 2002, p. 9.

Because they are habituated to seeing expatriates in the ranks of management and local staff in lower positions, seasoned interveners and populations in conflict zones automatically assume that foreigners know and decide, while local colleagues obey and execute. When I conducted a participant observation with an international peacebuilding NGO, I went to the field accompanied only by local staff members, and consequently everybody assumed that I was the team leader. Although I was the least knowledgeable of the project and was not even wearing the organization's official paraphernalia, people addressed their requests and questions to me merely because I was the only expatriate on site. Other foreigners have had similar experiences.[74]

In fact, most intervention structures value the expertise of local people only at the level of implementation, if at all.[75] An agency may recruit a local staff member familiar with a specific theater in order to ensure a successful execution of given strategies and projects, but it will not involve this person in the design of these initiatives. Similarly, as various interviewees and I experienced in UN agencies, diplomatic missions, and international NGOs, the role of the national staff is usually limited to collecting information that expatriates later analyze. Very few agencies build on local analytical capacity. This unequal relationship also prevails in the interactions between international and local NGOs, as the latter are "rarely" involved "in shaping strategy."[76]

This standard mode of operation is highly problematic because many inter-viewees justified the preference for thematic expertise in the recruitment of foreign staff members by explaining that there is an informal distribution of tasks in Peaceland. In their view, expatriates bring the technical and thematic skills, while national employees contribute their local knowledge. But this division of labor can work only if the two groups enjoy equal status and if they both participate in program design. Such a setup, though infrequent, does occasionally exist in Peaceland, among agencies that have decided to resist the trend, such as Catholic Relief Services (CRS).[77] As Chip Gagnon studied in Serbia and Bosnia, and as I observed in Timor-Leste, local staff and local NGOs conceived, designed, and implemented CRS projects.[78] CRS expatriates working in these countries viewed their role as "providing technical support, resources, and international connections."[79] In Gagnon's analysis, which cor-roborates what I heard in Timor from many difference sources, "reliance on

---

[74] A public source on this topic is an author's on-record interview with Christiane Kayser, Pole Institute and Service Civil pour la Paix de Pain pour le Monde, Goma, July 2011.

[75] For a public source on this issue (in Liberia and Sudan), see Sending 2010b (ed.), pp. 5, 24–25, 28–29, and 31–34.

[76] Keystone Accountability 2011, citation from p. 5; details on pp. 17–20, and 48. Also Keystone Accountability 2013, p. 6.

[77] On CRS' approach to partnership with local people, see Gagnon 2006, pp. 171, 174–176, and 180–181.

[78] On Serbia and Bosnia: ibid.

[79] Ibid., citation from p. 172.

local staff," "an intense research-and-needs assessment" at the very beginning of the intervention, and solicitation of input from beneficiaries during all subsequent phases of the project were key to ensuring the success of CRS' democratization and reconstruction efforts.[80] By contrast, the division of labor between international and local employees is likely to weaken peacebuilding effectiveness when one group conceives and creates the operations and the other merely executes them, as is usually the case.

Two other studies highlight similar findings. The independent evaluation of UN Peacebuilding Fund projects in Burundi emphasizes that the "most effective projects" were those that enabled "a relatively equal partnership and continuous dialogue between the national and international partners during the design *and* implementation of the project" and that "integrated non-governmental partners, civil society, beneficiaries, and/or community members in the design, implementation, and monitoring of the projects."[81] In fact, of the seventeen projects that the team evaluated, only those that presented a "balance" between national and international inputs made a "high" contribution to peace consolidation, and of the eleven projects that made only low or medium contributions, ten were found to have unequal partnerships that favored the input of either the national or international partners.[82]

The last example provides a model of how to balance the need to build both on the expertise and new ideas from outsiders and on the understanding of local people.[83] In the early 1990s, after the end of communism, Slovakia saw the arrival of a flurry of international experts. Slovaks initially received these outsiders "with open arms and unrealistically high expectations that they would solve all of" their country's problems, but then started to reject foreign expertise as local expectations remained unfulfilled.[84] One of the initiatives that avoided this disaffection was the Partners for Democratic Change. Unlike the others, this project did not rely primarily on outside expertise and foreign interveners; instead, it gave an equally important role to domestic institutions. Local organizations hosted foreign facilitators, and the project started by offering trainings where both domestic and foreign experts worked together.[85] As soon as local trainers "started to receive comparable or better feedback than foreign experts," the project moved to relying on local resources and inviting outsiders only when necessary to "introduce new methodologies or address specific issues."[86] Local participants saw this model as highly effective: It enabled them to benefit from external ideas and expertise while still providing them with peacebuilders

---

[80] Ibid., p. 172.
[81] Campbell 2010, p. 11 (emphasis in the original). Similar claims also appear on pp. 50 and 78.
[82] Ibid., pp. 52–59.
[83] This paragraph is based on Glick and Reynolds Levy 2009, notably pp. 43–44.
[84] Ibid., p. 43.
[85] Ibid., p. 43.
[86] Ibid., p. 44.

familiar with the "many different contexts and complexities" of their country that other international programs failed to apprehend.[87]

Recruitment of Local Partners and Conflict Dynamics

The tendency when hiring to privilege thematic expertise above all else, especially if this expertise is substantiated by scholarly degrees and experience with various intervention structures, also affects the recruitment of local staff members in intervening agencies. Unfortunately, in conflict zones, this preference can lead to bias in various dimensions, notably ethnic or geographic, thereby reinforcing some of the drivers of conflict.

For instance, in Burundi, where Tutsis have enjoyed privileged access to education and high-profile positions for several decades, using degrees and past experience as criteria for recruitment results in favoring the Tutsi minority over the Hutu majority. Several Burundians in fact mentioned offhand during interviews that a number of UN agencies and NGOs were "biased" and "pro-Tutsi" due to the ethnic identity of their local staff. A grassroots peacebuilder I interviewed demonstrated the extent of the problem: When she first arrived in Burundi in 1999 to work with a development agency, she "had almost no contact with Hutus."

Along the same lines, in Congo, a number of interveners complained that orders to ignore the ethnic dimension during recruitment and to focus exclusively on "merit" led them to hire an ethnically or geographically unbalanced staff, whom the communities in which they worked then rejected as biased. My discussions with ordinary citizens provided ample data to support this analysis. The inhabitants of Goma, for instance, complained that expatriates discriminated against them during recruitment. Interveners employed mostly ethnic Bashi from the neighboring province of South Kivu, as this province had better schools and universities and as NGOs had worked there for longer, enabling people from South Kivu to acquire more experience. Throughout eastern Congo, the value that expatriates placed on formal education and experience with intervention structures also led intervening agencies to privilege the urban elite, which created many tensions in the rural towns and villages where the peacebuilders operated (a problem that other researchers have also documented in countries as varied as Burma, Ecuador, Indonesia, and Kenya).[88] Local populations felt discriminated against, and some reacted by organizing violent protests and even riots against interveners.

The preference for thematic expertise has another widespread effect on the interveners' local counterparts that, while not as counterproductive as the others mentioned above, nevertheless decreases the efficiency of peace interventions. As

[87] Ibid., pp. 44–46, citation from p. 44.
[88] On Burma, Ecuador, and Kenya: CDA Collaborative Learning Projects 2010b, pp. 2–3. On Indonesia: Smirl 2008, p. 249.

both my contacts and the interviewees of the Listening Project lamented, when international structures select "local partners," they privilege those who "speak the international language" – meaning those who are conversant in the interveners' technical terms and acronyms, understand the logic of the international aid system, are familiar with its values, and know how to navigate complex international processes.[89] This preference regularly leads interveners to overlook grassroots structures that are embedded in communities and consequently have the deepest understanding of on-the-ground dynamics. In Congo, for instance, several contacts emphasized that "only the technocrats, the experts, and the members of the civil society who [...] master the international machinery" make the cut, even when they have a limited or nonexistent popular base and do little to actually help populations in need. The other peacebuilders – "the rural grassroots organizations" who are "very efficient in the field and have a large popular base" and "the communities, the small groups of people who are not formally organized, but who have real needs and do concrete actions" – do not benefit from international support, as they do not know how to navigate the complex international system. The situation seems similar in Cyprus: An NGO representative explained that "all the projects funded, all the ones that have chances to be funded," are the ones using the "key words" that international donors like, such as "'multiculturalism,' 'respect,' 'tolerance,' and so on."[90]

Outsider Bias

Beyond its impact on expatriate staff, local employees, and local organizations, the dominance of thematic expertise shapes the overall structure of the intervention. It generates an outsider bias, as Dennis Tull and Pierre Englebert trace in their study of state reconstruction in Africa. In their words, "The very nature of international reconstruction efforts suggests that the knowledge, capacity, strategies, and resources of external actors are crucial ingredients for success."[91] This bias is evident at the macro level, in the dominant explanations for peacebuilding successes and failures. Many scholars and practitioners indeed "assume that the chances of successful statebuilding increase with the intensity of outsiders' inputs such as per capita assistance or the strength and mandate of UN peacekeeping missions" (an assumption that Carrie Manning and Christoph Zürcher have convincingly rebutted).[92] The bias is similarly obvious at the micro level, in the implicit assumption that expatriates "have the answer" to local problems and can thus "save" host populations (see Chapter 6).

---

[89] CDA Collaborative Learning Projects 2010b, p. 6. The quotes come from my confidential interviews.
[90] Mitchell 2011a, p. 28.
[91] Englebert and Tull 2008, pp. 134–135.
[92] Ibid., p. 135; and Manning and Zürcher 2013, chapter 4.

Combined with the negative view of local counterparts detailed in Chapter 6, this pro-outsider bias entices international interveners to substitute themselves for local partners.[93] Admittedly, one could blame the persistence of this inefficient mode of operation on a selfish (if normal and understandable) desire by peacebuilders to preserve their employment. However, this objection does not stand, given that reorienting the expatriates' work toward training and capacity building would not leave them jobless.

That interveners substitute themselves for local partners is a frequent criticism directed at emergency relief efforts, and many UN, NGO, and diplomatic contacts working in conflict resolution provided examples from their own organizations.[94] A UN civilian peacekeeper, for instance, recalled that only when peacekeepers learned that they had to leave Chad – after they had already been on site for a year and a half – did they start training local people in the mission's activities. She also regretted that, in the new mission where she was now working, there was almost no emphasis on training local counterparts – whether local authorities and civil society structures or UN local staff – in domains such as organizing elections and protecting human rights. Another UN official emphasized that diplomatic missions also tend to think, act, and talk for local partners, and he illustrated this point with an anecdote. During the lead-up to the 2011 elections in Congo, certain embassies disapproved so strongly of the ruling president that they acted as if they were full, legitimate members of the domestic political opposition, organizing meetings among opposition leaders and drawing up action plans for them to win the elections. International NGOs are no exception. Two Congolese intellectuals provided numerous examples of NGOs running hospitals themselves instead of training local authorities to manage them, fighting against injustice themselves instead of training grassroots activists to do so, or carrying out state reconstruction projects themselves without even consulting state authorities.[95] In conclusion, one of these interviewees offered a striking remark: "With all their self-confidence, [interveners] think that they can construct the Congo without the Congolese."[96]

There were exceptions within all organizations – people who tried, at their own level, to share their knowledge with their local colleagues or partners, and to give them as much responsibility as possible, in the hope that these people would eventually take over their positions. As the section on ownership and authorship in Chapter 3 demonstrates, these individuals implemented initiatives

---

[93] On the relation between negative views of counterparts and lack of capacity building, see also McWha 2011, p. 36.

[94] On humanitarian aid, see, among others: Anderson 1999, pp. 47–49; Anderson, Brown, et al. 2012, pp. 21–23 and 67–69; Juma and Suhrke 2002; and Smillie 2001, pp. 1, 19 and 20. See also Branch 2009 on human rights.

[95] Author's on-record interview with Onesphore Sematumba (Pole Institute, Goma, November 2010) and Jean-Pierre Lindiro Kabirigi (Pole Institute, Goma, July 2011).

[96] Author's on-record interview with Sematumba.

that were, on average, more effective. However, they all emphasized the rarity of their approach. Although other expatriates were aware of the problems inherent in their tendency to substitute themselves for their local partners, they explained that the low capacity of these counterparts left them with little choice. Humanitarian aid workers underscored that relying on expatriates is often the only way to save lives during emergencies. In immediate post-earthquake Haiti, for instance, it made more sense for a foreign NGO to set up and run a hospital to do amputations rather than spend several years teaching local surgeons to do so, letting injured people die of gangrene in the meantime. The same reasoning holds for other medical, water, sanitation, or food emergencies. Peacebuilders stationed in weak states, such as Congo and Sudan, felt that they faced a similar dilemma. Overall, my contacts presented the situation as a catch-22: Either they did capacity building, which took an enormous amount of time and resulted in poorly executed programs – while intended beneficiaries continued to suffer from the continuation of violence – or they implemented the programs themselves, which was more effective in the short term but unsustainable in the long term and created dependency.

Templates and Preexisting Models

In addition to creating and perpetuating an outsider bias, the preference for thematic expertise, the view of knowledge as fungible, and the deep-seated belief that there are universal solutions to war and violence legitimize the use of nearly identical templates across conflict zones. Furthermore, the interveners' frequent rotations between countries and lack of local knowledge leave them no other choice but to rely on these external models. Other researchers have extensively analyzed the interveners' shared tendency to rely on templates and preexisting models, so it is necessary here to emphasize only the main ideas.[97]

At the macro level, interveners often use a checklist approach for their work. They view each situation as requiring the use of a toolkit that includes the deployment of peacekeepers; the disarmament, demobilization, and reintegration of combatants; the repatriation of refugees; the liberalization of the economy; and, above all, the organization of elections.[98] As was evident in many countries, from Afghanistan to Bosnia-Herzegovina to Timor-Leste, this approach to intervention

---

[97] The extensive literature on this topic includes, among many others: Anderson 2008, pp. 99–100; Anderson, Brown, et al. 2012, notably pp. 38–39 and 44; Autesserre 2010, chapter 3 (notably pp. 84–85); CDA Collaborative Learning Projects 2011b, p. 1; Chandler 2005, p. 308; Chopra and Hohe 2004; Coyne and Pellillo 2012; Duffey 2000, notably p. 144; Ellis 2005; Gilbert 2008, especially chapter 1; Hohe 2002; Mac Ginty 2006 and 2008; Ottaway 2003; Paris 2004 and 2010; Pouligny 2004, especially pp. 133–136 and 293; Salem 1997; and Verma 2011, pp. 64–67. See also the very interesting discussion of this literature in Moore 2013, pp. 29–30.

[98] Coyne and Pellillo 2012; Ellis 2005; Gilbert 2008, notably chapter 1; and Pouligny 2004, notably p. 293. On the creation and transformation of this toolkit, see Ottaway 2003.

can build neither sustainable peace nor functioning democracy because it is not adapted to situations on the ground.[99]

This approach entices interveners to rely on templates and models that are developed elsewhere and apply them to new situations without consideration for local contexts. My interviewees provided multiple examples, illustrating both the widespread use of templates and models and the fact that, contrary to the dominant claim in the literature, they are not necessarily linked to liberal ideas. Several contacts emphasized the "international approach to statebuilding," with its notion that "there is a correct," "very technocratic" way "to build a state and institutions." Others pointed to the "cookie cutter" approach to disarmament, demobilization, and reintegration in Sudan; the attempted application in Timor-Leste of a security sector reform agenda developed in Kosovo; the "logistical toolkit" that humanitarian aid workers bring from mission to mission; the Western gender norms promoted around the world; the untraditional food rationed to needy populations; the conventional model of toilets built to respond to water and sanitation emergencies; and the kits of basic necessities that aid agencies provide to resettled populations.

The detrimental impacts of using foreign models are obvious at the micro level. Because these templates are not adapted to local conditions, while some projects achieve their objectives, many others cannot reach their full potential, fail to accomplish their goals, or have counterproductive effects. For instance, interveners once attempted to introduce the "food for work" approach (paying people who contribute to public work in food rations) in Kalemie, a city in the Congolese province of Katanga, because this method had proven effective in promoting food security and building infrastructure in other countries across the globe. The project backfired because schoolteachers rarely received a salary in Kalemie. Local schools closed for the duration of the program as the teachers went to work on road construction projects. Even worse, initiatives based on external templates at times exacerbate the very problems that they aim to address. In Liberia, the implementation of a formal, modern justice system, which could not and did not work, alongside a traditional system that did not work well either, led to the hybridization of two incompatible logics, the delegitimization of traditional institutions, the implementation of ineffective formal structures, and a decrease in the overall provision of justice.[100] In Congo in 2011, interveners working in police reform tried to introduce the concept of community police, which had promoted better relationships between North American citizens and their police officers and thus ensured safer cities. Unfortunately, in a context where police officers survive on extortion and corruption, increased contact with police merely multiplied threats to ordinary people and boosted their sense of insecurity.

---

[99] Duffey 2000, notably p. 144; Hohe 2002; Moore 2013, pp. 7, 12, and 165; Paris 2010; Pouligny 2004, especially pp. 133–136; and Salem 1997.
[100] Neumann 2011.

Another important, oft neglected, negative consequence of interveners' reliance on universal models is that international peacebuilders regularly fail to address crucial issues and have little idea of how to act without these templates to rely upon. I have argued elsewhere that the absence of models and templates for local conflict resolution was one of the reasons for the paucity of international support to bottom-up peacebuilding in Congo in the 2000s, despite the critical need for such programs to promote sustainable peace.[101] Similarly, a UN official working in state reconstruction in Congo in 2011 noted that international efforts in this domain overlooked a number of essential problems, in large part because NGOs, UN officials, and donors lacked applicable templates. As other sources confirmed, the bulk of the efforts were devoted to basic economic recovery projects, return and resettlement of populations, and infrastructure-building – three areas in which interveners can draw upon an enormous stock of models and lessons learned. There was very little effort in areas such as training police and reconstructing the justice system, which were just as critical, but for which there were few preexisting formulas.[102]

Local populations, as well as scholarly and policy researchers, have criticized the use of universal models so frequently and for so long that interveners on the ground are perfectly aware of this problem.[103] The international peacebuilders I interviewed regularly brought up the need to adapt their templates to local contexts. However, they also said that they rarely had the opportunity to do so more than superficially, for several reasons. To begin with, they lacked time, as every moment spent adapting models is likely to mean lives lost. Additionally, they were afraid that, if they requested local input from the start, local stakeholders would manipulate the programs and bias them in favor of their political or ethnic groups. Finally, many interveners emphasized that, in spite of all the problems they encountered, they still firmly believed that their universal models provided the best answers to war and violence (a result of the politics of knowledge studied in this chapter). They therefore insisted on using these templates, genuinely believing it was in the best interests of the host populations.

Consequently, the processes used to implement templates minimizes local input.[104] As numerous interviewees in all my field sites deplored, meetings with populations and authorities aim at gathering the data necessary to tailor the models to local conditions and flesh out preestablished project proposals; they are not meant to question whether the programs themselves, and the

---

[101] Autesserre 2010, chapter 5.
[102] A public source on this unbalance is MONUSCO Stabilization Support Unit 2011.
[103] An early criticism was McDougal and Lasswell 1959 (cited in Miller and Rudnick 2010, p. 68). For subsequent criticisms, see, among many others, the sources cited in Note 97.
[104] For a similar claim, see Anderson, Brown, et al. 2012, pp. 70–78; Keystone Accountability 2011, pp. 5, 17–20, and 48; and Miller and Rudnick 2010, pp. 63 and 70.

templates on which they rely, are appropriate. More often than not, consultations instead take the form of "sensitization" (to convince authorities and populations that the program is good for them) or "mobilization" (to get the populations' support for the implementation of the initiative) rather than a genuine effort to collect the views of local people on whether a project is needed or how best to design and implement it. Thus, in most cases, local partners participate in the later stages of a program – during the validation of previously designed projects, the process of follow-up, and the evaluation of impact – but not in the early conception of the intervention.[105] There are only a few exceptions to this widespread practice: isolated efforts by select individuals, project staff (notably those working on community-driven reconstruction initiatives), and organizations (such as the Life and Peace Institute in Congo). Apart from these exceptions, the marginalization of local input is widespread. Tellingly, a number of interveners emphasized that "we cannot pacify Congo" (or Sudan, or Burundi) without the Congolese (or the Sudanese, or the Burundians), since "they are the ones who have the solution." To anyone outside of Peaceland, such a remark would have sounded like a truism. The interviewees, however, presented this argument as a profound conclusion born out of their long experience in conflict zones. To me, their statements merely highlighted just how much the standard practices of on-the-ground peacebuilding run counter to common sense.

Compartmentalization

The last key consequence of valuing technical knowledge over local expertise is the compartmentalization of the international system into several distinct components – such as development, humanitarian, and peace programs. Country specialists and local people often present all of the dimensions of a conflict as interlinked, emphasizing how economic, security, political, and social issues interact with one another in distinct ways in each specific area and advocating for holistic solutions in each particular locale.[106] In contrast, the thematic expertise that interveners acquire is usually compartmentalized: One can be an "expert" in economic development, or emergency humanitarian response, or political mediation, or human rights advocacy, but rarely, if ever, in all of these topics at once. This makes it difficult for international peacebuilders hired for their thematic expertise to consider all of the dimensions of a conflict together and to think that such an approach might be effective and legitimate.

The structure of the international aid system reflects this compartmentalization of knowledge. Each component has distinct actors, funding instruments, and meetings. Donor states, for instance, have separate budgets and structures for development, humanitarian, peacebuilding, and human rights initiatives.

---

[105] Also Anderson 2008, p. 102; and CDA Collaborative Learning Projects 2010a, pp. 6–8.
[106] For a public source, see among others: CDA Collaborative Learning Projects 2011b, p. 3.

Similarly, international agencies have specialized mandates, whether for development (such as the Coopération Technique Belge), humanitarian aid (like the United States Office for Disaster Assistance and Médecins Sans Frontières), peacebuilding (for instance, the UN Peacebuilding Commission and International Alert), human rights (such as Human Rights Watch), or political and military issues (like UN peace operations and the International Crisis Group). The UN cluster system clearly distinguishes between meetings appropriate for development organizations ("Early Recovery"), humanitarian ones ("Rapid Response to Movements of Population"), and peacebuilding ones ("Rule of Law").

In line with this structure, interveners regularly request that their local partners use a thematic approach rather than a geographic one. In Congo for instance, I witnessed on several occasions interveners pushing grassroots NGOs – whose original goals were to respond to the various needs of specific, geographically defined communities – to develop thematic rather than geographic expertise and thus focus on conflict resolution, human rights advocacy, or response to sexual violence over a broader geographic territory. The local organizations had to comply with this requirement in order to obtain funding. Grassroots actors were split on the merit of this practice: Some strongly opposed it, while others viewed it as valuable.

A few exceptional international actors have recently started to experiment with a different approach. NGOs like the International Rescue Committee and international organizations like the World Bank implement community-driven reconstruction programs, which focus on a geographic rather than a thematic specialization and respond to the needs of local communities as determined by those same communities.[107] Since 1999, the UN has also started to deploy integrated missions, which try to harness the power of all humanitarian, development, military, and political agencies for the greater goal of promoting stability in various countries around the world. However, these efforts to overcome the compartmentalization of intervention remain the exception rather than the norm – and, in the case of the UN tentative at integration, they face substantial difficulty.

Compartmentalization results in missed opportunities, so it tends to decrease the effectiveness of the peace initiatives. When interveners have both a political and development role, they can leverage both tools in peacebuilding negotiations: As a diplomat in the Palestinian Territories emphasized, it is more effective "to sit with a check on the table than with just words." This dual involvement enables interveners to be more critical of political and military issues without fear of losing partners, as development funds provide strong incentives for all local actors to remain involved in the discussions. Likewise, on the ground, by all accounts, conflict-resolution initiatives such as reconciliation workshops and peace education programs work best when combined with development or relief

---

[107] See King 2013 for an overview of such programs.

undertakings. Development projects such as building a market, a school, or a health center shared by two communities in conflict can help reestablish social and commercial links between them.[108] The new structure alleviates the tensions stemming from distrust and lack of communication, perpetuates the benefits of reconciliation workshops, and gives grassroots populations an added incentive to coexist peacefully with their enemies. A number of peacebuilders therefore deplored that the regulations on budgets they received for conflict-resolution projects prevented them from financing initiatives labeled as "development." In their views, these restrictions jeopardized the long-term sustainability of their projects.

Several Congolese grassroots actors also complained that the compartmentalization of aid efforts was downright dangerous. As they explained, it is much easier and safer for them to probe sensitive topics related to conflict or human rights violations when they concurrently implement development or aid activities. In these circumstances, their inquiries often seem benign, and they rarely raise suspicion among local authorities. In contrast, projects that require them to work only on peace or human rights issues significantly increase the risks they face.

Conclusion

In many respects, the professionalization of the peacebuilding field has increased the effectiveness of international efforts. It has also elevated thematic knowledge over local expertise for expatriate interveners. At the same time, it has generated a number of dominant practices – placing expatriates in management positions and local staff in subordinate ones, rotating interveners every couple of years, deploying interveners who are not familiar with local contexts and do not speak local languages, relying on universal templates and "lessons learned," overlooking local input for project design, and compartmentalizing the international system into distinct components – that are inefficient (except for the use of templates) and ineffective (except, to a certain extent, for the rotation of interveners).

Even more worryingly, some of these practices are counterproductive. The use of universal templates at times leads interveners to implement projects that actually fuel violence. Worse, the dynamics analyzed in this chapter – notably overlooking local input for project design and placing expatriates in management positions and local staff in subordinate ones – generate local resentment. Combined with the resource gap between local stakeholders and expatriates (see Chapter 6), these manifestations of the politics of knowledge entice the former to use "weapons of the weak": evasion, contestation, and resistance.[109] As the

[108] Public sources on this issue include Anderson 1999, pp. 34 and 48; and Prendergast 1996, pp. 115–116.
[109] On weapons of the weak, see Scott 1985.

next chapter demonstrates, local populations regularly perceive interveners as arrogant outsiders who are trying to impose their own ideas. Consequently, local people rarely feel ownership over international programs. In response, they ignore, distort, or oppose foreign peace efforts, thereby generating numerous obstacles to effective intervention.

The patterns documented in this chapter also result from and reinforce several elements that I analyze in the second half of this book. It is in part thanks to their financial, material, and symbolic resources that interveners have succeeded in constructing external expertise as more relevant and more useful than local knowledge. At the same time, valuing thematic knowledge over local expertise reinforces the socioeconomic and hierarchical differences between foreign interveners and local populations, and it perpetuates the view of intended beneficiaries as helpless people. This dominance also allows interveners to assume – and not doubt – that their narratives are fitting and their security and professional routines are appropriate and necessary.

3

Local Reactions

Time and again, across all of my field sites, I heard the same kind of criticisms levied against interveners, and so did researchers working in other conflict zones. Our local interviewees would complain that international peacebuilders were "arrogant," "condescending," and "paternalistic."[1] Certain phrases recurred constantly: Interveners were characterized as "bossy" and "preachy" ("*donneurs de leçons*") because "they arrive and immediately tell people what to do."[2]

My contacts then emphasized a point that is critical for the debates on international peacebuilding: They explained that the arrogance of foreign interveners resulted from their valuing thematic expertise over local knowledge. This attitude stems from the belief that outside approaches are better than local ones and from the attendant disregard of local ideas. For instance, a Congolese elite criticized the "pride" interveners take in seeing themselves as experts who employ a scientific approach to extricate people from crises and promote development. A Congolese grassroots peacebuilder concurred: For the international non-governmental organizations (NGOs) and the United Nations (UN) agencies, "there is conceit around this idea of assistance." To him, the "'I help you, I bring you aid' idea leads to arrogance" because the international expert "arrives with his methods and his knowledge, and tells you 'you should do this and not that'" and discounts local ideas and expertise. Recipients of intervention whom the Listening Project teams interviewed in Bosnia-Herzegovina, Ecuador, the Philippines, Sri Lanka, the Solomon Islands, and Thailand made a similar point.[3]

---

[1] For public sources, see Anderson 2008, p. 100; Anderson, Brown, et al. 2012, pp. 27–28; Anderson and Olson 2003, p. 39; CDA Collaborative Learning Projects 2010a, p. 8; McWha 2011, p. 33; and Sending 2009.

[2] Public sources include Anderson, Brown, et al. 2012, p. 28; and "South Sudan's reliance on NGOs," by Matthew Brunwasser, PRI's *The World*, April 15, 2011.

[3] CDA Collaborative Learning Projects 2008c, p. 6; and Anderson, Brown, et al. 2012, pp. 27–28 and 31.

They complained that "outsiders ignore their ideas and knowledge," a process that they found "fundamentally disrespectful."[4] A South African diplomat acknowledged that he and his colleagues were guilty of such prejudice, explaining: "We treat African counterparts with a lot of arrogance," based on the idea that "we know better, we know that this works so you should do this." He attributed this attitude to the politics of knowledge at work in Peaceland. In his words, "What people are doing is thinking that there is an international best practice. And when we do that, we trample on people's toes, so there is an accusation of arrogance."

I found another recurring pattern in my interviews, which was just as significant for the scholarly research on peace interventions, and which the rest of this chapter also elucidates. I heard the above criticisms in reference to all kinds of international programs, irrespective of their particular objectives. The reproaches were not limited to initiatives that were obviously shaped by liberal values, such as those dedicated to organizing elections or developing a market economy; they were also concerned with efforts like food distribution or latrine construction, which have no relationships with liberalism. This ubiquity of the censure challenges one of the core findings of the research on the liberal peace, which attributes the chronic problems of international interventions – including lack of local ownership, conflictual relationships between interveners and local stakeholders, and widespread phenomena of contestation and resistance – to the essential characteristics of liberalism as a political system (see Chapter 1). In this chapter, I identify these same problems and, while I agree that they strongly influence intervention effectiveness, I disagree as to their source. I contend that these problems are primarily due not to the imposition of Western or liberal templates and values, but to the imposition of foreign ways of thinking and working, whatever they might be. Through my own analysis, as well as that of other researchers whose studies I present in the following sections, I demonstrate that the persistent challenges that peacebuilders face in the field are rooted in the process, the "how," the everyday practice of peacebuilding, rather than in the intended outcome.

This chapter develops this argument by detailing the local reactions to international peace interventions on the ground. The first section emphasizes the resentment that the politics of knowledge at work in Peaceland engenders among local populations. I next show that the widespread tendency to promote and impose outside knowledge prevents local ownership and authorship, and I emphasize the negative consequences of this process for intervention effectiveness. The final section demonstrates that the prevailing practices generate local responses of evasion, contestation, and resistance, which pose significant obstacles to international efforts.

---

[4] Anderson, Brown, et al. 2012, p. 28.

Knowledge, Arrogance, and Resentment

As I did, the teams of the Listening Project (who interviewed more than 6,000 people in 21 countries to study perceptions of aid among intended beneficiaries) observed many crosscutting similarities in the way people in conflict zones perceive international interventions.[5] We heard a constant refrain, from Cyprus to Ecuador: Expatriates impose their ideas in a manner both disrespectful and humiliating.[6] The introduction to this chapter already provided a few illustrations of this perception. In this section, I present longer excerpts from my interviews to provide a fuller sense of how, from the point of view of local counterparts themselves, the politics of knowledge at work in Peaceland impacts their everyday interactions with foreign peacebuilders.

It is important to keep in mind two nuances when reading this section. First, it is certainly possible that the accusations that I report in this section may be exaggerated, or may result in part from preexisting biases against foreigners. However, the important point here is that my contacts' criticisms centered on the manner in which the interveners implemented their programs, rather than on the content of the initiatives. Second, although the intended beneficiaries can be very critical of international interventions, they rarely call for an end to all aid and peacebuilding efforts. Instead, they want to see initiatives that are more effective and have fewer counterproductive outcomes.[7]

Michel Losembe, a Congolese businessman, explained:

> Condescension does not express itself as a lack of politeness [...]. The social mannerisms are respected; when you arrive at a meeting, everything is "hello sir, hello madam." [...] Condescension is at the level of the message [...], and in not giving the opportunity to the Congolese to express their ideas.

He then gave a concrete example:

> The World Bank recently wrote a document called the Country Economic Report – it is the summary of all the action of the World Bank in Congo, and the last report was dated 1985, so it was about 25 or 26 years old. On this occasion, they organized a debate to which they invited different stakeholders. The idea was that the World Bank would do presentations on specific themes, such as infrastructure, financial inclusion, and then open up to Q&As after each presentation. But each presentation was about "Guys, what on earth have you done during all this time? Here is how it should go: step 1, step 2, step 3, step 4. . . ." It is a form of intellectual condescension that I find quite difficult to bear.[8]

[5] For concise statements on this topic, see Anderson 2008, p. 98, and Anderson, Brown, et al. 2012, p. 1; and for the details see the various issue papers from the project (available at www.cdacollaborative.org/publications/, last accessed in December 2013 – many are also listed in the bibliography of this book).

[6] Anderson, Brown, et al. 2012, pp. 27, 28, and 31.

[7] Also ibid., p. 3 and throughout the book.

[8] Author's on-record interview with Michel Losembe, vice president of the Fédération des Entreprises du Congo, June 2011, Kinshasa.

This attitude is not specific to Congo or to the World Bank. A Bosnian NGO representative interviewed by the Listening Project recalled having the same experience: She walked out of a presentation by an international organization because "she found it so arrogantly and condescendingly presented that she could not bear to stay."[9]

These anecdotes echo a discussion I had with a Timorese peacebuilder, who noted how the daily behaviors of his expatriate colleagues were often so humiliating and frustrating that they reminded him of the Portuguese and Indonesian colonizers who had only recently left his country. He felt that the international peacebuilders had "come in with an agenda": "They want to civilize the uncivilized." To him, this was a familiar attitude, which reminded him of the foreigners that had occupied his island in the past centuries – "the Portuguese, the Church, the Indonesians":

> They all come to Timor, picture us as uncivilized, indigenous, and they disrespect all the practices and concepts that we have. And it puts them in a superior position and us in a lower position. It also applies to the knowledge: Theirs is in a superior position; ours is in a lower position. [...] They think what they bring from the outside is better. [...] This idea that our knowledge is inferior; it is what colonialism does to the indigenous. [...] It creates a feeling of inferiority among the Timorese people. [...] Every time a Timorese person tries to come up with an idea, he is always wrong... In every Timorese, you have that, the feeling of inferiority. So sometimes, when you [expatriates] do not realize it, in your actions you reinforce the action of colonialism and imperialism, in your daily life.[10]

In his view, all kinds of international efforts warranted this reproach, whether they aimed at promoting democracy, defending human rights, or strengthening grassroots conflict-resolution efforts.

Other researchers documented similar complaints in Ecuador, Haiti, Kenya, the Philippines, and Thailand, regarding all kinds of international initiatives.[11] My contacts provided multiple additional illustrations of how good intentions, when they rely on the firm belief that internationals know best and are here to help, can lead to behavior that local counterparts perceive as arrogant. A Congolese employee of a humanitarian aid organization explained in a matter-of-fact voice that his international colleagues arrive as "conquerors," full of preconceived and flawed notions about Congo. When, during initial briefings, he asks new hires what they know about his country, many of the same phrases recur: "a very vulnerable country"; "high levels of corruption"; "People are unreliable"; "I am coming to teach you everything"; "Every second a Congolese steals or embezzles money. We have to keep an eye on that." This interviewee once worked with an expatriate originally from Sri Lanka who told him after a few minutes that he had come to fill people's heads with knowledge,

---

[9] Anderson, Brown, et al. 2012, p. 27.
[10] Author's on-record interview with Josh Trindade, consultant, Dili, Timor-Leste, February 2012.
[11] Anderson, Brown, et al. 2012, p. 31; and CDA Collaborative Learning Projects 2011b, p. 1.

and he was surprised that this local employee knew so much. Along the same lines, a diplomat recalled that she felt sorry for the head of the commission tasked with organizing the referendum on South Sudan's independence, because a lot of aid workers who were "a third of his age were coming to tell him how to do his work better." The expatriates thought that they were "trying to help the person," but they did not realize the impressions that this image left on their local counterpart.

My interviews also emphasized that the behavior of the host authorities can reinforce and legitimize the interveners' condescending behavior. Continuing the story of the World Bank conference that he found so shocking, Losembe recalled:

> I was very surprised to see that the [Congolese] ministers who were in the room agreed with the comments and with the manner in which they were given. And they all started their answers with 1- "Thank you to the World Bank," 2- "It is true that we have done poorly in the past," 3- "We will try to do what you say." I found it quite pitiful.[12]

This "beggars can't be choosers" problem is something I encountered often in my interviews (see Chapter 6 for further analysis). A number of contacts noted that, whether due to poverty or low state capacity, local stakeholders have so few resources – financial, logistic, or otherwise – to accomplish their goals that they have no choice but to request outside help. These appeals weaken their own position and strengthen that of the intervening organizations, which then perceive themselves to be taking on the core responsibilities of the state and, as a result, operate with increasing arrogance. Local NGOs and authorities often respond by behaving deferentially toward representatives of these organizations in an attempt to secure their aid. However, that conduct further undermines the authority of local stakeholders and fuels the interveners' beliefs that they know more than their local counterparts, which in turn reinforces the international tendency to value external knowledge over local input.

Even if the dynamics analyzed in this section are therefore most prevalent in poor and weak states, the case of Cyprus demonstrates that the interveners' attitude is an ingrained practice rather than a response to poverty and lack of local capacity. Although Cypriots were mostly indifferent toward international interveners and although the resource and education gaps between foreign and local actors were much smaller than in the other theaters of intervention I studied, these accusations of arrogance and bossiness were the main criticisms that Cypriots directed against international peacebuilders. As one of them explained:

> The foreigners, especially the UN, come with their ways of doing things. For example, they tell the Cypriot: You have to finish the negotiations by a certain date. The Cypriots resent that. In the middle class, on the street, you often hear "Oh, here come the foreigners who have come to solve us."

[12] Author's interview with Losembe.

Another Cypriot concurred, using virtually the same words as a Palestinian lawyer to express his opinion. In their views, one of the downsides to the international interventions in their countries was that there was "a perception of 'Who are you to tell me what to do?!'"

Virtually every single interviewee that I cite in this section identified exceptions to the dominant modes of operations that he or she criticized. The reports from the Listening Project similarly highlight exceptions to all of the broad patterns that they document. In all theaters of intervention, certain individuals or organizations try hard to engage with local ideas and to be respectful of their local counterparts. Their experiences are crucial to recognizing the impact negative perceptions of international interveners can have. Just like Anne Holohan established in her study of the international intervention in Kosovo, I demonstrate in the next section that the same policy or strategy leads to different outcomes when it is carried out under different kinds of everyday relationships – whether this policy and strategy is liberal or not.[13]

Lack of Local Ownership and Authorship

A large body of research has established the importance of involving local stakeholders in the design and implementation of international programs.[14] Building on this scholarship, this section explains that peacebuilding is more effective when it promotes both local authorship, meaning the constant solicitation of "local input on how to best proceed with a given set of goals," and local ownership, which entails "control over policy creation" and implementation.[15] Unsurprisingly, however, the widespread tendency to promote and impose outside knowledge regularly undermines both local authorship and local ownership, with serious consequences on peacebuilding outcomes.

Local Ownership, Local Authorship, and International Effectiveness

As I have documented, expatriates regularly discount local input (see Chapter 2). Worse, Mary Anderson and her colleagues at the Listening Project found that expatriates at times do not even solicit such input.[16] This practice significantly

---

[13] Holohan 2005, notably chapters 3 and 4.
[14] Anderson and Olson 2003, pp. 32–33; Anderson, Brown, et al. 2012, pp. 21–23 and 67–69; Campbell 2010, notably pp. 9, 10, and 52–59; CDA Collaborative Learning Projects 2008b and 2012 (pp. 8–9); Martin and Moser 2012; Richmond 2012; Sending 2009 and 2010b; and Wilén 2009. See also the Organisation for Economic Co-operation and Development's *Paris Declaration* (2005) and the *Accra Agenda for Action* (2008) for the policy perspective (www.oecd.org/dac/effectiveness/parisdeclarationandaccraagendaforaction.htm).
[15] The definitions come from Moore 2013, p. 121.
[16] Anderson, Brown, et al. 2012, pp. 14–15 and 26–31. Also Anderson 1999, p. 14.

impact of scale of organization

decreases the effectiveness of international efforts, given how important local authorship is in promoting successful peacebuilding.

A quantitative analysis of local involvement and international reconstruction efforts in Bosnia-Herzegovina (from 1991 to 1995) and Somalia (from 1987 to 1997) found that "phases in the peacebuilding process with high local participation are associated with lower levels of hostility, while phases with little local involvement tend to be associated with escalating violence."[17] The differing success of two consecutive international attempts at integrating schools in Brčko (Bosnia-Herzegovina) similarly demonstrates the importance of soliciting and integrating local input as well as the problems that occur when interveners fail to do so.[18] The first initiative occurred in 2000 "with little input from district officials or public discussion with concerned parents." It generated "massive protests" that "resulted in the temporary closure of the schools until changes were reversed." The second attempt took place a year later. It started with extensive consultations of district citizens, teachers, and officials, to discuss their concerns and gain their support for the proposed change. The subsequent implementation of the reform proceeded smoothly with minimal incidents or public protest. Beyond school integration, international staff based in Brčko worked on a daily basis with their local counterparts and took their suggestions into account. In Moore's analysis, the cultivation of local officials as partners in the peacebuilding process was one of the reasons for the success of reforms in this district, whereas efforts in the rest of the country widely failed.[19]

Chip Gagnon's study of reconstruction and democratization programs in the former Yugoslavia provides another clear demonstration of the importance of local authorship for intervention effectiveness.[20] When expatriates use their standard modes of operation and set up projects that they have designed without local input, those projects "often disappear" after the expatriates have left.[21] In contrast, the initiatives of a few organizations (like Catholic Relief Services) that "integrate the community and its own knowledge into the process" and keep them informed and involved at each step are "much more effective" and sustainable.[22]

It is not only local authorship that matters for peacebuilding. Other scholars, studying all kinds of international efforts around the world, have widely demonstrated that local ownership similarly increases the effectiveness of international initiatives, while its absence has the opposite effect.[23] Unfortunately, the

[17] Gizelis and Kosek 2005, citation from p. 364, demonstration throughout the article.
[18] The example of Bosnia-Herzegovina is based on Moore 2013, pp. 122–124.
[19] Ibid., p. 122.
[20] Gagnon 2006.
[21] Ibid., p. 175.
[22] Ibid., citations from pp. 174–175.
[23] Anderson and Olson 2003, pp. 32–33 and 43; Anderson, Brown, et al. 2012, pp. 21–23 and 67–69; Campbell 2010, notably pp. 9, 10, and 52–59; CDA Collaborative Learning Projects 2008b and 2012, pp. 8–9; Donais 2009; Martin and Moser 2012; Richmond 2012; Sending 2009 and 2010b; Wilén 2009.

same scholars have also documented that local stakeholders rarely feel in control of international programs. A few vignettes from my fieldwork will suffice to give a sense of how this issue plays out on the ground.

Local authorities and populations regularly view international peace initiatives as having been dictated by their foreign partners. Numerous Cypriots complained about how the whole idea of reconciliation and equality between Greek and Turkish Cypriots was "imposed" on them. Certain Congolese contacts used language that revealed a similar perception that the programs that they supposedly owned were in fact forced on them by internationals: They referred to aid projects as "the *muzungu*'s [foreigners'] projects." The lack of ownership reaches such a point that university students in Goma reportedly differentiate between human rights, which are "something linked to international NGOs" – something that interveners somehow work on – and the actual rights of the Congolese people, which local human rights activists promote.

A noteworthy theme constantly recurred throughout my fieldwork. In the interveners' discourse, "local ownership" could describe ownership by any actor, whether from the central government or a grassroots organization. While foreign interveners view ownership by the central government as key to respecting the sovereignty of the host states, their counterparts in the field regularly emphasize that achieving national ownership does not necessarily ensure local ownership.[24] For example, certain local authorities in Congo told me that they viewed the very presence of international actors as an imposition because only the central government had any say in whether interveners could come to their countries; they themselves were never consulted. The experience of the Joint Donor Team based in Juba (South Sudan) highlights the consequences of this practice. With the help of the central authorities, these international donors designed a large project to build primary schools throughout the country. Once they had completed the project, the donors noticed that, while some schools were functioning, others remained empty. Upon inquiry, they realized that the local governments objected to the locations of some of the schools and had thus decided not to use them.

The differing attitudes of Congolese communities toward the water sources that NGOs build for them illustrate how resentment that local stakeholders feel toward the imposition of foreign ideas leads to failure, whereas ownership promotes success. Several contacts explained that grassroots populations view water supply points built by most international NGOs, such as Oxfam, as the property of these NGOs instead of as new assets for their communities. Their reasoning is simple: Because the NGO never consulted intended beneficiaries on important issues such as where the supply point should be located, the project is not theirs; they have no stake in it. As a result, the stations fall apart quickly after international interveners leave. When the sources malfunction, nobody maintains or repairs them – local communities view this as the NGO's responsibility.

[24] On this topic, see also Richmond 2012.

However, certain organizations have a different approach – such as Caritas. This network of international and local church structures involves grassroots communities throughout the entire process. As a result, according to my interviewees, communities see themselves as the owners of the stations; they therefore maintain and repair them regularly, and Caritas's initial investment benefits these individuals for a long time.

Local communities in Cambodia, Ethiopia, Kenya, Thailand, and Zimbabwe told similar stories: They worked harder to ensure that a project succeeded and persisted when they viewed it as "theirs," while they did not "put [in] as much effort" when they perceived it as a donor's or NGO's initiative.[25] Extensive research by Mary Anderson and her coauthors around the world substantiated this evidence: They found that "when people participate in all phases of an aid effort, from conception of the idea, to the design and planning, to implementation, and through final evaluation, they will 'own' the process and therefore be more likely to maintain the results," and the reverse is also true.[26]

Dilemmas and Obstacles to Change

Expatriates are well aware of the obstacles that lack of local ownership and authorship pose to their efforts. Many of them have therefore tried to take steps to mitigate this issue. "Local ownership" is now a buzzword in development and peacebuilding circles, and interveners regularly consult with area authorities. Sometimes, they even organize local focus groups when developing a new program. However, these measures have only altered international efforts on the surface for three reasons.

First, the politics of knowledge in Peaceland, added to the foreign peacebuilders' negative perceptions of local populations and authorities (see Chapter 6), regularly counteracts the efforts to change. Two conversations with donors, one based in South Sudan and the other in Congo, encapsulated the dynamics at work. During our interview, the first noted the problems inherent to imposing foreign templates and ideas and mentioned how he and other interveners tried to promote ownership by their local counterparts. He then explained why they regularly abandoned these efforts: Expatriates get so frustrated at the behavior of their counterparts (their abuse of power, resource embezzlement, and disregard for the plights of their fellow citizens) that they eventually stop trying to involve them. The second interviewee described the same dynamics in much harsher terms. In her words, the "contempt for local actors" that most of her expatriate colleagues shared made it seem appropriate for interveners to "manipulate" local counterparts and try to impose programs and ideas on them.

---

[25] CDA Collaborative Learning Projects 2008b, pp. 4–5; also Anderson, Brown, et al. 2012, pp. 68–69 and 74.
[26] Anderson, Brown, et al. 2012, pp. 67–68.

Another main reason for the lack of reform is a dilemma that international peacebuilders face. On the one hand, there are normative and practical reasons to encourage local participation. The idea of integrating local people fits well with the liberal norms dominant on the international stage: The core idea of democracy (which the leading intervening organizations claim that they want to spread) means participation of local stakeholders.[27] The practical dimension is just as clear: As explained above, and as Anderson and her coauthors summarize, most interveners and local people know that "participation leads to ownership leads to sustainability."[28]

On the other hand, integrating local stakeholders may worsen the situation. To start, participation can slow things to a standstill. The more numerous the parties to a negotiation, the more difficult it becomes to reach an agreement, and the higher the likelihood that local spoilers will find an opportunity to hinder or even stall the peace process.[29] Furthermore, privileging local demands can lead to policy capture.[30] That is, local stakeholders regularly "game" the international system, interacting with interveners strategically in order to extract as many resources from outsiders as possible and to maintain or increase their existing power.[31] Since governments and civil society groups do not necessarily try to advance the welfare of the population, partnering with national and local elites may actually reinforce existing problematic structures rather than promote peace.[32] Besides, it is not often clear to interveners which local actors they should integrate. As I mentioned previously, there is rarely, if ever, one local perspective, or one actor that can represent the values and interests of all local stakeholders, but instead diverse and often conflicting local perspectives. In the highly divided and contentious environment of a conflict zone, integrating one set of actors may lead to favoring one side over another and thus reinforce tensions. Likewise, siding with local partners might mean ignoring the demands of the central government, or vice versa. Finally, in a number of situations, interveners face irreconcilable differences with local or national elite, whose perspectives on contentious issues (like democracy and women's rights) may elicit demands that are unacceptable for certain donors – as well as for certain foreign and local peacebuilders.

The last obstacle to change arises from the detrimental by-products of the politics of knowledge at work in Peaceland, which make it exceptionally difficult to move away from standard intervention practices. The experiences of NGOs (such as International Alert and the International Rescue Committee)

---

[27] On the dominance of liberal norms and the attempts to spread democracy, see Paris 2004, as well as all the authors who work on the "liberal peace" (presented in Chapter 1, section on "constraints, interests, and liberal values").

[28] Anderson, Brown, et al. 2012, p. 68.

[29] For instance, Belloni 2008, pp. 182–183 and 192–193; and Narten 2009, pp. 261 and 276.

[30] Barnett and Zürcher 2009.

[31] Ibid. For an alternative approach, see Peterson 2011.

[32] Anderson, Brown, et al. 2012, p. 84.

that have tried to promote local authorship and ownership by implementing community-driven reconstruction programs are telling.[33] According to staff working on such initiatives, local communities are so used to seeing foreigners arrive with a bossy attitude and set ideas that it becomes challenging to implement the new approach. Instead of giving their opinions and requesting what they actually need, a number of grassroots communities construct their appeals to reflect what they think the expatriates want to hear, as a way to ensure access to funding and help. In other words, despite considerable efforts, these interveners still often end up facing similar problems to those of their colleagues who use less progressive methodologies.

The various obstacles to actual implementation of the local ownership principle perpetuate reliance on external knowledge and ways of working. In turn, the reliance on outside input prevents the promotion of local expertise and local solutions, which would open up a valuable source of alternative ideas and options for resolving conflict. At the same time, the placement of expatriates in decision-making and leadership positions, as well as the interveners' tendency to substitute themselves for local implementers, impairs the development of local capacities. The resulting lack of local authorship and ownership decreases the incentives for the population and the authorities to learn how to perpetuate the international programs. Worse, in situations of protracted crises, when the message being communicated every day to local stakeholders is that only external models work and only external knowledge matters, local expertise and solutions become discredited. This undermines the authority of local people to frame and solve their own problems and decreases their confidence to command their destiny, further hindering local participation in international initiatives. To top it all off, throughout the theaters of intervention in which I worked, these practices regularly encouraged local stakeholders to adapt, contest, or resist international programs, even those that could potentially benefit them.[34]

Adaptation, Contestation, and Resistance

Existing research has shown that, in every country, elite and ordinary citizens interact with interveners through a wide variety of strategies, which reflect the local populations' infinitude of goals, beliefs, customs, and attitudes.[35] For this reason, local reactions to international initiatives depend on the given project and the country, province, or village in which it takes place. Countless other factors (including local cultures, governance structures, levels of poverty and

---

[33] See King 2013 for an analysis of these initiatives across various countries and organizations.

[34] Nathan 2007 develops an excellent case study of this process in Congo, with a focus on security sector reform.

[35] This paragraph draws on Acharya 2009; Barnett and Zürcher 2009; Mac Ginty 2010 and 2011; Pouligny 2004; Richmond and Mitchell 2011; and Trefon 2011, p. 11 and throughout the book. See also the special issue of the journal *Global Governance*: Hybrid Peace Governance (Belloni and Jarstad 2012).

education, and preexisting experience with international programs) also play a role. Nevertheless, as numerous scholars have documented, common patterns recur throughout areas of intervention.[36] Some actors, varying in number depending on the context, cooperate with certain aspects of the intervention, either because they believe in the programs or because they use them to reach their own goals. In many cases, local reactions to international peace interventions also include much less supportive responses, such as nonengagement, negotiation, renegotiation, adaptation, subversion, contestation, cherry-picking, outright resistance, and rejection.[37]

The way that local stakeholders react to international efforts reflects more than just the particular on-the-ground merits and shortcomings of an intervention. A number of authorities in post-war environments come from former armed groups, and many of them have a vested interest in prolonging the violence that enabled them to attain their positions of authority. They may decide to resist or reject international programs that run counter to their own goals, regardless of the value of these programs or the manner in which they are implemented. They may also engage in – or solicit foreign support for – initiatives that advance their own interests, but which fail to promote a sustainable solution to the conflict, and which may even fuel violence. Likewise, local partners may adapt, distort, or otherwise change international programs on account of their own personal agendas (whether political, economic, or social), or just because they lack the motivation to invest enough time, energy, and resources in the projects. In sum, existing local dynamics contribute to the opposition to and distortion of foreign initiatives as well as to the misappropriation of their accompanying resources. It was clear in all of the countries in which I researched that these behaviors regularly impeded the success of international efforts.

However, not all local authorities are interested in prolonging war. Likewise, not all local counterparts immediately prioritize their own interests over those of their broader communities. On the contrary, most local staff, civil society activists, and target communities would benefit from more stable conditions, and a number of local authorities and peacebuilders truly care about the well-being of their fellow citizens. It is therefore essential to understand why many of these people, who would in fact benefit from effective international efforts, reject or distort them.

As this section shows, although my fieldwork confirmed the findings from existing research that contestation, resistance, and adaptation strongly influence the effectiveness of international efforts, it also suggested an important nuance to these claims. In my analysis, the varying degrees of nonacceptance are not necessarily linked to the factors that extant research usually cites, such as the

---

[36] See the sources listed in the previous footnote, as well as Anderson, Brown, et al. 2012, pp. i, 1, 6, 21, and throughout the report.

[37] This sentence paraphrases Mac Ginty 2011, p. 17

local partners' lack of understanding of international strategies, the presence of vested interests, the financial and logistical constraints of the projects, or the Western and liberal characters of the programs. Instead, they are due to the very act of imposition and fueled by the power differential inherent to the daily practice of intervention on the ground.

Andrea Talentino reports a similar finding.[38] Through an in-depth study of local perceptions of eleven ongoing peace operations, she demonstrates that "actors resist change, even when they might objectively agree that it is positive, if it seems forced upon them."[39] In all her cases, even those where interveners were initially welcome (like in Kosovo and Liberia), she documents resentment at the imposition from at least some local groups – whether they were spoilers, elites, citizens, social groups, or, usually, a combination thereof.[40] In line with existing research, she also shows that this resentment results in obstructionism and thus poses significant obstacles to international peace efforts.

Talentino's work on the causes of resentment focuses on macro-level factors, such as the extent to which local groups agree with the overall values or wide-ranging reforms that interveners promote. I argue that we should consider an additional explanation: the pervasive international disregard of local knowledge and input, and the resulting perceptions of arrogance and lack of ownership. As one Congolese intellectual described:

> The programs are often good, if you read the documents from the UN and all the others – at the core they have good intentions. That is not the problem, really. The problem is the bad set-up; things are badly set up from the start, so they cannot work. People here, the supposed beneficiaries, are not consulted; they do not participate in anything. When [interveners design] a project, it is as if it fell on the heads of people here.[41]

This quote reflects what I heard throughout my interviews with all kinds of Congolese people. Employees of international agencies explained that they felt excluded from the decision-making process within their organizations and that this perception decreased their motivation to perform well in their jobs. Intellectuals and authorities regularly complained that interveners tried to impose their ideas, values, and standard operating procedures with no respect for local knowledge and customs. These local actors deplored their lack of influence over international strategies. Some of them overlooked these problems in order to benefit from the resources that interveners might provide, but others refused to participate in the international programs. The majority dragged their feet – by canceling meetings, forgetting to attend them, or creating state

---

[38] Talentino 2007.
[39] Ibid., p. 153. Also Nathan 2007.
[40] Talentino 2007, p. 161, especially table 2.
[41] Author's on-record interview with Lindiro Kabirigi.

structures for the sole purpose of pleasing international donors but then never using them.

Interviewees recalled witnessing similar dynamics in Burundi, the Palestinian Territories, and South Sudan. A former government official complained about interveners arriving with external systems and ideas that disregarded existing Burundian ones; he explained that this practice led to "revolt" by local people, either through violence or through "a certain lack of discipline." An American attorney working in the Palestinian Territories explained how her counterparts would listen to what she said, and then "do things their own way, ignoring the instructions or advice with which they disagreed." As her Palestinian colleagues themselves confirmed, they thought, "How dare she tell [them] what to do" in their own country, of which she knew nothing. A Sudanese civil society activist reported that "friction between the donor's perception of how things should look and the communities' perceptions" resulted in a number of local communities "reject[ing] the intervention," saying "to hell with their money." Alternatively, communities "abandoned the project, worked against [it] by creating lots of obstacles," or simply let it collapse when the donor left. He concluded that "this is why some projects fail – because communities have never owned them, they were always owned by donors. [...] It is very common."[42] Reyko Huang and Joseph Harris' analysis of capacity building by UN officials in Timor-Leste emphasizes a similar point. Expatriates making "direct or indirect attempts to impose" their ideas on national staff met with "frowning and resistance," which compromised peacebuilding efforts.[43]

Certain local staff and implementers also reacted to the perceived imposition of international programs by embezzling resources.[44] I heard countless stories about such problems during my fieldwork, across all types of organizations, engaged in all kinds of projects, in many different places. Admittedly, corruption is rife in a number of countries hosting international peacebuilders, so the diversion of resources cannot be attributed solely to the interveners' everyday modes of operation.[45] However, the way international interventions operate on the ground only compounds the problem of misappropriation, and this influence follows a recurring pattern. One expatriate who had managed to develop in-depth relationships with local populations in Congo, where embezzlement is pervasive, summarized arguments that I had heard from many other interviewees:

---

[42] Author's on-record interview with Edmund Yakani, Community Empowerment for Progress Organization, Juba, April 2011.

[43] Huang and Harris 2006, p. 83.

[44] Anderson, Brown, et al. 2012, pp. 99–102 makes a similar claim.

[45] On corruption in areas of intervention, see among many other sources ibid., chapter 8, as well as the yearly reports produced by Transparency International (available at www.transparency-usa.org).

> In general, the perception is that NGOs are here for a certain amount of time and with a certain amount of money, so what you do is get the money out. The programs are short term, not really relevant. [...] The perception is even worse in rural areas, because of the difficulty to understand the NGO strategies, unless you work with NGOs. So [local people] think "they are here, let's get whatever we can from them." [And with relief programs], a lot of it is, "take what you can get when they are here." Because NGOs rotate so much in different towns, it is not seen as something that communities have a stake in.

In other words, the buy-in for the international programs can be so low that local stakeholders will care mostly about the material benefits that they can get for themselves – the funds they can gain or steal, the bribes they can exact, the jobs they can provide to friends and relatives – and little about the actual impact of the program for the broader populations. This trend also reflects the feeling among host populations that "the NGOs have already decided what they want to do. They have money now, and we (local people) will take it when we can." As my contact explained, "It is a survival issue."

This logic is sometimes taken to its extreme. In Congo, for instance, certain local circles view embezzlement of resources from interveners as so "normal" that several contacts explained to me that stealing from an intervener or his organization "is not stealing" – a particularly striking statement when compared to the generally strong condemnation toward ordinary thieves (which occasionally results in lynching). This perception applies only to international aid agencies, and not to businesses, the logic being that aid funding is meant to help the Congolese, so those who help themselves to the money or material resources are just taking what is already legitimately theirs. In the eastern part of the country, local communities actually have a special label for the kind of cement used by international interveners to construct buildings and infrastructure. It is called "NGO cement" – cement that cracks after a few months because the builder has put in only part of the concrete that was necessary and that was paid for and has kept the rest for himself. A colleague reported hearing of similarly unapologetic behavior in Kosovo. Some of her respondents maintained that they had a right to "redistribute" the funds that, from their point of view, international organizations had allocated with too much bias.[46]

Although these various patterns clearly decrease peacebuilding efficiency and effectiveness, adaptation and subversion do not always lead to poor outcomes. In fact, local adaptation sometimes helps ensure that the projects will improve conditions on the ground, even if the eventual results deviate significantly from the interveners' original intentions. Oliver Richmond, Audra Mitchell, and their coauthors provide several examples of these positive dynamics in peacebuilding programs around the world, from Congolese nationals organizing street parliaments as a way to reclaim democracy in their everyday lives to

---

[46] Personal communication from Dr. Audra Mitchell, lecturer in international relations, University of York, May 2012.

Bougainvilleans spending large parts of their peace negotiations singing (thus making the outcomes of the negotiations more acceptable and legitimate).[47] The teams of the Listening Project found similar patterns at work in aid efforts. For instance, a donor agency program once brought cheese to the Samburu (a Kenyan nomadic tribe) "to increase the protein in [their] diet" as a way to promote the tribe's economic and human development. People melted the cheese "and put it on their skin to protect [themselves] from the sun instead."[48] A South Sudanese journalist I interviewed recounted another enlightening story about condoms that a humanitarian organization distributed in the late 2000s as part of an HIV prevention initiative in his country. People regularly lined up in large numbers to get the prophylactics. Naturally, the organization and its donor were thrilled – the program was working well, and the rural population was recognizing the importance of using condoms. The population was very happy too: Finally an organization understood their needs and provided them with durable plastic pouches in which to transport their tobacco crops. It took years for the organization to realize the misunderstanding. I heard similar stories in other countries involving different agencies and different uses for the condoms, such as to store water or transport homemade alcohol. Whatever the particular confusion was, the point is clear: Adaptation of international programs can be widespread, and the perspective from which a program is judged influences how "effective" it appears. What seems like a terrible result in the eyes of the implementing organizations may be quite a positive one in the opinion of the intended beneficiaries – and of course, vice versa.

Conclusion

The widespread complaints of local populations that external models are ill-adapted to local circumstances represent attempts to change the criteria that establish which knowledge is valuable and legitimate in Peaceland. It is part of a struggle to raise the status of local expertise and those who hold it. When these attempts fail, local actors feel humiliated at their presumed inferiority and resentful of the expatriates' oversight of their competencies. They perceive interveners as arrogant, resent the imposition of foreign initiatives – whether or not those promote liberal values and models – and feel no ownership over the international programs. These grievances regularly lead local stakeholders to evade, adapt, or resist international efforts. Although these reactions may at times help improve local conditions, overall they generate multiple obstacles to the implementation of international programs, thus decreasing their eventual efficiency and effectiveness.

---

[47] Richmond and Mitchell 2011. The Bougainvillean example comes from p. 97 (chapter by Volker Boege) and the Congolese example from pp. 146–161 (chapter by Meike de Goede).
[48] CDA Collaborative Learning Projects 2008c, p. 4.

These various dynamics can create a vicious cycle, as happened in Aceh (Indonesia) after the 2008 Tsunami and in Congo during the wars of the 2000s and early 2010s.[49] The lack of Congolese and Acehnese involvement in the design of the international programs led to local resistance and adaptation. The misappropriation of funds and the local reluctance to contribute to international efforts fueled the interveners' views of local populations and authorities as corrupt, lazy, untrustworthy, and incapable of sacrificing themselves for the public good. This negative perception – in addition to the delays, the resistance, and the fact that programs were not implemented as intended and did not achieve the desired results – reinforced the tendency of internationals to substitute themselves for their Acehnese and Congolese partners instead of engaging in capacity building, ensuring local authorship, and promoting local ownership. This reaction crowded out local initiatives, further decreased Acehnese and Congolese involvement, and thus led to additional local resistance and adaptation. Altogether, this entire process reinforced the negative perceptions that expatriates and local stakeholders had of each other, which further impaired collaboration.

Local partners' resistance and interveners' negative perceptions of their counterparts also reinforce the foreign peacebuilders' tendency to work in a bubble (see Chapter 5). A number of interveners explained that operating in a parallel structure enables them to cope with the challenges of working with unreliable and uncooperative partners. There is no need to wait months for local elites to approve or start programs; to convince anyone but other interveners that a specific strategy is the right way to proceed; to interact with leaders who might still be involved in violence; or to be accountable to anyone but donors. The interveners' propensity to work among themselves is all the more pronounced in weak or failed states – such as Afghanistan, Congo, or Sudan – where peacebuilders believe they lack counterparts with actual and legitimate authority. In turn, this practice reinforces the sense of alienation on the part of host governments and populations and thus their tendency to resist international efforts. A British intervener who had spent more than ten years in Timor-Leste and had become embedded in the local communities explained this process:[50] After the 2006 riots, a "parallel thinking" was taking place in international forums. Once every intervener had provided input on an initiative, UN officials would bring the resulting document to the relevant Timorese ministry. This practice puzzled and annoyed the staff at the ministry. They wondered what the initiative was about, and they resented having "pieces of policy fired at" them by foreigners. My interviewee emphasized that, from the Timorese point of view, the problem was not that the suggested policies "were bad or anything, but just that [the interveners] were working in isolation." Annoyed at this behavior, the ministry staff regularly ignored the international requests.

[49] On Aceh: Smirl 2008, p. 246.
[50] Author's on-record interview with Ben Larke, Dili, Timor-Leste, February 2012.

To top it all off, the unproductive relationships between interveners and local stakeholders, added to the undervaluing of local knowledge, have another pernicious consequence. As the next chapter demonstrates, they make it extremely difficult for external peacebuilders to make sense of the contexts in which they work, creating further impediments to effective intervention.

4

Fumbling in the Dark

Interveners used several analogies when they reflected on the process of trying to understand what was going on in their areas of deployment. To one diplomat, it was "like a puzzle." A United Nations (UN) official likened the process to that of "four blind men feeling an elephant." While the man touching the elephant's leg claims that they have arrived at a tree, the man touching the trunk retorts instead that it is a snake. Meanwhile, the man touching the belly argues that they have found a big balloon, and the one touching the ear maintains that it is in fact a giant palm leaf.[1] To that official, this was exactly the problem that plagued interveners deployed in Congo: "There are lots of perspectives that we can take on what Congo is and what its problems are." But, as he crucially added, foreign peacebuilders rarely considered the perspectives of the Congolese – for reasons analyzed in the previous chapters.

After working for many years in Peaceland, the analogy that came to my mind was the experience of standing in the dark with only a blinking flashlight. The fleeting illumination reveals one fragmentary image after another. The pictures are limited to the immediate surroundings, so the observer can make little sense of what lies beyond the circle of light. The scene as a whole is disjointed. At any moment, a change in one shadow can occur undetected while the flashlight is pointed somewhere else. Ultimately, this experience provides sparse and fragmented information, which cannot help one develop a clear image of the overall conditions.

Compounding this problem, foreign interveners and local populations often have different frameworks for interpreting this information. People with different cultures, political views, and ideologies apply distinct inferential patterns to the same evidence, producing contradictory accounts of a single circumstance. An Irish interviewee recalled that, once, in Iraq, while passing a series of soldiers, tanks, and buildings that bore the U.S. flag, his Iraqi driver pointed at them and bitterly spat: "Jews." The interviewee was baffled. For him, a U.S. flag obviously

---

[1] Eltringham 2003 develops a similar comparison to describe analyses of the Rwandan genocide.

indicated that the soldiers were Americans, but there was no suggestion that they might also be Jewish. He and his driver were living in distinct worlds, where meaning was constructed discordantly, and thus the same evidence signified something different to each of them.

In this chapter, I examine how interveners go about making sense of the situations in which they work, paying particular attention to the unintended consequences of the politics of knowledge and the local resentment analyzed in the previous chapters. In the first section, I analyze the data collection and analysis processes that interveners employ on the ground. I identify the main obstacles facing foreign peacebuilders and trace how expatriates try to overcome them, highlighting the ways in which these dynamics impede the interveners' understandings of their environments. In the second section, I show that these challenges encourage interveners to develop and rely on dominant, simple narratives concerning the causes of war and peace in their areas of deployment. Through a case study of the narratives that shaped the international intervention in Congo in 2010 and 2011, I identify the positive and negative effects of this practice: Using dominant narratives enables interveners to act, but at the same time, it can orient interventions toward strategies that are ineffective or even fuel violence. Finally, in the last sections, I demonstrate that the interveners' lack of knowledge and inefficient data collection techniques decrease the potential effectiveness of international efforts in two additional ways. First, they generate a number of misunderstandings. Second, they reinforce the interveners' tendency to approach their work in a top-down manner, thus failing to address critical bottom-up sources of violence.

Data Collection and Analysis

Given that they are recruited on the basis of their technical expertise rather than their country knowledge, interveners know very little about their area of deployment when they arrive in the field. There are a few exceptions: country experts who manage to get hired by an intervening organization and expatriates who stay in the same location for years, acquiring in-depth local knowledge over time. (Those interveners, when I interviewed them, developed highly insightful and original analyses.[2]) The vast majority, however, are in a different situation.

Newcomers receive a briefing before or upon their arrival, but these information sessions focus primarily on logistical, administrative, and security procedures. They also include contextual material on their area of deployment, but the scope is thematically specialized. Military peacekeepers, for example, learn only about military issues while their colleagues in relief work learn only about humanitarian ones. According to all of my interviewees, whether

---

[2] Pouligny 2004, pp. 186–187 makes a similar observation.

from peacekeeping missions, other UN agencies, foreign ministries, or non-governmental organizations (NGOs), the briefings they received devoted only a few hours (or, in rare occasions, a couple of days) to the political, security, economic, and humanitarian conditions. Obviously, such a limited overview cannot provide a thorough understanding of local contexts.

Once the initial briefing period is over, several elements analyzed in Chapter 2 – in particular the discounting of local knowledge, the framing of the interveners' role as primarily technical, and the insistence that expatriates remain on site only for a short period of time – discourage most foreign peacebuilders from deepening their contextual expertise. Moreover, expatriates regularly complain that they lack even the occasion to read the extensive literature available to them, including the many reports, articles, and books on macro-level dynamics that they receive during and after their briefings. In the face of multiple competing tasks and obligations, learning more about the local and national situations is not a priority.

To be sure, the interveners who work in leadership or political analysis positions in headquarters and capitals eventually develop a thorough command of the general context of their host country. They master the macro-level sociopolitical environment: They are experts in the geopolitical dimensions of violence and peacebuilding in the broader region, and they have a firm grasp on the histories and agendas of national leaders and significant groups as well as on the relationships among them. They develop this knowledge of the national and international situations with access to their organization's archives and, occasionally, with the help of country experts who work as consultants, informal advisors, or temporary staff.[3] However, as this section details, the obstacles to data collection and analysis in the field are such that this leadership staff rarely enjoys a comparable understanding of the micro-level factors at work in their theaters of deployment, especially in areas outside of the capital cities.[4] Worse, the material available to their field-based colleagues is even more limited.[5]

Obstacles to Data Collection

International interveners confront numerous challenges to collecting reliable information on the current events they are trying to influence. Researching dynamics of war and peace is inherently onerous because it requires gathering sensitive material. During interviews, local grassroots activists commonly reported facing difficulties, noting that their sources routinely change their stories, provide misleading information, or hide critical data because they are suspicious of outsiders or need to protect themselves and their kin. The challenge is even greater for expatriates.

---

[3] Pouligny 2004, pp. 184–185, develops a fascinating analysis of these dynamics.
[4] Ibid., pp. 186–191; and Coles 2007, pp. 28–29 develop a similar analysis.
[5] Also Pouligny 2004, p. 186.

Lack of linguistic competency is one of the most significant hindrances. People from conflict zones all over the world emphasize how "local language skills improve [expatriates'] ability to serve beneficiaries and to foster good relationships with community members and [local] staff."[6] However, due to the politics of knowledge at work in Peaceland, apart from rare exceptions, expatriates speak at best the official language of their country of deployment; they usually have no command of the local languages. As a result, they can communicate directly with only the educated elite and must rely on translators to interact with most ordinary people.[7]

An abundance of examples illustrate how the interveners' inability to understand their local counterparts fuels miscommunication and misunderstandings and, at times, leads to disastrous consequences.[8] In mid-2010, for instance, members of a local militia called Mai Mai Sheka gang-raped 387 civilians over the course of three days in Luvungi, a village located close to a UN peacekeeping base in Walikale territory (Congo). The victims were assaulted in their homes, in other semi-secluded locations, and in the bushes. A patrol of Indian peacekeepers actually passed through the village while the atrocity was ongoing. According to various interviewees, a UN internal inquiry cited linguistic barriers between Indian soldiers and the Congolese victims as a central reason for the peacekeepers' failure to recognize the events that were unfolding in their midst.

Unfortunately, the use of translators is not fail-safe. As I witnessed on numerous occasions, interpreters routinely make translation mistakes or omit vital information.[9] This can unintentionally create security hazards, as it did when a Congolese interpreter translated "We advise against circulation in town between 7 p.m. and 5 a.m." as "We advise against circulation in town after 9 p.m." I also observed several instances in which translation errors resulted in all parties feeling insulted, which created an entirely new conflict.

The interveners' lack of awareness of different cultural codes further compounds their confusion. Rwandans, for instance, tend to distinguish between public truth, which is uttered when speaking with a group, and private truth, which is conveyed only in one-on-one settings.[10] Hence, before the 1994 genocide, some Hutus who disagreed with the policies of their leaders nevertheless supported them in public. This discrepancy confounded expatriates deployed in Rwanda, who were unable to gauge antigovernment sentiment accurately or determine whose insights to trust. Likewise, while Europeans and North Americans assume that their counterparts will tell them when they are wrong, many Burundians view it as rude to contradict someone. Interveners who ask

---

[6] CDA Collaborative Learning Projects 2010b, p. 3.
[7] Also Ibid., p. 3.
[8] For other examples, see ibid., pp. 3–4; Coles 2007, pp. 28–29; Pouligny 2004, p. 194; and Toshiya and Konishi 2012, pp. 56 and 70.
[9] Also Pouligny 2004, p. 194.
[10] For a public source, see King 2009, pp. 132–133.

leading questions (such as, "Is this the road to Bujumbura?" or "Were your attackers Tutsi?") would therefore often receive misleading answers. Similar miscommunication occurs in Cambodia, where local people convey "their wants and likes in ways that they feel is direct," but that foreigners "don't get" because they "expect more [straightforward] communication."[11] Even definitions can vary along cultural lines, as an expatriate who had lived for dozens of years in Sudan explained: Many Sudanese nationals use English words differently from British or American people. Saying "he is very corrupt" is a typical way of blaming somebody, especially when the person is from another tribe, regardless of whether or not this person is involved in actual corruption. In addition, this contact said, Sudanese people can "talk very nicely about their worst enemy, because it is part of the politeness, but when you are alone with them they will tell you horrible things about the same person." As a result, foreigners who "take words at face value" get confused.

Two other elements discussed in subsequent chapters heighten the obstacles to information gathering. First, expatriates usually live, work, and socialize in privileged spaces (see Chapter 5). Their disconnection from the majority of the population limits their firsthand knowledge of local realities.[12] Second, strict security routines prevent interveners from accessing many unstable areas (see Chapter 7). These security procedures, when added to the discounting of local knowledge, the framing of the expatriates' role as that of thematic supervision, and the interveners' desire to preserve a certain quality of life (which tends to be much lower in rural areas), also decrease the incentives to live or travel outside of the main urban centers. As a result, in countries like Afghanistan, Burundi, Congo, Cyprus, Kosovo, Madagascar, Timor-Leste, and South Sudan, most foreign interveners are based in national or provincial capitals.[13] Only a few of them – usually humanitarian project teams, peacekeeping military units, and military observers – are stationed permanently in small, rural towns or villages.

The problem with this state of affairs is that humanitarian teams do not focus on collecting context information, nor are they trained in methods of doing so. As technical experts in areas like nutrition, health, water and sanitation, they do not even view context analysis as part of their jobs (another effect of the compartmentalization of knowledge in Peaceland). Admittedly, depending on their backgrounds, other civilian interveners sometimes have much better data gathering skills. Those in NGO and UN management positions, the diplomats, and the political and civil affairs officers of the peacekeeping missions often have training in the social sciences and instruction in proper information collection. However, these individuals are usually stationed in urban areas, like the national or provincial capitals, and while they do occasionally go into the field to supervise rurally-based teams, their visits are rare and last, at best, a

---

[11] Anderson, Brown, et al. 2012, p. 72.
[12] See also Verma 2011, notably p. 74.
[13] On Madagascar: ibid., p.74. On the other countries: author's field observations.

couple of days. Under these conditions, it is not possible to develop in-depth contextual analyses.

Most military observers are similarly ill-equipped to collect adequate material on local conditions. When accompanying military observers on routine data collection trips, I noticed that they made a number of basic mistakes. They drove straight to the place they wanted to investigate without stopping along the way, thus missing opportunities to gather useful contextual data. Then, they spent very little time in the area (of all the patrols I followed, most visits lasted less than half an hour, and the longest time spent in a village did not exceed an hour and a half). Moreover, they often stayed on the main road instead of entering villages, and they interacted mostly with local administrative and security officials. To top it all off, they publicly interviewed people on sensitive issues, asked leading questions, and failed to cross-check critical information or to probe important topics.[14]

It is not just military observers who employ these improper methods of data collection. I repeatedly witnessed peacekeeping units do the same, often to the detriment of both their mission and the civilians they were trying to protect. In a representative instance, I was conducting participant observations on a peace-keeping base. One night, we heard that a rebel group had attacked a nearby camp of the national army. The peacekeepers dispatched troops to help the soldiers under attack, but they arrived after the combat had subsided. The next morning, they sent two pickup trucks full of soldiers to investigate the incident, and I went with the patrol. As I recorded in my field notes at the time:

> We drive straight to the site of the fighting. We get off the trucks once we arrive near the camp that was attacked and see local soldiers walking on the side of the road. The local soldiers act as if they do not see the peacekeepers – they do not say anything to us and barely look at us. The peacekeepers do not try to speak with their local counterparts either. Instead, they stand guard on both sides of the gravel to secure the road.

The patrol was very conspicuous. The local soldiers were standoffish, almost defiant, and I worried that the peacekeepers' attitude was making the villagers uncomfortable. We were off to a bad start, and the situation did not improve:

> The local civilian translator that the peacekeeper brought with them runs after the officer in charge to try to talk to him, but returns to say that he seems very angry and does not want to say anything (apparently because his troops have suffered many casualties). The patrol leader decides to walk behind the local officer in charge, keeping some distance from him. After striding along for about two hundred feet, we arrive in the middle of the neighboring village. The interpreter goes a bit further to try to talk to the population. Villagers gather around us to look

---

[14] Jessica Hatcher, "Sleeping through the Slaughter," *Vice*, August 7, 2012 (available at www.vice.com/read/massacre-investigation-mission-un-congo, last accessed in December 2013) mentions several similar observations.

at the peacekeepers, who remain silent and still do not try to talk to anybody. After a couple of minutes, the interpreter returns and says that everything is now fine. Five people were killed and several injured during the nighttime fighting, but since then, there have been no abuses of local civilians.

At this point, the interpreter had talked with just a handful of people. Furthermore, he had done so in the presence of local soldiers, so, even if the troops had committed abuses, I doubt that any villagers would have dared mention them. I assumed, therefore, that we had only begun the investigation. Unfortunately, none of the peacekeepers tried to double-check the information with any other sources. We also still did not know what prompted the assault and whether the local soldiers expected further attacks or planned to retaliate, but the patrol leader did not ask the interpreter to talk with more people or pose any further questions – nor did he do so himself. Then, tensions began to escalate:

> Villagers on the side of the road start shouting at us angrily. The patrol leader tells his soldiers to get inside the vehicles quickly. We leave, with the population jeering.

Later, the interpreter explained to me that people were angry at the peacekeepers for not protecting the local army and for not fighting the rebel group. Yet, during the patrol, none of the peacekeepers informed the villagers that they had tried to help the previous night, but had arrived too late. To me, it was a missed opportunity: Mentioning that could have improved relations between the peacekeepers and the surrounding villages. Plus, any further discussions with the population might have yielded additional information on the events of the night. Once back at the base, reflecting on the whole experience, I concluded that the patrol could not possibly have brought back reliable information:

> We have stayed on the main road, and never set foot inside the village where the fighting took place. The entire data-gathering mission was extremely quick: We spent at most 20 minutes in the village. The interpreter had "extended" (a couple of minutes long) discussions with only two persons – the army commander and the chief of the village – and maybe a couple of sentence-long interactions with nearby villagers.

I also wondered what the point was in sending all these foreign soldiers rather than just the interpreter to conduct the investigation:

> All in all, the peacekeepers have had no interaction with the population. During almost the entire trip, it was the interpreter who decided with whom to talk and what to ask. The patrol leader did not stay with him, did not ask him what was going on, and did not provide him with any guidance.
>
> In fact, the patrol leaders and the other peacekeepers had a lot of trouble communicating with the interpreter because not only did they not speak any of the local languages, but also their English was weak or nonexistent. The interpreter received information from the population, but he barely mentioned anything to his foreign colleagues.

These poor data collection techniques should not be surprising. Military officers and soldiers are recruited for their military experiences, not their research skills, and they receive no training on how to gather sensitive data properly. Only the few individuals working for their countries' intelligence services have the necessary expertise to gather relevant information on sensitive political and military issues. Furthermore, the peacekeepers' translators – when they are available – obtain their positions based on their language skills, not their knowledge of research techniques. Besides, in places where all kinds of armed groups terrorize the population, sending soldiers in uniform to collect data hardly qualifies as a good idea: Even military interveners themselves, working in countries as varied as Congo, Georgia, and Haiti, reported in our conversations that host populations are just as afraid of peacekeepers as they are of local soldiers.[15]

Perhaps surprisingly, the obstacles to proper data collection are even greater in small countries like Burundi and Cyprus. Because one can cross these countries in a few hours, virtually all of the interveners are based in the capital cities – they make only day trips to the provinces. Such visits are too short to enable interveners to acquire a decent grasp of the complexities on the ground or develop trusting relationships with local people who could provide helpful information.

The interveners' tendency to congregate in national and provincial capitals, in combination with the poor data collection skills of the expatriates stationed in rural villages, creates what Robert Chambers and Stathis Kalyvas have aptly labeled an "urban bias."[16] International peacebuilders, like most conflict analysts, tend to focus on events in metropolitan areas, while many civil wars are predominantly fought in rural places, which are very distinct from urban ones.[17] Interveners also analyze problems and develop solutions based on research completed in urban environments while, as Ritu Verma notes, the distances between urban and rural settings "are not only geographic [...], but also social and cultural."[18]

One might think that local sources could compensate for the international deficiency in data gathering. However, as Chambers and Kalyvas have demonstrated, local conflict analysts also suffer from an urban bias: They are usually based in and more familiar with national or provincial capitals and have less information on and less experience in rural settings.[19] Furthermore, most conflict zones lack an independent and reliable media, which might otherwise function as an alternate source of material – although there are exceptions, such as Israel and Cyprus. Finally, the absence of sustained informal contacts and the

---

[15] For a public source, see Pouligny 2004, pp. 71–73.
[16] Chambers 1983, pp. 7–16; and Kalyvas 2006, pp. 38–48. For a related discussion of urban biases in economic development, see Bates 1981 and Lipton 1977.
[17] Kalyvas 2004 and 2006, pp. 38–39.
[18] Verma 2011, p.74.
[19] Chambers 1983, pp. 7–16; and Kalyvas 2006, pp. 38–44.

tense relationships between international peacebuilders and their local partners (as mentioned in Chapter 3 and further analyzed in Chapters 5 and 6) pose additional obstacles to the timely transmission of information from local sources to interveners.[20] For instance, in many places, peacekeepers complained that police and military counterparts would hide from or refuse to meet with them, and would turn off their cell phones to avoid peacekeepers reaching and reproaching them for their evasiveness. Civilian peacebuilders reported hurdles that were different, but just as problematic. Local people often told them what they thought the expatriates wanted to hear, or what they believed would help them achieve various goals, such as getting money or support. Additionally, in places where the resource gap between interveners and local people was particularly large and the relationships between the two groups especially distant or conflictual, the latter often preferred not to correct the former when they were wrong. From their perspective, there was no point in risking trouble as they felt that interveners never listened to them anyway.

Partial Material

As a result of their weak data-gathering skills, the expatriate bubble, and the restrictive security procedures that I analyze in Part II, interveners end up collecting information from a limited array of sources. Although there were exceptions, the large majority of foreign peacebuilders relied on the same contacts – other expatriates and local elites – a practice that may be efficient, but is clearly ineffective.[21]

In all of the countries in which I have worked or conducted research, requests for names of interesting people to speak with generally elicited a regurgitated list of a dozen or so individuals for each given location. International agencies trying to collect information on rural conditions would meet with local military and administrative authorities, with the other expatriate interveners deployed in the area, with one or two representatives of the local civil society if time allowed, and occasionally with a traditional or religious leader. They relied on these same types of informants when working in the national and provincial capitals. I observed this pattern across all kinds of intervening organizations – NGOs, UN agencies, peacekeeping units, donors, and subcontractors.

Interveners rarely hold in-depth discussions with ordinary citizens. They consult these people mostly through population surveys meant to inform relief aid programming. This research is useful, but limited. It provides data only on humanitarian conditions, not on the broader political, social, and military situations. There are a few exceptions. Just as they have stronger media,

---

[20] Also Moore 2013, p. 168.

[21] On-record sources include: Seay 2011, p. 77; and author's on-record interview with James Scambary, independent researcher, Australian National University, Dili, Timor-Leste, February 2012.

developed countries like Cyprus and Israel also have local research institutes that carry out useful opinion polls. In other conflict zones, interveners occasionally conduct in-depth quantitative and qualitative inquiries to produce perception surveys and write human rights advocacy reports.[22] A few grassroots peace-building organizations additionally produce bottom-up conflict analyses.[23] Academic researchers, particularly anthropologists, also write numerous studies based on in-depth interviews of ordinary citizens. (However, as mentioned at the beginning of this section, foreign peacebuilders rarely have time to read these reports.)

On the whole, though, the average local inhabitant has no voice. A 2010 UN report on the peacekeeping mission in Congo provides a typical example.[24] It mentions missions by several teams tasked with assessing, among other things, "the population's perception of the situation on the ground." To gauge these opinions, the UN teams met exclusively with members of the elite: "local government officials, customary chiefs, representatives of [the Congolese army], the [Congolese National Police] and other security services and civil society representatives."[25] They never actually talked with the ordinary citizens whose perceptions they sought to assess. In Afghanistan, Kenya, Mali, and Thailand, grassroots representatives similarly lamented that expatriates virtually never consulted directly with ordinary people.[26]

As the interveners I interviewed explained to me, they have legitimate reasons for meeting with authorities instead of ordinary citizens. Firstly, protocol demands it. Secondly, it enables international peacebuilders to get the official version of events. Thirdly, it is part of the basic security precautions that intervening staff should adhere to in all conflict zones, as state authorities are formally responsible for protecting them. Finally, my interviews made it clear that interveners (at times mistakenly) view state and nonstate elites, including traditional chiefs, elected political leaders, religious leaders, and civil society officials, as somehow representative of the broader population.

Unfortunately, meeting exclusively with these individuals creates a skewed sample that provides international peacebuilders with biased information. Frequently, in war and post-war settings, leaders of political parties and state administrations are party to the ongoing conflicts, as are security forces. In

---

[22] Examples of perception surveys include: the various reports written by Phuong Pham and Patrick Vinck on Cambodia, Congo, and Uganda (such as Pham, Vinck, et al. 2005, 2008, and 2009); and the protection investigations that Oxfam conducted in Congo between 2007 and 2010 (such as Oxfam 2010). Most reports by Human Rights Watch on conflict areas provide typical examples of human rights advocacy reports based on extensive interviews of ordinary people.

[23] For instance: Life and Peace Institute 2011 and 2012; and the projects of the NGO Local Voices (www.localvoicesproject.com).

[24] UN Security Council 2010b.

[25] Ibid., para. 71.

[26] Anderson 2008, p. 101; Anderson, Brown, et al. 2012, p. 15; and CDA Collaborative Learning Projects 2011b, p. 3.

places like Afghanistan, Burundi, Congo, Kosovo, and Sudan, they are often also responsible for the very problems that interveners are investigating, such as corruption and human rights abuses. Consequently, they have a strong incentive to misrepresent facts and events. Furthermore, regardless of the setting, the quest for reelection frequently drives political leaders to depict situations in the light most favorable to them. In Congo in 2010, for instance, the national and provincial authorities' official statements and statistics, both of which emphasized the improvement of security conditions in the eastern provinces in recent years, stood in stark contrast to the perceptions of the population there, who felt increasingly insecure with every year.[27] In other instances, leaders may wish to portray the situation as graver than it actually is in order to garner sympathy and obtain additional aid. Either way, interveners receive a biased picture of local conditions.

Civil society and religious contacts serve as correctives to this official bias, but they, too, do not necessarily represent the broader population.[28] Just like other leaders, they may misrepresent grassroots conditions to advance their own agendas – local NGOs, for instance, may paint a particularly catastrophic picture of the situation in order to raise funds. Moreover, civil and religious leaders are often wealthier and more educated than their fellow citizens, so their perspective on local problems and opportunities is different. The fact that interveners often prefer to meet people who speak their language and who, if possible, have also mastered the "international language" and its specific logic, references, and acronyms, further compounds the problem. In South Sudan, for instance, as several long-term peacebuilders explained, this way of working has led interveners to meet with people who had studied abroad, and thus spoke English, but who were regularly cut off from the concerns of their fellow citizens. Those who remained connected to their area of origin often spoke "with two tongues," one for "the international community" and one for "their own people," and they came "with very different messages for each audience." In Amboro and Jonglei (Sudan), this standard practice also led to the neglect of "large groups of communities," who did not have access to wealth and power. According to my interviews, whether in a wealthy and peaceful country like Cyprus or a poorer and more unstable one like Pakistan, the elite with whom interveners interact are often disconnected from the daily preoccupations of the population.

Another issue with the reliance on elites is that those located in provincial and national capitals are not necessarily well-informed about grassroots dynamics.[29]

---

[27] President Kabila's 2010 State of the Nation address to the parliament ("Discours de Joseph Kabila sur l'Etat de la Nation," December 8, 2010, available at http://radiookapi.net/docutheque/2010/12/16/discours-du-president-joseph-kabila-le-8-decembre-sur-l'etat-de-la-nation/, last accessed in December 2013) is a representative example of the discourse from national and provincial authorities. On the perception of the population, see the reports on Congo cited in Note 22.

[28] Also Richmond 2011, p. 72.

[29] Chambers 1983 (chapter 1) and 2006 develop many of the observations that I mention in this paragraph.

A number of intellectuals and civil society leaders have in-depth knowledge of rural areas, due to family ties, regular trips to the field, or cell phone communications. However, many of their peers lack such close understanding, due to the poor state of communication infrastructures in post-war environments, the above-mentioned urban bias of local intellectuals, and the presence of tensions between central government on the one hand and provincial authorities (especially those comprised of former rebel groups) on the other. Congolese people in Kinshasa, for example, are notoriously ill-informed about the situation in the eastern provinces. And the authorities based in provincial capitals (such as Goma and Bukavu) rarely travel outside of the cities, mostly because of security and logistical constraints. When they do, they are usually so well protected that they have very few interactions with the populations that they are supposed to represent. As a result, they, too, rely heavily on secondary sources, including both the same rural elite who inform the expatriate interveners and, occasionally, military allies from the area. During my interviews, provincial authorities thus proved routinely unable to supply even basic information on certain rural villages under their purview. This disconnect is even stronger in places where rebel groups control parts of the territory. A donor based in Sudan (before the independence of the South), for instance, marveled at how elite in Khartoum did "not have a clue about what [was] happening in Juba."

When questioned, local partners and local staff members could provide foreign interveners with richer data than the expatriates had collected for themselves, but this information was also often biased and incomplete. The fact that international actors prefer to support local peacebuilders – and hire local employees – who are thematic experts means that these local colleagues routinely suffer from the same kind of limitations that affect expatriates. They usually have to work in places different from their areas of origin, and as a result, local communities also view them as outsiders.[30] For instance, a Congolese peacebuilder explained to me that he also felt like a foreigner when he started working in a new local community, and he too "felt superior because he had technical knowledge." So he also had difficulties collecting information and integrating into local structures. Local contacts from Burundi expressed a comparable feeling, and an expatriate working in Somalia similarly blamed the emphasis on "technical knowledge" as the source of the distance she frequently saw between her Somali colleagues and the communities with which they worked. They would interact with intended beneficiaries on an equal basis and develop an amount of good will among local communities, but then lose the people's trust and attention as soon as they switched to using technical jargon. Local employees of NGOs operating in Istalif (Afghanistan) faced a related challenge: They had gained employment because they had received formal education and training abroad, and they had good connections in the capital Kabul, but they proved unable to develop political and social networks in the

---

[30] For a public source on this issue, see CDA Collaborative Learning Projects 2010b, pp. 2–3.

village where they worked.[31] Even staff or partners who work in their own district or province can confront this problem. The inhabitants of Ituri (Congo), for instance, confer trust and legitimacy on a village basis: They view and treat someone from a different village as an outsider, even if that village is in the same district.[32] Interveners rarely anticipate this distinction.

Relying on other international interveners for information poses its own set of problems. All of my expatriate contacts acknowledged that they had an incentive to depict local conditions in a way that suited their own objectives. Peacekeepers tasked with maintaining the peace present the state of affairs as calmer than it actually is, while NGOs trying to raise funds for their programs act overly pessimistic. During interviews, my contacts reported numerous stories of slightly distorting survey data to make it say what their chief wanted to hear (in Kosovo), "sanitizing" the information (in Bosnia), "sugarcoating it or making it worse to keep the money coming" (in the Palestinian Territories), or just trying to frame local conditions in the most useful light for themselves and their organizations (in Congo). A middle-ranked UN official emphasized the consequences of this way of working:

> I travel to [rural areas outside of the provincial capital] once every two months, and the rest of the time I receive reports that originate from a monitor, transit through our partner's antenna, then to our field office, and then arrive here. At each stage, I am sure that the information changes. And once I receive the information, before I give it to my head of office, I review the report and I put it in my own style, and there is a chance that in doing so I distort it.

Many interveners also use UN and NGO coordination meetings as a primary source of security information. These meetings, however, provide a similarly biased view of the situation. They usually cover any kind of episode involving interveners as well as the major security incidents affecting the local population – such as the displacement of hundreds of families, the looting of entire villages, or large-scale fighting among armed groups. The meetings do not, however, provide useful data on peaceful places, nor do they report low-level security issues that do not affect interveners. They therefore paint an accurate picture of security conditions for expatriates, but a distorted image of the challenges and opportunities facing host populations.

To make matters worse, expatriates are notoriously hesitant to exchange political and security information, even with colleagues from the same organization – and even more reticent with other agencies. I experienced (and shared) this reluctance when I worked as an intervener, and my contacts reported the same. Interveners prioritize protecting their organizational interests in the turf wars

---

[31] Coburn 2011, pp. 138–140.
[32] Personal communication from Sara Hellmüller (doctoral student, Swiss Peace), June 2013.

among peacebuilding organizations and ensuring their own security.[33] This diminishes the amount and quality of data available to each individual or organization.

Linguistic barriers among interveners further compound the difficulty of obtaining information from other expatriate sources. On many occasions, I witnessed UN staff members struggle to communicate even with their closest colleagues. Military observer teams, for instance, often had no language in common: One portion of the team would speak some English and the other some French (or Arabic, Spanish, or Swahili). Communication was similarly difficult within an entire peacekeeping mission. In Congo, for instance, the Uruguayan contingent spoke so little English that they were isolated from the rest of the mission, and civilians attending meetings with Indian and Pakistani military peacekeepers had to compare notes afterward to verify what their counterparts had said.

All in all, interveners often rely on the same flawed information. NGOs use UN and local official data along with other NGO reports; UN agencies base their analyses on local official data and NGO information; and diplomats use UN, NGO, and local official data. Audra Mitchell paints the same picture. Her survey of conflict analysis tools and databases (such as the Global Peace Index, the Human Security Report Project, the Conflict Trends Database, and early warning systems) shows that "many [. . .] are interlinked": "They draw on common sources of data," notably the Uppsala Conflict Data Program and the Economic Intelligence Unit, "or refer to each other in a self-referential loop."[34] Overall, Mitchell concluded, "It is a completely closed system."[35] This closed, self-referential network of information provides interveners with partial material and with superficial – and often distorted – understandings of the local contexts, none of which constitute a good enough basis to design effective peacebuilding initiatives. These inaccuracies are exacerbated in national and international headquarters, as information is repeatedly filtered out between field locations and capitals, and thus superiors routinely receive a fragmented and biased picture of the situations on the ground – a picture that is usually quite favorable to their subordinates.

Distorted Analysis

Not only is the material regularly poor and unreliable, but often the analysis that follows is similarly deficient. Meetings and reports provide factual information on security events but rarely put these facts into a broader context and almost never infer their meaning for the overall political, social, or economic

[33] Also Pouligny 2004, pp. 187–188.
[34] Mitchell 2014, pp. 110 and 125 (footnote 25); and personal communication from Dr. Audra Mitchell (lecturer in international relations, University of York), December 2013.
[35] Personal communication from Dr. Audra Mitchell, May 2012.

situations.[36] Interveners cannot always rely on in-house resources to compensate for this issue. Interviewees from NGOs or UN agencies routinely criticized the lack of analytical capacity both within their organizations and in the broader intervention circle. Diplomats deployed in the field usually have better analytical resources on macro-level events, thanks to their superiors stationed in the capital, but they too complained of a lack of analytical capacity from their counterparts on the ground.

Another significant obstacle to analysis is that the few expatriate teams based away from national and provincial capitals often lack the information on neighboring areas that is necessary to contextualize their local data. Many teams with whom I met or worked lamented the fact that their colleagues did not send them information on events in the rest of the country, or that their poor communication systems did not allow them to receive such material.[37] As a result, very few people possess both detailed and accurate information on local dynamics from a variety of sources and the ability to connect this local data with the bigger picture.

Because of the obstacles to data collection and analysis presented in this chapter, interveners usually end up with views of the situation that are more similar to one another's than to community perspectives – which are diverse and often distinct from those of the local elite.[38] In Laura Seay's words, expatriate circles in Congo resemble "a giant echo chamber in which the opinions of international actors are largely in line with one another, but far removed from those they intend to help."[39] Dan, an intervener who had spent so long in Sudan that his colleagues accused him of having "gone native," summarized the process: Expatriates "meet and attend the same workshops" and "they get more or less the same information."[40] In particular, they get "all their security information from the UN," but this information is misleading. Dan recalled that, when he would ask local contacts to verify reports from the UN, they would say, "No, it is not like that." The fact that interveners function in closed circles, however, often makes it difficult for them to recognize inaccurate data. The problem, as Dan described it, was that expatriates "tell the same story to each other" and then, having heard it from different contacts, believe it to be confirmed information. Hence, as I observed numerous times, rumors spread like wildfire among interveners deployed in a particular place – whether about a new coup, an impending attack, or new alliances among local armed groups.

---

[36] The weekly meetings organized by the UN Office for the Coordination of Humanitarian Affairs provide an excellent illustration of this claim. The main exceptions are the reports of the International Crisis Group and those of the UN Secretary General to the Security Council.

[37] A public source on this issue is Pouligny 2004, pp. 187–188.

[38] See also Seay 2011, pp. 77–78.

[39] Ibid., p. 77.

[40] Dan is a pseudonym, used to protect the identity of my interviewee.

The obstacles to data collection and analysis do more than just distort the perspective of interveners. When added to the politics of knowledge at work in Peaceland, they have another pernicious effect: People who lack a good grasp of local situations end up designing projects and managing missions. Robert Chambers reports having met one such individual, a UN senior adviser who was "drafting a national development strategy" for Afghanistan without ever having been outside of the capital, Kabul.[41] The problem is widespread. In the words of an intervener based in Congo:

> I have friends who are here to write proposals, and they do not know about specific villages, but have to write a proposal by a certain deadline anyway. It is a big, systemic problem. [...] All the projects are written by people like you and me. I may be educated and know about the region, but I would not trust my judgment about [the village of] Kirilino, and what impact a project will have on things I do not know about. So there is a failure at the level of designing programs.

Throughout my fieldwork, I regularly met people who were responsible for designing international projects but who knew little about the situations they sought to change. A few examples from Congo provide a sense of the magnitude of the problem. I lunched with two military officers tasked with deciding the "future planning" of the peacekeeping mission, despite the fact that they had no preexisting knowledge of the country and had never left the capital. I briefed a senior World Bank expert who designed million-dollar programs for the economic development of the eastern provinces, but who obviously had no idea about what life was like there. I had drinks with several NGO staff members whose jobs as "grant writers" included flying from one country to the next, spending two weeks on site researching local problems, and writing proposals for projects to address them. Each of these interveners felt that it was perfectly natural for them to be completing these tasks even with their limited knowledge. When necessary, they thought they could always ask their colleagues stationed in the area for contextual information – but, as I have shown, these colleagues too often lacked a thorough understanding of local conditions as well.

The interveners' poor data collection and analysis practices have three further, even more serious consequences, to which I devote the rest of this chapter. The lack of understanding of local conditions encourages international peacebuilders to rely on dominant narratives and to resolve conflict from the top down. It also generates numerous misunderstandings. The resulting modes of operation may be efficient, but they are also ineffective. Worse, they can be counterproductive because their reliance on simplistic narratives sometimes leads interveners to fuel the violence that they aim to combat.

[41] Chambers 2006, p. 10.

Main Consequences

Reliance on Dominant Narratives

The Power of Simple Narratives. Interveners cannot base their work on an in-depth understanding of their areas of deployment; thus they must rely on something else to make sense of local contexts and to design their intervention strategies. Usually, they turn to dominant narratives. Adopting dominant narratives offers a useful solution to foreign peacebuilders who must contend with the poor quality of information and analysis in many conflict zones. Such narratives emphasize a few specific issues on which to focus. Interveners can then believe that they have a grasp on the most important features of the situation, instead of feeling lost and deprived of the knowledge necessary to properly accomplish their work.

Multiple narratives on the causes of peace and violence abound in any conflict zone, but several elements enable certain discourses to gain dominance while others remain marginal. According to existing research, stories resonate more, and thus influence action more effectively, when they assign the cause of the problems to "the deliberate actions of identifiable individuals"; when they include "bodily harm to vulnerable individuals, especially when there is a short and clear causal chain assigning responsibility"; when they suggest a simple solution; and when they can latch on to preexisting narratives.[42]

As was evident from my fieldwork, the aspect of "simplicity" – notably an uncomplicated story line, which builds on elements already familiar to the general public, and a straightforward solution – is particularly important in enabling a narrative on a given conflict situation to achieve and maintain prominence. Media outlets need to find a story that fits in a few pages, or can be told in a few minutes, and that their audience can easily understand and remember. Policy-makers based in headquarters and national capitals, such as desk officers, intelligence staff, and advisors to foreign and defense ministers, face a similar challenge for internal bureaucratic reasons. They are granted only a few minutes or a short memo with which to brief their superiors, who decide on the main policy directions, but who usually have only a superficial knowledge of various conflict zones. They thus have to find a brief and straightforward presentation of the situation, with clear policy recommendations that their superiors can readily grasp and approve. Finally, aid organizations need to raise funds for their programs, and advocacy agencies need to mobilize followers. As numerous staff members have explained to me, fundraising and advocacy efforts succeed best when they put forward a simple narrative, and the story is most likely to resonate with its target audience if it includes well-defined "good" and "evil" individuals, or clear-cut perpetrators and victims. Most donors also want to fund projects that have realistic and feasible goals. Given the uncertainty and complexity inherent to peace work,

---

[42] Bakke 2011, pp. 6–8; Keck and Sikkink 1998, p. 27; and Lanz 2011.

the best way for funding applicants to give the impression that they match the donors' requirements is to simplify the story line.[43]

The need to find a simple narrative is all the more important in the cases of conflict and post-conflict situations like Afghanistan, Congo, Darfur, and South Sudan because both policy-makers and the general public usually perceive these wars as extremely complex and intractable. Virtually all of my interviewees complained about the multiplicity of foreign and domestic actors involved in the violence, the seemingly endless character of the conflict, and the blurred lines between victims and perpetrators. Simple narratives are essential to dealing with such complexity: They identify salient issues, dictate urgent action, and help determine who is worth supporting and who should be challenged.

In turn, the reliance on these narratives orients the process of knowledge construction in a way that James Ferguson best described in his landmark study of World Bank programs in Lesotho:

> [Intervening] institutions generate their own form of discourse, and this discourse simultaneously constructs [the target country] as a particular kind of object of knowledge, and creates a structure of knowledge around that object. Interventions are then organized on the basis of this structure of knowledge, which, while "failing" on their own terms, nonetheless have regular effects.[44]

In other words, narratives contribute to shaping both the agendas of the interveners at the macro level and their everyday actions at the micro level.[45] To illuminate how this process affects peacebuilding effectiveness, the next section develops a case study of the external efforts aimed at helping Congo build peace in 2010 and 2011.

Illustration: The Unforeseen Consequences of Dominant Narratives Concerning Congo (2010–2011). In 2010 and 2011, three narratives dominated the discourse on Congo and oriented intervention strategies there.[46] These narratives focused on a primary cause of violence, the illegal exploitation of natural resources; a main consequence, the sexual abuse of women and girls; and a central solution, the reconstruction of state authority.[47] This section considers each

---

[43] On the relationships between increased uncertainty and complexity of development on the one hand, and simplified implementation procedures and models of change on the other, see Mosse 2005, p. 3.

[44] Ferguson 1990, p. 14. Also Mitchell 2002, chapter 7.

[45] For fascinating analyses of this process at the micro level, see Carpenter 2003 and at the macro level, see Doty 1996; Kojan and Angelo 2005; and Mamdani 2009, part I.

[46] Autesserre 2012 presents a preliminary version of this section.

[47] The advocacy documents produced by Enough (www.enoughproject.org) and Friends of the Congo (www.friendsofthecongo.org) at that time provide a perfect illustration of this focus. For a claim similar to mine regarding the first two narratives, see the recurrent debates in the blogs *Texas in Africa* (by Laura Seay, texasinafrica.blogspot.com) and *Congo Siasa* (by Jason Stearns, www.congosiasa.blogspot.com).

narrative in turn. Building on the analysis developed in the previous section, I explain how these narratives achieved prominence: They provided straightforward explanations of the violence, suggested feasible solutions, and resonated with foreign audiences, including institutional and individual donors. I show that, thanks to the reliance on dominant narratives, foreign and Congolese activists managed to put the Congolese conflict on the agenda of influential policy-makers in head-quarters and national capitals. However, the focus on these narratives and on the solutions they recommended also produced results that clashed with their intended purposes, notably an increase in violence on the ground.

- The Cause: Conflict Minerals

The first dominant narrative held that the illegal exploitation of mineral resources was the main source of violence in Congo.[48] Revenue from Congolese minerals such as gold, diamonds, copper, and columbite-tantalite (usually called coltan) funded foreign and local armed groups who committed atrocities against the general population. The solution seemed straightforward: To end war and violence, interveners should stop the illegal trafficking of resources.

European advocacy NGOs, such as Global Witness, were the first to put forth this narrative in the late 1990s. Their campaigns led to the creation of a UN Panel of Inquiry that investigated the illegal exploitation of natural resources and other forms of wealth in Congo. Along with the efforts of European NGOs, the three reports that the Panel of Inquiry published between 2001 and 2003 put the topic of mineral resources firmly on the policy agenda.[49] From then on, media reports, as well as research on the link between mineral resources and violence in Congo, multiplied.[50] Newly created advocacy NGOs like Enough and Friends of the Congo then adopted the narrative and helped reinforce nascent interest in the subject in North America.[51] By 2010, conflict minerals had become a requisite topic at conferences and in writings on Congo.

Many of the Congolese people with whom I interacted supported this interpretation of the violence. They explained that the looting of their country's mineral wealth was at the heart of the civil and international wars that had plagued Congo since the mid-1990s.[52] However, along with think tanks, academics, and a number of interveners on the ground, they also routinely put forth several competing narratives. They pointed to the presence of foreign militias, the efforts of the Rwandan and Ugandan governments to eradicate these militias,

---

[48] For a similar claim and additional supporting evidence, see Laudati 2013, pp. 32–33; and Laura Seay, "Is Congo's Mineral Trade Really the Key to the Country's Conflict?," The Christian Science Monitor, April 29, 2011.

[49] UN Panel of Inquiry 2001 to 2003.

[50] International Alert 2010, pp. 10–11, provides a very helpful review of this literature.

[51] For a detailed analysis of Enough's positioning and strategy, see Seay 2012, pp. 9–10.

[52] For excellent analyses of this issue, see Fahey 2011; and Nest, Grignon, et al. 2006.

and the violent competition for power among Congolese leaders.[53] Grassroots peacebuilders emphasized instead local drivers of tensions, such as land issues and bottom-up antagonisms over traditional and administrative power.[54] Academics and local populations pointed as well to other economic sources of violence beyond conflict minerals, notably disputes over cattle, charcoal, hemp, timber, drugs, and taxation at roadblocks.[55]

In fact, according to the only overall statistics that I found on the causes of violence in Congo, a mere 8 percent of all conflicts were over natural resources.[56] Ann Laudati's extensive field and desk research yield a similar result: Minerals play just "a secondary role" in "stimulating the activities" of most armed groups active on Congolese territory.[57] Admittedly, taxes on the natural resource trade did provide most of the revenue for some of these groups, including the Democratic Front for the Liberation of Rwanda (up to 75 percent of revenue) and certain brigades of the national army (up to 95 percent).[58] However, other brigades of the national army had no income from minerals, and mineral trade comprised only 15 percent of the estimated revenue for the most high-profile Congolese spoiler, the National Congress for the Defense of the People – and even less for its successor, the M23.[59] There was also a wide variation in reliance on minerals for revenue, depending on whether the armed groups were deployed in mineral-rich areas or not. In sum, the illegal exploitation of natural resources was an important cause of violence in Congo, but it was certainly not the only one.

Although these competing narratives did influence the discourse on Congo, the conflict minerals narrative had become so prominent in 2010–2011 that it often eclipsed the others. The interviews I conducted with foreign interveners in headquarters and in the field made this abundantly clear. A number of these contacts presented mineral resource trafficking as the principal reason for Rwanda's involvement in Congo and the only funding source for armed groups – while, again, it was one among many factors and was often not the largest contributor.[60] Numerous interveners similarly emphasized that ending the violence required first stopping the illegal exploitation of resources, when, in fact, that was only one of several urgent steps necessary to end tensions. The only other measure that these interviewees regularly mentioned was reconstructing state authority, which they saw as essential to improving control over the minerals trade.

[53] Lemarchand 2008; Prunier 2008; Reyntjens 2009; Stearns 2011; Turner 2007; and Vlassenroot and Raeymaekers 2004.
[54] Autesserre 2010, chapters 2 and 4.
[55] Garrett 2009; and Laudati 2013.
[56] UN Integrated Bureau, Termes de Référence: Analyse des Conflits, Kinshasa, 2011, p. 3.
[57] Laudati 2013, pp. 33–35 and throughout the article.
[58] Garrett 2009; and Garrett and Mitchell 2009, p. 6.
[59] Garrett 2009; and Garrett and Mitchell 2009, p. 6. On the M23: Johnson 2013, pp. 6–7.
[60] Garrett 2009.

The actions of the countries and organizations most involved in Congo in the 2000s and early 2010s illustrate how powerful the influence of this dominant narrative was on international efforts. Both panels of experts that the UN created on Congo focused their investigations on the illegal exploitation of natural resources.[61] While countries and organizations outside of the African Great Lakes usually paid little attention to Congo, by 2011, Germany, the United States, the European Union, the Organisation for Economic Co-operation and Development, the UN, and the World Bank had all passed legislation or set up projects to reform the Congolese mining sector and help prevent the use of its conflict minerals.[62]

The conflict minerals narrative reached and maintained prominence in large part because it resonated with non-Congolese audiences. It latched onto a broader narrative about the economic dimensions of violence and the "resource curse," which dominated research on civil wars in the 2000s and led to high-profile policy initiatives such as the Kimberley Process.[63] It assigned the cause of the problem to the deliberate actions of identifiable individuals (soldiers in various armed groups), referenced bodily harm to vulnerable people (the Congolese population), suggested a simple solution to the complex issue of the Congolese conflict (to end the illegal exploitation of resources), and enabled the American and European publics to take action (by boycotting companies suspected of using conflict minerals). It also let journalists and advocates tell the story of Congo to the less-informed public in an easily understandable and relatable manner. As a journalist explained, "The fact that I say coltan is in cell phones and your cell phone is supporting the conflict in Congo is a simplification of the conflict, but I would say it anyway, because we as journalists are trying to make things less foreign to a foreign audience."[64] The reactions of large parts of the Congolese elite and diaspora further legitimized this story line. Many of them contended that their country was a victim of a global conspiracy in which Western powers supported neighboring states and foreign militias and fueled conflict on the ground in order to ease their access to Congolese natural

[61] After the previously mentioned panel of inquiry handed in its last report in 2003, the UN created another group of experts to monitor the application of sanctions it had recommended. The group's reports clearly illustrate its continued focus on mineral resources. See, for instance, UN Security Council 2010a.

[62] Arimatsu and Mistry 2012; Verbruggen, Francq, et al. 2011; and Thierry Vircoulon, "Derrière le Problème des Minerais des Conflits, la Gouvernance du Congo (blog post, International Crisis Group, www.crisisgroup.org/fr/regions/afrique/afrique-centrale/rd-congo/Derriere%20le%20probleme%20des%20minerais%20des%20conflits.aspx, 2011) provide very helpful overviews of these initiatives.

[63] Collier and Hoeffler 2001 launched this research program. Subsequent studies include, among many others, the works of: Paul Collier, Anke Hoeffler, David Keen, Michael Ross, Nicholas Sambanis, and numerous researchers affiliated with the World Bank.

On the Kimberley Process (an initiative in which governments, industries, and civil society representatives work together to stem the flow of conflict diamonds), see www.kimberleyprocess.com.

[64] Author's on-record interview with Michael Kavanagh, Kinshasa, September 2010.

resources.[65] In this story, conflict minerals were, again, at the heart of the violence.

Advocacy efforts that promoted this narrative and attempted to end the illegal exploitation of resources achieved considerable results. They helped bring international attention to Congo by "galvaniz[ing] grassroots activists" in Europe and the United States and "build[ing] a broad constituency around the situation."[66] They succeeded in increasing the news coverage of the Congolese conflict and in raising the number and amount of donations for aid organizations involved there.[67] They forced companies doing business in Congo to consider whether their actions fueled conflict.[68] They made it more difficult for neighboring countries to illegally exploit Congolese minerals.

However, this advocacy also had a number of perverse and unintended consequences on the ground. By focusing exclusively on one cause of violence, the dominance of this narrative diverted attention from other much-needed policy actions in the field, such as resolving land conflict, promoting intercommunity reconciliation, jump-starting economic development, and fighting corruption. In 2010 and 2011, as international regulations came into effect and international pressure persuaded President Kabila to impose a temporary ban on mining operations in the Kivus and Maniema, it became clear that, given the conditions in eastern Congo, such technical measures alone could not stop the illegal trade in minerals and the associated violence.[69] Even worse, as these measures were not accompanied by broader political, economic, military, and social reforms, they actually fueled the problem they purported to combat.[70] Since military leaders remained the principal power brokers in rural areas and since corruption persisted, the application of the technical measures deprived vulnerable populations of their sole means of livelihood, while allowing armed groups to continue and even further expand their mining operations.[71] At the

---

[65] Autesserre 2010, pp. 17–18, discusses these conspiracy theories in depth.

[66] Seay 2012, p. 9.

[67] Ibid., p. 9.

[68] Arimatsu and Mistry 2012, p. 29; and Levin 2012.

[69] A public source on this issue is de Koning 2011.

[70] The topics analyzed in the rest of this paragraph were at the heart of a heated debate, conducted in various blogs and newspapers, and focused on the merits of the U.S. regulation. The most useful contributions include: the blog *Texas in Africa* (by Laura Seay, http://texasinafrica.blogspot.com, notably the post dated December 13, 2010); the blog *Congo Siasa* (by Jason Stearns, www. congosiasa.blogspot.com/, notably the posts dated August 3 and 10, 2011); the blog of the *Enough* project (www.enoughproject.org/blog, notably the post dated October 26, 2011); "Africa and 'Obama's Embargo:' A Provision of Dodd-Frank Boomerangs on the Continent's Poor," *Wall Street Journal*, July 18, 2011; David Aronson, "How Congress Devastated Congo," *The New York Times*, August 7, 2011; and Mvemba Dizolele, "Conflict Minerals in the Congo: Let's be Frank About Dodd-Frank's," *The Huffington Post*, August 22, 2011.

[71] Arimatsu and Mistry 2012, p. 29; Pole Institute 2011b; Seay 2012, notably pp. 13 and 16; Vircoulon, "Derrière le Problème des Minerais;" and UN Security Council 2010a.

same time, the regulations resulted in a de facto ban on many Congolese mineral exports and an increase in fraudulent transactions, due to the near impossibility of implementing the required supply chain verification in the unstable conditions prevailing in eastern Congo.[72] This led to a permanent loss of revenue for many artisanal miners, their families, and the countless small businesses that depended on them.[73]

• The Worst Effect: Sexual Violence

Sexual abuse of women and girls was another core focus of many individuals who promoted the conflict minerals narrative.[74] These advocates emphasized that the armed groups responsible for mineral resource exploitation routinely raped women, presenting these violent assaults as the worst by-product of the conflict and, thus, the crisis most in need of attention.

Advocates concerned with natural resource exploitation were not the only ones calling attention to sexual violence. Across the board, journalists, policy-makers, practitioners, and even celebrities paid enormous attention to the problem of sexual abuse in eastern Congo, more than to any other form of violence.[75] In 2008, the *New York Times* Op-Ed columnist Nicholas Kristof dubbed eastern Congo the "rape capital of the world," a label that the UN special representative on sexual violence in conflict Margot Wallström applied after her 2010 visit to the area.[76] Journalists, advocates, and aid workers have employed this designation ad nauseam ever since, to the point that experts now view Congo as the second most dangerous country on earth for women, behind Afghanistan.[77] In 2010–2011, rape was the main theme of countless media

---

[72] Arimatsu and Mistry 2012, p. 35; Pole Institute 2011a and 2011b; Seay 2012, pp. 13–15 and 19–20; and UN Security Council 2011, para. 371.

[73] Arimatsu and Mistry 2012, p. 35; Atta-Asamoah and Githaiga 2012, pp. 1–3; Bouvy and Lange 2012, p. 39; Matthysen and Montejano 2013; Seay 2012, pp. 13–16; and UN Security Council 2011, paras. 339, 342, and 368.

[74] Representative examples of this focus, among many others, include the Enough Project strategy paper "Can You Hear Congo Now? Cell Phones, Conflict Minerals, and the Worst Sexual Violence in the World," by John Prendergast (dated April 2009, available at www.enoughpro ject.org/publications/can-you-hear-congo-now-cell-phones-conflict-minerals-and-worst-sexual-vio lence-world, last accessed in December 2013), and the *Enough Project Activist Brief* (available at http://enoughproject.org/files/certification_activist_brief.pdf, last accessed in December 2013). The post "Is my Cell Phone Full of Rape, Redux" on the blog *Wronging Rights* (by Kate Cronin-Furman, wrongingrights.blogspot.com/2011/07/is-my-cell-phone-full-of-rape-redux.html) provides links to many other examples. For a scholarly source on the link between mineral resources and sexual violence, see Samset 2012, pp. 230 and 242.

[75] Eriksson Baaz and Stern 2010 (pp. 15–16) and 2013 (pp. 89 and 94–95) make a similar claim.

[76] Nicholas Kristof, "The Weapon of Rape," *New York Times*, June 15, 2008; Margot Wallström, "Statement by UN Special Representative of the Secretary-General," Security Council Open Meeting on "Women, Peace and Security: Sexual Violence in Situations of Armed Conflict," New York, April 27, 2010.

[77] "Poll says Afghanistan 'Most Dangerous' for Women," by *BBC News*, June 15, 2011.

reports on Congo.[78] According to a UN insider, since 2009, there had been no interest in the Congo at the UN Security Council except when it discussed incidents of, and potential responses to, mass rapes. Similarly, top U.S. Department of State officials reportedly paid no attention to Congo except when sexual violence grabbed the headlines.

As a result, the number of NGOs working on sexual violence in Congo has skyrocketed.[79] The itinerary of foreign diplomats visiting the eastern provinces in the late 2000s and early 2010s inevitably included a stop at one of the hospitals dedicated to treating rape victims, such as the Panzi hospital in Bukavu or the Heal Africa hospital in Goma. (Aid workers on the ground found this practice appalling: In their view, visitors often behaved insensitively toward the victims, callously exploiting them for publicity or political gain.) Sexual violence has also become a requisite topic of expertise for all people who work on Congo. The Belgian foreign minister, for instance, reportedly felt obliged to react publicly to cases of mass rape in order to meet the expectations of his domestic audience. For several years, the Dutch foreign ministry ordered its embassy staff in Congo to take up the issue of sexual violence at all donor and coordination meetings. Ultimately, according to donors and aid workers, sexual violence became such a buzzword that many foreign and Congolese organizations began inserting references to it in all kinds of unrelated project proposals simply to increase their chances of obtaining funding.

Sexual violence did not always dominate the discourse on Congo. During the large-scale fighting that took place between 1994 and 2003, few people discussed sexual violence, even though it was perpetrated at a higher rate than in 2010 and 2011.[80] They talked instead about violence in general, and only a handful of humanitarian organizations had specific projects to help victims of sexual abuse. The 2002 report by Human Rights Watch *The War Within the War* was the first to draw attention to this specific form of brutality.[81] Journalists and news editors started favoring the sexual violence angle when reporting on the Congolese conflict. The attention to this issue prompted NGOs to initiate projects on sexual abuse and to launch fundraising campaigns that reinforced interest in the topic.[82] By all accounts, the visit of U.S. Secretary of State Hillary

---

[78] Examples include, among many others: "Rapes 'Surge' in DR Congo," *Al Jazeera*, April 15, 2010; Anne Mawathe, "Haunted by Congo Rape Dilemma," *BBC News*, May 15, 2010; The Associated Press, "U.N. Reports over 500 Rapes in Eastern Congo," *USA Today*, September 8, 2010; "DRC Army Raping and Killing, Says UN Envoy," *Radio France Internationale*, October 15, 2010; Jeffrey Gettleman, "Rapes Total in Millions in Congo, Study Finds," *The New York Times*, May 12, 2011; and Ben Brumfield, Azadeh Ansari, and Moni Basu "Attackers Rape More than 170 Women in Raids on Congo Villages," *CNN*, June 24, 2011.

[79] Eriksson Baaz and Stern 2013, p. 97.

[80] For a public source and a thorough statistical analysis of the number of U.S. official statements on Congo mentioning sexual violence between 1990s and 2012, see Crawford 2013.

[81] Human Rights Watch 2002.

[82] For a detailed account of the increase in NGOs working on sexual violence after 2002, see Douma and Hilhorst 2012, pp. 33–34.

Clinton to eastern Congo in 2009, which focused on victims of sexual violence and resulted in an offer of $17 million in aid, and which was followed shortly after by a trip by UN Special Representative Wallström, entrenched sexual violence as *the* frame to use when thinking about Congo. From then on, Congo and rape became inextricable for most foreign audiences.

Congolese populations on the ground and field-based interveners agreed that sexual violence was widespread and persistent in the eastern provinces and that every possible effort should be made to end it. However, a number of Congolese citizens, including many intellectuals and NGO actors, as well as select expatriates, also emphasized the many other consequences of violence: killings, forced labor, conscription of child soldiers, and nonsexual torture.[83] Furthermore, ordinary people (including women) deplored that the reduction of the complex Congolese problems to an overly simplistic rape narrative diverted aid and other resources away from the health issues that they viewed as the most urgent and important to address, notably food insecurity, as well as the physical condition, location, quality, and costs of hospitals and health centers.[84] They insisted that using the available funding to improve the overall health-care system would be more effective than helping victims of rape, given that, to them, "gender-based violence is just one [of the many issues] affecting women's health."[85]

Despite the presence of these competing story lines, there were several reasons the sexual violence narrative reached and maintained prominence. To begin with, the emotional impact of sexual abuse is particularly strong, because of several characteristics. Sexual violence involves intentionally inflicted bodily harm to individuals who are socially constructed as the most vulnerable (women and girls) and therefore the most worthy of assistance. It is viewed as the "ultimate violation of self."[86] The consequences of this form of violence are also worse than others as, in addition to being tortured, victims are often subjected to social stigma and rejection by their communities.[87] Most people thus react more strongly to cases of sexual violence than to other forms of abuse. The narrative also resonates with audiences from all nationalities, as sexual abuse occurs everywhere, and at the same time it fits perfectly with widespread stereotypes of Congolese people as savage and barbaric.[88] One journalist aptly explained that stories of rape are another way to make the Congolese conflict less foreign to their audience. The response of the public was unequivocal: Of all

---

[83] Also Eriksson Baaz and Stern 2013, p. 98.

[84] D'Errico, Tshibangu, et al. 2013; also Eriksson Baaz and Stern 2013, p. 95.

[85] D'Errico, Tshibangu, et al. 2013, p. 63.

[86] Justice Byron R. White, cited in many studies and articles on rapes, such as Baxi 1998; and Leone 1993.

[87] For more on this issue, see D'Errico, Tshibangu, et al. 2013, p. 52.

[88] Eriksson Baaz and Stern 2013, pp. 90–92; and Howard French, "Congo: Rape, Savagery, and Stereotypes, the Heart of Darkness," *YouTube*, www.youtube.com/watch?v=NXJEVoaHoHU). On the construction of the stereotyped view of Congolese people as barbaric, and the colonial roots of this image, see Dunn 2003 and Autesserre 2010, pp. 74–81.

of his articles on the Congo, this journalist's stories on rape got the highest number of hits.[89] Finally, the narrative included a straightforward, feasible answer to the problem – to provide medical care to victims of sexual abuse – and a possibility for people all over the world to get involved, by sending money for projects helping rape survivors. Working on sexual violence was also an effective strategy for humanitarian organizations. As an aid worker described, setting up projects on sexual abuse was some of the "most eligible programming" possible, as it was a combination of "pure" humanitarian work (treatment of the victims, with immediate, concrete results) and "protection" of the population, which had become a hot topic in humanitarian circles in the previous five years.

It is indisputable that everything should be done to stop the scourge of sexual violence in Congo. Tens of thousands of Congolese people are sexually assaulted every year; some of the rapes include horrific forms of torture, and they almost always destroy the lives of the victims. Advocacy efforts thus helped provide crucial assistance to the victims. However, this international focus also led to unintentionally counterproductive results on the ground, namely reluctance to deploy female peacekeepers, discrimination against other vulnerable populations, and at times, an increase in the use of sexual abuse by combatants.

The framing of the Congo as "the most dangerous place on earth to be a woman" led several organizations to refrain from sending female interveners to the eastern provinces, which ultimately diminished these agencies' capacity to respond to sexual abuse. In 2008 for instance, the relief NGO Action Against Hunger decided to avoid sending women to the Kivus in order to keep from placing them in danger. In the military contingents of the UN peacekeeping mission in Congo, women made up 2.26 percent of the troops as of August 2010 (approximately 42 percent fewer than in other UN missions), and the few female military personnel sent to the eastern provinces mostly worked in noncombat (administrative or medical) positions.[90] One of the commanders explained to me that the greater gender imbalance was intentional: The leadership of his army did not want to send female combatants to places where they might be sexually assaulted. The mass rapes that took place in August 2010 in Luvungi illustrate the negative effect of the lack of female soldiers among the peacekeepers. As previously noted, UN troops patrolled the area during the three days of the assault, and a team actually crossed the village where women were being raped. Local populations failed to alert the peacekeepers to the ongoing violence because they did not trust them. According to UN internal investigations, one reason for the population's reluctance, in addition to the language divide previously mentioned, was that the women could not find any female peacekeepers,

---

[89] Author's on-record interview with Kavanagh.

[90] Statistic calculated from the figures available in the factsheet "UN Mission's Contributions by Country" available on the UN Web site (www.un.org/en/peacekeeping/contributors/2010/missioncountry.zip, last accessed in December 2013).

with whom it would have been less embarrassing to raise the topic of sexual abuse.

In addition to decreasing the international capacity to respond to sexual assaults, the overwhelming focus on sexual violence against women and girls led to discrimination against vulnerable populations in two ways. First, the concentration on sexual abuse diverted attention from other horrific forms of violence, such as nonsexual torture, killings, and the recruitment of child soldiers.[91] For instance, the UN Development Program's support for the reconstruction of the justice system in 2010–2011 focused on enabling Congolese officials to respond to sexual abuses, instead of to all kinds of violent crime.[92] The police mission of the European Union had only one unit deployed outside of the capital, and this unit focused exclusively on the fight against sexual abuse, instead of on the fight against all illegal activities. During off-the-record interviews, Congolese and foreign aid workers regularly complained that they could not draw the attention of the media or donors to horrific events that had no sexual dimension. Some of them also lamented that they received more money than they needed to treat victims of sexual abuse, while they lacked funding to implement other crucial projects.[93] The focus on sexual violence actually shaped the provision of health and other social services to such a point that Congolese women knew that the best, and sometimes only, way to obtain care was to claim to have been raped.[94]

Second, while violence against women and girls received enormous attention, the sexual abuse of men and boys earned little consideration.[95] However, at least 4 percent to 10 percent of all rape victims were male, and their abuse carried equally terrible psychological and physical consequences.[96] Ignoring men and boys led to discrimination in the provision of support to rape survivors. Framing sexual violence as a women's issue was also counterproductive, as it often prevented constructive engagement with men – whether they were victims or perpetrators, power brokers or powerless – and thus could not halt the cycle of trauma and violence.

Even worse than discrimination against victims, another main unintended consequence of the dominant narrative was that armed groups began to perceive sexual violence as an effective bargaining tool. The singular focus on sexual violence sent the message that this form of abuse was particularly forbidden and punishable, creating incentives for various groups to exploit it. While this mostly

---

[91] French makes a similar point in "Congo: Rape, Savagery, and Stereotypes."
[92] UN Development Programme North Kivu, "Stabilisation et reconstruction de la RDC – Appui du PNUD," Goma, December 15, 2010, on file with author.
[93] Also Eriksson Baaz and Stern 2013, pp. 97–99.
[94] Public sources on this topic include Douma and Hilhorst 2012, p. 49; and Eriksson Baaz and Stern 2010 (pp. 61–63) and 2013 (pp. 99–100).
[95] Public sources for this paragraph include Cruz and Smits 2011; Dolan 2010; Eastern Congo Initiative 2011, p. 79; Eriksson Baaz and Stern 2010, pp. 50–55; and Lwambo 2011.
[96] Eastern Congo Initiative 2011, p. 79; and Johnson, Scott, et al. 2010.

took the form of rebels using the threat of rape to push for negotiations or request an end to military operations, there were also examples of those threats actually being carried out, such as during the August 2010 mass rapes in Luvungi. According to several sources, Sheka (the leader of the Mai Mai group responsible for this atrocity) ordered his soldiers to systematically rape women, instead of just looting and beating people as they usually did, because he wanted to draw attention to his armed group and to be invited to the negotiating table.[97] He knew that using sexual violence was the best way to reach this goal, as it would attract the attention of the international community, and various states and advocacy groups would put pressure on the Congolese government to negotiate with him – which is exactly what happened. Unfortunately, many other rebel leaders used the same reasoning as Sheka did, and, during the time of my fieldwork, humanitarian organizations observed an increase in the use of sexual violence by armed groups who had political claims.

This last unintended consequence would not have existed without the presence of a final problem: There was much more attention, and many more projects, devoted to the consequences of sexual violence than to its causes, such as poverty, land conflict, hostile civil-military relationships, disorganization of the army and the police, weakness of the justice system, physical and economic insecurity, and oppressive gender norms.[98] The massive media coverage in the aftermath of the 2010 mass rapes in Luvungi was a case in point. Nearly all news items focused on the horrific nature of the violence and on the UN's failure to respond, while virtually none tried to explain why the soldiers decided to rape (an oversight that illustrates the extent to which pervasive assumptions of Congolese barbarism impede foreigners' understandings of the conflict situation).[99] The International Security and Stabilization Support Strategy also provided a good illustration of how international contributions were used during that year: of the funds for sexual violence, 72 percent were devoted to treating victims of rape, and only 27 percent to preventing sexual abuse.[100] Both the multi-trust fund budgets and the UN strategy on sexual violence were similarly disproportionate in their allocations.[101] Regrettably, the millions of

---

[97] A public source is UN Security Council 2010a, para. 41.

[98] On the causes of sexual violence: Cruz and Smits 2011; Dolan 2010; Eriksson Baaz and Stern 2009, 2010, and 2013; Kelly 2010; and Samset 2012.

[99] Examples, among many others, include: "Reports of Mass Rape by DRC rebels," *Al Jazeera*, September 8, 2010; The Associated Press, "200 Women Gang-Raped Near Congo Base U.N. Says," *USA Today*, August 23, 2010; "UN Peacekeepers 'Failed' DR Congo Rape Victims," *BBC News*, September 7, 2010; Josh Korn, "At Least 150 Women Raped in Weekend Raid in Congo," *The New York Times*, August 22, 2010; and "242 Women Raped by FDLR and Mai-Mai, says NGO," *Radio France Internationale*, September 3, 2010. One of the rare exceptions was Jeffrey Gettleman, "Mass Rapes in Congo Reveals U.N. Weakness," *The New York Times*, October 4, 2010.

[100] 0.4 percent of the funds were devoted to data collection. Source: Système Intégré des Nations Unies 2010, p. 46.

[101] Respectively Solhjell 2010; and Douma and Hilhorst 2012, p. 37.

dollars spent on this problem had no chance of ever resolving it if they did not address its causes. Helping women who had been raped was imperative, but there is no doubt that the victims would have appreciated an effective prevention program, which would have spared them from assault in the first place.

• The Solution: Statebuilding

As was evident in my interviews, virtually all interveners saw the reconstruction of state authority as the most effective way to end violence, including sexual abuse, and to stop the illegal exploitation of natural resources.[102] Thus, one of the main priorities of the UN peacekeeping mission, as well as of numerous international donors and UN agencies, was to help the Congolese government extend its authority in the unstable eastern provinces.[103]

The focus on statebuilding as the central solution to the complex problems in Congo came from three sources. To begin with, as numerous scholars have documented, statebuilding became a classic element of peacebuilding strategies in the 2000s.[104] The rationale was simple and still holds much weight today: Effective, legitimate governmental institutions are indispensable for sustainable peace.[105] Without them countries can rarely escape the cycle of war and violence – not to mention poverty and underdevelopment.[106] In theory, interveners could foster a number of different institutional arrangements. In practice, however, as Roland Paris has convincingly demonstrated, the major powers on today's global scene "are predisposed to promote structures that fit their preconceptions of governance," namely "Westphalian-Weberian states."[107] These states should notably feature a "central authority capable of exercising exclusive control over a bounded territory," possess "a monopoly on the legitimate use of violence," and include "a centralized, hierarchical governmental apparatus in which political authority is attached to formal offices, not to the people who occupy those offices, and in which administrative tasks are carried out by a specialized bureaucracy."[108] The newly-formed (or reformed) states are expected to mobilize financial resources, regulate violence, generate legitimacy, provide public goods, and arbitrate between competing demands from its citizens.[109] In doing so, as the reasoning goes, these states will ensure both

---

[102] See also Cruz and Smits 2011, p. 1.

[103] For public sources, see among others: Trefon 2011; UN Integrated System 2009; and UN Security Council 2010c, section on stabilization.

[104] This paragraph draws on the enormous literature on statebuilding, of which Bliesemann de Guevara 2012, pp. 2–10; and Paris and Sisk 2009, pp. 1–3 and 7–15 provide very useful overviews.

[105] Fukuyama 2004; and Paris 2004.

[106] Chesterman 2004, pp. 82–88 and chapter 3; Fukuyama 2004; Paris 2004; and Paris and Sisk 2009, pp. 2–3.

[107] Paris in progress, citations from pp. 2 and 18, demonstration in the rest of the article.

[108] Ibid., p. 18.

[109] Ibid., p. 18. Also Mac Ginty 2012, p. 290.

domestic and international stability: They will protect their populations from fear and want, and they will take responsibility for respecting international rules and norms.[110] The preference for this specific form of governance is so strong that the sovereign territorial state has now become, according to Alexander Murphy and other scholars, virtually "the only imaginable spatial framework for political life."[111] Interveners often do not even recognize arrangements that do not fit these preconceptions, such as informal, personalized, or non-territorialized governance regimes, as proper forms of governance.[112]

The second reason for the international focus on statebuilding was that, from 2009 onward, international interveners believed that they had successfully implemented in Congo all the standard post-war solutions, notably general elections as well as national and regional reconciliation.[113] In their view, the remaining problems were due to criminality and other law-and-order issues, which Congo would be able to tackle if it were not a "failed state."[114] In other words, foreign peacebuilders attributed the problems of instability and violence to the lack of proper governance structures in the eastern provinces. Reconstructing state authority along a Westphalian-Weberian model was a way to give the Congolese government the capacity necessary to address these domestic matters. Along the same lines, many international NGOs and church structures saw themselves as providing services that should be the responsibility of the state, such as health care and education. Thus, they considered state-building a sustainable exit strategy.

The third and final reason for the international focus on statebuilding is that, as further detailed in the second-to-last section of this chapter, diplomats and the leadership of international organizations are most comfortable with a state-to-state approach.[115] They are trained to deal with state officials, and they see such interactions as the best way to respect the global norms of sovereignty and noninterference. It is therefore of utmost importance to these high-ranking interveners to ensure that they have counterparts with whom to interact.

The main problem with this strategy was that, in 2010 and 2011, the Congolese state was a predatory structure, on par with what it had been during most of Congo's history.[116] Governmental officials were often preoccupied with using public offices to accumulate personal wealth, even when doing so con-flicted with the pursuit of the public good.[117] State representatives, including

---

[110] Bliesemann de Guevara 2012, pp. 2–3.

[111] Murphy 1996, p. 91, cited in Paris in progress, p. 19.

[112] Paris in progress.

[113] A public source on this perception is International Crisis Group 2010.

[114] On the failed state label, see Titeca and De Herdt 2011. On the view of violence as criminality, see Autesserre 2010, pp. 72–74.

[115] Autesserre 2010, pp. 91–100.

[116] Trefon 2011. Also Hellmüller 2013, p. 224. On the Congolese state before the war: Reno 1998; and Young and Turner 1985.

[117] Transparency International 2010; and GRIP 2010, p. 6.

members of the army, the police, and the administration, were responsible for the largest part of all human rights violations.[118] Throughout eastern Congo, people wished that their state would eventually become a strong, functional, well-managed structure, working for their benefit. In the meantime, though, citizens often experienced it as an oppressive, exploitative, and threatening machine. Overall, large parts of the population survived in spite of the state rather than with its help.[119]

While policy-makers based in headquarters and national capitals often over-looked this problem, field-based interveners were painfully aware of it. There were thus nuances within the dominant narrative, notably different views of which components of the state structure interveners should prioritize reforming. On-the-ground interveners and Congolese activists requested a strengthening of the justice system in order to end impunity, and a reorganization of the armed forces in order to halt opportunistic violence. However, these advocacy efforts led to very few concrete results, as national and local authorities who benefited from the status quo met them with resistance. Worse, the dominant narrative insisted so strongly on statebuilding as the leading solution to violence that, despite their failure to promote accountability and respect for human rights, interveners preferred to implement any kind of state reconstruction project possible rather than no project at all. The international efforts thus focused on material reconstruction. Using funding from a number of bilateral and multi-lateral donors, UN agencies constructed roads and administrative buildings, and transported police and military forces to their new areas of deployment.

Unfortunately, extending the authority of a predatory state merely resulted in replacing one group of perpetrators (foreign and Congolese rebel groups) with another (state authorities and state security forces). Furthermore, it sometimes worsened living conditions for the population. For instance, Jeroen Adam and Koen Vlassenroot have masterfully demonstrated that the international efforts to reconstruct the taxation system became constitutive of the regime of preda-tion.[120] The aftermath of the 2010 mass rapes in Luvungi further illustrates how statebuilding initiatives merely replaced one form of violence with another. In response to the attack, the Congolese army deployed a battalion to ensure the safety of the population and to dismantle the bases of the armed groups respon-sible for the assault. This operation caused the displacement of hundreds of people and was marred by numerous human rights violations, including "rape, abduction and disappearance, perpetrated by [army] soldiers against civilians."[121]

---

[118] Public sources include, among others: International Crisis Group 2010, pp. 9–11; UN Human Rights Council 2011; UN Security Council 2010a; and the weekly reports of the UN Office for the Coordination of Humanitarian Affairs.

[119] A public source for this statement is an author's on-record interview with Onesphore Sematumba, Pole Institute, Goma, November 2010.

[120] Adam and Vlassenroot 2010.

[121] MONUSCO and UN Human Rights Office of the High Commissioner 2011, paras. 39–41 and 58.

Meanwhile, outraged by the news of the mass rapes, high-level diplomats and UN officials vowed to bring justice to the victims. The UN thus helped deploy Congolese justice officials to conduct the investigation, but the proceedings were so poorly organized that they resulted in perpetrators threatening victims with death to discourage their testimony.[122] To protect the victims, high-ranking interveners asked the peacekeeping mission to help station 100 Congolese police in Luvungi. Several field-based peacebuilders tried to stall the process, as they knew that these underpaid police would further perpetuate insecurity in the area in the long run, but they eventually complied under pressure, and the new deployment created another protection problem for an already victimized population.

Interestingly, nobody I met challenged the focus on statebuilding as the indispensable response to the ongoing conflict. There was no narrative emphasizing other modes of social organization beyond the state. Nobody mentioned the anarchist civilizations that James Scott studies: the societies that reject state-based organization and the woes associated with it, including conscription, taxes, famine, epidemics, servitude, and warfare.[123] Nobody pondered the pathways to state formation that Paul Staniland analyzes, and that have proved more peaceful than the "counterinsurgent Leviathan" and "government in a box" at the heart of current statebuilding templates.[124] Building on in-depth studies of conflict and post-conflict environments in Asia and elsewhere, Staniland demonstrates that "cutting deals with insurgents, propping up local power centers, and simply ignoring areas of resistance can all be more effective in forging stability" and reducing violence "than trying to bolster central state authority."[125]

This is not to say that stateless organization, indirect rule, informal governance, or wartime order would necessarily have minimized the costs of conflict more effectively than the dominant statist strategy.[126] Extensive research (beyond the scope of this book) would have been necessary to assess the benefits of each approach in the Congolese context. The important point here is that these alternatives did exist and could have inspired narratives countering the idea of statebuilding as the best and only solution to the Congolese conflict, but they did not. When I asked interveners why they persisted even when there was no evidence that the presence of state authorities would benefit the population and even when available data suggested that many state officials were likely to commit abuses, they answered that there was no alternative. Likewise, every Congolese person I talked to, from poor peasants to high-level policy-makers, presented the extension of state presence as an essential measure to end the

---

[122] A public source on these events is ibid., p. 5 and para. 45.
[123] Scott 2009.
[124] Staniland 2012, citations respectively from p. 244 and pp. 255–256.
[125] Ibid., citation from p. 244.
[126] On the first three options, see ibid., notably p. 256.

violence. Even if they did not trust the police and the army, even if they had been victims of abuses in the past, they still hoped that state reconstruction would eventually better their living circumstances.

Congo and Beyond. In sum, in 2010 and 2011, three related narratives dominated the discourse on Congo and eclipsed competing framings of the situation. These dominant narratives helped bring international attention to Congo. They challenged the view of the Congolese conflict as an intractable problem. They made it possible for international interveners to sidestep their data collection and analysis problems and to identify concrete actions to help improve the situation. These actions helped address some of the sources of violence, notably those linked to the exploitation of Congolese minerals. They also enabled agencies to raise the funds necessary to provide much-needed help to rape victims.

However, the focus on these narratives had a number of negative unintended consequences. It obscured most interveners' understandings of the multilayered problems of Congo, and it oriented the intervention toward a series of technical responses, hindering the search for a comprehensive solution. Even more disconcertingly, because of this narrow focus, international efforts exacerbated the very problems that they aimed to combat. The attempts to control the exploitation of resources enabled armed groups to strengthen their control over mines; the disproportionate attention to sexual violence raised the status of sexual abuse to an effective bargaining tool for combatants; and the state reconstruction programs boosted the capacity of an authoritarian regime to oppress its population.

It is not only the Congolese populations who have suffered from the unintended effects of simplistic narratives. The advocacy organizations that tried to raise awareness of the Darfur crisis painted a similarly distorted picture of the conflict there, which produced its own terrible consequences on the ground.[127] It involved oversimplification (presenting the conflict as an ethnic problem between "Africans" and "Arabs"), latching on to the preexisting frame of the Rwandan genocide, and advocating for quick and visible answers to the crisis. This advocacy strategy obscured many of the ongoing conflict dynamics, and it oriented most of the international efforts toward initiatives that failed to stem the violence and that also, at times, fueled it. The protection of noncombatants in the former Yugoslavia is another case in point.[128] The deeply ingrained idea that women and children are the most vulnerable populations led aid workers to evacuate them first from besieged areas. This operational decision had deadly consequences, as adult civilian men were in fact the most at risk of being killed during these wars. The Bosnian Serb Army and the Yugoslav National Army

---

[127] The example of Darfur is based on Hamilton 2011; and Mamdani 2009.

[128] The example of the former Yugoslavia is based on Carpenter 2003, which provides an article-length account of the problem I summarize in the next three sentences. On this topic, see also Jones 1994, pp. 121–126.

viewed all Bosnian Muslim and Bosnian Croat men as potential enemy combatants and thus massacred approximately 8,000 of them in the enclave of
Srebrenica alone.

The viral video Kony2012, which attracted considerable social media attention in early 2012, is another textbook example of advocacy organizations
relying on simplistic narratives to mobilize followers at the risk of hurting the
very people they intend to help.[129] This video was the cornerstone of a campaign
led by the NGO Invisible Children. It aimed at increasing the notoriety of
Ugandan rebel leader Joseph Kony in the United States alongside harnessing
support for the Ugandan army. It relied on a highly simplistic view of the conflict
in Uganda: A bad rebel leader was committing bodily harm against children.
It distorted many facts, for instance by suggesting that Kony was still in Uganda
(whereas, in reality, he was in a remote area of the Central African Republic) and
by depicting the Ugandan military as the "good" actor that international interveners should support (when the army, in fact, has a terrible human rights
record). It also disempowered local populations by portraying U.S. engagement
as the solution to the crisis. Furthermore, it diverted attention away from other
armed groups – such as various local militias as well as the Congolese and
Ugandan armies – that were perpetrating at least as widespread and serious
abuses of local inhabitants. To top it all off, the video advocated for action that
was highly problematic: Increasing support for the Ugandan army was more
likely to generate additional violence than it was to resolve the tensions.

Other dominant narratives that immediately come to mind when thinking
about specific conflicts include: drug trafficking in Afghanistan; amputations in
Sierra Leone; state collapse in Somalia; antagonisms between the "Christian
South" and the "Muslim North" in Nigeria; and blood diamonds in Angola,
Liberia, and Sierra Leone. Since they emphasized only part of the story, it is likely
that – just as in Congo, Darfur, Uganda, and the former Yugoslavia – these
narratives have obscured other causes and consequences of violence, shaped
interventions toward an exclusive focus on certain issues, and thus oriented the
international efforts toward counterproductive strategies.

A related problem in Peaceland, one that came up regularly in my interviews,
was the tendency of interveners to focus on issues that are "fashionable" on the
global scene.[130] Such "fads" include setting up power-sharing arrangements to
end civil wars, organizing elections and security sector reforms in post-conflict

[129] Video available at www.youtube.com/watch?v=Y4MnpzG5Sqc. The rest of this paragraph
draws on Bareebe, Titeca, et al. 2012; Taub 2012; Vlassenroot, Schomerus, et al. 2012; and
the post "Unpacking Kony2012" on the blog *My Heart's in Accra*, by Ethan Zuckerman
(available at www.ethanzuckerman.com/blog/2012/03/08/unpacking-kony-2012/). The first
and last sources make explicit the parallels with my analysis on Congo.
　　See Branch 2009 for a fascinating analysis of the narratives of intervention in Uganda before
Kony 2012 and their counterproductive effects.
[130] Also Anderson, Brown, et al. 2012, pp. 59–62; and CDA Collaborative Learning Projects
2008c, p. 4.

situations, and financing HIV-AIDS programs in peaceful areas.[131] All of these initiatives are certainly important, but, like dominant narratives, they privilege one focus at the expense of other equally necessary initiatives.[132] For instance, in Angola, Congo, Guatemala, Nicaragua, Rwanda, and El Salvador, among other countries, the international obsession with elections often displaced attention from other peacebuilding measures that would have addressed the roots of continued violence.[133] Resulting peacebuilding strategies therefore failed to address existing tensions. "Trendy" approaches to peacemaking can also worsen conditions on the ground, as power-sharing agreements illustrate perfectly. In theory, such agreements require elites to work together. In practice, however, many such collaborations are effective only in the short term and usually fail to produce widespread cooperation across society. Worse, elites regularly exploit existing antagonisms to buttress their claims to governmental positions, entrenching societal divisions.[134] The institutionalization of power-sharing agreements has also created an incentive structure that contributes to the reproduction of insurgent violence throughout Africa.[135]

In all of these cases, the dominant narratives brand the conflict in an instantly recognizable way. They evoke themes and frames that international peacebuilders can use to analyze the ongoing violence. From the interveners' point of view, the situation becomes a case of conflict minerals, state collapse, or ethnic war, which they can fix by using their general, technical knowledge of these issues and by drawing on their stock of best practices and lessons learned elsewhere. The dominant narratives thus enable thematic experts to take on situations that they would otherwise find too baffling to confront.

Top-Down Understanding, Top-Down Solutions

Another far-reaching consequence of insufficient local knowledge and data is the reinforcement of the interveners' tendency to approach peacebuilding in a top-down fashion, ignoring grassroots drivers of tensions.[136] (My previous book was entirely devoted to this topic, so this section will summarize the main ideas only briefly. Readers interested in the explanation, supporting evidence, and

---

[131] On power-sharing arrangements: Tull and Mehler 2005; and Roeder and Rothchild 2005. On the obsession with elections: Autesserre 2010, chapters 3 and 6; Coles 2007; Lyons 2002 and 2004; Ottaway 2002; Paris 2004; Snyder 2000; Stedman 1997, p. 50; Youngs 2004. On HIV/AIDS: Anderson 2008, p. 100; and Pisani 2008.

[132] See notably Autesserre 2010; Englebert and Tull 2008; Snyder 2000; and Tull and Mehler 2005.

[133] Paris 2004, chapters 4 to 7. On Congo: Autesserre 2010.

[134] Roeder and Rothchild 2005.

[135] Tull and Mehler 2005.

[136] For a practitioners' report that similarly identifies the interveners' lack of in-depth local knowledge as a reason for why they overlook local conflicts, see Bouvy and Lange 2012, notably pp. 6, 7, 31, and 49.

discussion of alternative analyses should look into my 2010 work, *The Trouble with the Congo.*[137])

Journalists, policy-makers, and even academics often portray war and post-war violence as resulting exclusively from top-down causes – an analytical take that regularly ignores critical bottom-up dynamics.[138] In Congo for instance, as my 2010 book has demonstrated at length, grassroots conflicts over land, decentralized power, and local economic and social issues fueled a large part of the violence that took place in the eastern provinces after the official end of the war.[139] However, interveners identified national and international tensions as the only causes of the continued fighting and massacres.[140] This top-down narrative was dominant whenever there were clear national and international dimensions to the ongoing fighting, most notably between 1994 and 2009 and again after 2011. (Since the macro-level sources of tensions were less obvious in 2010 and 2011, the top-down narrative became overshadowed by the three I analyzed in the previous section.)

Top-down narratives are common in contexts beyond the Congo as well. Despite evidence to the contrary, manipulation of the masses by ethnic entrepreneurs remains the dominant explanation for the 1994 Rwandan genocide, even though local antagonisms also provided a key motivations for the violence.[141] Along the same lines, media outlets and policy-makers often portray Muslim combatants in Afghanistan, Iraq, and other areas of the "global war on terror" as mere puppets of terrorist masterminds, like Al-Qaeda executives or other religious extremists, while they are, in fact, often part of small, unconnected networks of fighters who do not report to a higher authority.[142] Likewise, interveners in Timor-Leste understood the post-2006 violence to be a result of macro-level tensions between easterners and westerners, and between the police and the army, even though grassroots antagonisms have, in fact, caused more of the deadly violence.[143] Other scholars have similarly documented how international peacebuilders analyze violence in Afghanistan, Kenya, Sudan, and Uganda as top-down problems, thus overlooking crucial bottom-up dimensions.[144]

---

[137] Autesserre 2010. This section draws notably on chapter 6. For a critical evaluation of the book analysis, see the symposium on the book in African Security Review 2011.

[138] Kalyvas 2003 and 2006 (pp. 43–45). For additional details, see also Autesserre 2010, pp. 42–47.

[139] Autesserre 2010, chapter 4.

[140] Ibid., chapter 2.

[141] Examples of the dominant narrative include: Chrétien 1995; Des Forges 1999; and Prunier 1995. For an analysis of bottom-up dynamics, see Straus 2006.

[142] Hoffman 2008; Sageman 2008; Sageman and Hoffman 2008; and author's field research in Afghanistan, 2002.

[143] Scambary 2014; and author's on-record interview with Scambary.

[144] On Afghanistan: Coyne and Pellillo 2012; and Dennys and Zaman 2009. On Sudan: Sørbø 2010. On Kenya: Klopp and Kamungi 2007; and Klopp and Zuern 2007. On Uganda: Perrot 2010.

This way of understanding violence is often accompanied by a view of local tensions as unimportant and undeserving of international attention. In Chad, Congo, and Uganda for instance, interveners considered grassroots conflicts as private, criminal, and the consequence of the lack of state authority.[145] In addition, because the image of Congolese people as "inherently savage" has persisted since the Belgian colonizers constructed it a century ago, foreign actors often saw extensive local violence as a normal feature of life in a peaceful Congo – a perception that other scholars have noted exists both for Africa as a whole and for the former Yugoslavia.[146] All in all, foreign peacebuilders routinely perceive local conflict as a negligible cause of war hostility.[147]

This particular perspective reinforces the interveners' conception of their role as "naturally" focused on the macro levels. Diplomats and UN officials are trained to work on superstructures, such as national and international negotiations, and to seek out national-level counterparts. They are also socialized into focusing on predefined tasks and performance guidelines that do not consider local violence.[148] Accordingly, foreign peacebuilders usually adopt a state- or capital-centered approach, whether they are in Afghanistan, Burundi, Congo, Cyprus, Ethiopia and Eritrea, Liberia, Rwanda, Sierra Leone, Sudan, Somalia, or Timor-Leste.[149] There is only one overall exception: humanitarian aid workers – but these people do not address the causes of violence; instead they focus on its consequences.[150]

Ordinary citizens, civil society organizations, religious institutions and leaders, as well as select state and nonstate agencies have initiated extensive bottom-up peacebuilding projects in various places, such as Burundi, Northern Ireland, Somaliland, and South Africa.[151] These initiatives remain underfunded and underappreciated, but the few researchers who have evaluated them share one conclusion: "In order for peace agreements between warring parties to lead to durable peace, there needs to be, alongside top-down implementation of the

---

[145] On Congo: Autesserre 2010, pp. 68–74. On Chad: Debos 2008; and Vincent Hugeux, "Tchad. L'EUFOR a des faiblesses," *Le Vif / L'Express*, October 3, 2008. On Uganda: Perrot 2010.

[146] On Congo: Autesserre 2010, pp. 74–81; and Dunn 2003. On the former Yugoslavia: Woodward 1995 (pp. 19–20) and 1997 (pp. 19–20 and 30–31). On Africa as a whole: Shaw 2007.

[147] Kalyvas 2006, chapter 2 provides numerous illustrations, spanning continents and centuries.

[148] See Autesserre 2010, pp. 91–100 for an in-depth demonstration of this point.

[149] On Afghanistan: Coyne and Pellillo 2012; and Dennys and Zaman 2009. On Congo: Autesserre 2010, chapter 3. On Cyprus: Hadjipavlou and Kanol 2008. On Ethiopia and Eritrea: Terlinden and Debiel 2004. On Liberia: Alao, Mackinlay, et al. 1999; Bøås 2009; and Ellis 2002. On Rwanda: Jones 2001; and Paris 2004, chapter 4. On Sierra Leone: Johnston 2005. On Sudan: Berger 2009; Brewer 2008; International Crisis Group 2007; and Sørbø 2010. On Somalia: Adam 2004, p. 271; Duffey 2000, pp. 160–162; Elmi 2010, pp.141–142; Farah 2002, p. 3; and Menkhaus 1997, pp. 46–47. On Timor-Leste: author's on-record interview with Scambary. On Burundi and Cyprus: author's confidential interviews and field observations. Also Richmond 2011, pp. 5–6.

[150] Autesserre 2010, pp.116–120.

[151] For more details, and for bibliographic references, see ibid., pp. 248–252.

peace agreement, concurrent bottom-up processes aimed at constructing a new social contract and healing societal divisions."[152]

A handful of UN officials and diplomats have tried to advocate for their organizations to better address local issues.[153] Host populations and international NGOs that specialize in grassroots conflict resolution similarly often maintain that micro-level disputes do, indeed, fuel violence, and that the international role in a civil war situation should include support for bottom-up peacebuilding programs in addition to the ongoing initiatives at the national and international levels. However, these dissenting voices have thus far wielded little influence within their organizations or on the international scene. The strategies they advocate clash so fundamentally with existing cultural norms (notably the one concerning nonintervention in the domestic affairs of a sovereign state, which I discuss in my previous book) and so threaten key organizational interests that the contesters' colleagues regularly deride and marginalize them.[154]

The problem with macro-level understandings of conflict is that they overstate the importance of national, regional, and international tensions. These dynamics certainly fuel violence in most conflicts, but so do local antagonisms.[155] Thus, while top-down strategies are indeed crucial to building a sustainable peace, an exclusive focus on them is problematic. The detrimental consequences of such a narrow understanding of the sources of conflict are clear. They range from failing to stem ongoing violence (in Afghanistan, Congo, Somalia, Sudan, and Timor-Leste, for instance) to implementing reconciliation programs that win over the elite but do not change the attitudes of citizens living outside the capital city (in Cyprus).[156]

Ultimately, top-down understandings of violence are dominant narratives just like the others I have discussed – they produce both positive and negative consequences. Top-down analyses are a way for interveners who lack data on local dynamics, and who would otherwise feel overwhelmed by the complexity of a situation, to feel that they can get a grasp on the most important features of a conflict and design strategies to address them. Like the narratives analyzed in the previous section, top-down accounts emphasize certain reasons for violence and solutions to it and disregard others. They highlight national and regional

---

[152] Prendergast and Plumb 2002, p. 327. See also Anderson and Olson 2003; Lederach 1997; Leonard 2013; and all the case studies of the project Reflecting on Peace Practices (www.cdacollaborative.org/programs/reflecting-on-peace-practice/rpp-newsletter,-publications-and-services/).

[153] See Autesserre 2010, chapter 5 and p. 252 for an in-depth study of the process mentioned in this paragraph.

[154] Ibid., chapters 3 and 5.

[155] Ibid., chapters 2 and 4; Dennys and Zaman 2009; Fujii 2008; Kalyvas 2003 and 2006; Klopp and Kamungi 2007; Krämer 2006 and 2007; Straus 2006; and Sundh 2004.

[156] Public sources on Congo include: Autesserre 2010. On Somalia: Adam 2004, p. 270; Elmi 2010, pp. 21–22 and 141; and Menkhaus 1997, pp. 54–56. On Sudan: Sørbø 2010; also Berger 2009; and Brewer 2008. On Cyprus: Hadjipavlou and Kanol 2008. The rest of the examples are based on confidential interviews.

tensions instead of local ones and underscore statebuilding and international negotiations instead of grassroots conflict resolution. This diversion of attention itself is enough to jeopardize the effectiveness of interventions, but another factor exacerbates the harm: Top-down narratives reinforce two problematic dominant modes of operation I have already documented. First, they legitimize the understanding of "local ownership" as meaning ownership by the central government instead of by decentralized authorities and intended beneficiaries. Second, they fuel the interveners' tendency not to consult ordinary citizens and, instead, to interact mostly with the elite (as expatriates view elite as the key to peacebuilding and ordinary citizens as much less influential). This oversight prevents foreign peacebuilders from appreciating the importance of bottom-up tensions, reinforcing their view that top-down interventions alone are sufficient.

Misunderstandings

Interveners' superficial knowledge of their areas of deployment has one last main detrimental consequence: It regularly generates all kinds of misunderstandings that decrease the effectiveness of their efforts. Studies of humanitarian and development aid have widely documented how lack of expertise on local conditions often leads to inefficient, ineffective, wasteful, or even at times counterproductive relief projects.[157] This section develops a similar analysis on peacebuilding initiatives.

To begin with, the interveners' superficial knowledge of local contexts regularly leads them to misunderstand key dynamics of war and peace. Based on an in-depth ethnography of life and power in the Afghan village of Istalif, Noah Coburn masterfully shows that "many assumptions that have guided the international intervention" there – especially about "violence, stability, and state-building" – were fundamentally flawed.[158] In particular, interveners understood violence to be a "last resort" that occurs only "when other alternatives have failed." In fact, violence was "simply one of many political tools available to actors in certain settings." Consequently, when interveners chose strategies that provided political alternatives, like elections, they failed to address the main reasons why people might have been deciding to use force.[159] An interviewee who had deep roots in Congo, and who was working for the UN peacekeeping mission there, provided another representative example of such misunderstandings, about a small Congolese group that tried to achieve secession for the province of Katanga:

---

[157] Among others: Anderson, Brown, et al. 2012, pp. 25 and 36; CDA Collaborative Learning Projects 2008c (pp. 5–6) and 2011b (p. 11); De Waal 1997; Ferguson 1990; Pottier 2002; Scott 1998; and Uvin 1998.

[158] Coburn 2011, citation from p. 218.

[159] Ibid., citations from pp. 218–219.

These people know that they need an international audience. So, they bring a document [about their group to the UN mission], whose staff scan and e-mail their document to everybody. For me, when I receive the document, I see that it has been written with an old typewriter [...], so it is clear that these are people who have no means and no idea of how to communicate. On the list of leaders, [...] the people with decision-making power are perfect nobodies. I asked a friend, "Do you know so and so?" "Oh yes, he's [a distant relative], he is a joker." So we should not take this group seriously. But we do! We talk about it during senior management meetings, "There is a danger of secession in Katanga," while there is absolutely no reason to be worried.

As this interviewee concluded, not only did his colleagues give too much importance to an irrelevant militia, raising the profile of the group and providing them with an audience that they would never have obtained otherwise, but this focus also led them to overlook other local armed groups that posed a real danger to the stability of Katanga.

Moreover, in Afghanistan and Congo, expatriates regularly mistook formal power for real power.[160] The formal state structure, which mirrored those present in Western, Asian, or Latin American countries, in fact masked a different distribution of influence.[161] The person formally identified as responsible for a specific area – for example, the general in charge of reforming the army in Congo, or the district governor and the police in Afghanistan – might have little actual power, while someone without a formal position, such as an informal advisor to the president in Congo or informal leaders in Afghanistan, might actually be in control. Likewise, in Congo, although ministers formally directed their departments, the tradition of respecting one's chief dictated that they should not make a decision without first consulting the president. The dynamics were similar at the local level. In certain areas of the Kivus for instance, administrative authorities held formal command, while military leaders were often the primary decision-makers. There was even a power differential among administrative authorities because representatives of the state (like the administrator of the territory) had less clout than the customary chiefs. Consequently, expatriates in both Congo and Afghanistan routinely targeted the wrong person when they needed help from national and local leaders.[162] In Congo, many programs also failed to achieve their intended objectives because they tried to reform formal institutions but had no effect on the people who actually controlled the situation, or because they focused on formulating new legislation while the population would usually rather obey customary laws and a series of semi-formal rules.

---

[160] On formal and informal governance structures, see among many others: Bratton 2007; Englebert 2000; and Kassimir 2001. The Afghanistan example that I develop in the rest of this paragraph is based on Coburn 2011, chapters 6 and 7; the Congo example, on my own fieldwork.

[161] For more on the differing views of the concept of the "state" in Europe (or North America) and in other parts of the world, see Chabal and Daloz 1999 and 2011 (chapter 9); and Owen 2004.

[162] On Afghanistan: Coburn 2011, pp. 137–140 and 204.

Interveners in Timor-Leste made similar mistakes.[163] They failed to engage with the traditional power structure even though most of the population supported it. They also misidentified parties in conflict and consequently organized reconciliation workshops between friends, and they used traditional conflict-resolution mechanisms in a way that made no sense in the given situation.

Another issue in Congo was that interveners assumed that new state officials would carry on the work of their predecessors. They often did not realize that there had been no hand over between current administrators and their predecessors or that the former had not only left with all their archives but also failed ever to involve the rest of the administration in the project, in order to keep the perks to themselves. This created significant friction between high-level state officials, who would come to meetings without even knowing what topics they were expected to discuss, and their international counterparts, who complained that they had to start everything from scratch each time they had a new interlocutor – which happened frequently.[164]

Often, foreign peacebuilders also incorrectly interpret or fail to realize the symbolic dimension of their actions. I once observed an African peacekeeper, who had made the laudable effort to learn a local language, go around his area of operation shouting greetings in Kinyarwanda to every Congolese he met. Little did he know that, in a place where ethnic tensions between Kinyarwanda-speakers and other Congolese had caused tens of thousands of deaths in the past fifteen years, greeting people in the tongue of their archenemy was not a very good idea. A "well-known and distinguished" foreign peacebuilder encountered a similar challenge in Georgia.[165] He used an exercise based on the Prisoner's Dilemma to demonstrate the values of cooperation. (In this classic game, two prisoners accused of committing a crime together have to decide whether or not to confess, with an incentive structure that rewards cooperation but makes it very difficult to attain.) Unfortunately, this intervener did not realize how contentious the very subject of prison was in a country where many of the new political leaders had been incarcerated under the previous regime. Instead of promoting reconciliation, the "normally benign exercise" backfired, unleashing "hours of arguments" and unpleasant "clashes about history and justice."[166]

Yet another by-product of the interveners' poor understanding of local situations is that they regularly fail to appreciate the differences between their conceptions of peace, peacemaking, and peacebuilding and those of host populations. There is an extensive literature on how this blindness orients

---

[163] The Timor-Leste examples are based on on-record interviews conducted in Dili (Timor-Leste, February 2012) with two independent researchers: James Scambary from the Australian National University and Dr. Anna Powles from the University of New South Wales.

[164] A public source on this issue was an author's on-record interview with Dr. Arsene Mwaka Bwenge, professor at Kinshasa University, Kinshasa, June 2011.

[165] Glick and Reynolds Levy 2009, p. 44.

[166] Ibid., p. 44.

interventions toward unproductive approaches.[167] An illustrative example that recurred in my own fieldwork was that of interveners not only expecting local stakeholders to have the same understanding of security as they did but also assuming that the same needs called for the same social response. Foreign peacebuilders overlooked the fact that, while the presence of police and army forces usually provides increased security and order for Europeans and North Americans, it often incites fear among private Congolese and Sudanese citizens, given that police and army units are among the worst perpetrators of human rights violations in their countries.

Additionally, foreign peacebuilders often do not realize that ideas and concepts that are obvious to them might not be as clear to local populations. Sudanese officials explained to me that the concept of peacebuilding was "new" to them, and that "understanding of it by the communities require[d] time" – something to which their international counterparts were oblivious. A peacebuilder recalled his difficulties in implementing programs based on the idea of "community" in Georgia because the communist heritage there had rendered the very notion unfamiliar. A Cypriot interviewee mentioned a similar problem with the concepts of "bi-communality" and "federalism": These terms were buzzwords among international interveners and national elites working on the Cyprus problem throughout the 1990s and 2000s, but ordinary citizens rarely had a concrete sense of their meaning. An international intervener tasked with making the "Kosovo standards" (the criteria that Kosovo should meet in order to join the European Union, among other objectives) more popular on the ground encountered an unexpected challenge: Although Kosovars had strong opinions on what these standards symbolized, they had no idea what they implied in practice. The standards included respect for the "rule of law" and "free use of language," but nobody had bothered to explain to ordinary people what these concepts actually entailed or how they would affect everyone's daily lives.

Conclusion

A foreign peacebuilder I interviewed in Cyprus told me: "We are doing something we don't understand fully, and the best we can do is admit we don't understand it, and that we also don't have time to understand it." Sadly, this diagnosis applies broadly in Peaceland. Interveners start their missions minimally acquainted with their new area of deployment, and they have little opportunity to develop their understanding of local conditions once they are in

---

[167] Among others: Acharya 2009; Anderson, Brown, et al. 2012, pp. 24–25; Chopra and Hohe 2004; Duffey 2000; Englebert and Tull 2008; Fetherston and Nordstrom 1995; Heiberg 1990; Hohe 2002; Pouligny 2004, especially pp. 133–136; Rubinstein 2008, chapter 7; Salem 1997; and Winslow 1997. Mac Ginty 2008, pp. 147–149, also provides a very helpful review of the social anthropology literature on this topic.

the field. They stay for too short periods of time, their data collection techniques are deficient, and the politics of knowledge in Peaceland often hinders them from consulting local stakeholders programs. Moreover, grassroots partners feel sufficiently resentful and humiliated that, often, they hesitate to provide such input. As a result, expatriates rely on limited or incorrect information, and their analyses are often erroneous. They have an inadequate basis for affecting positive and sustainable transformations in their host country.

To overcome this problem, international peacebuilders regularly turn to two dominant modes of operation that are ineffective and, in the case of the first, may in fact fuel violence. To start, the obstacles to understanding encourage interveners to rely on dominant, simple narratives, which provide expatriates with the illusion of grasping the situations and suggest important issues on which to concentrate their efforts. The narrow focus on the issues that these narratives raise, however, routinely yields harmful, unintended consequences that may even run counter to the interveners' intended aims. In addition, poor comprehension of grassroots dynamics reinforces the peacebuilders' tendency to approach their work in a top-down fashion, thereby preventing them from addressing the numerous bottom-up sources of violence. Frequently, the lack of local knowledge also generates outright misunderstandings, which have their own detrimental impact on peacebuilding effectiveness. Altogether, the results of these two dominant modes of operation are as serious as they are pervasive. As the executive director of a Cypriot NGO explained forcefully: "The most dangerous thing is when you have somebody not informed and not knowledgeable who tries to intervene."

The second part of this book examines the everyday dynamics that make this situation possible. It explains how the interveners' daily professional, social, and personal routines, while perfectly understandable responses to the situation that international peacebuilders face, further hinder their acquisition of an in-depth understanding of local conditions and compound the separation between them and local counterparts. Part II also continues to unlock the puzzle of how so many expatriates can be intelligent, hardworking, caring people, and yet still find themselves following practices and implementing programs that so often miss the mark.

CONSTRUCTING AND MAINTAINING BOUNDARIES

The most enlightening Christmas party I ever attended occurred during my fieldwork in an unstable city in eastern Congo. The organizer, a civilian member of the peacekeeping mission, had gathered twenty of her closest friends on site: several military and civilian peacekeepers, a few officials from other United Nations agencies, several staff members of non-governmental organizations, and a diplomat. All in all, the guests were a perfect sample of the people I was studying. Permeating the gathering was a spirit that one of the participants captured: "Here we are all part of a club; we are all here to help Congo." The second part of my book is about this "club."

Noticing who was absent from the Christmas party was just as illuminating as studying the guests. Although the attendees came from all kinds of national, professional, racial, organizational, and religious backgrounds, they shared one characteristic: They were all expatriate interveners. No business expatriates had been invited, nor had any Congolese people, though they and their country were the subject of our conversations for most of the day. This particular marriage of diversity and exclusivity is common in Peaceland, and it engenders a specific pattern of interactions between members of the interveners' club and nonmembers. Accordingly, Part II of the book examines these relationships. I focus principally on how interveners interact (or do not interact) with the local populations and authorities who are their intended beneficiaries. I also study how these local people react to the efforts that some expatriates make to integrate locally.

In doing so, I identify the social and professional everyday practices that make possible not only the peculiar makeup of this Christmas party but also the politics of knowledge in Peaceland and its negative consequences for international interventions. I emphasize the intended and unintended effects of the interveners' daily personal, social, and professional routines on the ground. These practices have clear positive intended results: They enable interveners and their organizations to function in the difficult environments of conflict zones. However, they also have significant unintended consequences for the effectiveness of international efforts. They construct and maintain boundaries between expatriate interveners and other inhabitants of Peaceland, notably local stakeholders. These boundaries exacerbate the obstacles to data collection and analysis documented in Chapter 4, fuel the local resentment described in Chapter 3, and help justify the politics of knowledge studied in Chapter 2.

Chapter 5 studies the bottom-up, everyday processes that construct such boundaries. It presents the dynamics of integration and exclusion that shape the interveners' club. Chapters 6 and 7 then identify the top-down and bottom-up elements that perpetuate the boundaries and enable them to persist despite widespread recognition among interveners that the separation is counterproductive. These two chapters also illustrate how top-down instructions generate a number of daily habits and practices and how bottom-up processes reinforce the resulting dynamics.

My analysis emphasizes the personal and social dimensions of the interveners' behavior for good reasons. The specific conditions of most deployment areas blur the usual distinctions between one's work and social life. As a result, the professional and the personal are inextricably linked in Peaceland. Additionally, as many interveners know, their everyday personal and professional behaviors can, in and of themselves, promote peace or reinforce war.[1] Expatriates can "set out alternatives for acting, and 'model' peaceful ways of living and working," thus countering "the modes that characterize violent conflict."[2] Or they can do the exact opposite, feeding the mistrust, discrimination, dishonesty, and suspicion that fuel aggression.

---

[1] Anderson 1999, pp. 55–59; and Anderson and Olson 2003, chapter 4.
[2] Anderson and Olson 2003, p. 27.

5

The Interveners' Circle

During my formal conversations and in informal settings, certain phrases recurred that revealed how the inhabitants of Peaceland often perceived the interveners' identity. Foreign peacebuilders would start sentences with "we, the international community" or "we, the expatriates." They would refer to "the international system" or "the international machinery" and would mention their feeling of being part of a "huge family" that is here to help the country of intervention. The phrases that noninterveners – including local elites, business expatriates, or missionaries – used to refer to interveners were often less kind, such as "the humanoids" or "*les criseurs*" (those who come when there is a crisis, behave as though everything is an emergency, and act with reckless impatience to resolve a problem). Reflecting on her experiences in various conflict zones, including Juba (South Sudan) and Aceh (Indonesia), a peacebuilder working for a non-governmental organization (NGO) explained:

> It is personal and professional. When we talk about multiculturalism, there is a shared nod around the table: We are here as a bloc, as the international community; we operate as one. [. . . .] You just assume it. It is a given.

International interveners and local citizens have even created blogs that discuss – and mock – this community, such as *Stuff Expat Aid Workers Like* and *Stuff Malai Like* ("Malai" referring to expatriates deployed in Timor-Leste).[1]

This chapter demonstrates that interveners on the ground form a specific group – one that might be called a community of practice.[2] Four elements enable a group identity to develop in spite of internal differences and tensions: a shared

---

[1] Available at http://stuffexpataidworkerslike.com and http://stuffmalailike.wordpress.com/.
[2] When I use the word "community," I am building on the scholarly literature on communities of practice mentioned in Chapter 1. However, I also detail many features of this group that belie the positive connotations of the word community and make the terms "bloc" and "club" regularly more appropriate.

official goal (to help the host country and its people), a common experience of life in conflict zones, dense professional and social interactions, and the presence of an "Other" (host populations) against whom interveners can construct their identity.[3] This chapter analyzes the group's shared characteristics, its internal dividing lines, its relations with nonmembers, and the exceptions to its dominant trends. Throughout, I study not only the intended effects of the social dynamics I describe (to enable interveners and their organizations to function in conflict zones and to help the host country build peace), but also their unintended effects, particularly the construction of boundaries between international peacebuilders and local populations. The habitual patterns of cooperation and conflict among expatriates, and between them and local counterparts, are perfectly understandable responses to the situations that interveners face, but they have a significant and often detrimental impact on the potential effectiveness of international peace efforts. They make possible, perpetuate, and reinforce the politics of knowledge at work in Peaceland. They also have their own harmful by-products that further impede effective peacebuilding.

The Community

Interveners in conflict zones share a number of basic characteristics. They are foreigners who call themselves "expatriates." They are deployed by humanitarian, development, peacekeeping, or peacebuilding organizations in unstable countries for short periods of time – from a couple of months to three years, and on average a year or two. They often drive in big sport utility vehicles (SUVs) marked with the logos of their organizations and speak a language full of acronyms and technical terms that outsiders have difficulty understanding.[4] They have urban legends, inside jokes (such as calling Kenya's capital Nairobi "Nairobbery" and Save the Children "Save the Chicken") and favorite topics of discussion – notably the political and security situations in their area.[5] Even more importantly, as the rest of this chapter details, interveners have a social and professional life unto themselves, with its own cliques, romances, and disagreements.[6]

---

[3] This analysis partly draws on Tajfel 1974 and the social psychology literature that it has inspired.

[4] "The Jargon of Aid: Anyone here speak NGOish?" (*The Economist*, January 27, 2011, www. economist.com/node/18014068) has a humorous take on this issue.

[5] The project *Legends of Intervention* (available at www.legends-of-intervention.com/stories.php), by Berit Bliesemann de Guevara and Florian P. Kühn (Helmut Schmidt University Hamburg, Germany) presents an amusing collection of these urban legends.

   "Nairobbery" is a quote from the twelfth comment on the post "#12 – Establishing Field Cred" in the blog *Stuff Expat Aid Workers Like* (January 6, 2011, http://stuffexpataidworkerslike.com/2011/01/06/12-establishing-field-cred/).

[6] Fechter and Hindman 2011a; and Mosse 2011 (notably Harper's, Eyben's, and Rajak's chapters) present anthropological perspectives on this issue, and Cain, Postlewait, et al. 2004 a novelized version. On the romantic element, see also the site Humanitarian Dating (www.humanitariandating.com).

The introduction to Part I described the enormous variety in the personal, national, professional, and organizational backgrounds of international peacebuilders. This chapter addresses the elements that are particularly important in constructing a coherent interveners' group despite the diversity and internal tensions that nevertheless persist.[7]

A Shared Official Goal

The quote that I heard at the Christmas party ("Here we are all part of a club; we are all here to help Congo") illustrates that the sense of sharing a common official goal defines who belongs to the interveners' community. This narrative of interveners being "here to help" has clear, intended effects: It legitimizes and explains the expatriates' deployment in the host country. At the same time, it also has unintended effects on the ground. First, as I detail in this section, it delineates the boundaries of the "interveners' club." Second, as I explain in the next chapter, it participates in the construction of an image of the interveners as superior to local populations.

The statement that interveners had come "to help" the host country and its people pervaded the interviews I conducted for this project, from Afghanistan, to Congo, to Timor-Leste, whether with military peacekeepers or with civilian staff from United Nations (UN) agencies or NGOs. All my contacts viewed this justification for their presence as self-evident. Even certain diplomats – usually those in charge of political affairs, development, or peacebuilding – maintained that they were trying to help the host state in addition to protecting the interests of their home country and its citizens.

Admittedly, there were numerous differences in the way intervention groups sought to reach this goal. Each institution, and each subunit within an institution, defined "helping" in a different way. Helping might mean supporting the government (for the UN) or remaining as independent of the authorities as possible (for most NGOs), organizing high-level international conferences (for diplomatic and UN leadership) or implementing grassroots reconciliation projects (for agencies like Search for Common Ground and UN Habitat). Furthermore, most individuals also have personal motivations for choosing to work as peacebuilders. Some people go into it primarily to earn money, others to boost their careers, and a few for purely altruistic reasons; a portion seeks adventure or finds the job intellectually stimulating, while a number enjoy the prestige of being a "UN peacekeeper" or a "humanitarian aid worker." Many more are motivated by a combination of these factors.[8] As a result, not all peacebuilders are equally dedicated to their official tasks.

---

[7] See also Anderson 1999, pp. 62–63 for a fascinating analysis of some of the dynamics described in this section.

[8] For a fascinating study of altruism in relation to passions, power, privilege, and ideology among NGO aid workers, see de Jong 2011. For concurring analyses, see Fechter and Hindman 2011b, pp. 7 and

Despite these differences in personal motivations or dedication to the official mission, the fact that the "interveners' club" does not include all of the foreigners living in a specific country underlines the importance of the shared goal in constituting the boundaries of the group. Foreign businesspeople, for instance, are excluded. From the interveners' point of view, business executives just want to make money, regardless of whether their actions hurt the host populations.[9] As a result, businesspeople do not get to participate in any of the meetings mentioned below, do not benefit from any of the privileges granted to the in-group (such as the use of UN flights and the sharing of security information), and are rarely invited to the interveners' private parties. International peace-builders refrain from interacting with them and rarely view them as peers. Likewise, as was clear during my interviews, expatriates working in business usually felt the same distaste for interveners. In fact, I often noticed a striking similarity between their attitude and that of local populations toward foreign peacebuilders.

A Common Experience of Life in Conflict Zones

While the shared official goal of helping the host country delineates the boundaries of the interveners' club, the most important element promoting cohesion on the ground is the personal experience of living and working in a conflict zone.

It is a lonely thing to arrive in a new location as an intervener. At the start of every new position, a foreign peacebuilder moves to a country where he or she most likely has no friends, no family, and no contacts beyond his or her colleagues. Engaging with the communities that he or she wishes to help is tricky, for reasons detailed later in this chapter. The fact that most interveners are away from home for a long time compounds the sense of isolation. They do not enjoy a proper family life while in the field since, for security or logistical reasons, they are usually obliged to leave their loved ones behind in their home countries. They often feel, with good reason, that their friends or family at home cannot relate to what they experience on a daily basis: the constant fear and adrenaline rush inherent to working in dangerous settings, the regular lack of basic facilities (including hot water, reliable electricity, food that they are used to, and comfortable housing), and the emotional toll of working with perpetrators or victims of violence.[10]

The experience of an NGO worker, not yet 30 years old, illustrates well the enormous pressure that interveners face. As he confided in me one day, "This is

---

14; and Roth 2011, p. 162. For an example focused on United States diplomats in Afghanistan, see Chandrasekaran 2012; and for a fictionalized account see Cain, Postlewait, et al. 2004.

[9] For more information on this topic, see Mitchell 2011's (p. 22) study of the differences and lack of relationships between interveners and economic migrants in Cyprus.

[10] Roth 2011, p. 159; and Verma 2011, p. 77 develop a similar analysis. Connorton, Perry, et al. 2011 present a useful review of the existing research on the traumatic dimensions of aid work.

the first time that I have a job where I am making a series of decisions that are so important that, if I make a mistake, people may die, including members of my team." Even in relatively peaceful intervention settings such as in Cyprus, the political stakes of the job are so high that the personal strain is enormous. One of my contacts there described these constant feelings of precariousness and danger as being "like I am standing on top of a very narrow roof, and I am balancing millions of different lightning bolts, each of them can kill me and each of them is needed."

Since international interveners face common challenges and need outlets, they often turn to other expatriates for support. A UN official based in Goma perfectly captured what I heard, experienced, and observed in all of my field sites:

> In war situations, you are in it together, in a country that you do not know, where people speak other languages that you do not understand. We interact [with local people] all day long, but there are times when you want to eat your own food, listen to your own music, speak your own language. You and I have millions of things in common. You and the Congolese, you have two or three things in common apart from work. This is why expats go together, [because] the expats in any country need to have a place where they can go and sit down, just so that they are in their own world. [...] It is the only thing that helps them work in a country that is not their own. [...] I find that it is necessary to keep you sane and anchored.

As many contacts reported, and as I discovered personally, this common experience creates tight bonds among group members. The relationships are particularly intense in dangerous settings, where expatriates are usually fewer in number, more scared, and more isolated. In the words of a fellow researcher who is also, at times, part of the peacebuilders' world, life as an intervener is like "dancing on a volcano." Expatriates "are in a special situation, where everything goes very quickly." This whirlwind of stressful work, difficult living conditions, and much-needed revelry often results in a "work hard, play hard" mentality.[11] It also produces a significant and immediate sense of solidarity with other members of the community: In my experience, recognition as an insider was usually sufficient to gain invitations to meetings, parties, and dinners, or to be given confidential information and documents.

Tellingly, the seasoned expatriates whom I interviewed frequently used the term "family" to denote other interveners in the field – the people they understood and who could understand them. In contrast, the demands of the job are so high, and the field experiences so intense, that a number of interveners become estranged from their loved ones at home. Combined with the community's inherent position of power relative to local populations (see Chapter 6), these dynamics render life as an intervener intoxicating and difficult to leave. The vocabulary that expatriates use reflects this sense of addiction: Contacts

---

[11] Author's interview with Christiane Kayser, Institut Pole and Service Civil pour la Paix de Pain pour le Monde, Goma, July 2011.

self-identified as "humanitarian junkies" and recalled having "been bitten by the bug." Individuals who have completed several missions often encounter significant trouble readjusting to "normal" life, whether at home or in non-conflict zones. Those who do resume normal life continually complain that they miss the field, and a number of them report feeling like misfits for the first several months or years of their new lives. Difficulty proving the value of their work experience in foreign conflict zones to potential employers at home presents yet another challenge. Eventually, a number of former expatriates fail in reentry. After a few months or years, they take on another field posting, ultimately spending their entire careers going from one mission to another. Then, as their links to home become increasingly distended, their emotional ties to the broader interveners' group grow stronger.

According to my interviews, field observations, and personal experiences, five additional characteristics of life as an intervener further reinforce the feeling of being part of a specific group. First, even before their arrival in the field, certain interveners start to develop the sense of belonging, and to learn the habits, practices, and narratives of their new community. The training that future expatriates receive when they attend a graduate program in aid or conflict studies (such as those at Bioforce in France or Columbia University's School of International and Public Affairs in the United States) or a predeparture course (which a few agencies offer) fosters these processes in two ways. Preparation programs instill in students a belief in their uniqueness as members of a community of compassionate people who have sacrificed wealth to "save the world." Predeparture courses also introduce newcomers to the rules they will have to follow on the ground. In doing so, they create a distinction between interveners and local populations by teaching the former to respect a certain ethos and set of restrictions concerning how they interact with the latter. Upon arrival in the field, the sense of community persists because many expatriates underwent the same graduate or predeparture training, or knew of others who did.

Second, due to the lack of infrastructure and security in most conflict and post-conflict zones, expatriates usually have to live and work in walled and gated compounds that provide the amenities necessary for them to operate efficiently – including reliable communication systems, power generators, safe settings, and hygienic conditions that reduce exposure to local pathogens. Living in these enclosed spaces both facilitates the creation of relationships among interveners and hinders connection with local people. It also creates a spatial separation from the surrounding environment.[12] Third, when seasoned expatriates arrive in a new country, they often meet friends or acquaintances from previous missions, which strengthens the feeling of community. Fourth, a number of interveners regularly move from one employer to the next, which diminishes their loyalty to any one specific organization. This bolsters the impression that all agencies

---

[12] For more on these issues, see the fascinating analysis in Duffield 2010; and Smirl 2008, pp. 241–242. On the safety aspect, see also Chapter 7 in this book.

belong to a broader intervention circle, which helps interveners overcome the overwhelming sense of isolation inherent to starting a job in a new place and encourages the expatriates' tendency to turn to one another for support. Fifth and finally, the extent and frequency of interactions among interveners during their field deployments creates a definite, if loosely-bound and tension-ridden, community.

Professional and Social Interactions

In theory, a community of practice can exist without any personal interaction among its members.[13] This insight helps us understand how military observers deployed in a remote village, where they are the only expatriates, can nevertheless belong to the broader community of international peacebuilders. Most of the time, however, sustained professional and personal interactions take place among interveners from different countries, organizations, and professions, who are based in the same conflict zone. These interactions help not only disseminate and perpetuate shared practices, habits, and narratives, but also strengthen the boundaries between expatriates and local people.

Instances in which interveners with different backgrounds come together for work are as numerous as they are diverse. First among these are security and coordination meetings (as well as cluster meetings) organized by the lead UN agency – usually the UN Development Program or the UN Office for the Coordination of Humanitarian Affairs (OCHA). These assemblies take place in most deployment areas, be they large capital cities or small and remote field locations. All throughout the world, these meetings gather a similar group of participants (representatives of the main NGOs, donors, and UN agencies) and follow the same pattern. For instance, OCHA coordination meetings will include: first, a review of the security situation; then, an overview of humanitarian and development problems, followed by presentations on various issues, and finally, miscellaneous questions and answers. As I observed and experienced, the social opportunities these gatherings present are, in many cases, at least as important as the professional value they offer. They are ideal places to network, gossip, flirt, catch up with friends, or remind a donor that a funding application is pending.

Additional professional events include: briefings by peacekeeping missions, convoys for trips to unsecure places, and ad hoc reunions among interveners working on the same challenge, such as training the local police to respond to sexual violence in Congo or ensuring that elections proceed smoothly in Timor-Leste. Overall, the number of professional gatherings organized in national or provincial capitals is sometimes so enormous that, as an intervener based in Goma (Congo) jokingly put it, one could spend one's "entire time going from meeting to meeting."

[13] Adler 2005, p. 25; Pouliot and Adler 2011b (p. 24) and 2011a (p. 30).

In addition to these formal gatherings, in most conflict zones, interveners also have their own logistical systems to compensate for the poor quality of local infrastructure – or the lack thereof. For instance, they can use their own air transportation – usually inaccessible to noninterveners – with planes from UN organizations, like the World Food Program or the local peacekeeping mission; from other international agencies, like the International Committee of the Red Cross (ICRC); or from air companies specializing in humanitarian flights, like AirServ. They often rely on their own security monitoring structures, with phone trees to use in case of emergencies and daily radio checks. They circulate news of common interests to their own e-mail lists, like Goma-update or Juba-licious.

Interveners enjoy opportunities for more than just professional relationships. After-hours social events abound in many theaters of intervention. Although expatriates from the same organization, country, or language group tend to form "bubbles within bubbles" (see the next section), these social opportunities nevertheless facilitate interaction with the larger peacebuilding community in the area. Interveners from various nationalities and organizations patronize the same handful of upscale bars and restaurants, work out at the same gyms, attend the same private parties, and often share houses or compounds. Many hotspots feature weekly social gatherings where NGO staff members, UN actors, and diplomats mingle. In Juba (South Sudan) in 2011, for instance, the ICRC head-quarters was the place to be every Wednesday for evening drinks. On Saturdays, it was the main compound of the UN peacekeeping mission for the weekly dance party. In 2002 in Kabul (Afghanistan), the social event of the week centered around drinks at the World Food Program compound on Thursday evenings.[14] While these gatherings are usually private and hidden from the eyes of local people, some are quite public. For instance, inhabitants of cities that host large UN missions, from Kathmandu (Nepal) to Juba, can regularly witness a "hash": "Somebody in the international community sets up a run," and on the appointed day and time "a group of international joggers runs through the town" and then goes out for drinks.[15]

Of course, this kind of socialization is not absolutely universal. In the first place, not all theaters of intervention offer the same extensive opportunities for it. Some locations see little in the way of after-hours events: For example, the expatriate community stationed in Kisangani (Congo) in 2010 organized few parties. Others, however, boast an array of revelries: Pristina (Kosovo) in late 2000 often reminded me of life in an American college town. Furthermore, even in places where social

---

[14] For a publicly available source on these social events in 2010, see "Exotic Birds in a Cage: Criticism Grows of Afghanistan's Bloated NGO Industry," by Walter Mayr; *Spiegel Online*, October 20, 2010, www.spiegel.de/international/world/0,1518,718656-3,00.html.

[15] The "Hash House Harrier's Guidebook, Juba South Sudan – 2011 (Some Edition)" (unpublished document, on file with author) has an extensive presentation of the principles, spirits, and guidelines for these events. See also, for a public source, the blog post "#153 – The Hash Run," on the blog *Stuff Expat Aid Workers Like* (June 4, 2012, http://stuffexpataidworkerslike.com/2012/06/04/153-the-hash-run/).

gatherings abound, a number of expatriates purposely avoid these gatherings, as they prefer to try to integrate into local social structures.

When they do occur, the social events significantly influence the formal dimensions of the intervention for two reasons. First, social events provide forums for interveners to exchange information and analyses, brainstorm difficult decisions, and extend offers for collaboration, all of which help create and reinforce shared modes of thinking and acting. Second, what foreign peacebuilders do after work substantially affects local perceptions of their professional activities because host populations can easily identify who is a member of the interveners' club. When foreign peacebuilders engage in behavior that local people view as illegal, morally wrong, or socially inappropriate, they fuel local resentment and strengthen the barrier between themselves and their counterparts in the host populations. Conversely, when they respect local ways of life and spend some of their time after hours trying to integrate in neighboring communities, they make the boundaries more porous and help alleviate local frustration.

Overall, the formal and informal gatherings are not necessarily sufficient to coordinate and cohere various peacebuilding strategies, but they do offer interveners multiple settings in which to form, share, and disseminate common practices, habits, and narratives. They also foster a sense of community. As a result, after living for a couple of months in a field location, interveners often have the feeling that they know "everybody" there – however, they mean everybody who counts in the expatriate group.

Internal Tensions

The strong sense of an expatriate community coexists with deep-seated internal divides. This is far from specific to the interveners' club. As explained in Chapter 1, the presence of a community of practice is perfectly compatible with the existence of internal divisions. By the same token, the existence of internal tensions and variations within a group does not preclude members of that group from sharing a series of everyday modes of operation.

In Peaceland, the competition, rivalry, and even hatred between factions of the interveners' club are so powerful that they came up in my interviews more readily than any particular similarities did. During our conversations, interveners often referred in passing to "the international community" or "the expatriates," acknowledging the existence of a broad group. However, as soon as I delved deeper into the similarities and differences, most of my contacts focused on the latter, talking as if the commonalities to which they had alluded beforehand did not exist. What most likely accounts for this pattern is the fact that their similarities are largely based on practices and habits, which interveners take almost completely for granted. They do not even think about mentioning them – just as humans rarely consider it relevant to bring up the influence of the air we breathe.[16]

---

[16] This analogy builds on Pouliot 2010, p. 51.

This section documents the sources and consequences of the divisions within the intervention community.[17] As existing research indicates, the primary fractures run along national, regional, professional, and organizational lines – and most strikingly separate civil from military actors. On the whole, their negative impact on peacebuilding effectiveness is threefold. These internal rifts prevent the cooperation and coordination necessary to achieve coherent strategies. They hinder information sharing and increase the obstacles to data collection and analysis that interveners face. They also reinforce the broader trend of constructing and maintaining boundaries between foreign peacebuilders and local populations.

In all of my field sites, the divide between civilian and military actors, each of which has a unique culture, was the most visible of these fractures and had the greatest impact on the intervention's effectiveness.[18] Virtually all of my military contacts mentioned this separation, as did a significant number of civilian interviewees. Civilians lamented the unwillingness of their military counterparts to collaborate. They emphasized military reluctance to share security information, provide escorts to dangerous places where peacebuilding work was needed, or proactively protect populations, all of which regularly impeded their daily work. Soldiers and officers, for their part, complained of prejudicial behavior – such as social stigma, lower salaries and benefits, stricter security regulations, and disregard of military expertise and input during mission planning – noting that such discrimination from their civilian counterparts disincentivized putting any extra effort into their work. These grievances fueled the tensions between the two groups while strengthening the sense of community among military interveners from different countries.

In many conflict zones, differences in socioeconomic status widened the split between the civilians and the military. For states, deploying soldiers to peacekeeping missions garners a variety of material and symbolic benefits: financial compensation, training and equipment of domestic forces, and international recognition as key contributors to multilateral endeavors.[19] The vast majority of UN contingents are from the countries that stand the most to gain from these exchanges, namely developing ones.[20] The rank and file are often poor and uneducated, which makes them easy scapegoats for other expatriate peacebuilders. In informal settings in North Kivu, for instance, a default topic of conversation among interveners was making fun of the Indian contingent of the UN peacekeeping mission for their lack of proactive attempts to protect the

---

[17] See the section "similarities and differences" in Chapter 1 for a presentation and discussion of the extensive literature on this topic.

[18] On the divide, the unique culture of each group, and how it influences peace interventions: Duffey 2000; Rubinstein 2008, chapter 7; Slim 1996; and Winslow 2002.

[19] Bove and Elia 2011; Daniel 2008; and Sotomayor Velázquez 2010.

[20] For official statistics, see the monthly factsheets of Military and Police Contributions to Peacekeeping Operations on the official UN Web site (www.un.org/en/peacekeeping/resources/statistics/contributors.shtml).

Congolese population, poor fighting skills, dated equipment, linguistic insuffi-
ciencies, feeble understanding of the situation on the ground, and so on. Serbian
and Bangladeshi peacekeepers in South Sudan faced similar derision. This
ridicule often provides a means of bonding for expatriates who otherwise barely
know each other. It thus reinforces their own sense of belonging to a cohesive
group.

Internal splits also exist within military and civilian groups; nationality is the
clearest line of fracture among military actors. The structure of peacekeeping
missions usually hinders sustained interactions between national contingents.
National units or battalions arrive preformed and have their own commanders.
Furthermore, they are often deployed to remote areas, which afford little to no
opportunity to mingle with other expatriates. As a result, in my field sites,
soldiers and officers worked and socialized only with the members of their
own army, except for the leaders at the very top of the hierarchy. However,
they gladly looked past their national boundaries whenever they had the
opportunity – for instance, because they were organizing a large social gathering
or seeking help with their work. In both cases, they reached out first to other
soldiers (contingents from a neighboring base, or military observers) and otherwise to civilian expatriates, especially those who spoke their mother tongue.

It was different for the civilian interveners: National rivalries, although very
influential in headquarters and national capitals, seemed mostly subdued in the
field. Admittedly, conflict zones are rife with conspiracy theories about particular organizations or individuals spying for or secretly promoting the interests of
their home countries. However, only a very small minority of peacebuilders
whom I met on the ground actually seemed deliberately to be advancing their
national agendas. The overwhelming majority were instead trying to fulfill their
professional and organizational mandates to help the host countries, regardless
of whether those orders promoted or clashed with their countries' interests. It is
true that people from the same country flocked together now and then, but,
overall, civilians were split mostly along organizational, professional, regional,
and linguistic lines.

When socializing, interveners gravitated toward colleagues within their own
organizations, and professional groups – such as foreign diplomats, international NGOs, and UN actors – tended to mingle with each other. Within each
group, the most prominent divide manifested itself between those whom interviewees termed "Western" and "non-Western" (Western referred to people
from Europe, North America, and Australia). People's mother tongues also
routinely determined their social circles after working hours. However, these
various divides were present only where there was a large enough group of
interveners. In remote locations, where only a handful of civilian expatriates
were on site, they tended to socialize with each other regardless of their organizational, linguistic, professional, or geographic backgrounds. Significantly, none
of these social circles routinely included local counterparts, which further
strengthened the boundaries between interveners and host populations.

When at work, other dividing lines proved more important for civilian interveners. In professional settings, vocational differences pitted development, humanitarian, peacebuilding, and peacekeeping actors against each other. The divide between UN agencies on the one hand and international NGOs on the other was similarly clear.[21] Within each of these camps, distinct organizational cultures oriented the work of each agency, unit, and subunit. These dividing lines influenced whom interveners chose to invite when organizing convoys or exclusive meetings in which they shared and analyzed sensitive information. For instance, in addition to the above-mentioned coordination meetings, which included all types of interveners, NGOs would also hold private safety briefings, and UN agencies were similarly exclusive when discussing security. This practice decreased the quantity of information and analysis available to each individual actor, thus hindering efforts to understand local contexts (see Chapter 4).

On top of these divisions, all UN agencies and NGOs, as well as some less wealthy donor countries (such as South Africa), competed with one another to obtain a share of the limited pool of funding available for aid projects. This competition often led to strong personal and professional antagonisms. It added to less salient tensions, including those between large and small agencies, religious and secular organizations, and NGOs close to donor governments and those that strove to remain independent.

This rivalry fuels the host populations' "sense that 'someone else is in control,'" with all the negative consequences that this perception entails.[22] Based on extensive field research in conflict zones around the world, the teams of the Listening Project found that competition "for funding or publicity reasons" indeed requires interveners to position themselves as "more successful than other agencies," and thus to "claim ownership of the activities" funded or implemented "rather than ensuring that people own them."[23]

Worse, all of these antagonisms regularly preclude cooperation among actors who would otherwise be natural partners. For example, in Goma (Congo), the NGO Search for Common Ground and the section of the UN peacekeeping mission tasked with the demobilization, disarmament, repatriation, resettlement and reintegration of combatants were located in adjacent compounds. They worked on similar issues (such as informing rebel soldiers of opportunities to demobilize), with similar methods (including radio programs). However, they operated in two such different communities (NGOs and the UN) that they never exchanged ideas and information or coordinated their efforts. They initiated collaboration only years after they started their programs, when a common donor organized a dinner at which the heads of both organizations finally met.

---

[21] Pouligny 2004, pp. 173–184 provides a fascinating account of such everyday divisions within peace operations.

[22] Anderson, Brown, et al. 2012, p. 21.

[23] Ibid., p. 21.

All of these cultures and subcultures, and their accompanying tensions and antagonisms, also regularly prevent cooperation to achieve coherent strategies and thus decrease the effectiveness of international efforts. The training of the Congolese national army in 2010 and 2011 epitomizes this phenomenon. Various foreign armies, from Belgium, China, France, South Africa, and the United States, participated in this initiative. They never coordinated to devise a unified program for the training, nor did the Congolese government try to promote any comprehensive guidelines. Consequently, each foreign army used its own standards, models, and culture to train the Congolese forces under its particular command. The result was a patchwork force comprised of units that had different drills, disciplinary rules, and routines and even issued orders in different languages. Military experts often communicated doubts as to whether such an incoherent army could ever function as a whole. These problems are not limited to the intervention in Congo; I heard the same criticisms levied against the UN approach to police reform in Timor-Leste.

Of course, individuals navigate these divisions in various ways. Often, they strategically emphasize various facets of their identities, switching according to the situation.[24] For instance, a friend of mine would stress her West African origin when socializing with other Africans or when reporting the views of African expatriates, but she would highlight her French nationality whenever she needed to interact with "Western" interveners. Likewise, she drew on her UN affiliation when negotiating with other UN agencies and poked fun at the peacekeeping contingents when she needed to find common ground with NGOs.

Even more importantly, these internal dividing lines do not preclude the existence of broader underlying commonalities or, in many cases, a feeling of belonging to a unified group. Lisa Smirl noted as much in her study of international intervention in Aceh (Indonesia), and the following comments are typical of what I heard during my own interviews.[25] In the words of an American NGO peacebuilder based in South Sudan:

> There is a lot of divisiveness and organizational intrigue, and there is a contradiction of approaches between donors [... based on national interests], but even then there is still a sense that [we are all working toward] a peaceful and developed Southern Sudan.

One of her African colleagues working for the UN in Congo concurred:

> At the end of the day, we come to help the population, we are all expatriates, and a priori there are more similarities between African and Western expatriates than between them and local people. Because we are expatriates, there is a common mentality, even if there are no relationships [...] and even if each of us live in our own spheres.

[24] On the use of competing identities, see Sen 2006, notably pp. 29–32. For detailed examples, see Cook-Huffman 2000; and Posner 2005.
[25] Smirl 2008, p. 244.

His remarks encapsulated my findings: The sense of belonging often persists despite clear internal divisions because interveners share a common goal, a common experience of life in conflict zones, and, as the following section further details, a perception of themselves as markedly different from local people.

Separation from the Other

A key element in the formation of the boundaries around the interveners' club is the presence of an Other against whom interveners construct their group identity.[26] For interveners, local people are the primary Other. Various expatriate interviewees presented the situation quite starkly: "It is an 'us versus them' issue." Others voiced a much more measured viewpoint, but still emphasized the importance of local populations and authorities in the constitution of the interveners' club. This is not to say that foreign peacebuilders perceive host populations as a threat or a common enemy. As social categorization theory illuminates, intergroup differentiation does not necessarily rely on such perceptions, "previous hostility," nor "an 'objective' current conflict of interests."[27] Instead, the basic human need for "order, meaning and social identity" drives processes of social comparison.[28]

Two Different Worlds

An image I vividly remember from a friend's farewell party in Congo illustrates the split between interveners and local populations. This friend, an expatriate member of a UN agency, had invited about fifty people: all of the local staff of his organization as well as a few expatriates – people from his agency and a couple of NGO staff. There were seven tables under the thatched roof of the restaurant where the gathering took place. While Congolese guests occupied the first six, the expatriates all sat around the last table at the back of the room. Over the course of the evening, the two groups never mixed. A year later, while visiting another friend working for the UN peacekeeping mission in Timor-Leste, I observed a similar divide. The UN compound in Dili had two cafes: one that the Timorese staff frequented, and another that the expatriate employees used.

These experiences brought to mind a prior interview with a Sudanese contact working for a grassroots NGO. When I asked about the kinds of relationships international interveners have with Sudanese people, his response captured this very problem: "Actually I don't see any relationship. Although there is... I can't

---

[26] On the importance of "the Other" for identity construction, see, among many others: Foucault 1976; Lacan 1966; Lévinas 1974; and Said 1978. On interveners and the local Other, see Kapoor 2004.

[27] Tajfel 1974, pp. 66–67, 72, and 86; citation from pp. 67 and 72.

[28] Ibid., p. 75.

call it a relationship, but I can call it knowledge about the existence of the other."[29] A Congolese intellectual concurred, as did the local head of an Indonesian NGO: Interveners and local stakeholders live in "two different worlds."[30]

There are multiple sources of this separation. The classic phenomenon of "us versus them," which is often present where there is a minority, is particularly relevant to interveners, as they constitute a minority everywhere they are deployed.[31] Furthermore, interveners are usually much wealthier than local people, in part because they receive disproportionately larger salaries. Ishbel McWha estimates that they usually earn "10, 20, sometimes even 100 times the local salary."[32] This often produces considerable frustration among host populations, who believe this disparity is rarely justified.[33] This inequality also generates economic barriers between expatriates and local counterparts, distorts the local economy, and creates a separate economic market for interveners.[34] Interveners can afford to go to bars, hotels, and restaurants that are far beyond the means of ordinary local people. In places like Goma and Juba for instance, a dinner in one of the interveners' favorite restaurants costs approximately one month's salary for a local schoolteacher. Moreover, as they are comparatively wealthy, interveners can afford to live in the richest (and safest) neighborhoods of the cities in which they are based. They also have cars provided by their organizations, so they do not have to walk to work as many local people do.

Language issues create additional barriers from local populations and bolster the interveners' tendency to congregate together. Peacebuilders deployed in conflict zones usually speak, at most, one of the official languages of the country, but they very rarely know the local dialects (see Chapter 2). As a result, interveners may be able to communicate with the educated elite, but their interactions with the rest of the population remain limited.

The interveners' strict security procedures reinforce the segregation (see Chapter 7). This effect is particularly strong in cities like Nairobi (Kenya), Juba (Sudan), and Baghdad (Iraq), where, for security reasons, many interveners – notably diplomatic and UN staff – have to live in enormous secured compounds that host no local people. Reflecting on this experience, two interviewees deployed in South Sudan emphasized how it separated them

---

[29] Author's on-record interview with John Lwong, Fashoda Youth Forum, Malakal, April 2011.

[30] Smirl 2008, p. 236; and author's on-record interview with Jean-Pierre Lindiro Kabirigi, Pole Institute, Goma, July 2011.

[31] There is an enormous literature on this topic, but a particularly illuminating approach is the "blue eyes/brown eyes" lesson that schoolteacher Jane Eliott taught to her third grade class in 1968 (see the documentary *A Class Divided* at www.pbs.org/wgbh/pages/frontline/shows/divided/etc/view.html).

[32] McWha 2011, p. 30.

[33] Also Anderson, Brown, et al. 2012, p. 31; and CDA Collaborative Learning Projects 2010b, pp. 5–6.

[34] On the barriers: McWha 2011, p. 31. On the separate economies: Bøås and Jennings in progress.

from host populations. The first one explained: "Living on the compound for the UN was a very strange experience [. . .]. On many nights I could have been on a military base anywhere in the world." This "weird and alienating experience" made it difficult for her to do her job, which included engaging the population. The second concurred: "The whole perception that people are staying locked up all the time created a division between the real world and what was happening inside the camp."

To top it all off, the UN has recently put in place a series of measures aimed at preventing the abuse of intended beneficiaries by its staff (as further detailed in Chapter 7).[35] These regulations, in effect, forbid any kind of exchanges between expatriate staff and local women outside of the work environment, and thus further separate the interveners from host populations. The conversations I had with several commanding officers of Southeast Asian troops deployed in Congo aptly illustrate the perverse consequences of these rules. The officers proudly explained to me that they enforced such a strict discipline among their rank-and-file members that "social interaction with local masses for [their] troops [was] at the minimum." To avoid any problems, the orders were clear: Soldiers were forbidden to talk to local civilians; they had to refer any civilian who approached them to the officer on site.

The transient character of the interveners' experience further reinforces these barriers, as evidenced by the cases of Cyprus and Israel. Even in places where there are no major security barriers or socioeconomic differences between expatriates and local populations and where many local citizens have essentially the same educational background as expatriates, international interveners still tend to socialize mostly among themselves. As a diplomat working in Cyprus explained, in a way reminiscent of what I heard in Israel, "Diplomats and UN personnel [. . .] know they come and go, and they are used to a life where they change friends. [. . . So] they tend to stick to themselves, because first, it is a safe bet, and second, they have common interests."[36] Peacebuilders are aware that they will stay on site for a couple of years at most. This decreases their incentives to learn the local languages and to spend time creating a social network within host communities.

Local people share responsibility for their separation from the expatriates. There are countless dividing lines within local populations, due to political, economic, social, religious, and educational factors. Various groups and individuals therefore react differently to the interveners' presence.[37] However, there is often an underlying common denominator. Because foreign peacebuilders often live in the same bubble, share numerous practices, and enjoy massive

---

[35] For an analysis, see Simm 2013.

[36] Author's on-record interview with Costa Constanti, Australian High Commission, Nicosia, Cyprus, September 2011. See also Mitchell 2011a, p. 12.

[37] Richmond and Mitchell 2011; and Pouligny 2004 develop fascinating studies of this wide range of reactions.

capital (see Chapter 6), host populations often treat all expatriates as alike and as separate from themselves. This occurs regardless of the interveners' national origin, profession, or organizational affiliation. As a longtime intervener in Timor-Leste most eloquently voiced, "It is as if [they believe] we are a different species."

In Rwanda, Congo, and Burundi, local populations call every expatriate *muzungu* (a Swahili word that usually refers to any white person), whether the person appears to be Asian, African, Arab, Caucasian, or Latino. The terms *blan* in Haiti, *khawaja* in South Sudan, and *malai* in Timor-Leste similarly refer to all kinds of interveners, regardless of their nationality or skin color.[38] In the twenty-one conflict zones that Mary Anderson and her coauthors studied, aid recipients usually conflated all interveners under the label "donors," because they saw international, non-governmental, and diplomatic actors on the ground "as operating in very much the same ways."[39] Although certain local counterparts strategically exploit the divergences and tensions among expatriate peacebuilders, in many places even authorities and local elites seem to be unaware of the subtle differences between the various groups of interveners, such as NGOs and international organizations, let alone the differences between individual agencies or units of the same organization.[40] During my interviews, numerous contacts – including people who were important counterparts for international interveners, as well as local staff of intervening agencies – talked about the "UNGOs" or referred to an NGO as a UN agency and vice versa. Many interviewees were similarly unaware of the professional differences between civilians and members of the military or between humanitarian and peacebuilding actors. They regularly identified soldiers as working for one of the humanitarian agencies, and often cited humanitarian organizations in response to questions on peacekeeping actors. (Granted, many inexperienced interveners were similarly confused by the inscrutable differences among the various categories of international actors.)

In many conflict zones, the mere fact of being an intervener – driving in a car with the logo of an international agency or carrying the card of such an organization – provides expatriate peacebuilders with a higher social status than that of local people. As I witnessed, the Congolese, the Burundians, the Rwandans, and the Sudanese usually treat interveners as VIPs. Expatriate peacebuilders have reserved seating in official tribunes during functions, they interact with and are treated with respect by the highest authorities in their area of deployment, and rural leaders clear their agendas to meet with them whenever they appear.[41] According to other researchers, international interveners enjoy

---

[38] On Haiti: Pouligny 2004, p. 173.
[39] Anderson, Brown, et al. 2012, pp. 4 and 51.
[40] On local elites who strategically exploit the differences among interveners, see Pouligny 2004, pp. 128–141.
[41] On Rwanda, see also King 2009, p. 133.

similar social privileges in Cambodia and Cyprus.[42] Even more strikingly, as I experienced in South Sudan and most of Central Africa, merely looking like an expatriate working for an intervention agency provides a degree of protection against harassment and violence by armed groups, who know that troubling such foreigners would lead to many more problems than attacking local populations. In places where international peacebuilders are seen as a party to the conflict, such as Afghanistan, Darfur, and Iraq, an opposite phenomenon prevails: Looking like an expatriate is enough to provoke an attack. Both situations, however, result in the same effect: The sense of community among interveners intensifies and the split between them and local populations widens.

While most expatriates enjoy the social privileges they receive, there are clear downsides as well. In Israel, for instance, the general populations so strongly dislike international interveners, whom they each see as working for their enemy, that they prefer to avoid any contact with them. The limited number of Israelis sympathetic to the international approach have their own friends, their own lives, and they do not incorporate foreign interveners into their circles. If they wish to socialize with a colleague, they often favor a fellow Israeli who speaks Hebrew over an expatriate who speaks only English.

Worse, virtually everywhere I researched, expatriates mentioned being tired of host populations constantly staring at them, scrutinizing their actions, and considering them oddities. A number of interviewees also complained that, in places like Congo and Burundi, local people treated them like walking money-bags whom one could always ask for donations or handouts. The following comments are typical:

> In their minds, as soon as they see someone from [my organization], they think money, so they will find every possible way to extract money from you. (African peacebuilder based in Burundi)

> What I found striking is that, since I started working for [this intervening agency], I get asked for money from dawn till dusk. [...] Even people I have never met come to request money. It's a problem because it prevents relationships with people: We know that if we are nice, we will get the bill. (European peacebuilder based in Congo)

> When you are with a Congolese person, he will always request favors from you that are impossible to grant. And I know that if I go to the home of a Congolese person, he will request impossible favors from me, and I will say no, and it will be an offense. (African peacebuilder based in Congo)

The reaction of a European policeman deployed in Congo illuminates the perverse consequences of this phenomenon. When I asked him if he had ever been invited to a Congolese home, he responded that he had not and, anyway, he would not want to be. If he had a local friend, the person would eventually ask

---

[42] On Cambodia: McWha 2011, p. 34. On Cyprus: Mitchell 2011a, pp. 20–23.

him for something, and in the end, he would never know if the person had befriended him genuinely or to get something out of him.

Ritu Verma describes the effect of these dynamics as "the fishbowl syndrome."[43] Through a case study on development workers in Madagascar during the late 2000s, Verma demonstrates that the "general feeling" among aid expatriates "is one of alienation, isolation, and the sense that they are living in a fishbowl where they are constantly being observed and speculated about."[44] In these circumstances, "intense social relations with other expatriates [help] counter feelings of vulnerability and alienation" and reinforce "social barriers of misunderstanding with" local people.[45] Verma also makes a useful distinction between professional and social behaviors. She notes that development practitioners "may attempt to bridge cultural differences in their work relations to varying degrees, [but,] in their personal lives, they tend to buffer, isolate, and cocoon themselves from the social and cultural worlds" of the surrounding populations.[46]

Although Verma focuses exclusively on aid workers, her analysis captures what I observed throughout my own fieldwork with peacebuilders. In a given locale, the social world of the interveners usually includes a handful of bars and restaurants where the clientele is overwhelmingly foreign, the one or two safe neighborhoods where all the international peacebuilders live, and a couple of shops that sell imported products. A handful of local elite – usually the significant others of interveners, and sometimes wealthy businessmen, important employees of international agencies, or leaders of prominent local NGOs – hang out in these circles, but otherwise they are reserved for expatriates.[47] All in all, as an interviewee from Congo summarized, the metaphor of two "fishbowls" perfectly describes the distance and impervious barrier between the interveners' and the Congolese's worlds. At best, he explained, expatriates will look in one aquarium and go back to the other to recount what they witnessed in the first.[48] Another contact emphasized that the reverse is true: The Congolese will look into the expatriates' fishbowl and then return to their own.

These patterns are so entrenched that the international peacebuilders I met who did try to integrate into host communities complained of the tremendous difficulties they faced in this process. In Congo, for instance, several of the exceptional interveners I interviewed explained that Congolese people imposed strong obstacles to their efforts to become part of the local fabric, essentially

---

[43] Verma 2011, p. 69.

[44] Ibid., p. 69.

[45] Ibid., p. 72.

[46] Ibid., p. 75.

[47] On the leaders of local NGOs accepted in the international circle, see the humorous post "Sexy Local NGOs (SLoNGOs)," dated March 23, 2011, on the blog *Stuff Expat Aid Workers Like* (stuffexpataidworkerslike.com/2011/03/23/37-sexy-local-ngos-slongos, last accessed in December 2013).

[48] Author's interview with Michel Kassa, head of mission of the Initiative pour un Leadership Cohésif en RDC, Kinshasa, October 2010.

forcing them to remain foreigners forever. Take the experience of Alain.[49] In the eight years he spent in Congo, Alain had done his best to stay away from the expatriate bubble. He had learned local languages, studied local cultures and histories, tried to develop strong friendships with Congolese people, married a Congolese woman, and had a child who was half Congolese. However, Alain felt that only his wife and his immediate relatives fully accepted him and deserved his confidence, while none of his other contacts did:

> I gave an enormous amount of trust, but almost without exception, they have betrayed that trust. [...] I have been betrayed almost systematically by people that I loved. [...] It has been a very hard experience to constantly realize that what I believed was authentic was not. I have lost so much faith in people, in Congolese people. [...] I have come to the thorough understanding that whatever you try, they don't trust you completely; they don't let you in. Congolese populations can be extremely warm, but it does not mean that they let you into their circles, that you become family. Even me, they still consider me a foreigner.

Alain agreed that his efforts to integrate locally gave him a much better understanding of the context and overall made him a much more effective intervener, but he still felt that he had to be on the lookout, as his counterparts would inevitably try to take advantage of him one day.

Compared to his colleagues, Alain went to extraordinary lengths to integrate locally. However, the sadness and frustration he expressed during our meeting were reminiscent of what I heard from several other exceptional interviewees and what Lisa Smirl discovered when studying the memoirs of interveners working in Timor-Leste and Cambodia.[50] Admittedly, some expatriates believed that they had been fully accepted by their communities, thanks in part to the kindness of what one of them called "cultural guardian angels": local people who had taken it upon themselves to teach the foreigner how to behave in their culture, what to expect in a given situation, and what the appropriate and inappropriate ways to respond to various circumstances were. However, many other contacts felt that personal associations had been determined for them prior to their arrival: The patterns of interaction between expatriates and local partners were so firmly established that escaping the interveners' circle was nearly impossible.[51] Because they are the exception and not the norm among peacebuilders, the individuals who reject the dominant practices fail to change the host populations' perceptions and face tremendous difficulties in earning the local people's trust. Yet, at the same time, they have rejected the support network that the expatriate bubble provides, leaving them unhappily isolated, caught between the two groups.

---

[49] Alain is a pseudonym, used to protect the identity of the protagonist in this story.

[50] Smirl 2012, p. 242.

[51] An interviewee who spoke on record about this issue was Véronique Isenmann (Goma, February 2011).

Variations

Several elements account for most of the variation in the firmness of the boundaries between interveners and host populations. The first is the institutional settings in place for each international organization. In his comparative study of intervention in two Bosnian cities, Adam Moore shows that the unusual concentration of decision-making authority and policy formulation responsibilities in the hands of the Office of the High Representative supervisory regime in Brčko promoted the development of "effective international – local cooperation."[52] In contrast, the exact opposite happened in Mostar, where international peacebuilders were insufficiently independent from their headquarters, and thus local elites preferred to bypass them and deal directly with the interveners' Sarajevo-based superiors.[53] In sum, the variation in institutional settings strongly affected the quality of the professional relationships that interveners could develop with their local counterparts.

Another element, local perceptions of foreigners in general, accounts for some of the variation, as it can motivate a reluctance to interact with interveners. In Congo, like in several other African countries, the history of the slave trade and colonization has created a strong distrust of foreigners, coloring current relationships with many types of outsiders, including international peacebuilders. Views of interveners as corrupt (as in Bosnia) or as the enemy (as in Iraq) similarly decrease incentive for local people to break the boundaries between themselves and expatriates.

The last element is the presence or absence of cultural, social, and economic differences between interveners and host populations. To begin with, the divide is starker in places where international peacebuilders come from cultures that are very distinct from local ones. Some of the most extreme examples of this are found in countries that follow a form of Sharia law, such as Somalia, (North) Sudan, and Afghanistan. An interviewee recalled that, when she was with other interveners in Khartoum, it was "quite lively, there were a lot of parties, crazy parties," but when she left this world she "entered into the wider society that had very little to do with what [she] had experienced." She emphasized that the divide was particularly large because "the fact that you are leaving a party drunk" means that you have done something illegal. Her analysis perfectly encapsulates the feeling I had when attending expatriate gatherings in Afghanistan. A Pakistani intervener occasionally working in Somalia made a related point. He resented the countless barriers that Somali people placed against the possible integration of interveners. By expecting female expatriates to wear the hijab and by making virtually no efforts to compromise on their strict cultural and religious requirements, his Somali contacts prevented the formation of productive relationships with their international counterparts. In contrast,

[52] Moore 2013, pp. 5 and 117.
[53] Ibid., pp. 117 and 121.

having fewer cultural and socioeconomic differences between the two groups diminishes the divide between them, as I observed in Cyprus and Israel, and as is reportedly the case in Colombia.

Women interveners face particular challenges in conservative societies, such as Afghanistan. There, traditional views cast friendship between men and women as improper, making it difficult for expatriate women to socialize with their male counterparts. Yet, female interveners have little to no opportunity to develop the social relationships that tradition would deem acceptable because local women are generally excluded from the political, military, and public scenes. My experience is representative of those of my friends and contacts. During my three months in Kabul, the only Afghan women I met were the two cleaners who worked for my organization and the family members of one of our guards, who had invited me to his sister's wedding. Sadly, my Afghan acquaintances and I had no languages in common and could hold no meaningful conversations. Although the situation in the Palestinian Territories was not as bleak, a Swedish woman, who had spent a year working for an international organization there, complained of a similar challenge. She rarely met local women in the course of her work, so her only sustained interactions with Palestinian women were in places like the hairdresser's, where she too faced an insurmountable language barrier.

The causes of the separation between the expatriates' and the host populations' worlds, although present in capital cities to some degree, are particularly obvious in provinces and rural areas, due to the heightened cultural, social, and economic differences between interveners and the inhabitants of these locales. The general populations of capitals are more used to foreigners, treat them less as aliens or VIPs, and grant them fewer special privileges. In the many countries where the capital remains the center of political and economic power, capital-based elites are also more educated, wealthy, cosmopolitan, and "Westernized" than rural elites. One contact of mine, a 35-year-old European woman who had worked for several years in Central Africa, described how this difference influences the ability of expatriates to integrate into host communities. She explained that, during the couple of years that she had lived in the Burundian capital, Bujumbura, she had developed close friendships with several local women. However, when she moved to a provincial town of eastern Congo, she had a different experience. Even after a few years, she had not managed to make a single Congolese friend – despite the fact that people from Burundi and eastern Congo relate to strangers in very similar ways. The main reason, she explained, was that she shared few common interests with people of her age and gender in eastern Congo. My own experience, as well as those of my contacts, confirms this pattern. The opportunities to develop friendship – or at least relatively respectful and trusting relationships – are greater in contexts where local counterparts have a comparable socioeconomic and educational status to that of the interveners. In developing countries, such settings are more common in capitals than in rural areas. In the countryside, the socioeconomic gap between expatriates and local elites is often so enormous that socializing proves difficult and unappealing.

The divide is compounded by the fact that, during wartime, local elites often flee the provinces and rural areas for the capital or other countries in order to avoid violence and find better work opportunities. As my interviewees made abundantly clear, expatriates suspect – often with good reason – that those who remain have gained their positions of authority through violent means or retained them through negotiations with armed groups. Interveners therefore refuse to associate with these local leaders in order to protect the image of neutrality that they view as indispensable to their jobs (see Chapter 7).

The dynamics are the opposite in extremely isolated field locations. Within remote villages, where only a couple of foreign interveners are deployed, expatriates often develop close relationships with local elites, notably their local staff and local counterparts. This happens regardless of whether the expatriates are based there permanently or on a temporary basis. The reason, according to several contacts, is that in such settings the distinction between work and leisure disappears, and interveners tend to "work all the time." On top of that, when they do take time to relax, it is only possible to socialize with local people. However, this proximity is the result of a dearth of other options. When these individuals return to locations that have a larger number of expatriates, they behave exactly like the other international interveners.

Unintended Consequences: Isolation and Its Costs

The previous sections have established that most interveners find integrating into local societies extremely difficult, while they feel that working and socializing with other expatriates is much easier. Reproducing the dominant practices and habits is also often the only way for interveners to keep functioning in the stressful conditions that they face. This section shows that, in addition to this positive intended effect, the various dynamics described in this chapter have important unintended consequences: Because they construct firm boundaries between interveners and local people, they decrease the effectiveness of the international efforts.

The Expatriate Bubble

The boundaries between the two groups are at the root of the widespread criticism that interveners live in a social and personal "bubble." Expatriate peacebuilders and host populations discussed this problem at length during our conversations, in every conflict zone in which I worked, from Afghanistan to Burundi, Congo, Cyprus, Israel and the Palestinian Territories, Kosovo, South Sudan, and Timor-Leste.[54] Interviewees and various scholars have also mentioned this issue when talking about Bangladesh, Bolivia, Cambodia, the

---

[54] On Cyprus and Afghanistan, see also respectively Mitchell 2011a, pp. 12–15; and "Exotic Birds in a Cage," by Walter Mayr.

Comoros Islands, Ivory Coast, Nepal, Madagascar, Sierra Leone, Sri Lanka, and Vietnam.[55]

Numerous interviewees additionally emphasized that, professionally speaking, UN agencies, NGOs, and diplomatic representations form a "parallel system" of governance, disconnected from that of the country of intervention. A case in point, only foreigners may attend some of the interveners' professional gatherings. No Congolese – not even local staff members – participate in the tri-weekly management meetings of the UN peacekeeping mission in North Kivu. Likewise, the chiefs of the humanitarian NGOs based in this province and in the neighboring province of South Kivu have organized bi-monthly expatriate-only sessions to complement the weekly coordination meetings that Congolese representatives can attend. For security reasons, foreigners did not want to share sensitive information in settings where Congolese might hear them. A Kosovar government official and a Sri Lankan civil society leader deplored similar phenomena in their own countries, where international actors coordinated among themselves without inviting any local partners.[56]

The design of the UN support plan for stabilization in eastern Congo, dubbed plan "I4S" (for International Security and Stabilization Support Strategy), aptly illustrates the functioning of the parallel system. According to several interveners involved in the process, in early 2008, UN civilian peacekeepers wrote multiple versions of a plan to support the Congolese government in its efforts to pacify eastern Congo, but they did not involve Congolese officials in the drafting process. Meanwhile, unbeknownst to the designers of the international strategy, the host government had already started constructing a stabilization plan of its own. Once UN officials realized this, they had to spend a lot of time trying to harmonize the two stabilization plans and attempting to convince the government to cooperate with theirs. By 2010, however, the disconnect between the government and the interveners was still such that Congolese representatives were not invited to the high-profile meeting organized to debate the I4S. It was not until February 2011 that Congolese stakeholders could actually participate in such gatherings. Up to that point, interveners had designed a strategy to support the government without actually involving national or local representatives in the process. According to several interviewees, there was a similar situation in Timor-Leste for several years after the 2006 crisis. Interveners met on a biweekly basis in the UN compound. There, they planned the future of the country without communicating with or implicating any local partners.[57]

[55] On Bangladesh, Vietnam, and Sri Lanka: Rajak and Stirrat 2011. On Bolivia: Eyben 2011. On Cambodia: McWha 2011, pp. 33–35; and Rajak and Stirrat 2011. On Madagascar: Verma 2011, pp. 67–74. On Nepal, Harper 2011; and Shrestha 2006 cited in Verma 2011, p. 75.
[56] CDA Collaborative Learning Projects 2010a, p. 9.
[57] A public source for this anecdote is an on-record interview by the author with Ben Larke, Dili, Timor-Leste, February 2012.

The tendency to congregate and socialize with people who speak the same languages and share the same experiences is a common trend for expatriate communities everywhere, not just within conflict zones. However, several elements specific to international interventions, such as the transient feeling mentioned in this chapter and the security procedures detailed in Chapter 7, further reinforce this segregation. More importantly, while some expatriate communities – such as foreign construction workers building roads and other infrastructure – may not need to fully integrate into local societies to accomplish their work, interveners do.

Learning from the Exceptions

Moore's case study on Bosnia clearly demonstrates the importance of breaking the boundaries and promoting good international–local interactions. In his analysis, unusually "close and productive" relations between international and local actors in Brčko were key to the relative success of peacebuilding there compared to the rest of the country.[58] Summarizing the findings of their discussions with more than 6,000 people from 21 different conflict zones, Anderson and her coauthors similarly observed that "every story of effective aid" that aid recipients mentioned "included a description of particular staff who worked in ways that developed respect and trust with" the intended beneficiaries.[59]

In fact, several of the requirements for successful peace programs are only attainable when interveners develop sufficiently good rapports with their local counterparts. Based on extensive interviews in Cambodia and on a review of literature on the topic, McWha has established that "relationship building," including communication, friendship, reciprocal learning/teaching, and confidence, is "the most important factor contributing to the success of capacity-development initiatives."[60] Other researchers have shown that one of the most effective ways for interveners to mitigate security concerns is through gaining the acceptance of local communities.[61] People from conflict zones all over the world regularly emphasize that they appreciate the expatriates who "spend time in the field getting to know the people they [aim] to assist and the contexts in which they live" much more than they value the many peacebuilders who show little interest in learning firsthand about the realities on the ground.[62] Such appreciation diminishes the local populations' incentives to distort, contest, resist, or evade the interveners' efforts.[63]

[58] Moore 2013, pp. 15 and 31 for the citations and chapter 7 for the demonstration.
[59] Anderson, Brown, et al. 2012, p. 144.
[60] McWha 2011, pp. 29–31.
[61] Public sources include, among others, Egeland, Harmer, et al. 2011; and Roth 2011, pp. 162–163. See also the Conclusion of this book.
[62] Anderson 2008, pp. 101 and 103; and CDA Collaborative Learning Projects 2008a and 2010b (citations from p. 2).
[63] Ibid.

Stuck in Cyck

This research acknowledges in passing an essential, but often overlooked, idea. It is not sufficient to have good working relationships with local counterparts; personal and social interactions are also critical. McWha's interviewees on capacity-building programs, for example, were not merely interested in professional ties, but rather regularly insisted that "friendship" was one of the keys to successful initiatives.[64] The UN advisors and Timorese counterparts that Reyko Huang and Joseph Harris interviewed in Timor-Leste similarly emphasized that capacity building was effective when trainers built relationships and fostered trust, notably by getting to know their partners personally.[65] A Filipino city official interviewed by the Listening Project explained that "relationships are crucial" in his country, that "trust is a huge part of the success factor," and that if people "like the person" they are "more willing to cooperate."[66] In his in-depth analysis of village life in Afghanistan, Noah Coburn similarly underscores the crucial nature of social contacts based on reciprocity and trust in political life and shows that the reason international military forces and NGOs failed to exert much influence on local politics is that they lacked such personal relationships.[67]

As a result, the same initiative varies widely in effectiveness depending on whether its implementers socialize with their local counterparts. Anne Holohan demonstrates that the existence of informal and personal contacts largely contributed to the success of democratization programs in Banshik (Kosovo), while the same democratization initiatives remained unsuccessful in the neighboring municipality of Thezren, where interveners had only formal, professional relationships with one another and with local people.[68] Moore similarly stresses that international officials based in Brčko, where peacebuilding was mostly successful, regularly socialized with friends or colleagues from the district on weekends, unlike their colleagues based elsewhere in the country, where peacebuilding largely failed.[69]

The story of James Scambary, an intervener in Timor-Leste, also illustrates how after-work interactions can help expatriate peacebuilders both overcome challenges to data collection and analysis and increase their effectiveness. As I explained in the Introduction, the riots that erupted in 2006, which almost destroyed the Timorese peace process, took virtually all interveners by surprise. James was one of the few foreigners who had predicted a deterioration of the situation, thanks to the in-depth personal relationships that he had developed with his neighbors.

Throughout my fieldwork, I found many other illustrations of the positive impact that social and personal relationships can have on professional

---

[64] McWha 2011, pp. 29–31.

[65] Huang and Harris 2006, pp. 86 and 89–90.

[66] CDA Collaborative Learning Projects 2010a, p. 4.

[67] Coburn 2011, chapter 6, notably p. 139.

[68] Holohan 2005, pp. 74–85. Holohan changed the name of both municipalities for reasons of confidentiality.

[69] Moore 2013, pp. 123–124.

interactions. To start, it was much easier for foreign peacebuilders with extensive social networks to obtain official approval or cooperation for their programs than it was for their fellow expatriates. An Israeli contact emphasized, in a way reminiscent of what I heard in many other countries, that "when something works, it is because you know people." Personal contacts were also crucial to promoting one's security. Well-integrated interveners living in violent environments recalled how much safer they felt compared to other expatriates, as their local friends and acquaintances made a point of keeping them informed of recent developments and, when necessary, protecting them.

Additionally, for obvious reasons, it is much easier to get an appointment with a member of the local elite if he is a friend, an acquaintance, or a friend of a friend. I experienced this phenomenon myself countless times in Congo. Along the same lines, one Timorese authority insisted that the importance of socializing in his country was "huge," explaining that he responded "very fast" to people with whom he usually socialized and that personal interactions provided "very easy access" to the highest-ranking members of the government. In all my field-work sites, the exceptional interveners who had managed to develop an extensive social network in their area of deployment described countless instances of quickly scheduling meetings with whomever they needed while their colleagues had to wait for months.

The benefit of social connections extends across the board. Strong personal relationships can significantly improve the comfort level of both local and expatriate staff in intervening agencies, thus encouraging them both to perform highly.[70] The importance of social interactions with colleagues is actually not specific to conflict zones: Research on human resources management in the United States notes that workplace camaraderie increases productivity and facilitates employee retention.[71]

In fact, the importance of good social and personal relations with local colleagues and counterparts seems like common sense. Throughout the world, business professionals insist that networking is the key to success – to get a job, a contract, a favorable deal, and so on. Interveners themselves emphasized during interviews and informal discussions that networking with other international actors is critical to secure funding, information, and other perks necessary for the successful completion of their projects. It would seem obvious that the importance of networking should extend to relationships with local people. However,

---

[70] Also Anderson 1999, pp. 62–63.

[71] Among many others: Cohen and Prusak 2001; Lin, Cook, et al. 2001; Nohria, Groysberg, et al. 2008, notably pp. 2 and 4; Riordan and Griffeth 1995; "Top 10 Mistakes Managers Make Managing People," by Susan M. Heathfield, *About.com Human Resources Guide* (http://human resources.about.com/od/badmanagerboss/a/mistakes-managers-make-managing-people.htm, last accessed in December 2013); and "Should Co-Workers Become Friends?" by Rebecca Hastings, *Society for Human Resources Management.* September 29, 2011 (www.shrm.org/hrdisciplines/employeerelations/articles/pages/coworkersfriends.aspx, last accessed in December 2013). For an international perspective, see Fukuyama 1995.

the opposite habit is so ingrained that interveners rarely put this idea into practice – they do not even talk about it. Out of the hundreds of expatriates I interviewed, only a handful ever mentioned it. The reason is straightforward. The sense of being a minority in tough circumstances, the strong bonds between members of the interveners club, and the firm boundaries that separate foreign peacebuilders from host populations make it very difficult to escape the expatriate world. In the field, a sense of familiarity renders relationships with other expatriates easier and more comfortable. As a Western diplomat based in Goma acknowledged: "It takes a certain amount of effort, as you know, to force yourself to get out of the expat circle where it is relatively easy to speak with and understand each other." As a result, the majority of interveners spend their time immersed in the expatriate world.

Identifying the Exceptions

The exceptional individuals who resisted these tendencies, eschewing the practices, habits, and narratives analyzed in this chapter – and, at times, some of the other dominant modes of action described in the book – did not belong to a specific geographic, professional, or gender group. Instead, they usually shared one of two characteristics. Either they had particularly strong ties to the host country, or they were newcomers to Peaceland.

In the course of my fieldwork, I met a number of interveners with very close connections to their country of deployment. Some were foreigners who had married a local person and had stayed in the country ever since. Others were members of the diaspora, such as a Timorese man who fled his country during the war, grew up abroad as a refugee, and came back home as an intervener for a large international organization. A few were researchers doubling as consultants, who had set up residency in the country they studied and had lived there for years, or kept coming back to the same area. Still others were typical interveners who one day fell in love with a location, did everything they could to remain there, and slowly built a life and a home in this new place.

Because of their local ties, all of these individuals integrate more easily with host populations. They often spend more time socializing with their families and local friends than with other interveners. This offers them a different form of knowledge about the country of intervention – one based on local perspectives. They also gain a more personal appreciation of the detrimental impact of the dominant international practices. As a result of this different socialization pattern and this distinct view of intervention, individuals with strong ties to the host country are more likely to stand on the margin of the interveners' club, challenge its dominant ways of thinking and acting, and attempt to find alternatives.

The most extreme cases are missionaries. They, too, are foreigners who share the interveners' common goal of helping host populations. However, they usually stay for dozens of years in their country of deployment, and they voluntarily reject participation in the interveners' club. They rarely, if ever, choose to attend its professional and social gatherings, as evidenced by the fact that I never met a missionary at any of the hundreds of events that I attended. They often have a poor opinion of international peacebuilders, which was clear during my interviews. (Admittedly, the feeling is often mutual – many interveners I met were suspicious of the overtly religious objectives of local missionaries.) Missionaries also follow distinct practices and habits. They do not use the governance or security procedures that interveners deem necessary. They are usually fully integrated within local communities, living with them and speaking local languages. All in all, missionaries form a separate group.

In theory, newcomers to Peaceland should be another group in which exceptions abound. Novices are better placed to see the contingent, bizarre, and detrimental character of dominant modes of operation, as they do not yet take practices for granted the way seasoned interveners do. In fact, however, most beginners try to fit into their new world as quickly as possible, and thus strive to adopt – or at least mimic – the dominant modes of operation. A minority nevertheless tries to resist. The problem is that newcomers are often relatively young and inexperienced, and thus they lack the status and credibility that would make their contestation more likely to succeed. Furthermore, just like the other exceptions mentioned above, they face suspicion from local people, as well as massive resistance from other expatriates who view their own dominant practices as the only proper and legitimate ones. Finally, newcomers, like the other contesters, must confront strong pressure from their superiors, who discourage dissent because their organizations rely on routines and stability to function.[72] An excerpt from an interview with a Timorese citizen, who worked as an intervener in the past, illustrates this process well:

> Every time we have a good operator, they get knocked so hard by other aid professionals that after a year they give up. "I came here to help, but I can't do so." [...] You cannot come up with your own analysis, your own research, because you have to follow the organizational line. You cannot speak your mind because of the obligatory contract to the organization. Young volunteers who do not fit in the box, who want to leave a mark somewhere in the world, to have made an impact, they get broken, and their lives get shattered. We have seen that over and over. And they become bitter. And to see that [...], it is sad. Because they were not that when they arrived, and it is not [local populations] who did it to them; it was the other internationals. [...] They almost cry when they tell you. [...] And then [their] own views start to suffer; they do not believe in their strengths, in how effective they are at creating change, and then, the next mission, they are broken.[73]

As he and I experienced, and as other interviewees confirmed, newcomers who question the dominant modes of operation often end up either forced to fit into

---

[72] Autesserre 2010, chapter 5 provides several detailed examples of this process in Congo.
[73] Author's on-record interview with Jose Kai Lekke Sousa Santos, Dili, February 2012.

the mold, or so frustrated that they change careers and leave Peaceland – to the relief of their colleagues and superiors.

Scholars and practitioners to whom I presented my research often asked whether certain regional, professional, or gender groups exhibited the interveners' dominant modes of operation to greater or lesser degrees. Notably, they wondered whether regional expatriates (for instance, African peacebuilders deployed in Africa), women interveners, and humanitarian aid or long-term development workers might be regular exceptions. As I show below, the fact that these people follow the dominant trends as much as the other expatriates do further demonstrates that the practices, habits, and narratives I identify characterize the broad interveners' group, despite its internal dividing lines.

The section on the two separate worlds already explained that local populations see little difference between interveners from their own continent and expatriates from other parts of the world. Béatrice Pouligny reports similar findings from her research in El Salvador and Haiti.[74] This observation should not be surprising given how diverse African – or American, Asian, European, or Pacific – countries are. Many local interviewees explained that "a foreigner is a foreigner," and thus regional interveners suffer from the same limitations as other expatriate peacebuilders. They too lack local knowledge and legitimacy; they too fail to take grassroots inputs into account and are perceived as arrogant. They also follow the other detrimental practices that this book studies, such as socializing mostly with other interveners, valuing thematic expertise over local knowledge, and using intervention routines and techniques that have unintentionally negative consequences. The fact that African, Asian, and Latino interveners share practices and habits with their European and North American colleagues indicates that the common modes of action cannot be dismissed as mere remnants of colonial or neoimperial mentalities. It also implies that the idea of adopting regional approaches, such as "African solutions for African problems," which is a popular alternative to current practices on today's global scene, would not alleviate the problems detailed in this book.

On the whole, my research identified only one significant comparative advantage for regional interveners: They can convey sensitive messages more effectively than other outsiders. For example, African peacebuilders are better positioned than their European or North American colleagues to voice critical arguments against African counterparts, because their countries face similar challenges – such as a history of colonization and arbitrary borders. By way of illustration, a Senegalese peacebuilder mentioned that he regularly told his Congolese counterparts to stop using colonization or ethnicity to explain the existence of dismal poverty and war in their country. Senegal faces the same problems and yet fares much better. According to my interviews, Congolese authorities view such statements as unacceptable when they come from former colonizers, but they accept them more easily from African contacts. Beyond this added capacity to convey

---

[74] Pouligny 2004, p. 173.

sensitive messages, however, regional peacebuilders are just as effective (or ineffective) as interveners from other parts of the world.

One may wonder whether the habits and practices I study have a gender dimension. Gender issues are certainly prominent in Peaceland since, as mentioned above, military peacekeepers are overwhelmingly male. Marsha Henry, Paul Higate, Gurchathen Sanghera, Liora Sion, Sherene Razack, and Sandra Whitworth have convincingly demonstrated that this gender imbalance creates a male-oriented culture within UN missions and that masculinity is central to how military peacekeepers understand themselves.[75] Many interveners I interviewed also complained that gender politics frequently led male peacekeepers to discriminate against their female colleagues. Women deplored that a number of coworkers assumed they were less skilled and less important than their male equivalents and treated them as second-rate associates who had obtained their jobs based on connections instead of competence. Tensions were even higher in interactions with contingents from countries where women have a much lower social status than men. Indian soldiers, for example, often felt uncomfortable when engaging in joint work with female colleagues, while Pakistani peacekeepers at times flatly refused to let female members of the UN mission stay overnight on their bases. On a daily basis, these attitudes regularly interfered with the UN mandated work of promoting women's rights and responding to sexual violence. The overrepresentation of men in these forces also heightens fears that sexual abuse may occur, which in turn results in strict regulations of relationships between peacekeepers and local communities.

Gender issues thus strongly influence peacekeeping missions. However, they do not shape the practices, habits, and narratives of the broader interveners' group. There is nothing specifically masculine (or feminine) in the shared modes of action I detail in this book. This may be due to the fact that, as detailed in the introduction to Part I, the gender distribution of expatriates overall (including other UN agencies, NGOs, and diplomatic delegations) is more or less balanced at any given intervention site. At the end of the day, gender remains just one of the many dividing lines in the interveners' club – one that often widens the split between military and civilian peacekeepers.

Aid experts occasionally wonder whether humanitarian and long-term development workers belong to the interveners' club. They note that humanitarian aid actors do not share a common goal with other interveners. A number of relief workers actually oppose the use of their work as part of stabilization efforts, as their primary goal is to respond to humanitarian emergencies rather than to build peace. It is true that relief aid expatriates have goals, practices, habits, and narratives that are specific to their action. However, the boundaries between humanitarian, development, and peacebuilding work have become increasingly

---

[75] Enloe 1993, notably chapter 1; Higate and Henry 2009, chapter 8; Razack 2004, notably pp. 39 and 70; Sanghera, Henry, et al. 2008; Sion 2008; and Whitworth 2004. On masculinity and military forces in general, see Enloe 1993 and 2000.

blurred since the 1990s, a trend identified by numerous scholars.[76] Even more importantly, as detailed in the previous section, local people fail to perceive significant differences between international humanitarian staff and peacebuilders. The reason is simple: Both kinds of interveners use the same approach to construct knowledge on the country of intervention. They participate in the same governance structure, they use the same security and visibility procedures, and they socialize with the same kinds of people. Altogether, they have countless practices, habits, and narratives in common. Humanitarian aid workers are thus one of the subgroups of the interveners' community of practice, on par with other professional categories like human rights advocates, journalists, or soldiers. Among the hundreds of people I encountered across nine conflict zones, the exceptions were as frequent among relief aid workers as among the broader interveners' club.

The same reasoning applies to development actors. These expatriates usually pride themselves on being different from emergency aid workers, peacekeepers, and diplomats. From their point of view, their command of local languages and their longer-term deployments enable them to integrate into host communities. However, the development workers Rosalind Eye studies in Bolivia, Ian Harper researches in Nepal, Ritu Verma observes in Madagascar, and Dinah Rajak and Jock Stirrat analyze in Bangladesh, Cambodia, Vietnam, and Sri Lanka are just as socially disconnected from local contexts as their humanitarian, peacekeeping, and peacebuilding colleagues.[77] Tellingly, Verma's analysis of the fishbowl phenomenon is in fact predicated on her study of expatriates working on long-term grassroots projects for a small development NGO. As I observed, development workers regularly attend social and professional meetings for expatriates, benefit from the privileges accorded to the in-group, use the same security, knowledge, and governance practices, and adhere to the same narratives. Overall, they are full members of the interveners' community of practice. The only caveat is that those who do spend a relatively long period of time in their area of deployment are more likely to form strong ties with the host country and to eventually challenge the dominant modes of international action, for reasons explained at the beginning of this section.

Conclusion

Despite internal differences and tensions, interveners form a distinct community that is defined both by what binds its members together and what sets them apart. Dense interactions, a common experience of life in conflict zones, and the reactions of local people all foster the internal cohesion of the interveners' club, while creating a division between them and the host populations.

[76] Curtis 2001; Duffield 2001; Fassin and Pandolfi 2010; Macrae 2002; Macrae and Leader 2000 and 2001; and Rieff 2002.
[77] Eyben 2011; Harper 2011; Rajak and Stirrat 2011; and Verma 2011. See also Roth 2011.

The interveners' personal and social practices promote peacebuilding effectiveness in two ways. They enable expatriates to function in the difficult conditions of conflict zones. They also facilitate collaboration of distinct actors and organizations, and they are the primary mechanisms through which foreign peacebuilders can attempt to coordinate their efforts to help the host country.

Unfortunately, these benefits are not without costs. The same everyday dynamics that enable action and cooperation also construct firm boundaries between local populations and the international peacebuilders deployed in their communities. Interveners tend to live and work in an expatriate bubble. Consequently, they enjoy limited opportunities to develop personal relationships with local counterparts – relationships which would encourage the kind of collaboration that can crucially bolster peace interventions. Moreover, this segregation renders data collection and analysis yet more difficult

To make matter worse, several related forces that I analyze in the next two chapters fuel the interveners' isolation and its detrimental impact on peacebuilding effectiveness. Chapter 7 shows that the expatriates' security, visibility, reporting, and impartiality routines increase the salience of the separation from local people. These dominant modes of operation further encourage foreign peacebuilders to spend most of their time socializing with other interveners, and further hamper possibilities for collaboration with local stakeholders. The politics of knowledge at work in Peaceland, as well as the structure of inequality that I discuss in Chapter 6, aggravates these divisions by elevating expatriate interveners to positions of relative dominance over host populations. These various elements also make it harder for interveners to contest the dominant ways of living and working, and they encourage expatriates to perpetuate boundaries instead of challenging them.

Taken together, these dynamics create a vicious cycle. No matter how hard interveners try to integrate into the communities they are trying to help, fellow expatriates and local populations persistently remind them that they are outsiders who can and should claim unique privileges. Interveners grow frustrated by the disparity between the intensity of their efforts and the sustainability of their results, and they gradually start to resent local partners. At the same time, socioeconomic differences, professional routines, and security rules limit opportunities for socializing with local contacts, so those feelings of resentment go unchecked. Eventually, even the many people whose value systems run counter to the interveners' prescribed way of life begin to abandon their ideals. A few individuals resist, but most adopt the expatriate identity in time. Thus, international peacebuilders usually arrive in new theaters of deployment with a clear sense of belonging to a specific group – a group markedly different from local populations.

6

A Structure of Inequality

A non-governmental organization (NGO) once sent its human resources director, Philippe Rosen, to visit its mission in Kenya. Upon arrival, Philippe was
impressed by the progressive management style that the country team had
adopted. The expatriates did everything they could think of to promote leadership by the local staff. One of their initiatives empowered Kenyan employees,
even the lowest-ranking ones, to chair the biweekly coordination meetings on a
rotating basis. Despite these efforts, Philippe heard multiple complaints about
the international staff from the local personnel. He found most worrisome the
various grievances indicating that expatriates inadvertently abused their position of authority. They would, for instance, ask Kenyan colleagues to run an
errand; the Kenyans would accept with a smile, not daring to explain that doing
so would mean forfeiting their lunch break, given their schedule. Then, they
would run the errand and lose the opportunity to eat and rest during the day.
The problem, Philippe realized, was that the Kenyan staff felt that they could not
refuse to do anything the expatriates requested. Philippe brainstormed how to
address this issue with the country management team, but even he did not
appreciate just how insidious the problem was. One morning, he arrived in the
office, entered the kitchen, and grumbled upon discovering that there was no
coffee left. Ten minutes later, the cleaner told him that he could now have a cup.
Philippe later realized that the cleaner had been so scared at the idea of having
upset an expatriate (especially one sent by the headquarters) that she had
dropped everything she was doing to run and buy coffee. "And yet," Philippe
said, "I had not requested anything. I had just showed that I was annoyed."[1]

Philippe had experienced firsthand the difficulties that interveners face when
they try to create balance in power dynamics and change the way international
interventions operate in the field. A structure of inequality permeates relationships

---

[1] Author's on-record interview with Philippe Rosen, New York, January 2012.

between expatriates and their local counterparts. It strengthens the boundaries between the two groups (thus decreasing the effectiveness of international interventions, as explained in Chapter 5) and antagonizes local populations (thus reinforcing the counterproductive effects analyzed in Chapter 3). Worse, it hinders change on the ground. The patterns of interaction between interveners and local people are so entrenched that even the most progressive individuals may inadvertently wind up perpetuating some of the very practices that they wish to avoid.

In this chapter, I successively analyze the three main elements that constitute Peaceland's structure of inequality, and I illuminate their impact on peacebuilding efforts. First, the narrative of interveners coming to "help" host populations enables expatriates to claim the moral high ground. Second, the massive resources that international peacebuilders bring to conflict zones also create a significant power gap between them and local people. Third, the accountability mechanisms in Peaceland reinforce existing imbalances by making interveners responsible to donors and headquarters rather than to local populations. By precluding equal relationships between international and local partners, these three elements all buttress the boundaries between interveners and local counterparts and fuel local resentment. In this situation, on-the-ground interveners have two choices in their everyday life and work: They can either reproduce the structure of inequality or undermine it. Throughout the chapter, I show that, although a few expatriates actively contest the structure of inequality, most interveners employ dominant modes of operation that perpetuate it.

The Ethics of Care

There are two important dimensions of the "here to help" narrative. First, it delineates the boundaries of the interveners' community and unites diverse groups of expatriates in one "club," as I discussed in Chapter 5. Second, it embodies a claim to the moral high ground, as I analyze in this section. My interviews amply illustrated this claim. For instance, in discussions with my Burundian, Congolese, and Sudanese contacts, I often heard the saying "The hand that gives is always higher than the hand that receives." The idea that expatriates arrive "to help" host countries also suggests that local people and authorities are "beneficiaries" or "recipients" of that assistance – two terms that, as Silke Roth notes, imply "an unequal relationship between donors and recipients of aid."[2]

It is worth noting that not all cultures assume that the giver is superior to the receiver. In Buddhist societies for instance, "the giver of alms to monks is the supplicant, asking for the privilege of giving to someone who is seen as more holy."[3] Even more importantly, the explicit goal of "helping" does not, in itself,

---

[2] Roth 2011, p. 167n6.
[3] Anderson 2008, p. 99.

create inequality.[4] Admittedly, people across many cultures find it embarrassing to ask for help, even when they know that the assistance is not intentionally debasing. This phenomenon is not limited to Peaceland: It takes place in many parts of the world and in many different settings – in social work, education, counseling, and even among colleagues, friends, or spouses.[5] However, based on several thousand interviews around the globe, the teams of the Listening Project found that recipients of aid "understand and accept the impulse to help people in need as a natural [one]," and as something that they too would do, if they were in a similar position.[6] Whether in Peaceland or outside of it, help-seekers do not feel belittled just because they happen to be on the receiving end of a given exchange.[7]

This is especially true when beneficiaries can somehow reciprocate.[8] The analysis of "the gift" that the anthropologist Marcel Mauss developed in the early twentieth century is particularly helpful to understand this process.[9] To Mauss, a gift comes with obligations and generates new forms of dependency. When a gift is reciprocated, the outcome of the exchange builds mutual bonds between people. In Mauss's analysis, returning a gift shows that one's honor is at least equivalent to that of the original giver and that one deserves as much respect. However, problems arise when the relationship remains one-sided, as usually occurs in Peaceland. A city official in the Philippines, for instance, deplored that he and his fellow citizens were only ever on the receiving end of the relationship and lacked opportunities to "give back in some form."[10] A Burmese leader made a similar point: Aid programs should be "much more of a give and take."[11] For both, a "true partnership" – as the city official put it – would establish mutual exchange, enabling local people to regain some dignity in the process.[12]

The process of helping can therefore accommodate both relatively equal and starkly unequal relationships. It is the ways in which givers execute their mission on an everyday basis that produces or does not produce imbalanced power dynamics. As this section elucidates, the interveners' dominant practices and narratives foster inequity, while the exceptional expatriates' alternative modes of operation promote more equitable and thus less demeaning relationships.[13]

---

[4] The rest of this paragraph was inspired by ibid., notably p. 99.
[5] Bohns and Flynn 2010; and Fisher, Nadler, et al. 1982.
[6] Anderson 2008, p. 99.
[7] Ibid., p. 99; Fisher, Nadler, et al. 1982, pp. 38–51; and Greenberg and Shapiro 1971.
[8] CDA Collaborative Learning Projects 2010a, p. 4. See also Fisher, Nadler, et al. 1982, pp. 28–31 for a critical overview of psychological research on this topic.
[9] Mauss 1923–1924.
[10] CDA Collaborative Learning Projects 2010a, p. 4.
[11] Anderson, Brown, et al. 2012. p. 23.
[12] Citations from CDA Collaborative Learning Projects 2010a, p. 4.
[13] For a similar claim, see Anderson 2008, p. 99.

Interveners' Narratives

The international peacebuilders' narrative that they are "here to help" has two components: First, interveners are altruistic, and second, local people lack capacity.[14] Interveners working in the field usually view themselves as outsiders who give up their own comfort, and often their family lives, to address the problems of strangers – a discourse that, to be fair, is perfectly consistent with their actual experience of life in conflict zones. In many areas of intervention, the expatriates' conception that they have come for altruistic reasons frequently results in puzzled reactions when host governments ask them to pay taxes or when host populations act aggressively toward them. From the expatriates' point of view, they have already sacrificed a lot to help the host populations, so why would the authorities request additional contributions, and why would beneficiaries resent them?

On the whole, interveners do not see their local employees or counterparts as making comparable sacrifices or being similarly motivated by a desire to do good. In my fifteen years of interacting with Peacelanders, I almost never heard expatriates refer to local employees in their organizations as people who wanted to help their fellow citizens or their home countries. Instead, interveners regularly portrayed their local colleagues as individuals whose motivations were primarily financial or professional. For local people in most conflict zones, intervening agencies provide the highest paid jobs, whereas the state usually cannot pay its employees much (if anything at all), and few individuals are able to make a decent salary in the private sector. This creates an observational equivalence problem: It is impossible for foreign peacebuilders to know whether local employees are working for international agencies for the sake of the cause or for the sake of the salary (and status) – or simply because it was the only job they could find. However, instead of recognizing this ambivalence, the dominant narrative reserves the moral high ground for expatriates and denies local staff members a claim to altruism.

In addition to the view of international peacebuilders as altruistic, the second component of the "here to help" narrative is that host populations lack the expertise or opportunities necessary to solve their own predicaments. Two seasoned expatriates for example pointed out that the very term "capacity building" – a buzzword among interveners across all conflict zones – implies that there is little to no capacity to begin with.[15] A UN peacekeeping officer deployed in eastern Congo told a fellow scholar: "We are dealing with people who are helpless [. . .]. The mass of this country is illiterate [. . .]. There are no real political parties here; we are trying to build this country from scratch."[16] A

---

[14] See Mutua 2001 for a related analysis on human rights.
[15] McWha 2011, p. 36; and blog *Stuff Expat Aid Workers Like*, Post "#62 Proper word choice" (June 6, 2011, http://stuffexpataidworkerslike.com/2011/06/06/62-proper-word-choice/).
[16] Iniguez de Heredia 2011, p. 14.

French NGO intervener working in a neighboring province voiced a similar perception, using it to reinforce the narrative that only interveners can save host populations. In his words, Congolese leaders are unreliable – "State structures are very weak," "there is a lot of poor governance," and authorities must strike shady deals just to survive – "so only the [. . .] foreigners are capable of enacting reforms." A longtime expatriate development worker in Goma lamented that the prevalence of this attitude produced significant inequality. For more than seventeen years, this interviewee had seen thousands of peacebuilders arrive in the city. She explained that, although there are exceptions, the general perspective of interveners in crisis situations is that "these poor, helpless, catastrophic people need our expertise," so "we will do this for [them]." Owing to this attitude, foreign peacebuilders "totally disregard capacities already here on the ground." This phenomenon is especially prevalent in crisis situations. Beneficiaries in conflict and post-conflict settings are in situations of extreme vulnerability and in need of help, so "almost automatically there is [a] power imbalance." As she concluded, "It is like 'these people have no power, so they have no voice.'"

Despite the admittedly condescending undertone of these various remarks and attitudes, the large majority of expatriates know perfectly well that "respect for differences and the willingness to work with people" should be one of their central values if they wish to accomplish their objectives of building sustainable peace.[17] An interview I conducted with Ben Larke, a peacebuilder with twelve years of experience working for a variety of UN agencies and NGOs in Timor-Leste, illuminates the process through which interveners come to adopt a perspective and series of behaviors and attitudes that differ from and, at times, oppose the ones they aim for.[18] No matter how hard Larke and his colleagues tried to use "the most empowering methodologies," the "classic, almost paternalist thinking" that permeates aid efforts "crept into the psychology of everyone."[19] To Larke, this patronizing attitude was rooted in the very fact of being "brought in from the outside with the idea that we are here to help – that people are needy and lack capacity."

Postcolonial feminist theorists would identify one additional source for this attitude and its associated narratives: In their analysis, "charitable impulses" are often "reliant on the denigration of those [being] helped."[20] Peacebuilding is no exception. Expatriates not only discount the knowledge of local people, but they also often disparage the people themselves. I heard pejorative statements about local populations and authorities from all kinds of interveners, regardless of their national origins, professions, and organizations. In Congo, for instance,

---

[17] Anderson and Olson 2003, pp. 30–31.
[18] Author's on-record interview, Dili, February 2012.
[19] For a theoretical discussion of paternalism as a central organizing concept of aid efforts, see Barnett 2011, pp. 34–35; also Barnett 2012.
[20] Presented in de Jong 2011, p. 32.

many interviewees – including African contacts – deemed local and national authorities incompetent, uneducated, corrupt, dishonest, insensitive to the sufferings of their populations, and incapable of long-term planning. Some of them also described Congolese people as poorly educated, lazy, self-centered, violent, or untrustworthy, and this perception extended to Congolese associations and civil society organizations.[21] Perhaps most disturbingly, this negative view of the host population effectively desensitized expatriates to otherwise shocking crimes and scandals. Widespread sexual violence, looting, entrenched corruption, complete disorganization – many interveners reacted to such events with a disabused remark: "That's the way it is in Congo."[22]

In all of the conflict zones in which I worked, I heard certain foreign peacebuilders express some form of this same dismissive attitude. Some interveners painted the Sudanese people as lazy, inept, hopeless, and aggressive, while others branded Timorese nationals as backward, corrupt, and incompetent. Several interviewees deemed Burundians hypocritical, untrustworthy liars, and other contacts thought Albanians to be violent, mean, self-interested Mafiosi; such derogatory comments were also widespread in Nicaragua and Afghanistan. My contacts described the same phenomenon in Azerbaijan, Chad, and Rwanda, and a fellow researcher observed it in Liberia.[23] Admittedly, expatriates and immigrant communities often criticize the citizens of the foreign countries in which they live, whether in the United States, Europe, or Africa. However, criticisms are particularly harsh and widespread among interveners deployed in conflict zones.

There was substantial variation in the validity of the accusations that expatriates voiced against local authorities and populations. Some of these comments were supported by a wealth of evidence. For instance, there is no doubt, that, at the time of my fieldwork, a large number of local and national authorities in Congo, Burundi, Timor-Leste, and Sudan were indeed corrupt, and some of them were incompetent, uneducated, dishonest, and insensitive to the sufferings of their people. However, other comments were blatantly racist and shockingly offensive, such as the "jokes" and offhand remarks I heard in informal settings among some South Asian and European peacekeepers stationed in Congo.[24] A Pakistani unit thought it witty to name their little pet monkey after then-president Joseph Kabila. French and Belgian officers used an "amusing" metaphor to explain to me over drinks the state of affairs: "In Congo, only the forests are virginal, and only the wood works." While those who made these jokes might protest that they meant no real harm and were not actually bigoted, such "humor" unquestionably reinforces feelings of discrimination and inequality.

---

[21] See also Dietze 2010.

[22] On the sources of the view of the Congolese population as inherently violent, and on the international habituation to abuses against the Congolese population, see Autesserre 2010, pp. 74–81; and Dunn 2003.

[23] On Liberia: Sending 2010b, pp. 26–28.

[24] Razack 2004 develops an in-depth study of racism in peacekeeping operations and provides many additional examples of such "jokes" and informal comments.

In each of my field sites, I met expatriates who contested these narratives and tried to rein in these types of careless comments. They reminded their colleagues that blanket statements about entire populations were bound to do injustice to many people. They pointed to the numerous local individuals they knew who defied the stereotypes and who had proved competent, intelligent, selfless, reliable, honest, hardworking, and fully dedicated to bettering the lives of their fellow citizens. They praised the resilience of host populations and emphasized that few individuals back home would have been able to endure the hardships that local people faced with such strength. However, at best, these interveners were able to prevent one conversation or another from getting out of hand. They rarely managed to improve the overall image of local people.

Sadly, at the other end of the spectrum, there were a number of individuals whose privileged positions led them to adopt condescending behaviors that they would have found shocking in other settings (These are examples of how prejudice "creeps in," regardless of one's good intentions). Interviewees in each of my field sites, except Cyprus, told stories of interveners from all walks of life and all geographic origins yelling at their local staff in a degrading way, speaking disparagingly to them, providing advice in a belittling tone, forgetting basic manners when interacting with high-level authorities, and driving so fast on dirt roads that they sprayed people walking nearby with dust or water. At times, these humiliations amounted to the dehumanization of the host population. Congolese regularly complained that South Asian military peacekeepers treated local people like animals, throwing biscuits on the ground for children to pick up.

That international peacebuilders come to belittle their intended beneficiaries so pervasively is puzzling given the patent contradiction between such attitudes and the values to which the vast majority of international peacebuilders say they subscribe. The behavior surprises – and distresses – even the individuals who themselves engage in it. During a party I attended with other interveners in eastern Congo, a friend of mine went on a lengthy diatribe about how he could not stand local people anymore. After a while, he paused, became very sad, and remarked on how he had changed in the year that he had spent in the field. All his ideals of equality, respect, and fairness had crumbled. He had become the very kind of person he used to hate. Only leaving Peaceland, he thought, would enable him to return to normal.

While the reasons for this deleterious process are not the focus of my analysis, my field material has provided the basis for a tentative explanation. Frustration and cultural misunderstandings are two key factors contributing to the profound personal change that my friend described, and that other contacts and I also experienced.[25] As I have discussed, life as an intervener is tough and requires many personal and professional sacrifices, but aid efforts often fail to achieve

---

[25] Thanks to Danielle Boyda for first suggesting to me the ideas I develop in this paragraph and the next one (personal communication, December 2012).

their intended results, generating considerable frustration. The fact that interveners are divorced from the host populations' aspirations and struggles, use inadequate evaluation techniques (as explained at the end of this chapter), and trust that their models and standard approaches will work – since they are based on a great amount of technical expertise and have been validated by research and lessons learned in numerous contexts – makes it difficult for them to identify flaws in their own practices or programs. At this point, it is only natural for them to think that local people deserve the largest part of the blame.

The cultural misunderstandings resulting from the interveners' lack of local knowledge further reinforce the problem, as Kalervo Oberg's work on the phenomenon of culture shock elucidates. In Oberg's analysis, when people living abroad are unable to derive meaning from their surroundings, they enter the "crisis" stage of culture shock. At this point, they reject their environments and take "refuge in the colony of [their] countrymen and its cocktail circuit, which often becomes the fountainhead of emotionally charged labels known as stereotypes."[26] In Peaceland, the stress leads to outbursts against local populations and reinforces the interveners' tendency to stay in the expatriate bubble.

Irrespective of its sources – be they misunderstandings, personal frustrations, culture shock, or other factors altogether – the denigration of local populations and authorities clearly impacts peacebuilding efforts. It legitimizes the narrative that target populations are unable to help themselves and need international expertise and assistance. In doing so, this disparagement perpetuates the entrenched inequality between interveners and their host populations. It also further prevents national employees from obtaining management positions in international structures in their country of origin and further reinforces the expatriates' tendency to impose their ideas and assume that local counterparts will obey.

Local Reactions and Counter-Narratives

These narratives and attitudes create two more pernicious consequences: They solidify the boundaries between interveners and host populations and fuel local resentment, because local counterparts are often aware of how the expatriates view them. A Congolese businessman emphasized that, when he and his fellow citizens interacted with foreign interveners, they felt:

> imprisoned in a sort of cliché that makes you feel uncomfortable: You are incompetent, corrupt, inefficient, and you cannot work in a group. When you are a Congolese today, and you [arrive in a meeting], you have to overcome this conception and make an effort to tell yourself 'I am not incompetent, I am not corrupt, I am not inadequate' even before you can start talking.[27]

[26] Oberg 1960, p. 178, cited in Irwin 2007, p. 2.
[27] Author's on-record interview with Michel Losembe, vice president of the Fédération des Entreprises du Congo, June 2011, Kinshasa.

He also admitted that there were many problems in Congo, but objected to the expatriates' blanket judgments of Congolese elites. A Cameroonian lawyer reported similar feelings: He recalled being "very ill at ease" when he was attending informal gatherings of expatriates and "very frustrated" by what he heard, wondering "who these people were to talk about [his] country in this manner." A Sri Lankan friend had the exact same reaction while attending interveners' parties in her country and in the United States.

In Congo, Sudan, and Timor-Leste, a number of local interviewees noted that the interveners' behavior reminded them of what colonialism must have been like – a feeling that other researchers have documented in conflict zones from Nepal to Madagascar to Haiti.[28] In the words of my contacts, just like the colonizers, foreign interveners "know what is best for local people" and come to teach host populations what to do. Colonizers were historically always in the leadership ranks, and the expatriates that the local populations see in NGO, UN, and business circles similarly hold management positions. Also like the colonizers, interveners socialize among themselves. In Congo, Timor-Leste, and Madagascar, they actually formed the main client base of the same bars, restaurants, and clubs that had previously served as exclusive social spaces for colonizers.[29]

These local reactions fuel several dynamics that profoundly and detrimentally impact peacebuilding effectiveness. To start, as explained in Chapter 3, resentment regularly leads host populations and authorities to evade, contest, or resist international programs. Moreover, humiliation occasionally generates violent forms of protest, as it has in Congo, Timor-Leste, and in other conflict zones. An interviewee attributed the many incidents of Congolese rioting against interveners and stoning their vehicles to their "anger at this disrespect." A Timorese citizen similarly explained that aggression against foreigners increased after 2006 as a reaction to incidents of interveners behaving in racist and demeaning manners.[30] Finally, across conflict zones, local people counter the "here to help" narrative and its inherent inequality with their own critical narratives. They

---

[28] The interviewees who spoke on the record about this issue were: Onesphore Sematumba (Institut Pole, Goma, Congo, November 2011); Reverent Tut (deputy director of the Peacebuilding Commission, Malakal, South Sudan, April 2011); and Josh Trindade (consultant, Dili, Timor-Leste, February 2012).

Marten 2004 develops a fascinating comparison of the nineteenth-century colonizers and the contemporary interveners in Haiti, Bosnia, Kosovo, and Timor-Leste. So does Dietze 2010 on Congo; Hindman 2011, p. 185 on Nepal; and Verma 2011, p. 73 on Madagascar. Dunn 2003 also presents very useful analyses of the persistence of colonial imagery in contemporary discourses of intervention in Congo. For a particularly insightful evaluation of the scholarly literature on the similarities between colonialism and today's peace interventions, see Paris 2010, pp. 344–346 and 348–350.

[29] On Madagascar: Verma 2011, p. 73.

[30] Author's on-record interview with Jose Kai Lekke Sousa Santos, Dili, Timor-Leste, February 2012.

point out the selfish motivations of interveners in an attempt to deny them the moral high ground and to emphasize that expatriates also reap large benefits from the aid relationship. From Congo to Afghanistan to Kosovo, these criticisms reinforce the tensions and barriers between foreign peacebuilders and their local counterparts.

In Congo, for instance, while recipients of humanitarian assistance are usually grateful to their benefactors, many other citizens emphasize that expatriates have come not to help local populations but to help themselves.[31] In this counternarrative, expatriates enjoy much better lives than they would in their home countries, by having better jobs, better salaries, better houses, and better cars. To further deny interveners any claim to moral superiority, certain Congolese interviewees noted how deeply the expatriates' lifestyle shocked them. They objected to the fact that some women dress in a manner the population considers indecent, criticized the interveners for partying or going to bars too often, condemned their lack of religion, deplored that too many men interact with prostitutes, and, as detailed earlier in this chapter, complained that expatriates treat them in a disrespectful and humiliating way. They also maintained that Western powers, motivated by greed and a desire to control Central Africa, were behind the Rwandan and Ugandan invasions of their country in the late 1990s. They argued that interveners still acted as spies or agents for their home country and thus fueled arms trafficking and illegal exploitation of natural resources. Finally, many Congolese portrayed expatriates as wasting the money earmarked for their country, arguing that they can see no obvious results from all the international aid and peacebuilding programs: Violence continues, and most of the population remains in dire poverty. These perceptions have engendered the widespread idea that foreigners must make it up to Congolese: In other words, Congolese are entitled to aid, which is not an act of charity by the interveners. Unfortunately, this exact attitude provokes the ire of frustrated expatriates, generating a vicious cycle.

Across the board, while many individuals feel grateful to a specific doctor for saving a child, or to a specific agency for protecting them or providing basic necessities, those sentiments do not necessarily extend to interveners as a group.[32] Afghans, Bolivians, Bosnians, Burmese, Burundians, Cambodians, Congolese, Ecuadorians, Filipinos, Indonesians, Kenyans, Kosovars, Lebanese, Palestinians, Malians, Thais, Timorese, Sri Lankans, and Sudanese reproach international agencies for using funds inefficiently, allocating money either toward perks for intervention staff or toward projects that intended beneficiaries view as pointless.[33] Jokes about peacekeepers illustrate how populations view

---

[31] See also Dijkzeul and Wakenge 2010.

[32] Also Anderson, Brown, et al. 2012, pp. 30–32 and 35.

[33] On the perception by Bolivian, Bosnian, Indonesian, Lebanese, Malian, and Thai people: CDA Collaborative Learning Projects 2010b, p. 7. On Burmese, Ecuadorians, Filipinos, and Sri Lankans (and also on Bolivians, Bosnians, Cambodians, Kenyans, Lebanese, Malians, and

them as a waste of resources: Salvadorians nicknamed the 1990s UN mission in their country "*Vacaciones Unidas*" ("United holidays," a play on the Spanish translation of United Nations, *Naciones Unidas*); Africans note that UN soldiers in Cote d'Ivoire are supposed to observe breaches of the ceasefires but in fact they "*n'y voient rien*" (a wordplay on the name "Ivoirians," which is pronounced in French like the words "do not see"); while Cypriots present those stationed on their island as doing "beach keeping" rather than peacekeeping.[34]

Conspiracy theories are equally common. Afghans tend to view all kinds of peacebuilders – whether from the UN or from the North Atlantic Treaty Organization (NATO) – as invaders advancing Western economic, geostrategic, or religious agendas.[35] Contesting the narrative that the NATO intervention is aimed primarily at protecting them, Kosovars similarly emphasize the peacebuilders' geostrategic and economic interests. Somalis accuse interveners of perpetuating protracted state collapse in their country in order both to punish them for the losses incurred in 1993 and to avoid moving their organizational headquarters from comfortable Nairobi to much rougher Mogadishu.[36] Certain Timorese allege that interveners, notably Australians, fuel instability in order to maintain control over Timorese oil reserves. Laurent Gbagbo's supporters in Cote d'Ivoire reproach the UN for supporting the "recolonization" of their country, and Cypriots often suspect that foreign funding has underlying imperialist motives.[37]

In addition to these geostrategic considerations, host populations emphasize that the interveners' "amoral" everyday behavior conflicts with their official "moral" objectives. Just like in Congo, local people in other conflict zones – especially those belonging to traditional, conservative, or deeply religious societies – regularly criticized the interveners' lifestyle during both formal and informal discussions. They derided the expatriates' dress codes, patronage of bars and clubs, and sexual behaviors.[38] Many populations, from West Africa to

---

Timorese): Anderson, Brown, et al. 2012, pp. 35–39 and 108–109. On Indonesians: also Smirl 2008, pp. 244 and 246. On Cambodians and Kosovars: CDA Collaborative Learning Projects 2008a, p.8. On the other countries: author's formal interviews and informal communications, 1999–2012. On Afghans, see also "Exotic Birds in a Cage: Criticism Grows of Afghanistan's Bloated NGO Industry," by Walter Mayr, *Spiegel Online*, October 20, 2010 (www.spiegel.de/international/world/0,1518,718656-3,00.html).

[34] The Salvadorian example comes from Pouligny 2004, p. 15.

[35] For public sources, see among others Egeland, Harmer, et al. 2011, p. 16; and Marine Corps Intelligence Activity, 2008, p. 8.

[36] Ken Menkhaus, Davidson College, during panel "The Politics of International Intervention in Africa" at the International Studies Association annual meeting, Montreal, April 2011.

[37] Public sources on Cyprus include Mitchell 2011a, p. 7; Papadakis 1997, pp. 356–357; and author's on-record interviews with Bulent Kanol (executive director of The Management Center, Nicosia, September 2011) and Dr. Costas Constantinou (professor of political science at the University of Cyprus, Nicosia, September 2011).

[38] Cain, Postlewait, et al. 2004 and Chandrasekaran 2012 paint a useful picture of the social and personal characteristics of the interveners' lives that local people object to.

Bosnia, also pointed to sexual abuse by interveners as further evidence of their moral failings.[39]

Even in places like South Sudan, where, at the time of my fieldwork, international peacebuilders were generally quite popular (as they had just helped achieve independence from the North), I heard numerous complaints. Local contacts bemoaned the way that interveners wasted assistance funds, did little that actually benefited surrounding populations, encouraged prostitution, or acted as spies for their home countries.[40]

While the local peoples' counter-narratives highlight real issues with the behavior of some interveners, they too overstate and overgeneralize their cases. Most expatriates do try to improve conditions for local populations. Most of them also try to alter their usual behavior – changing their dress codes, drinking alcohol only behind closed doors, and relating differently with persons of the opposite gender – when the norms of their host societies so require, and even when doing so violates their own norms. Many also attempt to resist the regrettable attitudes adopted by some of their colleagues, and a number of individuals actually attempt to promote different kinds of interactions between external and local counterparts. More importantly, the interveners' goal of helping people is certainly a worthy one, even if the dominant narratives tend to blind expatriates to both what local people have to offer and to the hurt and resentment of host populations. Overstating the negative behavior of some interveners or understating the good intentions and propriety of others therefore exaggerates the responsibility of foreigners for the failures and tensions that exist in Peaceland. Regardless, the narratives detailed in this section have significant unintended effects on the ground: They further reinforce the boundaries between international peacebuilders and their local counterparts, and they fuel the resentment of the former by the latter.

The Interveners' Resources

The structure of inequality in Peaceland is predicated not only upon the "here to help" narrative, but also on the resource gap between interveners and local populations. International peacebuilders enjoy massive material, social, and symbolic advantages when they work in conflict zones. While the policy and scholarly literature on international intervention emphasize that the peacebuilders' lack of necessary resources decreases the effectiveness of their actions, I emphasize here a different point: The resources that do exist on the ground

---

[39] Simm 2013 details and evaluates these local accusations in greater depth. Also Higate and Henry 2009, chapter 8.

[40] A semi-public source on most of these perceptions is the debate that took place on the NGO Forum in April 2011 in response to the article "South Sudan's Reliance on NGOs," by Matthew Brunwasser, PRI's *The World*, April 15, 2011.

are so comparatively vast that they further instantiate a structure of inequality, which has serious consequences for peacebuilding efficacy.[41]

As explained in the previous chapter, membership in the community of interveners endows expatriates with social capital – resources that are linked to social relationships and networks.[42] Chapter 5 has also shown that the social superiority of the international peacebuilders is manifest in most areas of operation. Interveners are treated like VIPs in many theaters of deployment and, because of the salary gap, they enjoy a quality of life much higher than that of their local peers.

In addition, in the eyes of host populations, foreign peacebuilders enjoy the symbolic clout that comes with representing "the international community." Even in Cyprus and Israel, where socioeconomic differences between interveners and local populations are relatively small, the former still enjoy distinct prestige and social standing due to their international affiliations.[43] In Israel, in the words of a local peacebuilder, "The power [interveners] have is mainly the legitimacy they can give or take." Acquiring UN recognition – receiving the mission's backing, earning seats at the negotiating tables, having appointments with delegations, or getting visits from UN officials during formal events – was also central to local politicians' and armed groups' quests for legitimacy in many countries, from El Salvador to Cambodia and from Mozambique to Haiti.[44] Furthermore, in Cyprus, Bosnia-Herzegovina, and Kosovo, the foreign peace-builders' prestige rests on the fact that they "contribut[e] to the production of a better form of life and transcendence of the conditions that foster and result from violence."[45] The consequences, in the words of an expatriate peacebuilder reflecting on her experience in Cyprus and central Asia, are that "there is a sort of awe of the foreign community." Importantly, foreign and local sources confirmed that only interveners benefit from this prestige: For instance, Cypriots do not necessarily regard the businesspeople or the retired foreigners who reside in their country in this manner.

Interveners also enjoy significant material resources, notably economic funds. Donors often provide extensive bilateral and multilateral aid to the governments of host countries, totaling more than 60 percent of the gross domestic product in places like Burundi, Iraq, Liberia, and Timor-Leste.[46] In addition, in most conflict

---

[41] Examples of the classic policy and scholarly literature on the impact of lack of resources on peacebuilding operations include, among others: Doyle and Sambanis 2000 (p. 780) and 2006; Kim and Metrikas 1997, pp. 127–128; and Stedman, Rothchild, et al. 2002, notably pp. 44 and 57–58. For an approach related to mine, see Anderson 2008.

[42] On social capital, see Bourdieu 1980.

[43] For a public source on Cyprus: Mitchell 2011a, pp. 20–21.

[44] Pouligny 2004, pp. 238–245.

[45] Personal communication from Dr. Audra Mitchell (lecturer in international relations, University of York), May 2012.

[46] Lavers 2008.

zones, foreign donors finance humanitarian, development, and peacebuilding efforts through international agencies and NGOs. These contributions are quite substantial: In some places, the combined operating budgets of intervening organizations are comparable to that of the state. For instance, in 2010, non-governmental and international organizations in Congo administered projects totaling close to $2.8 billion, whereas the Congolese government directly managed $3.1 billion.[47] In some cases, a single NGO can carry tremendous economic weight in a given region. In the eastern Congolese province of North Kivu in 2011, for instance, local officials expressed suspicion that some international NGOs had budgets that were larger than those of their entire province. They were right. According to confidential sources, the 2011 budget for the province of North Kivu was officially $110 million, but was in practice closer to $35 million. During the same year, Doctors Without Borders (all sections combined) spent approximately $73 million in Congo, the International Rescue Committee about $70 million, and the International Committee of the Red Cross $63 million.[48]

In all of these cases, greater funding means more and better logistical assets, such as cars and other means of transportation, as well as nicer and better equipped offices – all very visible manifestations of the disparity in resources between interveners and their local counterparts. In addition, international interveners sometimes enjoy sizeable military assets. In conflict zones such as Cyprus and Kosovo, international peacekeepers are a force at least as powerful as the domestic armies or the armed opposition groups.

In the eyes of local people, the interveners' enormous economic resources are among their most significant contributions.[49] For one, they provide certain local peacebuilders with the funds and logistical assets necessary to implement their programs.[50] International funding also encourages the creation, growth, professionalization, and expansion of local civil society groups, who then make crucial contributions to peace initiatives, as happened in Cyprus and Burundi.[51] Furthermore, employment opportunities with intervening agencies regularly provide a useful economic stimulus for local communities.[52] That stimulus can have important conflict-resolution dimensions, as it did in Aceh (Indonesia): The injection of international funds following the 2004 tsunami generated jobs that, incidentally, proved very effective at reintegrating former combatants. Researchers estimate that this process of job creation was so important that it

---

[47] Coalition of thirteen international and Congolese civil society groups 2012, p. 19n2 and author's confidential interviews. Official Congolese budget data available at www.ministeredubudget.cd.

[48] Demian 2012, p. 15; and International Committee of the Red Cross 2012, p. 109. The figure for Doctors Without Borders comes from confidential communications, May 2012.

[49] Also Pouligny 2004, pp. 245–251.

[50] Also Anderson and Olson 2003, p. 40.

[51] CDA Collaborative Learning Projects 2012, p. 4.

[52] CDA Collaborative Learning Projects 2010b, pp. 7–8.

"probably played a larger role in contributing to peace than the dedicated reintegration programming."[53]

While these positive contributions cannot be discounted, the disparity in resources reinforces the sense of inequality between interveners and their local counterparts. Using the same words as a Filipino city official interviewed by the Listening Project, a Kenyan peacebuilder I interviewed explained that, in the cases of countries with weak state structures and few material resources, "beggars cannot be choosers."[54] In Haiti, the government has to comply with donors' conditions and suggestions because that is the only way it can get the financial resources it needs to govern.[55] In Congo, state capacity is so low that the government cannot oversee the actions of international interveners. At the same time, the need is so high that, as several Congolese officials noted, they "have to agree to anything" in the hope that it might "get [them] out of the ditch."[56] Interveners can thus – in the words of one of them – "set any kind of unreasonable rule [they] feel like" and impose the projects they want on their local counterparts. Select local peacebuilders are, in fact, so wary of the strings attached to external funding that they occasionally refuse foreign contributions simply to preserve the independence they need to implement their programs.[57]

The very words that certain local populations use to address foreign interveners are indicative of how they view the resulting power asymmetry in Peaceland: South Sudanese call expatriates "*khawaja*," which means "lord" or "master" in Arabic, and populations of Central Africa often call foreigners they do not know "chief" or "boss" (when otherwise they would typically reserve such terms for those who appear wealthy and powerful). Altogether, as an expatriate working for an international NGO summarized, interveners in conflict zones "represent power and authority."

There is one series of exceptions to these deeply unequal relationships: countries that enjoy wealth, well-functioning state structures, and diplomatic influence. These are rare conditions in war zones, but they do occasionally exist in places such as present-day Cyprus and Israel. In these circumstances, the relationship between interveners and host government can be more equal. During my fieldwork in Cyprus in 2012, all of my interviewees enthusiastically praised the ongoing peace negotiations for being a "Cypriot-led" process. Many local stakeholders similarly reported feeling that expatriates listened attentively to their arguments and took them into account. My expatriate contacts emphasized one main reason for the Cypriots' relative success at resisting international imposition: The high level of education of their Cypriot

---

[53] Barron and Burke 2008, pp. 53–54.
[54] The Filipino city official is cited in Anderson, Brown, et al. 2012, p. 61. On this topic, see also Anderson and Olson 2003, p. 40.
[55] Sending 2010b, p. 18.
[56] Citation from author's interview with Losembe.
[57] Also Anderson and Olson 2003, p. 40.

counterparts was enabling a constructive dialogue. Interveners would offer suggestions, and Cypriots would engage with their ideas, analyze them, and offer constructive feedback on how to change or adapt them. Even in this context, however, as an employee of a local Cypriot NGO explained, "When you hear the word 'international' in front of anything, an NGO or an organization or whatever, it gives a different status, a status of envy, of like, having your way in other countries."[58]

Accountability

Upward Accountability

The resource disparity that gives such advantage to interveners on the ground also gives enormous leverage to the donors that finance international work. Because they control the funds, donors can decide what to do with that money, based on criteria they establish themselves. They can also refuse to back initiatives of which they disapprove. Consequently, even remote donors can shape conflict-resolution projects on the ground. One of the important consequences, which the scholarly and policy literatures on aid and peacebuilding have widely documented, and of which host populations are perfectly aware, is that, for all interveners, accountability structures are oriented toward external entities, not toward beneficiaries.[59] As an international NGO official summarized, based on her experience in various conflict zones, foreigners "drive things with their money." They "decide what to fund, what activities will get supported, and which ministries will get assistance."

Indeed, NGOs are accountable to their donors – which are UN agencies, as well as European and North American states, organizations, and private funders. One of these donors stationed in Sudan captured what I heard during many other interviews: NGOs "are so keen to get funding; they are led more by funders and donors than by the realistic needs of the communities that they are working with." NGOs usually take donors' priorities into account when designing their intervention strategies, and they keep their funders informed of their progress while implementing projects. In contrast, as I witnessed numerous times, they strongly (and usually successfully) resist whenever a host government or local authority – whether Afghan, Congolese, or Sudanese – asks them to report on their activities and their uses of aid monies.

Likewise, government donors are accountable to their taxpayers and legislators, rather than to beneficiaries. Peacekeeping missions report to the UN

---

[58] Mitchell 2011a, p. 22.
[59] Jacobs and Wilford 2007 presents a very useful review of the scholarly literature. For representative analyses on aid, see among others: Eyben 2006; Smirl 2008, pp. 242–243; Stiglitz 2003; and Wenar 2006. On peacebuilding: Aoi, De Coning, et al. 2007, part V; and Woodward 2003. On the perception of host populations: Anderson, Brown, et al. 2012, chapter 5 and pp. 91–93.

Security Council, UN agencies report to their headquarters in New York and Geneva, and these headquarters report to the UN member states. A disillusioned peacekeeper based in Congo summarized what I observed during many meetings and field visits:

> The whole mission is solely accountable to New York. As soon as the [Congolese] government or the population says something, we raise the issue of the mandate: 'We can't do this or that.' [...] What the population says is of no importance, except if they literally throw stones at us. [...] The mission is responsible neither to the [Congolese] population nor to [their] government. This is the crux of the problem. There is no cooperation with the government to accomplish any specific goals together.

In the end, he concluded that "journalists from *The New York Times* or *The Washington Post*" had much more influence in setting the mission's agenda than local counterparts. This was painfully accurate. In confidential meetings and interviews, I saw how fear of foreign public opinion clearly influenced which issues peacekeepers prioritized. While the troops feared particularly the reactions of their home countries, the whole mission also worried about the opinions of the Security Council countries. Anxiety over what the international media might say could prompt actions that peacekeepers knew were pointless. For instance, in response to media-fueled public outrage in Europe and North America, a UN operation sent a Joint Protection Team to investigate a massacre that had taken place so long ago that it was impossible for the team to obtain useful data. Another launched an inquiry on accusations of corruption that everybody knew were unfounded, but that a foreign journalist had mentioned.

A related problem is that the indicators used to evaluate success do not measure the satisfaction of the beneficiaries or the actual impact of the project on the ground. Instead, they evaluate whether the donor's money has been spent appropriately, for instance by checking whether the agreed-upon number of local officials have been trained or relief items distributed.[60] A Cypriot NGO peacebuilder cited the 2006–2009 UNDP project to increase the capacity of civil society in her country as a prime example of such detrimental procedures, as did many other Cypriots I interviewed. The project aimed at training local NGO staff in technical skills, such as project management and writing proposals, while at the same time promoting collaboration between Turkish and Greek Cypriots. According to the evaluation guidelines, the project was effective: Participants from both communities attended the trainings. According to civil society actors, the project was in fact ineffective. It did

---

[60] On peacekeeping operations: Meharg 2009, notably pp. 8–11. On development programs: Birdsall 2004, section 3, and Easterly 2002. On aid and peacebuilding projects in general: Anderson, Brown, et al. 2012, pp. 36–37 and 41–42.

nothing to promote the broader goal of reconciliation because participants did not continue collaborating beyond the initiative's activities. Ole Jacob Sending and his coauthors observed the same phenomenon in Haiti, and I heard similar complaints in Congo.[61]

There, a state official also lamented that donors "do not try to find out what the level of satisfaction is among us beneficiaries." A striking demonstration of this oversight occurred in the projects to reconstruct state authority in the eastern provinces in the early 2010s. Because prevailing narratives emphasized statebuilding as the main solution to the complex problems of Congo, donors and UN agencies devoted a great deal of funds and efforts to developing infrastructures, transporting police officers and other state officials, and helping state representatives regain authority over rebel-controlled territory. However, despite repeated requests, not once did I find an intervener who had tried to assess whether or not surrounding populations were satisfied with these actions. The only assessment available detailed the actions that international actors had taken – the number of buildings constructed, the number of state officials trained – but it gave no sense of whether the program had actually changed conditions on the ground, or whether the population in the target area was satisfied with these efforts.[62] An independent evaluation of the UN Peacebuilding Fund projects in Burundi documented similar dynamics, deploring that "staff were pressured to and held accountable for spending money more than they were [...] for delivering results."[63]

Overall, many interveners I met over the course of my research wanted to improve the lot of host populations and genuinely tried to do their best, but they equated the betterment of local life conditions with the success of their projects. Because the indicators they used to measure the effect of these programs reflected external priorities instead of local ones, the evaluations regularly failed to assess the actual impact of the international initiatives on local conditions.

Change and Pushback

Since the 2000s, a number of researchers and practitioners have advocated for greater evaluation of the actual difference projects make in the lives of target populations.[64] Upon the request of various NGOs, academic researchers have studied the impact of community-driven reconstruction projects in various countries, demobilization and reintegration programs in Liberia, and grassroots

[61] Sending 2010b, p. 4 (and case study on pp. 15–22).
[62] MONUSCO Stabilization Support Unit 2011.
[63] Campbell 2010, citation from pp. 68–69; other supporting evidence on pp. 10, 18, 19, and 24–25.
[64] For an overview, see Meharg 2009 (see especially the introduction); and Menkhaus 2004 (especially on pp. 1–4).

conflict resolution initiatives in Liberia, Rwanda, and Timor-Leste.[65] A number of organizations have signed on to international charters to improve quality and accountability, such as the Humanitarian Accountability Partnership and the Accountability Charter for international NGOs.[66] Some of these agencies have also developed mechanisms to gather feedback from local stakeholders about the effectiveness of their efforts, including participatory evaluations, complaints and response systems, perceptions studies, community scorecards, citizen report cards, and storytelling.[67]

When successfully implemented, these mechanisms have significantly improved the effectiveness of international initiatives. A multi-country, multi-organization study found that the aid agencies that "maintained on-going primary stakeholder feedback mechanisms throughout the cycle of a project reported greater results and higher satisfaction compared to prior projects that did not include as much recipient feedback."[68] The changes that the beneficiaries requested were often easy to implement, and they led to "significant improvement in recipient satisfaction."[69] In a separate evaluation, Susanna Campbell found that, in Burundi, certain interveners managed to establish strong informal accountability mechanisms with beneficiaries and other important stakeholders to counterbalance their formal accountability mechanisms, which prioritized responsiveness to headquarters, donors, and the Burundian government.[70] In Campbell's analysis, these "downward accountability" mechanisms strongly increased the efficacy of peacebuilding efforts. In contrast, the many other initiatives relying solely on upward accountability remained much less effective.[71]

Despite these encouraging results, however, the organizations that routinely measure the on-the-ground impact of their actions, or the satisfaction of their beneficiaries, are still the exception rather than the rule.[72] Most of the initiatives with that aim have remained ad-hoc, isolated, and limited to specific projects. They are also often incomplete, as many organizations failed to change their

---

[65] On community-driven reconstruction projects: Fearon, Humphreys, et al. 2009 and 2011; Humphreys, Sanchez de la Sierra, et al. 2012; and King 2013. On programs to reintegrate former combatants: Blattman and Annan 2011. On grassroots conflict-resolution initiatives: Blattman, Hartman, et al. 2014; Levy Paluk and Green 2009; and the confidential evaluation of the Catholic Relief Services' *Laletek* (Bridge) program on communal conflicts in Timor-Leste (2010–2012).

[66] On the Humanitarian Accountability Partnership, see www.hapinternational.org (last accessed in December 2013). On the Accountability Charter for international NGOs, see CDA Collaborative Learning Projects 2011a, p. 1 and throughout the report. Also Jacobs and Wilford 2010.

[67] CDA Collaborative Learning Projects 2011a, pp. 2, 9–10, 14–19, and 22–23; and IRIN 2012, pp. 7–10. See also the material available on the Web site Listen First (www.listenfirst.org, last accessed in December 2013).

[68] CDA Collaborative Learning Projects 2011a, citation from p. 6, detailed examples on pp. 14–19.

[69] Ibid., citation from p. 6.

[70] Campbell 2014. Also Campbell 2010, pp. 50–51.

[71] Campbell 2010, pp. 50–51; and Campbell 2014.

[72] See Anderson, Brown, et al. 2012, p. i for a similar analysis.

policies and strategies based on the suggestions they received. Alternatively, when they did make adjustments, they rarely informed host communities, and thus local people eventually lost faith in the feedback process and stopped contributing to it.[73] Although donors' guidelines increasingly mention the need for downward accountability, few donors actually provide funding to implement such feedback processes.[74]

The predominance of upward rather than downward accountability is among the key obstacles to change on the ground because this configuration attenuates the impact of ineffective or counterproductive programs on expatriates. In the first place, it gives intended beneficiaries no power to hold interveners responsible for the outcomes of their efforts. Furthermore, it deprives both donors and interveners of powerful incentives to reform detrimental modes of action. Most evaluations fail to show donors that, although their funds have been disbursed appropriately, the programs may not have made the intended impact on the ground. The fact that expatriates stay in their areas of deployment for a short period of time means that the lack of improvement – or the deterioration – in local conditions affects them only briefly.[75]

An additional element that hinders the attempts to mitigate the structure of inequality is that certain interveners regularly use the power differential as a strategic resource. This happens particularly often with individuals who otherwise would not command the respect necessary to work effectively, for example because they are female in a male-controlled environment, young in a country that defers to elders, or of the wrong skin color in a racist society. One such expatriate captured what many of my contacts and I experienced. In her words,

> When a 24 year old finds herself getting deference in a room of ministers because she is from an NGO with money attached, she may strategically use that to 'get her job done' on a specific issue. I have definitely found myself [doing this], and using small things to my advantage in order to make my funder and boss in the United States happy.

These individuals, as well as their more privileged colleagues, use the structure of inequality to their advantage in pursuit of their programmatic or policy goals. However, even when it comes from the best of intentions – to more effectively help host populations – this strategy still perpetuates the entrenched inequality between interveners and their local counterparts, along with all its detrimental by-products.

Interveners who develop long-term sentimental relationships with members of the host populations also benefit from the structure of inequality, but at the

---

[73] CDA Collaborative Learning Projects 2011a, pp. 2, 11–14, and throughout the report; Jacobs and Wilford 2008, pp. 4 and 47–49.

[74] CDA Collaborative Learning Projects 2011a, p. 21.

[75] Also CDA Collaborative Learning Projects 2008a, pp. 4–5.

same time they are uniquely placed to challenge it.[76] Although media reports and local populations often focus on sexual abuse and prostitution, in virtually all theaters of deployment there are also expatriates (usually men) who develop noncoercive and nonabusive relationships with local inhabitants (usually women). Some of these relationships stem from ordinary attraction. In other cases, the attraction is more complicated: Irrespective of their professional disregard for host populations, the foreign peacebuilders may view the local Other as exotic and thus particularly desirable. Simultaneously, the power, prestige, and resources inherent to their status makes interveners especially attractive to local women and men – and more acceptable to the families of their local partners. As a result, from Haiti to Sri Lanka to Somalia, certain members of the interveners' club cohabitate with an educated local woman, marry a local aid worker, or have children with a local lady.

When they stay in their partners' countries of origin, these expatriates can challenge the firmness of the boundaries between international peacebuilders and host populations. A portion develop in-depth personal relationships with their new family members, stepping outside of the expatriate bubble and beginning to integrate in the local social fabric, with all the positive effects that it entails (see Chapter 5). The large majority also becomes more attuned to the consequences of ineffective or failed programs, since they see their partner suffering from the lack of improvement in local conditions. They therefore develop stronger incentives to change the status quo, and eventually, some of them start to challenge the ineffective modes of operation and suggest alternative strategies. Often, however, these expatriates eventually move on to another posting, sometimes bringing their partner along the way – and then both fall back into the expatriate bubble in their new country of deployment.

Conclusion

Throughout Peaceland, inequality permeates the relationships between interveners and local stakeholders. The massive material, social, and symbolic resources at the disposal of foreign peacebuilders create a significant power imbalance. The "here to help" narrative – and its inherent implications that host populations need assistance and their elite lack knowledge and capacity – perpetuates the imbalance and widens the chasm between the two groups. There are a variety of ways that international peacebuilders could bridge this gap. They could promote narratives that paint a more positive image of local people. They could also step out of the expatriate bubble and put local people in a position to "give back" to them in some fashion. Above all, they could ensure that they and their organizations become accountable to their intended beneficiaries. A few

---

[76] The entire paragraph builds on – and sometimes paraphrases – a personal communication from Nimmi Gowrinathan (independent researcher, March 2013).

interveners actually do so, and the increased effectiveness of their initiatives underscores the value of their alternative approach.

Unfortunately, instead of following the example of these exceptional interveners, most of their colleagues remain accountable only to outside donors and foreign governments. It is true that this is the only way for international peacebuilders to continue to raise the funds necessary for their actions, funds that local people see as one of the main contributions that interveners bring to conflict zones. However, the detrimental and counterproductive effects of the narratives and practices analyzed in this chapter offset these positive intended consequences. The moral implications inherent to the claim of "being here to help," the massive resources that interveners control, and the pattern of upward accountability solidify the boundaries between interveners and host populations. This sustains and promotes the expatriate bubble, which hinders the effectiveness of international efforts across the board (see Chapter 5). These modes of operation also fuel the resentment that entices local people to evade, contest, or resist international programs, thus aggravating the counterproductive dynamics documented in Chapter 3. To top it all off, as the next chapter explains, it is because interveners are accountable to donors instead of beneficiaries that they follow intervention rituals, such as visibility and security procedures, and favor short-term and quantifiable results. Sadly, the ways in which most interveners on the ground handle the demands of donors and headquarters further strengthen the boundaries between expatriates and local people, and these daily work routines also create their own impediments to effective peacebuilding.

7

Daily Work Routines

It took an interview with a Kenyan expatriate for me to realize that the daily work routines that I had taken for granted as an intervener – routines whose effects I once thought limited to the lives of Peaceland's inhabitants – in fact directly influenced peacebuilding effectiveness. Following a prevalent line of inquiry in peacebuilding scholarship, I asked this interviewee if he thought that Western or liberal ideas shaped the international efforts in South Sudan, where he was working. He evaded my question and cut to the core of what he, as a former recipient of intervention, found more important:

> People do not like those camps [in which peacekeepers live]: They are closed, barricaded; [interveners] come out of them all armored. It is not a good system, but it will not change because it is the United Nations' system. [...] Like the security system, you have to constantly listen to a handheld radio, so people appear very divorced from reality. [...] When they move, they move in big vehicles – two vehicles, five vehicles – and in every vehicle there is only one person, even though one vehicle could have taken ten people. And [the local people] do not understand [...] because there are 30 of them in a bus – some even hanging off the back or on the side of the bus – so they look at [the interveners] and think 'maybe they are just another kind of human being.'

I had followed these procedures countless times in the past while working for various non-governmental organizations (NGOs), but I had never realized how strong their impact was on local perceptions of interveners. It had not occurred to me that these routines could transform me into "another kind of human being," different from the people I was trying to help. Above all, I had not previously appreciated that my interview questions about the broad character-istics of international interventions, their values, and their structures had, just like existing scholarly research on the subjects, overlooked an equally crucial dimension of peacebuilding effectiveness: daily work routines.

This chapter focuses on the everyday routines that recur throughout conflict zones, that interveners viewed as evident and commonsensical, and that significantly influence the effectiveness of international action. In addition to the security procedures to which my Kenyan interviewee alluded, I analyze the impact of three other shared intervention rituals: the foreign peacebuilders' advertisement of their work, their relentless attempts to be neutral or impartial, and their regular writing of reports about their actions. I also highlight the influence of the expatriates' preference for quantifiable and short-term results.

All of these practices and habits result from a combination of top-down instructions and bottom-up processes, and all have both positive intended impacts and detrimental unintended consequences. The prevailing modes of operation aim to promote intervention effectiveness and to enable interveners to function on the ground, through providing for their safety (by following security routines), ensuring their access to all parties in conflict (by remaining impartial), and securing continued funding for their projects (by raising visibility, constantly reporting their actions, and striving to attain quantifiable and short-term results). However, in addition to these positive dimensions, the way in which the top-down instructions are put into practice on the ground has a number of unintended consequences that decrease the potential effectiveness of international efforts. These everyday practices perpetuate and bolster the firm boundaries between foreign peacebuilders and host populations, compounding the interveners' difficulties in collecting and analyzing data and in developing good relationships with their local counterparts. Worse, these practices are regularly counterproductive. They construct an image of the interveners as superior to host populations – thus regularly alienating the latter –, reinforce the disregard of local input, and create numerous additional obstacles to everyday peace efforts on the ground.

Security Routines

Widespread Security Procedures

Security procedures consist of a number of actions that are relatively identical across conflict zones. They include, among many other things, hiring security advisors; briefing new arrivals on security; informing the base of any and all staff movements; using code names to identify individuals, organizations, and locations when using radio communication; driving with doors locked and windows closed; letting only people from one's organization or other expatriates enter the interveners' vehicles; never traveling to the field at night; never walking around outside the compound after dusk (or, in places like the Congolese capital Kinshasa and the Afghan capital Kabul, never walking around outside at all); respecting curfews, even when the local authorities do not impose any; living in designated safe neighborhoods; attending regular security meetings; and writing security and evacuation plans.[1] These shared practices are behavioral, but many are also physical, embedded in material objects, like the walkie-talkies that many expatriates must carry or the barbed wire that protects their compounds.

In certain settings, women expatriates also have to comply with additional precautions. When I worked in Afghanistan, for instance, my NGO's internal rules forbade foreign female staff members from leaving our compound, whether on foot or by car, unless accompanied by a male colleague. In eastern Congo, many agencies also have "stricter security protocols for women than men" due to the fear of sexual violence.[2]

The security restrictions extend to information sharing. UN agencies, NGOs, and diplomatic missions usually classify their security reports as "confidential" and restrict dissemination to members of their own organizations. The confidentiality requirement is so strong that even organizations working together on an initiative are reluctant to exchange security information, and they rarely do so without assurances that both the data and its sources will remain confidential.

Interveners also have zones that are off-limits – places they are never supposed to visit unless for imperative operational reasons and, then, only while following stringent security procedures. These areas – notable among them the United Nations (UN)-designated "red" zones – can encompass entire transportation routes, villages, or districts. The Road Security Assessment maps, which the local UN security offices draw for each province where its personnel are deployed, illustrate how small the approved territory can be for expatriates. For example, in November 2010, the staff evaluating conditions in North Kivu (Congo) deemed only two short roads safe enough for expatriates to travel freely on. These roads were respectively about ten and twenty miles long, and both departed from Goma.[3] The security officers viewed about a third of the other thoroughfares as relatively secure, as long as expatriates used them during daytime and with many precautions, such as in convoys of two or more cars. They categorized the rest, meaning the majority of the roads in the provinces, as dangerous enough to require military escorts. Even worse, as the security situation deteriorated in late 2010 and early 2011, several relatively safe roads were recategorized as perilous, and updated Road Security Assessment maps showed the vast majority of routes as requiring military escorts.[4]

Of course, there are variations in the degree to which interveners design or implement such security routines. Three factors account for most of the differences. The first is the type of agency for which expatriates work. Diplomatic and

---

[1] Also Roth 2011, p. 160.

[2] Egeland, Harmer, et al. 2011, p. 32.

[3] Road Security Assessment Map, GIS Unit-Goma, UN Organization Stabilization Mission in the Democratic Republic of Congo, updated November 2010, on file with author.

[4] Road Security Assessment Map, GIS Unit-Goma, UN Organization Stabilization Mission in the Democratic Republic of Congo, updated June 2011, on file with author.

military structures always follow tight security procedures, even in places that are objectively safe for interveners, such as Cyprus in 2011 and Timor-Leste in 2012. By contrast, NGOs, especially small ones, are usually less rigid, partly because they have fewer resources to design and implement strict security protocols, and partly because some exceptional ones handle security concerns differently, using the acceptance approach described later in this chapter.[5] The second factor is that, in all organizations and contexts, certain individuals vocally challenge the security procedures, refuse to abide by them, or both. However, managing staff usually try to reign in such behavior and penalize those caught breaking the rules. In unsafe contexts, violating security regulations (even with the best intentions, and even if the rule seems counterproductive) can actually be a sufficient reason for receiving a warning or being fired.

The third and most important factor that accounts for variation is perceived peril. Interveners will religiously follow most or all security routines when they feel in danger, and apply much fewer and much looser procedures when they think they are safe. The height of the walls and the density of the barbed wire surrounding their compounds similarly reflect the degree to which expatriates perceive the surrounding environment as threatening. During my fieldwork in Afghanistan, Congo, and South Sudan, for instance, the expatriates' compounds looked like fortresses in besieged territory. In contrast, in Cyprus in 2011 and Kosovo in 2000, civilian interveners tended to live in private homes that more closely resembled those of local elites (although they still adopted some standard security precautions, such as the use of full-time guards).

Acceptance and Bunkerization

During interviews and informal discussions, my contacts presented their security routines as given and their justification as self-evident: It was a natural response to the risks that they faced. However, the prevailing security procedures are not the only possible responses to perceived threats. They are, in fact, a relatively new development in Peaceland.

There are two primary approaches to risk management in conflict zones, which essentially represent two ends of a continuum. The first, which is predominant in Peaceland today (and which I described in the previous section), consists of isolating oneself as much as possible from local sources of risk – hence the use of fortified compounds, guards, locked vehicles, and other procedures. It is a strategy that military forces always use and that Jan Egeland and his coauthors aptly label "bunkerization."[6] The second, which was more popular among development and humanitarian aid workers in the 1980s and 1990s, centers on "acceptance" by local stakeholders and reliance on their support. In this model, expatriates try to assimilate into local populations so that they are not

---

[5] Also Duffield 2010, pp. 463–464 and 470.
[6] Egeland, Harmer, et al. 2011.

conspicuous targets of attacks. They also strive to develop good relationships with local power brokers – including those whose interests might be threatened by the expatriates' programs – and with their neighbors and beneficiaries, so that these local counterparts will help protect them should anything occur.[7]

According to my interviews with seasoned peacebuilders and to the scholarly research on humanitarian aid, intervening agencies started favoring bunkerization over acceptance due to three concurrent developments that took place in the 1980s and 1990s: The areas in which they worked were increasingly dangerous; conflict, as they understood it, changed in its very nature; and warring parties began perceiving them as proxies for foreign governments, rather than as neutral agents.[8] The steady rise of robberies, kidnappings, and killings of expatriates since intervening agencies started to compile such statistics in the mid-1990s, as well as a number of particularly high-profile attacks – such as the murder of NGO staff members in Rwanda in 1994 and 1997, the assassination of International Committee of the Red Cross (ICRC) employees in Burundi and Chechnya (1996) and in Congo (2001), and the bombing of the UN and ICRC headquarters in Iraq in 2003 – increased the interveners' feeling that they had to find new and better ways to protect themselves.[9] In reaction, they and their organizations developed a "predilection toward risk-aversion."[10] The professionalization of aid and peacebuilding (discussed in Chapter 2) further reinforced this tendency. As the recruiters I interviewed emphasized, their new recruits – who were now highly trained, highly specialized staff – had much higher expectations than their predecessors regarding the level of safety that their employers would provide.[11]

These expectations and this risk aversion, when added to insurance requirements (notably the interveners' agencies' desire to avoid litigation over lax safety measures), led to the establishment of stricter security procedures and new structures.[12] The ability to protect its field-based staff became one of the criteria by which to judge an organization's professional standing. (This was evident in security meetings and informal discussions over drinks, when seasoned interveners routinely reproached small NGOs that struggled with security as "amateurish.") As a result, security breaches had increasingly detrimental effects on both the reputations of the organization that suffered them and the careers of the people in charge when they occurred. In Peaceland today, agencies have to mitigate potential threats as much as possible in order to attract

---

[7] For more details on the acceptance approach, see ibid., pp. 18–22; and Fast 2014, pp. 217–223.

[8] Also Curtis 2001, pp. 9–10; Duffield 2010, pp. 457–459 and 463–464; Macrae and Leader 2000, pp. 9–11 and 14; and Rieff 2002, chapters 5 and 6. For a critical discussion of these developments as the cause of increased insecurity for aid workers, see Fast 2014, chapters 4 and pp. 175–185. For a refutation of the claim that the nature of conflict changed in the 1990s, see Kalyvas 2001.

[9] Also Egeland, Harmer, et al. 2011; Fast 2014, pp. 175–185; and Roth 2011, pp. 151–154.

[10] Duffield 2010, citation from p. 464.

[11] Also Fast 2014, pp. 173–174.

[12] On insurance requirements, see Duffield 2010, pp. 463 and 470.

qualified staff and maintain the image of professionalism that is indispensable to fundraising.[13] Accordingly, those responsible for the safety of on-the-ground interveners – such as country directors, security officers, and headquarters staff – tend to impose a conservative approach to risk management. The aversion to danger is now so strong that, as many expatriates complained during interviews and informal discussions, security officers prefer to minimize risks even at the expense of operational goals.[14]

One last factor reinforced the departure from the acceptance approach. In the early and mid-2000s, scandals involving the sexual exploitation of beneficiaries by NGO workers and UN personnel (both civilian and military) led to the design and implementation of stringent policies to prevent such events from recurring.[15] While thwarting such abuses is of the utmost importance, the chosen solution – a move toward greater isolation – caused its own problems. In the UN, the new procedures added further constraints to the already strict security guidelines. In Congo in 2010 and 2011, for instance, staff members were forbidden to meet with any local people of the opposite gender outside of their work environments. They were also prohibited from frequenting bars and restaurants that prostitutes patronized – which, to their great annoyance, tremendously reduced the number of approved places where they could relax after work. A concurrent development across many conflict zones and intervening organizations was that supervisors drilled into expatriates' heads the idea that relationships with local people were usually unequal, so they should avoid romantic entanglements. Interveners – notably peacekeepers, against whom accusations of exploitative behavior were most widespread – ultimately came to regard any personal interactions with host populations as hazardous, regardless of their nature: If something went wrong, they might lose their jobs. In Liberia in 2006, for instance, Save the Children released a report documenting the sexual exploitation of children by aid workers and peacekeepers.[16] At the time, there were several false accusations against expatriates in addition to these confirmed cases of abuse. As a result, interveners there showed a lot of trepidation in interacting with local people. A number of young men were uneasy at the very idea of going out, for fear of being wrongly accused of assault. Even worse, they "would avoid stopping their vehicles to assist women at the side of the road or in villages who looked as if they were in difficulty" for fear that it might be a "setup."[17]

---

[13] Also ibid., p. 470.

[14] Public sources on this issue include Chandrasekaran 2012, para. 10; and Roth 2011, p. 160.

[15] Save the Children-UK and UNHCR 2002 produced the first report that led to the investigation and discovery of such abuses. For a thorough analysis of the various scandals that ensued and the procedures that intervening organizations put in place to prevent sexual exploitation of local populations, see Simm 2013.

[16] Save the Children-UK 2006.

[17] Higate and Henry 2009, p. 147.

Due to these various developments, the intervening agencies' use of acceptance measures progressively decreased, and in the 2000s bunkerization procedures became standardized and commonplace, even in areas where interveners faced little danger.[18] Expatriates increasingly considered these routines the only effective ways to protect themselves, a constraint to which they see no alternative. In Peaceland today, although many NGOs continue to use some components of the acceptance model, most other civilian interveners – and all military peacekeepers – isolate themselves from their surroundings.[19] Compliance with these protocols has even emerged as one of the core components of the interveners' identity and standing. As was evident during my interviews and field observations, carrying a handset, living in a protected compound, driving a large, safe car, and having to respect curfews signaled their privileged status as interveners in a perilous conflict zone.[20]

Despite their prevalence, these dominant security procedures are not necessarily the most effective way to protect interveners in conflict zones, as evidenced by the experiences of the individuals and organizations who reject the bunkerization method. Jan Egeland, Adele Harmer, and Abby Stoddard's large-scale study of the risks facing aid workers finds that the few organizations that have managed to maintain or expand their operations in the most dangerous environments are those that employed an active acceptance approach to security.[21] My fieldwork provided numerous anecdotes that support and illustrate this finding. In Congo, Caritas (a religious NGO that works in close partnership with local churches) uses none of the habitual security procedures that other interveners follow. It instead relies on assimilation into the community. While all of the NGOs that use the bunkerization approach in Congo have faced security incidents in the late 2000s and early 2010s, Caritas, according to my sources, has had only one security problem during that period (a highway robbery), which the local authorities resolved in a few hours. Across the board, in various conflict zones, other researchers and I heard frequent stories about interveners who, having rejected the dominant modes of operation and constructed close personal and social networks among local populations, evaded danger thanks to these local connections.[22] Friends or contacts warned them ahead of time that an attack was going to take place in the village in which they lived or at the location to which they planned to travel, thus protecting them from getting caught in the fighting. In other stories, exceptional peacebuilders would end up in the midst of

---

[18] Also Duffield 2010, pp. 465–466.

[19] Ibid.; and Egeland, Harmer, et al. 2011.

[20] *Stuff Expat Aid Workers Like*, post "#71 – Motorola Handsets," (July 6, 2011, http://stuffexpa taidworkerslike.com/2011/07/06/71-motorola-handsets/) has a humorous take on this issue.

[21] Egeland, Harmer, et al. 2011, pp. 2 and 18–22. Also CDA Collaborative Learning Projects 2011a, p. 6. For a fascinating discussion of security incidents against interveners using an acceptance approach, see Fast 2014, pp. 189–192 and 217–233.

[22] Public sources include Egeland, Harmer, et al. 2011, p. 19; Fast, Rowley, et al. 2011, p. 16, and Fast 2014, pp. 217–225.

ongoing fighting, but local villagers mobilized to keep them safe, at great personal risk. One community in east Africa even "formed units to protect aid workers" living in their villages "in case of attacks."[23] Several expatriates also said they owed their lives to local contacts who warned them that an armed group was targeting them or intervened with belligerents on their behalf.

Admittedly, in the most dangerous environments, interveners cannot rely on a pure acceptance approach: As I discuss in the Conclusion, adding a measure of bunkerization is indispensable to ward off at least some security threats. However, the current levels of bunkerization fail to take into account that perceptions of danger levels are often inflated or out of proportion because of a climate of fear that prevails among interveners.

A Climate of Fear

Insecurity is one of the main topics that foreign peacebuilders discuss, whether during official meetings or when relaxing after work. Admittedly, in informal settings, such as dinners and parties, interveners usually mention danger only casually: Ignoring it is a way to show that one is experienced, resilient, and professional.[24] However, my fieldwork material suggests that, despite their attempt at nonchalance, expatriates who are part of the interveners' club perceive danger in a much more acute way than those who are not. Foreign businesspeople and scholarly researchers, for instance, regularly remarked during formal interviews and informal conversations that their views of risk levels were at odds with those of foreign peacebuilders: What the former would consider to be a somewhat risky area the latter would perceive as a very hazardous zone. My husband, several other contacts, and I also noticed that when we were attached to an intervening organization in a conflict zone, we felt much more scared than when we worked in the same area for other reasons. This held true regardless of whether the actual security conditions were better, worse, or similar.

One would expect that, in unstable environments, soldiers – who have been trained to defend themselves – would be more comfortable than civilians; however, the climate of fear affects military interveners as well, sometimes to problematic extents. In compliance with the security protocol for traveling to red zone areas, several UN police officers once requested an escort from the nearby peacekeeping contingent to go to a specific Congolese village. The answer from the unit they contacted was: "And us, who will escort us?" The soldiers were so afraid of their environment that they felt they too needed protection. Along the same lines, when I spent time embedded with military observers in a rural Congolese area, I observed that only one of them occasionally left his protected compound on foot; the other four did so only by car. As the one who walked

---

[23] Fast 2014, p.222.
[24] Roth 2011 develops a fascinating analysis of this topic.

explained to me, his colleagues were too afraid to wander around, even though no security rule prohibited doing so, and, moreover, as both of us experienced and as many colleagues confirmed, there was absolutely nothing threatening in the village. Such anecdotes were not unique – I heard many similar stories across the globe.

The primary source of this climate of fear is the widespread perception that peace-related work is a dangerous business.[25] It is true that interveners face multiple security challenges. Expatriates can be the targets of attacks, and a number of them are killed, kidnapped, or injured every year.[26] They can catch tropical diseases or be hurt in car crashes, with a heightened risk that the injuries will be fatal or permanently disabling given the lack of quality health care in most conflict zones.[27]

These risks do exist, and it is perfectly understandable that they frighten the international peacebuilders. But there are also three elements at work in interventions that may make conflict zones seem even more dangerous than they actually are. The effect of the first element is, fortunately, relatively short-lived. Before interveners arrive in their host countries, foreign media are often their main sources of information on their areas of deployment. These news sources usually paint an intimidating (and incomplete) picture of the situations in conflict zones. Their coverage focuses overwhelmingly on any ongoing violence rather than on the aspects of life that remain normal despite tense security conditions, such as business, everyday politics, and cultural events. As a result, I met numerous newcomers who were especially frightened during their first few weeks (or months) in a new place. The head of a prominent U.S. agency, for instance, had heard so many horror stories about Congo that she was afraid even when staying in Kinshasa (which experienced criminality, but no war-related violence) and was too scared to travel to the eastern provinces. Similarly, a UN peacebuilder recalled seeing new colleagues arrive in Darfur with such preconceptions of terrible danger that they did not want to leave UN-protected areas. In my own experience, and in that of several of my contacts, security conditions always sounded much scarier from afar than when we were actually on the ground – whether in Afghanistan, Congo, Kosovo, the Palestinian Territories, or South Sudan.

The fear that results from lopsided and imperfect information about a conflict zone might therefore abate fairly rapidly upon arrival, were it not for the other two elements that distort interveners' perceptions of danger. In the field, several rituals amplify the feeling of insecurity among international peacebuilders.

---

[25] Ibid. makes the same observation on development aid.

[26] An excellent source on this issue is the database Peacemakers at Risk, compiled by Sara Lindberg and available at www.pcr.uu.se/research/ucdp/program_overview/current_projects/peacemakers_at_risk/. For statistics focused on humanitarian aid workers, see Egeland, Harmer, et al. 2011, pp. 11–16.

[27] This sentence builds on the analysis developed in Roth 2011.

Mandatory security trainings instill and reinforce the idea that expatriates "face pervasive threats" from faceless, calculating enemies.[28] Moreover, a number of formal coordination meetings and informal networks center on the sharing of security information, making it impossible for international peacebuilders to forget the risks they face.[29] Interveners also regularly honor the memory of those who lost their lives during field deployment, either through formal ceremonies or by recounting their stories in informal discussions, thus keeping these traumatic events fresh in everybody's minds.

One last element perpetuates these perceptions of constant peril. Interveners do not have much opportunity to confront their fears and realize that some are unfounded because their lack of in-depth understanding of local contexts and their practice of living in a bubble, separated from host populations, prevents them from experiencing the actual conditions on the ground.[30] The result is a marked difference between the expatriates' and the local populations' perceptions of danger, as evidenced in Egeland, Harmer, and Stoddard's 2010 survey on security threats facing aid workers.[31] Most national staff they interviewed "felt that internationals tended to overestimate the risk" in the local security environment.[32] Only in a few countries – Afghanistan, Iraq, Pakistan, and Somalia – did local respondents define their conditions as "'somewhat' to 'highly' insecure."[33] This stood in sharp contrast with the views of expatriate aid workers, who categorized many more areas of deployment as extremely unsafe.

The climate of fear has two consequences. First, it inhibits the deployment of development organizations, which have particularly low danger thresholds and usually require safer conditions than peacebuilding and humanitarian agencies. This creates a catch-22. Development actors will deploy only in stable environments, but creating such environments requires development initiatives – for instance, to build a state or fight against poverty and unemployment. Admittedly, the actors present on the ground try to fulfill these tasks. However, they often complain that they lack the necessary skills. In interviews, they regularly emphasized that they were trained in responding to emergencies and in handling difficult security conditions, not in implementing long-term development initiatives. The second consequence of the climate of fear is that it reinforces the interveners' perception that they need ever more security measures to protect themselves, which encourages further bunkerization. It was clear throughout my time in Peaceland that the feeling of being in constant danger was the main reason that interveners followed the dominant

---

[28] Duffield 2010, p. 461.
[29] For a public source on U.S. expatriates in Afghanistan, see Chandrasekaran 2012, para.11.
[30] Pouligny 2004, p. 190 develops a similar observation.
[31] Egeland, Harmer, et al. 2011, pp. 41–43 and 59–79.
[32] Ibid., p. 41.
[33] Ibid., p. 41.

security procedures; it was also why so few individuals challenged the burdensome policies, and why these methods therefore persisted.

Negative Consequences

Bunkerization-style security routines have clear benefits: They keep expatriates relatively safe and enable them to work in unstable settings. However, as already discussed, they are not necessarily more effective in protecting interveners than are acceptance-style measures. Moreover, they have costly side effects, which aggravate several problems that I have documented in this book, including segregation of interveners and host populations, portrayal of the former as superior to the later, and difficulty in collecting reliable material on conflict dynamics. Consequently, excessive bunkerization impedes the effectiveness of the very people and initiatives it is meant to protect.

Bunkerization procedures generate a physical and symbolic separation between international peacebuilders and local populations. The high walls, security guards, and other barricades that surround expatriate residences make interveners seem remote and difficult to access. Several interviewees particularly regretted the message conveyed by the use of barbed wires (a standard practice often required by the security offices of many agencies). To an intervener working in Sudan, it signaled to her neighbors that she viewed them as dangerous. A Congolese and a Timorese intellectual concurred: The high walls and other precautions meant that interveners were "afraid of [local] people."

The strict security procedures that most NGO, UN, and diplomatic compounds require for entrance have the same effect. Whether in Abidjan (Cote d'Ivoire), Juba (Sudan), or Nicosia (Cyprus), one has to verify one's identity, contact one's host, wait for an escort to his or her office, and – in the most protected places – undergo a thorough search of one's belongings, plus pass through a series of checkpoints. Although such stringent security may not surprise visitors to protected sites in North America and Europe, it is less familiar to some host populations, and they dislike having it imposed on them in their own countries. Worse, while such safety routines may be inconvenient for airports, museums, or foreign ministries outside of conflict zones, in Peaceland, they actually hinder the interveners' peace efforts. As I experienced, and as many interviewees confirmed, these procedures are time-consuming, intimidating, and often so unpleasant for visitors that they feel unwelcome. The nickname that local Burundians gave to the main UN camp in their capital city, Bujumbura, encapsulates this sentiment: They called it "Guantanamo" (after the name of the infamous US maximum-security detention center). National authorities shared this frustration with the expatriates' bunkerization measures. During a group interview, Sudanese high-level ministry staff members complained that the protocols prevented necessary interactions with international partners and regularly made these Sudanese authorities late for meetings. Altogether, the result of these security procedures is relatively similar across all conflict zones. A UN policeman deployed in Congo captured the extent of the problem: Interveners "are completely shut off from the outside world"; it is virtually "impossible" for the population to interact with international staff or to convey their concerns to expatriates.

The security routines reduce interactions between interveners and host populations beyond the compounds as well. For instance, an African peacebuilder working for a UN agency lamented that respecting curfews and no-go areas prevented him from socializing after work with his local colleagues and counterparts, who lived in neighborhoods considered too unsafe to visit at night. Likewise, a European NGO worker objected that the security constraints upon her movements made it "difficult to meet Congolese."

The use of cars as the preferred means of transportation further separates expatriates from local populations, as Lisa Smirl observed in Aceh (Indonesia) and as the case of peacekeeping units working in Ituri (Congo) illustrates.[34] In 2011, the UN peacekeeping mission in Congo had deployed Bangladeshi, Guatemalan, Indonesian, Moroccan, and Nepalese units in the district of Ituri. One would expect that the Moroccan units, whose officers spoke French (the lingua franca in Congo), would be closer to the population than their English- or Spanish-speaking colleagues. In fact, the Guatemalan units were the most popular, and the best integrated, for one main reason: Unlike the other units, the Guatemalans conducted their patrols on foot. When people saw them walking around day and night, they reportedly trusted the Guatemalan soldiers more and felt more secure than when they saw peacekeepers cross their villages in the safety of vehicles.

Not only do the various security routines strengthen the barriers between host populations and interveners, but they also reinforce the latter's tendency to interact mostly with their peers. Rajiv Chandrasekaran's provocative account of embassy life in Afghanistan demonstrates how onerous security rules prevented American expatriates from interacting with Afghan people except on rare occasions and restricted their professional and social contacts to fellow interveners. Expatriates could leave their protected compound only if they had official business, obtained permission from the security office, went to a preapproved location, and submitted a report afterward on the content of their discussions with any Afghan person.[35] An interview I conducted with an experienced African peacebuilder similarly encapsulates the crucial role security measures played in creating the expatriate bubble analyzed in Chapter 5. From his point of view, "security restrictions" are so extensive that expatriates "tend to live together" and to "frequent the same places," regardless of national or organizational background. In turn, by living and socializing in the same places, expatriates "develop a certain culture." Based on my fieldwork, I would add that not only are interveners restricted to the same safe areas, but it is also much

[34] Smirl 2008, p. 242.
[35] Chandrasekaran 2012.

easier for them to enter other expatriates' compounds and vehicles than it is for local people. Carrying the card of an intervention agency, or even just looking like a foreigner, usually eases many of the security procedures. All in all, as many other interviewees confirmed, interacting with other interveners is simpler because they share the same living and social spaces.

The security procedures also emphasize the image of the interveners' superiority over their local counterparts. The barricades around the expatriates' compounds proclaim the importance of the foreigners. The enormous level of protection that surrounds expatriates sets them apart from ordinary members of the host community, who go about their lives with few such defenses, and stands in sharp contrast to the safety measures established for local staff members and partners.[36] On a day-to-day basis, even local employees of intervening organizations tend to have "less access to security training [...] and to psychological or stress counseling [...] than their international counterparts, [...] lower levels of physical security measures for residences and vehicles, and little access to off-hours telecommunications."[37] In case of major security problems, there are provisions for evacuating the expatriates, but often not for rescuing the local staff.[38]

Many interveners are uncomfortable with this unequal treatment of their local colleagues, but two narratives, based on false assumptions, help to perpetuate it nonetheless.[39] The first stems, in part, from the tendency of interveners to define insider status based on national origin. Among foreign agencies, a pervasive misconception regarding security is that "a national will be able to work more securely anywhere in the country because he or she does not stand out as being visibly foreign."[40] In fact, aggressors may perceive a fellow citizen who is from another region, province, or even village as "just as much of an outsider."[41] The second assumption, which frequently recurred in my interviews, was that a local person would know how to survive in his or her own country – where to hide, whom to avoid, how to find basic necessities – and thus needed less support than expatriates in times of crisis. This overlooks the fact that the local employees' ethnic, clan, family, or religious affiliations – or their privileged economic status as holders of coveted jobs at international agencies – often put them at risk. Thus, the foreign interveners' practice of providing higher levels of protection to expatriates results from inadequate understandings of local contexts and of the risks that local employees face, not from insufficient care for the lives of those employees. Nonetheless, the message is harsh and its effect clear: To many local staff members, and to a number of their expatriate colleagues, these

---

[36] Also Pouligny 2004, p. 313.
[37] Egeland, Harmer, et al. 2011, pp. 40–47 (citation from p. 40).
[38] Also Anderson 1999, p. 58; and Roth 2011, pp. 152 and 157–158.
[39] The analysis of the false assumptions is based on Egeland, Harmer, et al. 2011, p. 40.
[40] Ibid., p. 40.
[41] Ibid., p. 40. See also Chapter 4 in this book.

disparities in security stress the preciousness of an intervener's life and the comparable expendability of a local one.

In addition to fueling the social dynamics at play in Peaceland, the culture of insecurity heightens the foreign peacebuilders' difficulties in collecting information on their locales of deployment. The reluctance to share potentially sensitive data reduces the contextual material available to each individual and organization. By thwarting the development of in-depth, informal relationships between expatriates and host populations, the safety procedures also decrease the quality and reliability of the material that foreign peacebuilders can gather. They make it exceptionally difficult for interveners to interact with ordinary citizens, who usually do not live in wealthy and "safe" neighborhoods and often feel too intimidated to try to enter the expatriates' compounds. This further reinforces the foreigners' tendency to associate with and gather information from, at best, local elites only. Finally, as the procedures prevent trips to the most dangerous places or permit them only with armed military escorts that frighten local inhabitants, they curtail the international peacebuilders' knowledge of local conditions in areas most in need of their work.

The experience of an academic collaborating with the UN Development Program (UNDP) in Liberia is representative of how severely all of the constraints that ensue from these security measures affect data collection by expatriates. My colleague had to conduct her research that was "'with' UNDP, separate from UNDP," (meaning, in a non-UNDP vehicle and with funding that appeared separate) because "abiding by the UNDP rules would have made [her] research nearly impossible." I had the same experience while working on a previous book.[42] The NGO with which I originally partnered – an emergency organization that prides itself on its fearless approach to aid – put so many security restrictions on where I could go, whom I could meet, and what I could discuss, that it was only after I ended our arrangement and started working quasi-independently that I could collect useful data on sensitive issues of conflict and violence.

The burdensome security procedures have one last detrimental effect: They force interveners to follow complicated guidelines that stall reactivity and often leave them frustrated. In Congo in 2010 and 2011, for instance, UN peacekeepers had to request military escorts a week beforehand and helicopter transportation two days in advance – a requirement that made it impossible to respond quickly to crises. For each movement to a new area, they first had to wait for the UN Department of Safety and Security to assess the security situation. I observed numerous times that this modus operandi further lengthened the lag between an incident and the deployment of response personnel. On occasion, it even prevented deployment all together. This problem is not limited to Congo. In conflict zones around the world, UN staff members must regularly cancel or delay planned missions, sometimes for months, because security rules

---

[42] Autesserre 2010.

require helicopter transportation, military escorts, or convoys of several vehicles, all of which are regularly in short supply. To make matters worse, the safety procedures also oblige UN military forces to focus most of their assets on the protection of personnel and material, at the expense of the rest of their mission. As I witnessed during my fieldwork, peacekeeping troops regularly must cancel patrols aimed at protecting the population because they are asked to escort NGOs or UN agencies. Burdensome security procedures similarly affect NGO personnel. During formal and informal conversation, numerous NGO staff members working in various countries complained that security protocols required them to travel by car (as opposed to by motorcycle, for instance), during daytime and, in unsecure places, in convoys of at least two vehicles. This created countless constraints on their movements and regularly prevented them from reaching the places where they needed to work in a timely manner. Finally, interveners working for all kinds of agencies deplored that security rules precluded long-term deployment in highly unsecure areas, significantly constraining work in the places most in need of peacebuilding. It is no surprise, then, that many interviewees blamed these security procedures for creating some of the most tangible obstacles to effective peacebuilding.

Intervention Rituals

Beyond their use of similar security methods, interveners from all kinds of organizations engage in three rituals that profoundly influence their daily work: publicizing their actions, reporting incessantly on their efforts, and striving for neutrality or impartiality. Just like security routines, these rituals not only make visible and perpetuate the boundaries between interveners and local populations, but also emphasize the superiority of the former – two consequences that significantly impede the effectiveness of the international efforts.

Visibility

Interveners of all kinds promote "visibility" – a concept that, in Peaceland, means deliberately advertising one's actions. As a result, conflict zones throughout the world are covered with the emblems of international intervention structures. It would be common to see, for instance, a mayor's office with logos explaining that the building was funded by the UN Development Program and constructed by the UN Office for Project Services, near billboards emphasizing that a road was rehabilitated by German Agro Action, thanks to a grant from the U.S. Agency for International Development. This could be next to a hospital whose entrance bears the insignias of Doctors Without Borders and its donor, the European Commission. Even more ubiquitous and noticeable are the white sport utility vehicles (SUVs) that most intervening organizations use, and which are instantly recognizable to both local people and to anyone familiar with aid work.

The idea that help should be "visible" is not a given one, and, in fact, this standard practice starkly contrasts with classic ways of providing help to people in need. The three major monotheistic religions, for instance, emphasize that charity should remain hidden, for fear of creating an obligation in the mind of the receiver. The Bible, the Mishneh Torah, and the Quran all explain that the best way to dole out charity is to do so "in secret."[43] The teachings of Hinduism and Buddhism emphasize a similar point: A benefactor should not humiliate a recipient of charity or make him feel indebted.[44] A *hadith* (saying) from the Prophet Muhammad summarizes the spirit of the endeavor: "The hand that gives should not be higher than the hand that receives." In Peaceland, however, an assertion of fact has replaced this normative prohibition. As I mention in Chapter 6, many of my African contacts characterized the interveners' work by saying that "the hand that gives *is* always higher than the hand that receives."

When I asked NGO and UN officials why their routine modes of operation seemed to disregard the importance of discretion in charity, they typically blamed their donors. In their view, they had no choice but to respect visibility requirements when they used institutional grants. Project proposals, whether to the French government, the European Union, the U.S. Agency for International Development, or the UN, must outline tangible strategies to broadcast their efforts and carry out these plans if awarded funds.[45] Budget requests must even include specific lines devoted to covering the costs of T-shirts, stickers, and billboards with the logos of the donor and the implementing agency.

My interviewees also emphasized that relying on private funds similarly requires them to publicize their actions, even if for a different reason. In their experience, individuals send contributions only to agencies they know. The more visibility an organization achieves on the ground, the more publicity it obtains in international media. Widespread exposure increases the likelihood that people will remember an organization when deciding where to direct their charitable donations.

When I asked state donors – such as the American, Australian, Dutch, European, and Japanese aid offices – why they attached visibility requirements to the funding they gave to international organizations and NGOs, all my respondents emphasized a similar dynamic, again linked to funding issues. Their governments have many competing priorities to finance, so it is important for aid offices to show concrete results if they want to sustain large budget allocations for their activities. The citizens of their countries also support aid initiatives much

---

[43] *The Bible*, Matthew 6:1–4; *The Holy Quran*, 2:262; and Rabbi Moses Maimonides' *Mishneh Torah* ("The Torah Reviewed," dated 1180), section *Laws on Gifts for the Poor*, 10:7–8.

[44] *The Bhagavad Gita*, "Threefold Faith," 17.20–17.22; and *The Sutta Pitaka* (a scripture from Theravada Buddhism), Anguttara Nikaya 5.148.

[45] European Commission 2010; UN Democracy Fund 2006 and 2007; and United States Agency for International Development – Office of United States Foreign Disaster Assistance 2008 provide representative examples.

more when they can see their tax money at work – for instance by seeing the logo of their country's aid office on pamphlets or during TV reports on initiatives to help war-affected populations. Furthermore, donors want to avoid criticisms from host authorities and populations that their promises of aid never materialize, so they need to clearly show the tangible impacts of their investments.

Interviewees from international agencies, NGOs, and donor structures emphasized three additional reasons for their dominant mode of operation. Some of them believed that publicizing their efforts helped win over the hearts and minds of local populations.[46] Others mentioned the hope that, in situations of intense violence, putting their logo or flag on a building, a car, or the vest of a staff member would provide a certain level of safeguarding, as armed groups would think twice before attacking foreign-protected assets.[47] Still others explained that they had to put their insignia on any installation that they helped build and any structure or endeavor that they supported in order to show that their organizations were actually doing something with the funds they received.

All of these motivations for operating conspicuously are so fundamental that the large majority of international agencies forgo the constant branding only when it puts their staffs in danger. Various aid agencies use a low-profile approach in certain high-risk contexts to decrease the likelihood of attacks on personnel and material.[48] Most organizations, however, consider this strategy suboptimal, as it may generate suspicion among the neighboring population and prevent the public and donors from recognizing the agency's work. The large majority of interveners therefore abandon visibility only as a last resort, and a temporary one at that.[49] After the 2006 riots in Timor-Leste, for instance, the unpopularity of foreigners reached such a point that angry mobs attacked several expatriates. Australian Aid then took down all its banners and logos, in the hope that it would reduce the risk of attacks against its staff and implementing partners. However, extensive criticisms accumulated within a few years. The Australian government wondered why nobody could see the results of its investments and requested a return to past practices. The Timorese president accused Australian Aid of misappropriating the funds rather than using them to deliver concrete results. By 2011, Australian Aid staff had to return to standard visibility procedures.

The visibility routines produce a number of positive intended consequences. They have the crucial effect of enabling intervening agencies to maintain good

---

[46] For public sources on visibility as a way to win hearts and minds, see among others Fishstein and Wilder 2012; and the official Web site of the United States Agency for International Development, section Branding (www.usaid.gov/branding, last accessed in December 2013). For discussions of the effectiveness of foreign aid in winning hearts and minds, see Brunner and Nada 2012.

[47] See Fast 2014, pp. 186–197 for a discussion of how (in)effective branding is in protecting interveners.

[48] Egeland, Harmer, et al. 2011, pp. 27–28.

[49] Ibid., p. 28.

relationships with the host governments and to obtain the funds they need to function. However, these routines are also inherently harmful to peacebuilding.

The standard practice of publicizing one's actions makes visible and embodies in a very material way the superiority the claim of "being here to help" gives to outsiders. The logos and banners constantly remind host populations that they are the recipients of international charity. They further distinguish interveners (the givers) from local people (the receivers). In doing so, they widen the gap between expatriates and local stakeholders, with all the problems that this rift entails.

Moreover, as programs visibly originate with expatriates rather than local partners, this ritual affirmation of the external contributions decreases local ownership and thus, following the process analyzed in Chapter 3, creates local resistance. A political affairs officer with the UN peacekeeping mission in Congo, for instance, deplored that his colleagues always tried to play up their contributions in conflict negotiations. He saw several deals collapse "just because it was said that the agreement had been reached thanks to" external interveners – such as the European facilitators or UN peacekeeping sections – "and thus the parties in conflict did not want to implement it because, from the start, from their point of view, the agreement was dictated by an outsider." In contrast, he emphasized that other initiatives, which came from the same intervening organizations but kept the external contributions as discreet as possible and emphasized local initiatives, were much more successful.

My fieldwork in other countries confirmed that interviewee's claim. Although exceptions to the visibility practice remain rare, the few organizations that have decided to act as discreetly as possible have noticed that doing so boosted the impact of their work. In Israel and the Palestinian Territories for instance, the staff of one such agency – which, in keeping with their low-profile approach, requested not to be named – explained that they have much more influence and much better access to all sides of the conflict than they would have if they were visible. Local interviewees confirmed that the few intervening structures using this low-profile approach were much more effective than the other peacebuilding organizations on site.

Other researchers report similar findings. Based on a systematic assessment of foreign efforts in Aceh (Indonesia), Patrick Barron and Adam Burke have ascertained that one of the "key practical attributes" of the international agencies that productively supported the 2005–2006 peace process was their adoption of a "low-key approach."[50] Mary Anderson and Lara Olsen conducted several years of in-depth interviews, program evaluations, and workshops with peace practitioners all over the world. Like my Congo-based interviewees, their contacts emphasized that letting local officials take credit for ideas and achievements often promoted sustainable solutions to conflict, while publicizing the leadership role of external actors generated antagonistic reactions among local

[50] Barron and Burke 2008, pp. xiii, 56–57, and throughout the book.

partners.[51] Ultimately, these researchers concluded what I witnessed in my own fieldwork: "Working quietly and not broadcasting achievements" – whether a new building or a ceasefire agreement – is the most effective way to support local actors.[52] This should not be surprising, given the significant toll that the unintended consequences of promoting visibility exact on peacebuilding efforts.

Neutrality and Impartiality

In addition to the desire for visibility, another institutional imperative that influences many interveners' daily routines is the search for impartiality: the adherence to objective standards or rules, applied equally to all parties. Certain organizations add to such impartiality requirements an accompanying search for neutrality: the abstention from undertaking or enabling activities that might contribute to the warring efforts of any parties to a conflict.[53] UN peacekeeping upholds impartiality as one of its three core principles.[54] The UN Development Programme, which regularly implements peacebuilding projects, prides itself on maintaining a "neutral presence" in developing countries.[55] The charters or mission statements of many emergency relief agencies – such as Action Against Hunger, Doctors Without Borders, the International Committee of the Red Cross, and the UN High Commissioner for Refugees – mention one or both of these principles.[56] Across the board, peace practitioners from NGO, donor delegations, and UN agencies agree that "impartiality on the politics" – meaning, not supporting the political positions of any party to conflict – is essential.[57]

These principles of neutrality and impartiality are not merely symbolic; they actively shape the daily work routines of international peacebuilders in the field. My contacts regularly emphasized this impact. In a representative statement, one high-ranking official from the UN mission in Cyprus stressed:

[51] Anderson and Olson 2003, pp. 32–33.

[52] Citation from ibid., p. 33.

[53] The definitions are based on Weller 1998, section "The Definition of Neutrality and Impartiality in General." For an insightful discussion of the meaning of both concepts, see Weller's article; and Donald 2003.

[54] Principles of UN Peacekeeping as presented on the UN Web site, www.un.org/en/peacekeeping/operations/principles.shtml, last accessed in December 2013.

[55] "UNDP at a Glance" (available at www.undp.org/content/dam/undp/library/corporate/brochure/w-undp_brochure_2012-Eng-final.pdf, last accessed in December 2013).

[56] Action Against Hunger's International Charter (available at www.actionagainsthunger.org/about/acf-international/international-charter); Doctors Without Borders/Médecins Sans Frontières's Charter (available at www.doctorswithoutborders.org/aboutus/charter.cfm); the International Committee of the Red Cross's Mandate and Mission (available at www.icrc.org/eng/who-we-are/mandate/overview-icrc-mandate-mission.htm); and the UN High Commissioner for Refugees' Mission Statement (available at www.unhcr.org/4ec230e8e.html) – all Web sites last accessed in December 2013.

[57] Anderson and Olson 2003, p. 32.

When we do our peacekeeping business with both sides, we treat them exactly the same way. [...] We do not discern between the Greek Cypriot National Guard and the Turkish forces in the north, [even though the latter] are, by international law, part of an illegal occupation of Cyprus. That [distinction] does not make a difference on our peacekeeping task on the ground. We are watching. There is a set of rules, a code of conduct, and whether the National Guard breaches it, or the Turkish forces do, we respond in the same way.

Donors and NGO employees similarly explained that they take pains not to be seen as favoring one camp, meeting too often with one side, or selecting their beneficiaries exclusively from one group.

As my interviewees constantly reminded me, and as the scholarly and policy research on intervention has extensively documented, there are multiple reasons for this dominant practice.[58] Being perceived as impartial – or, even better, neutral – decreases the likelihood that the parties in conflict may view interveners as supporting their enemies. Upholding these principles therefore eases the peacebuilders' relationships with the various sides of a dispute, enables international agencies to access contested areas, and helps protect staff members. In other words, at the most fundamental level, adhering to these principles makes the interveners' work possible.

There are two caveats, though. To begin with, most interveners recognize that, despite their influence, the ideals of neutrality and impartiality are unattainable on the ground.[59] The expatriates' work often requires them to take a side, if only to defend their beneficiaries against perpetrators of human rights violations or against those who want to deny them aid. Individuals working in the field also cannot help but resent the groups that harm the people they try to assist, whether or not the rules require fair treatment of all warring parties. Many interveners are so shocked by the horrors they witness that they form strong opinions in favor of or against certain belligerents. In informal settings and off-record interviews, numerous contacts pondered whether the neutrality and impartiality principles are at all useful or relevant.

The second caveat is that, in theory, neutrality and impartiality are not prerequisites for efficient peacebuilding work. Mediation, for instance, can be "outsider-neutral" (the model that dominates in Peaceland) or "insider-partial" – an approach that, as Paul Wehr and John Paul Lederach have studied, proved highly effective in helping end the Nicaraguan civil war in the late 1980s and early 1990s.[60] Espousing neutrality or impartiality can even be counterproductive because it may further deteriorate the relationships between

---

[58] For public sources, see among others: Curtis 2001, p. 13; Fast 2014, chapter 4; and Macrae and Leader 2000, p. 59.

[59] Seybolt 1996 and Weiss 1999 provide excellent overviews of this quandary. Other key texts include Anderson 1999, chapter 4; Barnett 2011, pp. 37–41; Duffield 2001, chapter 4; Macrae and Leader 2000, pp. 56–59; Prendergast 1996, pp. 9–12 and 38–42; and Rieff 2002, chapters 4 and 6.

[60] Wehr and Lederach 1991, pp. 86–98. Also Mason 2009.

expatriates and their intended beneficiaries. Host populations often complain about the interveners' attempts not to take sides. A South Sudanese journalist, for instance, spent most of our interview reproaching international peacebuilders for being neutral, arguing that his country does not need neutral interveners but rather people who support them in their fight against the "genocide" committed against his fellow citizens by North Sudan. Several Palestinian NGO representatives used a sarcastic (perhaps apocryphal) quotation from Desmond Tutu to illustrate a similar viewpoint: "If an elephant steps on a mouse, the mouse will be very thankful for your neutrality." I heard the same kind of discourse about interveners in all of the conflict zones in which I worked: Target populations prefer organizations that side with them to nonpartisan actors.

As a result, several intervening agencies have abandoned the impartiality and neutrality principles and instead espoused "solidarity." This approach entails aligning themselves with particular categories of people – usually those who are poor and oppressed – as a way to pursue peace or justice.[61] For instance, in 1986, as war in Sudan was raging, Norwegian People's Aid decided to side against the Khartoum-based government, establishing itself in areas controlled by the rebel group the Sudan People's Liberation Army. It has remained "in solidarity" with these people ever since. A number of organizations deployed in the Palestinian territories similarly pride themselves on standing in solidarity with Palestinians, rather than being neutral or impartial.

This approach has one clear advantage: The supported populations appreciate the efforts of the solidarity organizations much more. By all accounts, individuals working for such agencies are in a much better position than other expatriates to develop close personal, social, and professional relations with their local counterparts. According to such contacts, these privileged relations in turn make their intervention much more effective. In other words, adopting the solidarity principle helps weaken the boundaries between interveners and local people as well as the problems inherent to these boundaries.

However, abandoning impartiality and neutrality in favor of solidarity is not the silver bullet, as it generates a number of serious problems. Understandably, the parties on the other side of the conflict resent the solidarity organizations' position, and they view them as enemies – a perception which generates many challenges for the intervening agencies. By way of example, consider Israel's treatment of solidarity organizations working in the Palestinian Territories. According to my interviews, Israeli officials view these agencies as a threat and thus create tremendous visa difficulties, strictly control their movements, and overall create a number of obstacles to their everyday work. Israeli people also view these agencies as biased in favor of their enemies; these expatriates therefore cannot play an effective mediating role in the conflict. To top it all off, because of these problems, and because international peacebuilders view

---

[61] Minear 2002, p. 79.

impartiality and neutrality as such a constituent part of their identity, interveners ostracize NGOs that publicly reject these principles. A staff working for the Norwegian People's Aid in Sudan explained the reactions his solidarity approach usually generated among his colleagues on the ground:

> Many people, NGOs, internationals, they say: "Are you not neutral?!" It is a shock for them [...] because they think that to be neutral is something very holy. [...] A Japanese organization came to me and said: (*mimicking someone whispering*) "Is it true that you are not neutral?" "No, we are not neutral." "Is it true that you are smuggling weapons?" "No."

The reaction of the Japanese organization that this interviewee cited is typical: As I heard throughout many conflict zones, agencies that forgo neutrality and impartiality are often accused of a number of ills, notably weapons smuggling. Additionally, these principles are such staples of intervention work that abandoning them means relinquishing some of the privileges attached to the status of an aid or peacebuilding agency, such as access to many donors' funds. As my interviewee lamented, "For funding, the donors want neutral organizations."

The experiences of the organizations that have abandoned the neutrality and impartiality principles are conclusive. Neutrality and impartiality may be neither indispensable to peacebuilding nor fully attainable on the ground, but there is no better way to facilitate both fundraising and the everyday implementation of peacebuilding programs. As a result, emphasizing impartiality or neutrality has remained the dominant practice for intervening agencies. These norms are in fact so strong that the punishments for breaking them are stiff: In most intervening organizations, a staff member caught supporting one side of a conflict, whether through direct or indirect channels, runs the risk of immediate dismissal.

Despite their benefits, the principles of neutrality and impartiality have unintended effects when put into practice on the ground, like the other routines analyzed in this chapter. They make the everyday relationships between interveners and local counterparts even tenser. It is not only that certain local stakeholders resent the interveners' refusal to take their side, as detailed above, but also that expatriates' incentives to interact with local people decrease as a result of these principles. Whether in Afghanistan, Congo, the Palestinian Territories, or Timor-Leste, various interveners explained to me that they preferred to distance themselves from local political or military actors in public for fear that the population might perceive them as biased. Certain expatriates even tried to limit their social contacts with local people altogether.

The everyday pursuit of these principles also reinforces the structure of inequality that characterizes Peaceland. The interveners' claims that they are neutral or impartial further enable them to claim the moral high ground.[62]

---

[62] Also Marriage 2006.

Valuing these principles also justifies placing foreign peacebuilders in leadership roles, given that expatriates usually have few preexisting links to the parties in conflict. Altogether, the daily emphasis on impartiality and neutrality, while extremely important in facilitating the interveners' work, reinforces the segregation of expatriates and local populations and the pervasive inequalities in Peaceland.

Reporting

The last significant ritual that many interveners working for non-governmental and international organizations share is what several interviewees labeled "a reporting culture." Most of the people I met spent a lot of time writing accounts of their actions. This practice results primarily from demands of superiors and donors, who use these documents to check that the project has proceeded (or proceeds) as planned, without mismanagement, that it has served the intended population, and has achieved the original goal.[63] Reporting therefore satisfies the essential goals of ensuring continued funding for the peacebuilding projects and enabling supervision by capitals and headquarters. Secondarily, on-the-ground interveners also use reports to keep track of their own actions, reflect on their work, and create archives that preserve institutional memory and that they can draw on for ideas at a later date.

While NGO employees usually get away with writing these documents weekly – in addition to compiling a myriad of reports for their donors – some UN officials deployed in the field must send daily updates to their superiors. The first in-depth interview I ever conducted with a field-based UN peacekeeper (in 2004) provides a telling illustration. During our discussion, I kept asking my contact what she did every day and what her schedule looked like on a daily basis, and I felt that I never received a straight answer. I left the meeting puzzled. It seemed as if the only thing she did with her time was write reports. Although I quickly learned that the reality was more complicated than it appeared, this first interview was nevertheless representative of what I heard in many subsequent meetings. A civilian peacekeeper deployed in Congo illustrated the problem in an interview I conducted in 2011, explaining that:

> What prevents us from being closer to local realities is [. . .] the fact that we are stuck in our offices and obliged to write reports. I have to write a daily report, so I cannot go out. When there are two people, you can alternate. But when you are alone, you only see your computer. Sometimes you can go and conduct an interview, but every day you are stuck in the office.

A former staff member from a UN agency voiced a similar complaint, explaining that most of this agency's staff spent the first three months of any year writing

---

[63] For a public source, see Anderson, Brown, et al. 2012, p. 78.

internal reports, so the actual work only started in April. Likewise, certain NGOs in Cambodia deplored that they "had to spend more time and effort writing progress reports than focusing on the projects."[64]

Although the reporting requirement constrains the staff of other intervening organizations to a lesser extent, the same themes recurred in formal and informal discussions throughout all my field sites. Many contacts complained that their reporting routines ate up their schedules, forcing them to spend too long in their offices at the expense of interacting with local partners and beneficiaries. Those in leadership positions (usually the expatriates, as explained in Chapter 2) have to allocate their time toward bureaucratic procedures and working with headquarters, leaving the field visits to those lower down in the hierarchy (the local staff). In the experience of many of my interviewees, this contributes to maintaining the gap between them and host populations and to preventing them from better understanding local contexts. All the more frustrating was that my contacts rarely received feedback on their reports or suggestions to improve their actions, so they often felt that the time and energy spent on reporting was a waste.[65]

Reporting requirements also reinforce three other dynamics analyzed in this book. First, because they curtail the expatriates' opportunities to collect first-hand material on their areas of deployment, they reinforce the expatriates' tendency to use data from other UN, NGO, or governmental agencies when writing their reports, and thus fuel the closed, self-referential system mentioned in Chapter 4. Second, they encourage the preference for projects that fit neatly within certain reporting frameworks, and therefore promote the interveners' tendency to use preexisting models and templates.[66] Third and finally, the very necessities of reporting exacerbate the demand for quantification that I describe in the next section. A UN actor deployed in the Palestinian Territories for instance explained that indicating "how many meetings we attended, reports we wrote, e-mails we sent, phone calls to parties we gave, and news articles we read" was an essential part of the regular updates he wrote on the work of his team.

Preferred Results

In addition to these shared intervention rituals, there are two similarities in the types of results that peacebuilders from all kinds of organizations, backgrounds, and walks of life pursue. Ideally, these results are quantifiable and attainable in the short term – a preference that has significant impact on the overall effectiveness of international efforts.

---

[64] Ibid., p. 81.
[65] Neumann and Schia 2012, p. 36 documents similar complaints.
[66] See Anderson, Brown, et al. 2012, pp. 79–81 for a similar claim.

Quantifiable Outcomes

In their study of how NGOs, UN agencies, and donors monitor and evaluate sexual violence programs in Congo, Serena Cruz and Rosan Smits remark:

> The current approach heavily emphasizes quantitative results as a measure for success. [...] Programmatic success is tied to reaching specific numbers of those assisted and punished. This promotes a dependency on quantifiable efforts, such as tracking the number of rape victims receiving medical, psychosocial, legal, and economic assistance. Conversely, it also pushes for higher conviction rates for sexual assault offenders and monitoring the number of perpetrators incarcerated.[67]

Their observation is relevant to many programs beyond sexual violence. In their study of international peace and aid work around the world, Mary Anderson, Dayna Brown, and Isabella Jean emphasize that "donors and operational agencies" usually "focus on quantifiable results that can be documented, often in yearly (or more frequent) reporting cycles."[68] Keith Brown and his coauthors note a similar push from donors toward measurable outputs from democracy promotion programs in the Balkans in the late 1990s and early 2000s.[69] In their study of peacebuilding in Haiti, Amelie Gauthier and Madalena Moita emphasize "the pressure from donors" to achieve "results that can be measured quantitatively" and note that "possibilities for individual promotion are very much linked to measurable results and outputs."[70] Likewise, a donor involved in the prevention of mass violence explained to me that she and her colleagues preferred to fund "technical projects that are easy to measure." When they took on "soft" issues, they tried "to frame and implement them" in a way that was quantifiable. According to this donor, this common tendency stemmed from "a desire to claim impact and change."

When asked for the reasons behind this preference, my respondents explained that quantitative indicators were more "objective," "neutral," and "universal" than qualitative data. Other researchers have widely studied the historical process that led to this perspective.[71] In the reference book on this topic, Theodore Porter demonstrates that mathematics has "long been almost synonymous with rigor and universality" because "reliance on numbers and quantitative manipulation minimizes the need for intimate knowledge and personal trust."[72] The language of mathematics is "a highly disciplined discourse" that "helps to produce knowledge independent of the particular people who make it."[73] This advantage helps explain why quantification was so successful in the study of

---

[67] Cruz and Smits 2011, p. 4.
[68] Anderson, Brown, et al. 2012, p. 45.
[69] Brown 2006, notably pp. 24–25 and 70.
[70] Section "Haiti" in Sending 2010b, p. 21.
[71] Notably: Desrosières 1993; Mitchell 2002; and Porter 1995.
[72] Porter 1995, citation from p. ix, demonstration throughout the book.
[73] Ibid., citation from p. ix, demonstration throughout the book.

nature. Social scientists decided to use the same approach in order to emulate this achievement. Industrialized countries, mostly in Europe and North America, first designed and used quantitative concepts and measuring tools for public and social issues, and then began exporting them to developing countries.[74] Progressively, quantitative measurements became so dominant that doubts about their suitability subsided. Debates on their weaknesses – such as the inappropriateness of the proxies used to measure complex social concepts and the distance that increasingly sophisticated methods produce between "the real world and the world as represented by figures" – disappeared from mainstream public discourse (although it has persisted in academia).[75] By 2012, the public reliance on quantitative data and indicators had become so entrenched that various researchers labeled it a "practice of number worship."[76] This preference is quite prominent in Peaceland, given that interveners tend to view peacebuilding as a technical problem requiring a technical solution, which one might expect would generate a measurable result.

There is no doubt that measurable indicators are indispensable in identifying inefficient or wasteful initiatives. Since quantitative gauges are less subjective than qualitative measures, they allow for better comparisons across programs. They are thus particularly useful for measuring the relative effectiveness of various projects and comparing their "value for money" – their efficiency, calculated from the "costs of delivery relative to how many people they help."[77] As my interviewees emphasized, quantitative indicators also allow interveners to present "concrete" successes to funders and to the general public in donor countries. Finally, they make evaluation easier: A funder or supervisor just has to check that the adequate number of items have been constructed or distributed, which is much quicker than talking with people to gather their views on a program.

Problems arise, however, when the focus on numbers becomes so imperative and so habitual that the ritualistic search for quantifiable indicators leads to meaningless evaluations.[78] A Canadian defense official who served in the

---

[74] The rest of this paragraph draws extensively on the call for papers for the conference "Measuring Development – How Science and Politics Work Together," UNESCO, Paris, February 1 to 3, 2012, distributed by e-mail. On the appearance of quantitative concepts in industrialized countries, see also Desrosières 1993, chapters 1, 5, and 6; on exportation to the rest of the world, see Merry 2011, pp. S83–S85 and S89.

[75] Citation from the call for papers for the conference "Measuring Development." For a useful overview of the academic debate, see Green and Shapiro 1994, notably chapter 3, and a rejoinder in Friedman 1996. For more recent sources, see Bryman 2012, especially pp. 178–179; Merry 2011; and Moore 2013, pp. 11–14.

[76] Call for papers for the conference "Measuring Development."

[77] Anderson, Brown, et al. 2012, p. 35.

[78] Meharg 2009, introduction; Pérouse de Montclos 2012, pp. 8–11; and Pisani 2008, especially pp. 48–51 and chapter 3 present fascinating analyses of this issue, focused respectively on peacekeeping, development, and HIV prevention.

NATO and UN missions in Kosovo deplored that "the planners who typically produce initial [Measure of Effectiveness] programs [...] tend to start at the wrong end – with what can be measured, rather than what should be measured."[79] A peacebuilder working in Burundi explained that the UN mission evaluated the success of its Disarmament, Demobilization, and Reintegration program by counting the number of arms that it had collected. This indicator was irrelevant in a country where most people owned guns, weapon caches abounded, and borders were so porous that it was easy to import more. A proper evaluation of the program should therefore have studied whether people wanted to use arms and still viewed violence as an acceptable strategy – something that, according to my interviewee, "nobody knows how to measure."

Additionally, the everyday focus on measurable outcomes can become such an obsession that it orients intervention efforts away from methods that defy numerical evaluations but that may be just as necessary. I have argued in my previous book that the need for quantifiable results was among the reasons interveners, who were tasked with promoting peace and democracy in Congo between 2003 and 2006, devoted the large majority of their time, efforts, and resources to the organization of elections. This endeavor provided easily quantifiable data, such as the number of officials elected and the percentage of citizens who participated in the polls. Unfortunately, this focus detracted from local conflict resolution, which was also critical, but which gave rise to results that interveners found much harder to quantify.[80] A UN peacebuilder I interviewed faced the same issue in South Sudan. Although he viewed long-term grassroots peacebuilding as essential to successful conflict resolution, he spent little time working on this task, partly because it produced outputs that were "not easy to quantify."

Cruz and Smits document a related problem in their analysis of international responses to sexual violence. The interveners' "dependency on quantitative results" decreases "opportunities for recognizing strategies that also incorporate qualitative methods." It thus "encourages a focus on women survivors of sexual violence rather than addressing the broader gender dynamics underlying violence against women and men in Congolese society."[81] In other words, it reinforces the interveners' tendency to focus on consequences of violence rather than on its causes, as analyzed in Chapter 4. More broadly, as I have explained elsewhere, the obsession with quantifiable results is arguably one of the reasons why so many interveners still focus on reacting to problems rather than on preventing them in the first place.[82] An interview with a high-ranking peacekeeper encapsulated the issue: She blamed the shared perception that "prevention cannot be easily measured" as the main obstacle to her attempts at

[79] Cited in Meharg 2009, p. 8.
[80] Autesserre 2010, chapters 3 and 5.
[81] Cruz and Smits 2011, p. 4.
[82] Autesserre 2014.

convincing her colleagues that they should act preemptively rather than reactively.

Finally, as is true of all of the practices studied in this chapter, the emphasis on numbers reinforces the power dynamics at play in Peaceland. To begin with, it creates incentives that directly oppose involving local stakeholders in the design of international initiatives. In the words of an aid agency staff member in Thailand, "Placing ever-greater value on quantifiable results [...] makes it difficult to justify substantial expenditures on more participatory efforts, whose benefits are often hard to reflect in numbers."[83] Furthermore, expatriates are usually better equipped than host populations – especially those living in poor countries like Congo, Haiti, or Sudan – to access and produce quantitative data because of their privileged financial, logistical, and educational positions. At the most basic level, consulting or generating such material involves costs, from paying database access fees to funding the administration of surveys. It also requires command of digital media (to preview the material or disseminate the results) and statistical literacy. As a result, the obsession with numbers reinforces the superior position of expatriates relative to their local counterparts.

In contrast, privileging qualitative monitoring and evaluations promotes more reliance on local people, who have the necessary skills – notably the command of local languages and the knowledge of local histories, politics, and customs – to conduct such research.[84] All in all, complementing quantitative measures with qualitative ones helps rebalance the relationships between expatriates and local people, allowing each group to draw on its comparative advantages in different kinds of expertise. This also leads to better, more holistic assessments of programs.[85] Finally, it makes it easier and more legitimate for interveners to use peacebuilding approaches that are necessary but defy quantitative evaluations.

Short-Term Mindset

Interveners not only prefer quantifiable results; they also favor short-term ones. The brief deployments of most expatriates make it difficult for them to commit to long-term actions. In addition, mandate and funding constraints force them to try to attain results as quickly as possible.

The UN Security Council authorizes peacekeeping operation mandates that last six months to a year. Even if staff members on the ground are often confident that their missions will be renewed for years, many of those I interviewed still lamented that these limited time horizons led them to adopt a short-term perspective, which precluded a more long-term, structural view of their roles. Employees of other international organizations, such as the European Union's

---

[83] CDA Collaborative Learning Projects 2008b, p. 6.

[84] For an example of such an approach, see Life and Peace Institute 2011 and 2012.

[85] Millar 2014 provides a book length demonstration of this point. See also Bryman 2006; Cook 1997; and Rao and Woolcock 2004.

missions in security sector or police reform, voiced similar concerns. In May 2011, for instance, a staff member in one of these delegations explained that he and his colleagues were "working against a September 2011 deadline," so they avoided launching initiatives that went beyond that date, as they were not sure that their program would still be present in the country afterward.

International funding patterns reinforce the focus on the short term. Development donors, who grant one- to five-year contracts, are usually too wary to make investments in unstable situations.[86] As a result, most funds available for war and immediate post-war settings come from emergency donors, who usually finance projects for six months at a time.[87] While these programs are potentially renewable, donors require that implementing partners submit a continuation application at the end of the original grant period before they consider disbursing additional money. Funding for the evaluation of project results also typically expires on the official end date of the project, making it virtually impossible to assess an initiative's long-term impact (one, five, or ten years after the completion of a program). These modes of operation force all agencies dependent on such patronage, including NGOs and most UN organizations, to orient their work toward the immediate future.

This short-termism has several negative consequences on the effectiveness of international efforts, which other scholars have widely documented. Researchers agree that, while delivering "quick fixes" to problems might be possible for purely humanitarian projects – such as distributing emergency food rations to refugees to avert starvation – reconstructing post-war environments, establishing state authority, rebuilding social relationships, and promoting democracy are endeavors that must span several decades.[88] Consequently, long-term planning increases the chances that international efforts will succeed.[89] A leading donor in Cyprus, for instance, emphasized that his organization's involvement in the same peacebuilding program for more than ten years had enabled the staff to learn lessons that helped increase the effectiveness of their initiatives as time went on. In Jordan and Tunisia, long-term programs have proven much more efficient at promoting democracy than the projects that promise short-term results, which donors usually prioritize for funding.[90]

Even more importantly, short-termism fuels several problems analyzed throughout this book. It reinforces the international peacebuilders' tendency to use templates, as expatriates lack the time necessary to design projects specifically tailored to local conditions.[91] Short-termism also prevents foreign actors

---

[86] For a public source on the standard length of time of development, peacebuilding and human rights programs, see Anderson, Brown, et al. 2012, p. 40.

[87] See also Cooley and Ron 2002, p. 16; Garb and Allen Nan 2009, p. 12; and Verma 2011, p. 72.

[88] See, among others: Cooley and Ron 2002, notably p. 38; Garb and Allen Nan 2009, p. 12; Paris 2004, conclusion; and Pritchett, Woolcock, et al. 2010.

[89] Manning and Zürcher 2013, notably pp. 18, 161, 163, and 263–264.

[90] Bush 2011.

[91] Also Anderson, Brown, et al. 2012, pp. 25, 40–41, and 72–73; and Call and Cousens 2008, p. 15.

from engaging in the slow process of building trust with their local counterparts before taking on sensitive projects together.[92] It strengthens the interveners' propensity to bypass local partners, as they find it quicker to do things themselves than to involve their counterparts.[93] Finally, it creates such enormous time pressure on interveners that it adds to their already high levels of stress. As I experienced and witnessed, and as numerous contacts similarly noted, a number of us became progressively so focused on getting results quickly, and on ensuring that our programs were technically sound, that we "forgot to be decent human beings" (as a friend working as a donor in South Sudan put it). In other words, we engaged in some of the condescending and humiliating behavior detailed in Chapters 3 and 6.[94] In many cases, our conduct exacerbated our already tense relationships with our local counterparts and reinforced the boundaries between us and them.

Finally, the search for quick results often generates frustration and fatalistic and pessimistic attitudes among expatriate interveners. In post-conflict settings, apart from clear landmarks such as the signing of a peace agreement or the holding of post-war elections, improvements are small and incremental in comparison to the overwhelming nature of the problems at hand. As a result, it is difficult for interveners who are on site only for a short time to notice them. Peacebuilders deployed in Congo, for instance, often asked me informally whether I thought that things there would ever improve. In their view, there had not been any positive changes since they had arrived, and they doubted that the situation would ever get better. I, in contrast, saw tremendous improvements between the situation that I first witnessed in early 2001 (full-scale war over the entire Congolese territory, a divided country, unsafe areas almost everywhere beyond the centers of the main towns) and the scene in 2011 (civil war only in a few eastern provinces, a reunified country, and relatively safe territory with remaining pockets of insecurity). In Burundi, long-term interveners similarly observed both that tremendous progress had been made and that their colleagues on short-term deployments were unable to get a clear sense of how much the country had improved. This raises an important point: In addition to harming host populations, the short time scales of projects and deployments also detrimentally affect interveners, who dedicate their lives to helping others only to become discouraged and disheartened because they do not have the opportunity to see the value of their work.

Conclusion

Foreign peacebuilders deployed in conflict zones have to follow a number of routines to remain safe and to ensure that their donors will continue funding

---

[92] Also CDA Collaborative Learning Projects 2011b. p. 4; and Huang and Harris 2006, p. 84.

[93] Also Anderson, Brown, et al. 2012, pp. 126–127.

[94] Also Anderson 2008, p. 100.

their programs. Although these procedures achieve their intended results, they also have serious unintended consequences that fuel many of the problems analyzed in the previous chapters. The standard security procedures reinforce the boundaries of the expatriate bubble and decrease opportunities for the collection of reliable information on peace and conflict. Moreover, the security procedures, the visibility rituals, the search for neutrality, and the privileging of quantifiable and short-term results perpetuate and widen the chasm between international peacebuilders and their local counterparts. Altogether, these dominant modes of operation make it particularly difficult to break the boundaries between the two groups, even for the expatriates who are most motivated to change the system.

All of these routines also create additional constraints on the peacebuilders' daily work. The security procedures stall reactivity and, combined with the demands for quick results, generate significant frustration among interveners. The obsession with short-term and quantifiable outcomes also regularly orients peacebuilding efforts away from other, more effective strategies.

Certain individuals and organizations eschew the dominant modes of operation and suggest alternative ones, such as promoting security based on acceptance by local populations, maintaining a low profile, and valuing qualitative measurements on par with quantitative ones. As the next chapter explains, it is by looking at these exceptional cases – and the other ones described throughout the book – that we can learn how to reform the dominant practices, habits, and narratives in a way that will make the boundaries between interveners and local people more porous and thus less harmful.

CONCLUSION

Transforming Peaceland

Every morning, when Véronique arrived at the office of the Congolese human rights agency where she volunteered, Deo, the janitor, would be hard at work scrubbing the floor. Half an hour later, one of the Congolese lawyers would come in and see the young man cleaning. Every time, the passing lawyer would kick Deo's bucket of water over, forcing him to start scrubbing all over again. Every senior member of the office participated in this routine, so that whoever arrived first and saw Deo finishing his work would carry out the ritual of kicking over the bucket. Véronique was outraged. She was also puzzled: Why did the young man not protest? Above all, how could lawyers dedicated to the defense of human rights behave this way? Her first reaction was to put an end to the injustice (as most other expatriate interveners would have done). Then, Véronique stopped herself. She was a newcomer to Peaceland. She had just arrived in Congo, and she did not know the culture there. Her husband came from a developing country, and he had seen firsthand the problems that well-meaning interveners who knew little of local conditions could create. That, plus Véronique's extensive interactions with other cultures in her previous professional life, had made her wary of using her own Franco-Swiss frame of reference to judge the practices of others. Besides, as a subordinate of the organization's Congolese leadership, she had an unusually low rank for an expatriate, which deprived her of the power and legitimacy to sanction her colleagues. So, instead, she waited.

After numerous discussions with the janitor and his employers, she understood. If Deo went back home at 9 a.m., he would lose face. From his neighbors' point of view, people who earned little money and who returned home early lacked proper employment and thus stood at the bottom of the social ladder. The young man possessed no other characteristics that might have raised his status. He had no second job – such as driving a moto-taxi, like the other underemployed male youths of the neighborhood did – and he was unmarried. Furthermore, he lived with his sister, who resented having someone around during the day as she needed to take care of her house. In sum, when he went back home, and especially if he returned early, he was a nobody. So, without saying anything, without coordinating, the human rights lawyers had found a way to ensure that Deo was occupied for the whole morning. Admittedly, they might have come up with an alternative means of accomplishing this. Véronique never quite grasped why her colleagues had selected this particular method – it was not particularly sustainable, nor was it respectful. But, the system worked.

Eventually, Véronique joined in the game herself. She began to criticize Deo's performance – "It's still dirty here" – and realized that he was grateful for any pretext to stay longer at work. Véronique concluded her story with these words:

> For me, it was a shock to my understanding of the world. It changed the way I relate with people. Instead of coming with my good intentions – respect for human rights, justice, equity – and challenging what I perceive as injustice, I started wondering: If I kick the ant hill, what will happen to all these people? They have a specific place in the society, and if I take it away, in my awkward but well-meaning way, what else do I have to offer?[1]

Just like Véronique, most interveners in conflict zones arrive with good intentions. They may pursue additional selfish motives, but they do want to help improve local conditions. Many times, however, unlike Véronique, they use their own categories of meaning to interpret the foreign situations in which they work. Moreover, many of the challenges they face require quick responses, so most interveners cannot weigh the merits of their decisions over months. They follow the routine modes of actions that they have acquired through previous deployments and that other interveners also use. As a result, their good intentions often lead to ineffective strategies and regularly have pernicious consequences.

This book started with a question and a puzzle: Why do peace interventions regularly fail to reach their full potential? Why do international peacebuilders continue to reproduce even those practices, habits, and narratives they know to be ineffective or, worse still, counterproductive? In response, I proposed that everyday elements strongly influence the effectiveness of international initiatives. They shape international interventions on the ground, orienting them toward approaches that fail to stem ongoing violence or, worse yet, fuel it. These everyday elements also enable the perpetuation of dominant modes of operation, even those that interveners themselves view as detrimental to their efforts. The first section of this chapter summarizes this argument, and the second discusses its wider applicability beyond the topic of international interventions, suggesting avenues for further research. The rest of the chapter draws on the experiences of Véronique and the other exceptional individuals and organizations mentioned throughout the book, offering policy recommendations to improve international peace efforts.

---

[1] Author's on-record interview with Véronique Isenmann, Goma, February 2011. Deo is a pseudonym, used to protect the identity of the other main protagonist of this story.

The Argument, in a Nutshell

The question of how to build a sustainable peace is of critical importance to scholars, policy-makers, practitioners, and, above all, people living in conflict zones. The dominant explanations for international peacebuilding effectiveness focus on material constraints, vested interests, or the imposition of liberal values and templates. While these analyses are certainly important, they do not entirely explain why peace interventions often fail to reach their full potential. We need a new lens with which to approach the study of international peacebuilding – one focused on the everyday lives and work of expatriates deployed on the ground.

Individuals from all parts of the world and all walks of life, who would have little in common outside of Peaceland, exhibit a number of similarities when they serve as interveners in conflict zones. Despite their internal rivalries and antagonisms, and despite their notorious lack of coordination, they share a broad official goal: to help build peace in the host country. To do so, they value thematic expertise over local knowledge. They favor technical, short-term, and top-down solutions to complex social, political, and economic problems, and they orient these solutions toward quantifiable results. They compartmentalize the various elements of peacebuilding and preoccupy themselves with remaining impartial. International peacebuilders also have many personal and social experiences in common, such as a lifestyle that includes constant fear, enormous pressure to demonstrate results quickly, little chance for a family, and a job that is emotionally draining. For social, economic, and security reasons, they tend to socialize among themselves. These personal and social dimensions of the interveners' behavior are particularly significant because the living conditions in most theaters of deployment blur the usual distinctions between work and relaxation.

All of these standard modes of operation enable interveners to function in conflict zones, making possible the international efforts on the ground. The personal and social habits of expatriates are perfectly understandable responses to the stressful environments that they face. Most professional routines are reasonable answers to the security, logistical, and informational challenges inherent to operating in war and post-war situations. Dominant rituals such as visibility, neutrality, reporting, and quantification practices are crucial to ensuring continued funding for peacebuilding projects, as they stem from donor requirements. The interveners' reliance on thematic knowledge results from the professionalization of the peacebuilding field, a process that has increased the efficacy of many peacebuilding initiatives. Yet, in addition to these positive intended outcomes, the expatriates' practices, habits, and narratives also generate unintended results that decrease the effectiveness of international peace efforts.

The interveners' personal and social practices create boundaries between them and host populations. Several elements solidify these boundaries, increasing the salience of the divide between the two groups and further hampering possibilities for cooperation. The expatriates' narrative that they come to "help" host populations enables them to claim the moral high ground, while symbolic and material resources place expatriates in a dominant position. The triumph of thematic expertise legitimizes overwhelming reliance on external knowledge and solutions. The security routines, the obsession with quantifiable outputs, and the rituals of visibility, reporting, and impartiality further widen the chasm between interveners and their local counterparts, often emphasizing the superiority of the former.

These dominant modes of operation prevent local authorship and decrease local ownership. In addition, they generate widespread feelings of humiliation and resentment among host populations, encouraging local stakeholders to evade, adapt, or resist international programs. Although these reactions help improve local conditions at times, they often render potentially constructive projects ineffective or unsustainable. Moreover, they further solidify the boundaries between interveners and local counterparts. Local contestation, resistance, and rejection fuel the interveners' negative view of their counterparts. At the same time, local people regard expatriates with a high level of suspicion. They routinely interact with all types of foreign peacebuilders in a similar fashion and view them as interchangeable. This attitude promotes the internal cohesion of the interveners' club and exacerbates the foreigners' difficulties in integrating into local communities, thus encouraging them to live and work in expatriate bubbles.

The interveners' lack of local embeddedness prevents them from building the trust and personal networks that are vital to productive professional relationships. Moreover, it inhibits their ability to collect in-depth or even reliable data on dynamics of peace and conflict. In doing so, it reinforces a detrimental by-product of the triumph of thematic expertise, which justifies the deployment of foreign peacebuilders who possess little to no familiarity with their areas of intervention, no grassroots contacts, and no command of local languages. Consequently, expatriates too often lack an adequate grasp of the contexts in which they work, when in fact it should go without saying that effective peacebuilding requires a nuanced understanding of the dynamics of violence on the ground. This dearth of local knowledge encourages interveners to rely instead on dominant narratives – such as the idea that the illegal exploitation of natural resources is the main cause of violence in Congo. While useful, these narratives routinely paint oversimplified and, at times, biased pictures of local conditions. They also shape responses that are often ineffective and may potentially aggravate the very problems that interveners are trying to solve.

To make matters even worse, all of these dominant modes of operation orient intervention efforts toward specific strategies and methods and away from others that are just as necessary. The interveners' lack of local knowledge and deficient data collection techniques reinforce their tendency to use universal templates and to approach their work in a top-down manner, thus failing to address critical bottom-up sources of violence. The focus on thematic expertise leads to a compartmentalization of different aspects of the international efforts, even though the various dimensions of peacebuilding are inherently linked and mutually reinforce each other. The emphasis on short-term and quantifiable results regularly orients intervention initiatives away from strategies that are long-term or impossible to quantify but nevertheless crucial to building peace.

A number of interveners – most notably people with particularly strong ties to their host countries due to personal or family histories and, to a lesser extent, newcomers to Peaceland – resist and challenge the dominant modes of thinking and acting. They socialize with local people rather than with other expatriates, stay on site for years and develop an in-depth understanding of their area of deployment, use an acceptance approach to security, forgo visibility routines, and build primarily on local input to design their programs. Their peacebuilding efforts are usually more effective than those of their peers who follow the prevailing modes of operation.

Thus far, these challengers have not managed to accomplish broad change in intervention approaches. There are few incentives for their colleagues to reform the dominant modes of operation. The prevailing practices may be ineffective or counterproductive, but international peacebuilders rarely suffer the consequences: They are not accountable to their intended beneficiaries, and their short deployments expose them to the cost of continuing instability and violence only briefly, until they leave for another theater of intervention. Furthermore, since the dominant modes of operation enable international interveners to function on the ground, the large majority of expatriates considers these dominant practices the only proper and legitimate ones and, thus, resists attempts at reform. At the same time, local people are often so wary of interveners in general that they pose additional obstacles to the exceptional interveners' efforts to operate differently. To top it all off, the dissenting expatriates must often confront continual pressure from their superiors, whose organizations rely on routines and stability to function. As a result, many who question the dominant modes of operation end up either forced to fit into the mold or so frustrated that they change careers and leave Peaceland. Despite their marginalization, these dissenters are tremendously important: It is by looking at their alternative modes of operation that we can begin to specify the conditions under which peace interventions can be more effective.

Beyond Peace Interventions

Although this book has focused exclusively on one specific type of international actors (foreign peacebuilders), preliminary research shows that my critique and theoretical insights may be fruitfully applied to many other kinds of international action, from diplomatic engagement to business to counterinsurgency. Based on discussions with audience members at the various seminars where I have presented this manuscript, certain evidence offered in the previous chapters, and the relevant policy and scholarly literatures, it appears that peace interveners are an example of a much broader group.

The democracy makers studied by Anne Holohan and Kimberley Coles, the humanitarian aid workers examined by Mark Duffield and Lisa Smirl, and the development experts described by Robert Chambers, James Ferguson, Anne-Meike Fechter, Heather Hindman, Albert Hirschman, David Mosse, and Janine Wedel all present habits and practices similar to those of international peacebuilders.[2] They too value thematic and technical expertise over local knowledge, lack understanding of local contexts, live and work primarily in an expatriate bubble, focus on quantifiable and short-term results, and frequently follow the same security and visibility routines. Mary Anderson and her colleagues also explain that, due to a preference for top-down approaches, a lack of meaningful relationships with local partners, and a pattern of upward accountability, expatriates working in humanitarian and development aid regularly generate inefficient, ineffective, and counterproductive initiatives.[3] Just like I do, several of these researchers advocate greater inclusion of local people in the design of the international programs, and they too emphasize that individuals and organizations that challenge the prevailing practices tend to implement much more effective initiatives.[4]

Several other categories of expatriates who are deployed to conflict zones also present similarities to the international peacebuilders that I have analyzed. Take the US military and diplomatic officials that Rajiv Chandrasekaran and Rory Stewart depict.[5] They also fumble in the dark as they try to understand the local situations in Iraq and Afghanistan, and they too live and work in a self-referential international world.[6] Local knowledge is just as important for successful combat operations as it is for peacebuilding, as stated in the counterinsurgency manual that the U.S. Department of Defense drafted in 2006 under the impetus of General Petraeus.[7] Yet, like peace interventions, counterinsurgency efforts struggle with biased processes of knowledge construction, problematic boundaries between foreigners and local people, burdensome security procedures, and top-down approaches to bottom-up sources of violence.[8] Attempts at drawing on in-depth understanding of local conditions in addition to thematic knowledge, and trying to break the boundaries between foreign soldiers and local people, show as much promise for

---

[2] Chambers 1983 and 2006; Coles 2007; Duffield 2010; Fechter and Hindman 2011a; Ferguson 1990; Hirschman 1981, pp. 297 and 303–304; Holohan 2005; Mosse 2005; Smirl 2008 and 2012; and Wedel 1998.

[3] Anderson, Brown, et al. 2012.

[4] Ibid.; and Chambers 1983 and 2006.

[5] Chandrasekaran 2012; and Stewart 2007.

[6] On Afghanistan, see also Coburn 2011, chapters 6 to 9.

[7] Petraeus 2006, notably paras. 1–124, 1–125, 1–157, and chapter 3.

[8] Jones and Smith 2010, notably pp. 83–84; Kipp, Grau, et al. 2006; Lyall and Wilson 2009; Marston and Malkasian 2010; Petraeus 2006, para. 1–149; and Steve Featherstone, "Human Quicksand for the US Army, a Crash Course in Cultural Studies," *Harper's Magazine*, September 2008.

counterinsurgency operations as they do for international peace initiatives.[9] For instance, combat teams throughout Afghanistan reported up to a 60 percent decrease in the need for combat operations once local conflict experts (called "human terrain teams" in military lingo) joined their ranks.[10] However, these initiatives were isolated exceptions. The broader mission suffered from "a lack of understanding of Afghan society" and a "short-term" outlook that sharply decreased the potential effectiveness of the counterinsurgency efforts.[11]

According to my interviews and informal communications, the book's analysis also resonates with the experience of people not directly involved in war and peace, such as business expatriates working for commercial companies in places like Angola, Congo, and South Sudan. They too are sent to places about which they know little, due to the assumption that their technical skills will compensate for any deficiency in local understanding. Many of them interact primarily with other foreigners, bypass local people, and make mistakes similar to those that I have documented in this book. And, according to my contacts, just as with peace interveners, the businesspeople who break the boundaries between themselves and local populations and develop an in-depth understanding of their areas of deployment are much more effective in their operations.

The issues I note throughout the book are not even limited to international relations in the twenty-first century. Today's international interveners present a number of similarities with the colonial officials who lived overseas a century ago, as Gabrielle Dietze and Reo Matsukazi have noted.[12] In many aspects – the expatriate bubble, the boundaries between foreigners and local people, the politics of knowledge, the ethics of care – my description of Peaceland is reminiscent of the description of colonial society in Edward Said's *Orientalism* and in classic novels such as E. M. Forster's *A Passage to India* and J. M. Coetzee's *Waiting for the Barbarians*.[13]

This very brief overview is not meant to be exhaustive but rather to open areas for further study. Researchers need to analyze the aforementioned examples in much greater depth and consider the influence of everyday practices, habits, and narratives in these and other contexts. Virtually all issues that international relations scholars examine, from war and peace to financial markets to international law, are dealt with by communities of people who speak their own languages, have their own everyday modes of operation, and construct their own

---

[9] See Autesserre 2010, pp. 249–250 for more details. Also Lyall and Wilson 2009, pp. 96–101; and Marston and Malkasian 2010.

[10] David Rohde, "Army Enlists Anthropology in War Zones," *New York Times*, October 5, 2007. Also Anna Mulrine, "The Culture Warriors," *US News and World Report*, November 30, 2007.

[11] Paris 2013, p. 545. Also Chandrasekaran 2012; Coburn 2011, notably chapter 6; and Suhrke 2011.

[12] Dietze 2010; Matsuzaki in progress.

[13] Coetzee 1982; Forster 1924; and Said 1978.

systems of meaning.[14] To be sure, the challenges in looking ethnographically at macro-level topics – or at organizations that have a culture of secrecy – are such that international relations may not seem amenable to the ethnographic gaze.[15] However, this book and the works cited in this section demonstrate that it is possible and even necessary to conduct more ethnographic research on the everyday dimensions of international and transnational processes, and that our understanding of them will be richer as a result of it.

These additional inquiries would further help identify alternative modes of operation that are more effective than the prevailing narratives, practices, and habits. While awaiting these research results, the rest of this chapter suggests concrete ways for policy-makers and practitioners to reform the dominant modes of operation documented in this book so that their efforts can reach their greater potential.

Ongoing Challenges and Potential Responses

Given the harmful consequences of the intervention efforts that I have analyzed, one may wonder if it would be best to eliminate support for international peacebuilding altogether and let local populations build peace on their own. This solution is decidedly inadvisable because it would deprive people in conflict zones of all the advantages and assistance that expatriates offer (see the introduction to Part I). International actors ought not to terminate their peace-building efforts but rather eliminate their negative impacts while preserving their positive outcomes. *not possible*

Such reform would involve addressing the detrimental everyday elements of peacebuilding that I have documented in this book. As these elements stem from both top-down instructions and bottom-up responses, the impetus for change must come from both ends.[16] For instance, policy studies of the attempts to improve interveners' accountability to local people clearly illustrate that feed-back mechanisms imposed by donors are much less effective than initiatives coming from the bottom or mid-range up.[17] At the same time, there needs to be buy-in and support from the senior management – and, ideally, monetary support from funders – for these accountability mechanisms to be effective and lead to meaningful strategy changes.[18] The scholarly literature on organizational

---

[14] Thanks to Jonathan Blake for first mentioning this point and those that I develop in the rest of this paragraph. For book-length demonstrations of this claim, see Pouliot and Adler 2011b; and Schatz 2009. On financial markets, see also Ho 2009.

[15] Abrahamsen and Williams 2011.

[16] On the role of elites in policy change: Domhoff 1990; and Mills 2000. On the role of grassroots communities: Alinsky 1989; and Biklen 1983. For a useful brief on the main theories of policy change, see Stachowiak 2007. For an insightful case study of change and obstacles to change within international organizations, see Weaver 2008.

[17] CDA Collaborative Learning Projects 2011a, pp. 6–8 and 20.

[18] Based on ibid., notably pp. 2, 8, and 12.

change in international relations similarly emphasizes the need for both a top-down and a bottom-up approach to any reform process.[19]

There are numerous top-down factors that can help change everyday modes of operation. They may include revised instructions from the top-levels of the peacebuilding and donor organizations, for example. They may also comprise policies and rules that alter the material incentives of on-the-ground interveners, so that international peacebuilders see a personal benefit in adopting the recommended changes – or face sanctions when they persist in employing detrimental modes of operation. In particular, high-ranking policy-makers could use their influence over budgets to incentivize change by increasing funding for the initiatives recommended in the next subsections and decreasing funding for counterproductive processes. Moreover, these same policy-makers can require their employees to adopt the concrete measures detailed in the following sections.

From the bottom up, facilitating change involves, among other things, creating reasons for international peacebuilders to think of themselves in new ways, in order to diminish the perceived usefulness of established practices, habits, and narratives.[20] It is also essential to ensure that the rewards for following alternative modes of operation are greater than the sanctions for challenging them (or that the professional cost of persisting to use harmful practices is greater than its benefits). Donors, management staff, on-the-ground expatriates, and local stakeholders all have a role to play in this bottom-up process.

As I detail in the coming pages, there are two particularly important "fronts" in the struggle to encourage both top-down and bottom-up change and to overcome elements that perpetuate the status quo.[21] The first is the ideas front, which entails convincing stakeholders that the changes being advocated are worth implementing. The second is the practical front, which involves translating these ideas into action through new or revised training programs, recruitment and promotion patterns, resource distributions, policies, and standard operating procedures.

Admittedly, the whole process will be difficult, lengthy, and will face a great deal of organizational resistance. It will not guarantee that every single

---

[19] Demers 2007, notably parts II and III; and Fernandez and Rainey 2006 provide very useful reviews of the vast literature on organizational change. For studies on this topic in international relations, see among many others: Barnett and Finnemore 2004; Campbell 2012; Farell 2013, pp. 17–18 and throughout the book; Helfer 2006, especially pp. 657–669 and 722–726; Howard 2008; Rotmann, Tohn, and Wharton 2009; and Weaver 2008, pp. 178–179 and throughout the book. Thanks to Susanna Campbell (post-doctoral associate, the Graduate Institute, Geneva) for her help in navigating this literature.

[20] This idea builds on the research by Alexander Wendt mentioned in Chapter 1, notably Wendt 1992, p. 419.

[21] This paragraph builds on Weaver 2008, chapter 2, and at times paraphrases p. 39. Weaver draws on Bebbington, Guggenheim, et al. 2004; and Bebbington, Woolcock, et al. 2006. On the elements that promote a perpetuation of the status quo, see Chapter 1 in this book.

international initiative will be invariably successful. As explained in the Introduction and Chapter 1, the everyday elements on which this book focuses are only some of the factors that influence peacebuilding effectiveness. Correcting the harmful habits, practices, and narratives that prevail in Peaceland is a necessary but insufficient condition for ensuring intervention success. It is insufficient because vested interests, material constraints, and the imposition of liberal values can still thwart international efforts. It is necessary, however, because even the best-designed and the best-funded initiatives will never reach their full potential if such insidious practices persist.

Continuing the Battle Over Ideas

The first step in the process of reform is to raise awareness of the existence of these problems and their potential solutions. This includes calling attention to the serious flaws in the dominant everyday practices, emphasizing that the impact of such routines and habits is actually quite significant, highlighting the existence of alternative approaches, and stressing the absolute need for change.

Media outlets have a critical role to play. Many interviewees acknowledged that they and their organizations pay more attention to issues that are widely covered in the press than to those that are not. Publicizing the problems posed by the interveners' everyday habits, practices, and narratives would help reinforce nascent interest in these topics. At the same time, journalists could follow success stories, showcasing alternative approaches to everyday peacebuilding and emphasizing their effectiveness. The individuals and agencies who already reject the dominant practices are the best equipped to start raising interest among journalists, who could in turn induce other actors and media outlets to consider further action.

Researchers – including think tanks, academic scholars, and policy analysts – can also contribute to this process by inquiring further into the ways everyday modes of operation influence international peacebuilding effectiveness. This book along with the scholarship that I mentioned in the previous section and in the Introduction all represent a first step toward that goal. It would be fruitful to expand and deepen the exploration of the interveners' shared practices, habits, and narratives, in more places around the world, to fully appreciate how they influence the effectiveness of international peace efforts. This would contribute to further explaining which everyday strategies can promote successful peacebuilding and what the main obstacles to change are. It is also crucial to develop systematic studies of the individuals and organizations who suggest alternative modes of operation, not only to help identify which factors produce such exceptions, but also to better understand how exceptional actors manage to overcome existing obstacles and why certain individuals eventually integrate into local communities while others never do.

Increased awareness of the problems and potential solutions would facilitate the translation of these ideas into action by encouraging reformers, providing them with ideas, and delegitimizing resistance to such transformation. However, raising awareness alone would not be sufficient. Producing concrete and feasible suggestions for improving everyday practices is also critical. As mentioned throughout the book, a number of interveners are uncomfortable with the prevailing modes of operation. However, the vast majority either do not have the time necessary to come up with alternative approaches or cannot determine how best to proceed.

Researchers can thus help translate ideas into action by generating detailed policy recommendations that interveners and host populations have vetted. The Collaborative Learning Projects provide a useful model on how to do so: It could take the form of a group effort that involves researchers from every part of the world – including from countries of intervention – and constantly solicits the input and feedback of policy-makers, practitioners, and local people through interviews, workshops, and online interactions. Whether developed in this way or not, policy prescriptions would, of course, need to ensure the long-term cost-effectiveness of proposals. (The reform process would inevitably require an important investment of time, effort, and money in the short term; however, I believe that, in the long term, the changes can make international peace interventions less costly overall, or at least much more efficient, as I explain in the following sections.) Finally, to be effective, those who generate policy prescriptions should frame their message in a way that resonates with existing ideologies, norms, interests, and routines.[22] For instance, they could show that the new directives will help ensure better security for the staff on the ground. They could also underscore the fact that these changes will essentially bring the reality of peacebuilding in line with the rhetoric that many organizations already espouse about promoting local ownership and rejecting one-size-fits-all templates for intervention.

While we await the findings of this research, the next sections outline tentative suggestions to address the two main sources of dysfunction identified throughout the book: the politics of knowledge at work in Peaceland and the firm boundaries that exist between interveners and local stakeholders.

Rebalancing the Values of Local and Thematic Knowledge

Part I emphasized the dangers of overreliance on thematic expertise and highlighted the absolute necessity of building more extensively on local knowledge. International peacebuilders can take a number of concrete measures to address these issues. Importantly, they need and ought not disregard the value of thematic competency in order to promote that of country expertise. As explained throughout the book, both forms of knowledge are necessary for the design and

---

[22] Based on Weaver 2008, p. 39. On how messaging and frameworks influence decision-making, see Tversky and Kahneman 1981.

implementation of effective peacebuilding initiatives. What peacebuilding needs is a rebalancing so that the two forms of expertise are similarly valued.

Intervening organizations could model their restructuring on the various agencies that have already adopted such an approach. I mentioned some of these in Chapters 2 and 3, including Caritas, the Eastern Congo Initiative, and the Life and Peace Institute in Congo; Catholic Relief Services in Serbia; some of the UN structures studied by Susanna Campbell in Burundi; and certain international agencies examined by Adam Moore in Bosnia. The common characteristic of these otherwise diverse organizations is that they base their actions on in-depth local knowledge and reject universal approaches to peacebuilding. The most successful among them rely on local employees supervised by a few foreigners (who often have extensive preexisting country knowledge). Local staff and counterparts are in charge of conceiving, designing, and executing the projects. They regularly solicit the input of intended beneficiaries and community members (including ordinary people) throughout the planning and implementation process. The expatriates view their roles as that of "providing technical support, resources, and international connections" to the agendas, goals, and implementation plans formulated by the local stakeholders.[23] These interveners stay for several years and focus on developing their knowledge of local conditions and their network of grassroots elites.

The recommendations below are meant to provide suggestions of how to revise existing policies, recruitment and promotion patterns, training programs, resource distributions, and standard operating procedures for organizations that wish to adopt this model.

- Change Recruitment and Promotion Practices for Interveners

Intervening organizations should initiate changes in the recruitment and training of expatriates. To begin with, though they should continue to hire individuals with thematic expertise and technical skills, they should also recruit foreign staff with in-depth understanding of local contexts and knowledge of local languages. In addition, they should include these latter criteria in the periodic evaluations of their staff. When considering promotions, they should value the time spent in a given area of deployment over the number of missions completed in different countries. Donors could encourage this process by requesting that their implementing partners value local knowledge in recruitment and promotion of foreign staff, or even by demanding to vet the expatriates employed to work on the projects they fund (for instance by looking at the CVs of applicants and approving or denying their appointments).

This shift, in turn, would signal to prospective interveners – and their preparation centers or universities – that their education should include extensive coursework on specific countries and cultures. It would also help decrease the detrimental turnover of expatriates, as interveners would be enticed to stay

---

[23] Gagnon 2006, p. 172.

longer, and organizations would have incentives to deploy their staff for a lengthier period of time.

It would be important to keep certain positions for outsiders with no preexisting knowledge of the area in order to benefit from a fresh look at problems and to avoid the accumulation of bias. For certain highly specialized positions, intervening agencies may also have difficulty finding people who possess both the necessary technical skills and some understanding of local conditions. Intervention structures should consider reviewing the induction process for these newcomers and offer them briefings modeled on those of the Peace Corps: months-long trainings devoted to learning the local languages, history, politics, and cultures.[24] (These briefings would be even better if local employees took charge of them, as this would provide newcomers with information from firsthand sources, offer an opportunity to impress upon incoming interveners the value of the local staff's expertise, and help develop stronger working relations between expatriates and local colleagues from the start.) Changing induction in this way would help ensure that foreign peacebuilders recruited for their technical skills have the necessary foundation upon which to build local knowledge as well as the cultural understanding that would facilitate improved personal and social relations with local stakeholders, which I discuss later in this chapter. Whenever necessary, these training programs could also include classes on context analysis and proper data-gathering techniques both tailored to local conditions. Short-term emergency staff, who do not have sufficient time to participate in lengthy induction processes or training programs, could at least benefit from a one-day or one-week seminar on cultural issues, so that they avoid the worst errors and misunderstandings.

Donors could make this reform possible by funding the training programs for each implementing agency – or (even better and more cost-effectively) by financing training centers that all organizations could use in the various countries of intervention – and by covering the trainees' salaries throughout their instruction. They could also forcefully promote this shift by making the induction training obligatory for any expatriate working on projects that they finance, unless the new recruit passes a test proving sufficient preexisting local knowledge. To ensure that expatriates take these preparations seriously, donors and employers could condition deployment on an end-of-training exam, and request that people who repeatedly fail the test reimburse the training costs.

Admittedly, this practice would be too expensive and time-consuming if interveners spend only a few months to a year in a given country, as most currently do. However, it would make much more sense if the lengths of the expatriates' deployments were extended to several years.

It would indeed be important for the UN and NGOs to offer longer-term placements to their staff instead of the standard six-month contracts that employees renew, at most, a few times (admittedly, this change is dependent on having

---

[24] Details on these training are available at www.peacecorpswiki.org/Training_by_country (last accessed in December 2013).

new, longer-term budgets for peacebuilding programs, as recommended in the section Facilitating Factors). Recruiters could insist on hiring staff for at least two to three years, or even five years when possible. Foreign and defense ministries could also extend the standard term of deployment for negotiators, special envoys, on-the-ground diplomats, and peacekeeping contingents in conflict zones. It is true that living conditions in war and post-war situations are such that long-term assignments are taxing on the staff, but they are not impossible. Certain business expatriates live in the same conflict zones as peacebuilders and face approximately the same risk levels; yet, as I observed and as my interviewees confirmed, they usually stay on site much longer than interveners. One significant change that superiors could institute to make long-term positions more attractive would be authorizing employees to bring their families with them – a measure that would have a number of other positive consequences, as explained in the next section.

These reforms would increase the time and impetus for foreign interveners to learn local contexts, as they would reward expatriates who prioritize understanding their host communities and penalize those who do not. Another consequence would be a change in the profile of the interveners: Expatriate jobs would now attract people interested in a specific country and its population rather than in the technical aspects of a position. Given their distinct motivations, these people would likely be more inclined to develop an in-depth expertise on their area of deployment and to integrate locally, thus reinforcing the changes that this section recommends.

These reforms would also facilitate the expatriates' integration in local social structures, for three reasons. First, it is much easier – and much more enjoyable – for foreigners to socialize with members of their host countries when they speak local languages and understand local cultures than when they do not. Second, recognition that they are on site for an extensive period of time would increase the expatriates' incentives to integrate into the surrounding communities and would encourage them to build better relationships with local counterparts, if just to ensure a decent social life. Third, longer-term deployments would provide the time indispensable to the development of trusting relationships. In turn, this higher level of integration and longer deployments would promote greater accountability because expatriates would endure the effects of continued violence or see the toll it takes on people they care about. This would give expatriates a stronger stake in the futures of their host countries and boost their desire to see their programs make a significant difference.

Finally, having interveners on site for longer periods of time would decrease the frequent loss of institutional memory, especially if human resources departments eliminated the problematic practice that currently occurs in some NGOs, embassies, and UN offices in which all expatriate staff positions can turnover at the same time.[25] Staggering the turnover of staff such that newcomers do not all

---

[25] Chandrasekaran 2012, para. 21 is a public source on turnover at the same time affecting virtually all the expatriate staff of an organization.

arrive at once would have an additional benefit, as it would help organizations ensure that new arrivals would act as a check on their colleagues who, having been on site longer, might be more at risk of developing local allegiances.

• Rely More on Local Employees

Another essential measure would be for intervening agencies to progressively replace most of their expatriates with local staff, including for management and leadership positions, and pay these staff an equivalent salary. Instead of automatically placing outsiders in high-level positions, as they currently do, international and non-governmental organizations could retain expatriates only in posts that no local person can fill: in jobs where local people would face too much pressure and too great a risk of becoming biased, or in cases where the agency can find no local person with the requisite skills or expertise.

UN peacekeeping missions would be prime targets for this reform, given the high number of expatriates they employ for jobs that local people can easily fill. In all of the support sections, such as administration and movement control, expatriates could retain only the positions in which local employees might be subject to too many inappropriate demands and stressors – like in the top ranks of the finance and human resources departments. The "substantive" sections – such as Civil Affairs or Demobilization, Disarmament, and Reintegration – could also replace many expatriates with local staff members and give them much more responsibility. Other UN agencies and NGOs could follow a similar process.

All of these organizations should also try to ensure that at least some of their local recruits come from the specific area where they will be working, as employees from a different part of the country will not have the same relevant local knowledge, legitimacy, or network.

Concurrently, intervention structures should invert the prevailing practice of expatriates making decisions while local people merely assist or execute orders. Although this mode of operation is sensible for diplomatic missions seeking to uphold their country's interests, it is actually inefficient and ineffective for NGOs and international organizations. Local staff and counterparts should be in the driver's seat, getting to do things themselves and acting as the primary decision-makers; expatriates should remain in the shadows to help and advise. With this change, instead of imposing or strongly advocating for one idea, interveners could use their technical expertise in a different way: to suggest several options, explain the pros and cons of each, and offer support in implementing whichever plans local partners agree upon.

Augmenting the reliance on local employees would increase the effectiveness of knowledge transfer, empower local actors (and thus decrease the power differential with expatriates), expedite the eventual exit of interveners, and ensure greater sustainability of initiatives after the foreigners' departure. Given the cost associated with the deployment of expatriates in conflict zones (in terms of insurance, salary, in-kind benefits, and bonuses paid to reward placement in

dangerous areas), relying more on local employees would also make intervention efforts cheaper.[26] Additionally, it would further ensure the safety of the
interveners, as the organizations that extensively rely on local employees to
manage their security have a better track record of protecting their staff and
beneficiaries than those who primarily count on external experts.[27] Finally, as
local staff in higher positions would command better salaries, this reform would
help decrease the economic differences between expatriates and their local
employees, thus alleviating some of the concerns that this disparity generates.

[handwritten: but other neg side effect of that]

- Involve Local Partners and Communities in Novel Ways

Recognizing the importance of country- or village-specific knowledge would
incentivize more thorough consideration of local input by interveners. To further facilitate this process, experts could create guidelines, mechanisms, procedures, and structures to consult beneficiaries from the initial stages of program
design – instead of waiting to solicit their input until feasibility assessments,
project implementations, or end-of-program evaluations, as is current practice.
They should pay particular attention to ensuring that foreign peacebuilders
consult not only their usual biased sample of informants, but also ordinary
citizens. They could also suggest that any field team include at least one local
staff or stakeholder in an instrumental position – not, as is usually the case, as
just a driver or translator.

Several exceptional organizations have already implemented such an
approach and evaluated what worked and what did not. CDA Collaborative
Learning Projects has developed thorough guidelines concerning how to collect
and integrate feedback from local stakeholders.[28] Peace Direct has crafted similarly useful advice regarding how to determine when one can build on local
capacities (and how to identify appropriate and trustworthy local partners) and
when one should bring in external expertise and resources.[29] These resources
offer in-depth examples drawn from a variety of conflict zones around the world
as well as a nuanced discussion of the challenges inherent to their approaches and
potential ways to overcome them.

Donors could promote this approach in five ways. They could offer seed
funding for interveners to organize the necessary local consultations. They could
also revise their application templates, adding a section appraising the involvement of local stakeholders and intended beneficiaries in the design of the project,
and then use this assessment as part of their selection criteria. They could include
indicators that measure the level of satisfaction of target populations in their
standard evaluations. They could condition funding on a demonstration of need:

---

[26] For a preliminary evaluation of the savings associated with a more extensive reliance on local
partners, see McGuinness 2012, pp. 24–26, 57, 105–107, 127–128.

[27] Egeland, Harmer, et al. 2011, pp. 45–46.

[28] CDA Collaborative Learning Projects 2011a.

[29] McGuinness 2012.

Existing local capacities cannot address a given problem without external assistance. Lastly, as mentioned below, they could offer longer-term budgets, so that their implementing partners have the time necessary to gather meaningful local input.

Another more radical, but more effective, measure would be for donors to compel all interveners to work with a local partner (an NGO, civil society structure, religious agency, or local authority) to implement projects – as, again, peacebuilding organizations like Caritas or the Life and Peace Institute are currently doing, and as certain development funders already require.[30] Donors could request that project proposals include plans and budgets not only for technical, financial, administrative, and logistical training for local partners, but also for a handover lasting several years. They could condition the disbursement of funds on the signing of a partnership agreement between international and local counterparts. Of course, the agreement would need to be tailored to suit the conditions of each particular intervention, but one example might be to have international and local partners agree to a multiphase partnership for a particular project. In the first phrase, each party would enjoy equal authority over programmatic decisions and the allocation of financial and logistical resources. In the second phase, the local partner would take the lead, but the international organization and its staff would remain actively involved. In the third phrase, the expatriates would still monitor the project, but they would reduce their involvement, providing support (whether logistical, financial, administrative, or technical) only upon the request of local counterparts. Once ready, the local organization would take over the operation entirely, completing the partnership. If any concerns that the local and international partners might not be fully committed to the project arise, donors may ask them to find funding themselves for a small percentage of the budget or to contribute other assets (such as people or material resources).

To further sustain civil society organizations and to facilitate the identification of reliable local partners, donors could also establish support programs for local structures, with training in administrative, financial, and thematic and technical issues. The local agencies that are selected for training and pass the end-of-training tests would then be vetted to serve as local partners for international agencies. A list of these approved partners could be made publicly

---

[30] Examples of development donors including such a requirement in their call for proposals include: European Commission, *Cofinancing with European Development NGOs – Actions in Developing Countries (PVD) (Projects) – Guidelines for grant applicants responding to the call for proposals for 2006 – Restricted Call for Proposal – Budget line 21-02-03, Reference: EuropeAid/124568/C/ACT/ Multi* (available at http://ec.europa.eu/europeaid/tender/data/d98/AOF71698.doc); the UK Department for International Development's Common Ground Initiative (overview of the program available at www.gov.uk/common-ground-initiative-cgi); and Australian Aid's Africa Community Engagement Scheme (www.ausaid.gov.au/publications/web/aaces-annualreport/Pages/transforming-communities-changing-lives.aspx#approach) – all Web sites last accessed in December 2013.

available – on the Web sites and at the offices of donors, international implementing partners, and host government structures. An additional idea would
be to replicate in other conflict zones the mapping of community-based organizations that the Eastern Congo Initiative has completed, which provides a
thorough listing and evaluation of local organizations throughout the region,
along with a database that intervening agencies can use to identify potential
collaborators.[31]

All of these measures to reform the politics of knowledge in Peaceland might
raise a concern about expediency. Critics may argue that training interveners in
local languages and contexts, and involving local communities in novel ways,
would lengthen the response time to crises, and the time spent adapting
peacebuilding strategies to local conditions would mean lives lost. However,
my proposed reforms still allow for rapid deployment in case of emergencies in
new contexts, as intervening organizations will continue to have thematic
experts with transportable expertise on staff. Even in these circumstances, it is
true that the proposed reforms would slow down the initiation of peacebuilding
programs a bit. This is deliberate. Beneficiaries themselves advocate for such a
change and contend that they are willing to bear the consequences, given how
hurtful the current focus on speed is for them.[32] The thousands of "people who
had suffered rapid and extensive emergencies" that Mary Anderson and her
colleagues interviewed developed "a reasonably argued plea to slow down and
take time before delivering or acting."[33] Just like I have argued throughout the
book, they emphasized that without local knowledge, "outsiders make numerous mistakes that cannot be compensated for by speediness" – mistakes that
"could have been prevented with just a little more time spent in getting to know
local realities."[34] International peacebuilders need to find the right balance
between doing things quickly when required and taking the time necessary to
contextualize their actions and ensure that they do not generate more harm than
good.[35] My proposals are an attempt at finding this proper balance.

At the cost of a somewhat slower response time, the measures to rebalance the
values of thematic and local knowledge would enable foreign peacebuilders to
design more effective and appropriate intervention strategies. Better context-
specific knowledge would oppose and undermine the pervasive idea that there is
a recipe for peacebuilding that works in all situations and contexts. It would
provide foreign peacebuilders with the information they need to select and tailor
outside ideas and models to each specific situation, prevent misunderstandings
rooted in superficial knowledge of local conditions, and alleviate the interveners'

---

[31] Eastern Congo Initiative 2011; database available at www.easterncongo.org/success-stories/cbo-
database (last accessed in December 2013).
[32] Anderson 2008, pp. 99–103.
[33] Ibid., p. 101.
[34] Ibid., pp. 100 and 101.
[35] Also ibid., pp. 99–100 and 103.

need to rely on simplistic narratives regarding the causes of peace and violence. Increased local expertise would also promote context-specific evaluation measures, which would help allow for greater use of qualitative indicators, while increasing their reliability. This shift, in turn, would make it possible to use strategies that are necessary for successful peacebuilding but do not generate quantifiable outputs. Additionally, more attention to local contributions and greater allocation of responsibility to local staff and counterparts would promote local ownership and authorship, encourage downward accountability, and help decrease the power differential existing in Peaceland. Finally, this shift would help promote quality interactions between interveners and local counterparts, reduce the power imbalance between the two groups, and defuse the pervasive feeling of humiliation among the latter.

Breaking Boundaries between Interveners and Local Counterparts

The second part of the book has identified the firm boundaries between interveners and local populations as another key reason for international ineffectiveness and for the perpetuation of detrimental modes of operation. Reforming the politics of knowledge in Peaceland would already help break down some of these boundaries and reduce the perceived superiority of the international peacebuilders. In addition, the following measures would help initiate the types of changes necessary to further promote productive relationships between the two groups.

• Increase Professional Interactions

A first step would be to increase the on-the-ground presence of existing expatriates. To do so, intervening agencies could request that their foreign staff deployed in the field spend more time outside of their offices – and outside of capital cities and headquarters. As mentioned in Chapter 5, one of the central findings of the Listening Project is that host populations value the mere physical presence of expatriates.[36] To local citizens, presence shows respect, enhances protection, promotes mutual learning, better enables foreign interveners to understand local realities and implement worthwhile projects, and facilitates monitoring (thus helping to prevent or detect cases of corruption and embezzlement).[37]

Importantly, the suggestion is not to send more expatriates to conflict zones but rather to request that those on site allocate their time differently. One way to facilitate this shift would be to ease the reporting requirements, which, according to many interveners, force them to spend an inordinate amount of time in the office and serve little purpose given that few people actually use these reports.

Organizations could also embrace another, more ambitious measure by taking material steps to foster respect and collaboration between international and local partners. Instead of having separate offices and interacting only during ad

---

[36] CDA Collaborative Learning Projects 2008a.
[37] Ibid., pp. 2–8.

hoc meetings, foreign peacebuilders could make it a habit to combine facilities with their local counterparts (and if it were to become compulsory for international interveners to partner with local peacebuilders, then joint offices could be made a requirement). This would promote the sharing of financial and material resources, make both parties more aware of the daily challenges that their counterparts face, decrease the likelihood of parallel governance structures forming, and offer more opportunities for formal and informal interactions between the two groups.

• Facilitate Socialization

It is also critical for intervention structures to encourage after-work interactions between expatriates and host populations, instead of discouraging relations for the sake of appearing neutral and promoting security. As I explained in Chapter 5, good social and personal relations with local colleagues and counterparts are essential to ensuring the success of international efforts. Measures to promote such personal interactions could include opening as many social and professional events as possible to local staff and local counterparts; organizing weekly or monthly social gatherings with the specific purpose of bringing together expatriates and local contacts; removing the safety rules preventing after-work socialization (including the prohibition of travel to poor neighborhoods at night and the interdiction of nonprofessional meetings with local people of the opposite gender); considering skills for relationship-building with local partners and attitudes toward local people as one of the criteria for recruitment and promotion of interveners; and, during induction briefings, explaining the benefits of social interactions and reminding expatriates that networking matters just as much inside Peaceland as outside of it. The leadership of each organization could also budget time for their expatriate staff to interact with and learn from local counterparts.

In addition, international agencies should consider making it possible for interveners to bring their families into the field with them – something that many interveners and their significant others desire. Beyond greatly contributing to the expatriates' sense of well-being, having one's spouse (and, possibly, children) on site would help the interveners to integrate locally. As occurs in immigrant communities around the world, expatriates would have the opportunity to develop relationships with the colleagues of their spouses and the parents of their children's friends, and they would be more readily invited to family events. Having their families with them would also provide powerful incentives for interveners to stay on site for several years, as leaving would no longer mean returning to loved ones, but rather uprooting them – disrupting their children's educations, forcing their spouses to abandon their jobs and find new positions elsewhere, and upsetting the social life of the whole family.

A drawback of this proposed reform is that it would create significant hurdles in terms of logistics, administration, finance, and security. Intervention structures that currently allow expatriates to bring their families with them to the field incur significant costs, notably related to the provision of housing, transportation, and insurance for the family members, as well as education for the children. These organizations also face increased workloads for their human resources, logistical, and administrative staff, as each additional person on a mission creates additional visa, medical, security, and transportation matters to organize. However, diminishing the total number of expatriates on site (as recommended in the previous section) would decrease the number of accompanying people and thus lessen the financial and logistical burdens resulting from this suggested change. Furthermore, the organizations that already authorize interveners to bring their families have found effective ways to overcome these challenges, proving that the organizational and security obstacles are surmountable.[38] Admittedly, some intervention settings are too dangerous to bring children to or lack medical and educational facilities of sufficient quality. A compromise in this case would be to offer interveners the option to bring their families to the nearest possible place that offers safety and adequate social services, so that expatriates could see them more regularly than they do under the current system.

Regardless of whether or not their families are on site, expatriate interveners could help break the boundaries by following the examples of the exceptional individuals mentioned in Chapters 5 and 6. They could make it a point to spend time socializing with local people rather than with other interveners. They could start with their staff, neighbors, and counterparts, and then, if possible, extend their network to friends they meet through common acquaintances or through religious, social, or cultural groups. To facilitate these relationships, they could make an effort to learn the local languages and customs. Finally, they should take care not to belittle local partners – not even for fun or to let off steam – and instead should openly praise and acknowledge their counterparts' positive attributes, including their altruistic motivations. They could also reign in any expatriate colleagues who behave in disparaging and humiliating ways toward host populations.

The socialization efforts should include a diverse array of local people, so that interveners avoid being unduly influenced by one party of a conflict or perceived as biased. The induction training mentioned in the previous section would provide expatriates with a clear understanding of the social, ethnic, political, religious, economic, and other significant lines of fractures in the society, giving interveners the information needed to ensure that their socialization attempts include people from all relevant groups.

superficial

---

[38] Examples include the International Assistance Mission in Afghanistan (www.iam-afghanistan. org/sites/default/files/annual_report_2012.pdf, p. 27), the Agency for Technical Cooperation and Development for positions in the capital cities of sensitive security areas (www.acted.org/en/work-acted), as well as most UN, donor, and diplomatic missions in countries safe enough to be categorized as family duty stations (for instance, www.unhcr.org/4b82a19222.pdf) – all Web sites last accessed in December 2013.

To facilitate these informal interactions, recruiters for international agencies could put greater emphasis on human and social skills in the hiring, retention, and promotion processes, instead of focusing solely on knowledge and experience. Selecting people with greater capacity to empathize with host populations – or, in the words of the friend quoted at the end of Chapter 7, with greater potential to remain "decent human beings" in the stressful context of a conflict zone – would go a long way toward promoting trust, socialization, and overall good relationships with local counterparts. Staff evaluation forms could request that managers flag any disrespectful or demeaning behavior, with the understanding that such occurrences would hinder reemployment or promotion.

One more way for interveners on the ground to help bridge the power differential and to improve the quality of their social and professional relationships with host populations would be to acknowledge the benefits that they receive from their work, such as financial compensation, travel opportunities, rewarding relationships, and career bonuses.[39] Local peace activists indeed emphasize that "the offers of assistance that they most appreciate come from those who are up-front and honest about what they have to offer and, even, what they expect to get out of their work in that conflict."[40] Recognizing that there are compensations for the personal and professional sacrifices that interveners make on behalf of beneficiaries would defuse the expatriates' claims to the moral high ground – as long as expatriates make sure they do not go overboard and appear to be gloating or lording their wealth over local people. This would also deflect one of the criticisms levied by host populations, who often emphasize the distance between the image of selfless interveners and the advantages that these expatriates enjoy.

Local people, too, have an important role to play in improving the relationships between themselves and international interveners. Local staff and local counterparts should take the time to clarify their cultural practices to expatriates, identifying and explaining the do's and don'ts and letting the foreigners know when they make a cultural misstep. They could offer interveners opportunities to socialize with them, including invitations to meet their families and friends over coffee, over a meal at home or in a local restaurant that everybody can afford, or at cultural, sporting, or religious events. They could introduce newly arrived foreigners to local people with whom the newcomers might share interests or hobbies. Importantly, they should be careful not to use these interactions as opportunities to get something from expatriates, as interveners quickly become wary of invitations to socialize when they are inevitably accompanied by requests for fellowships, money, promotions, or other perks. Instead, local people should treat these invitations as a way to "give back" to foreign peacebuilders and to reestablish relations based on mutual exchange and mutual

---

[39] This idea was inspired by de Jong 2011, p. 32.
[40] Anderson and Olson 2003, p. 28.

benefits. To facilitate the expatriates' integration further, the local elite in areas where foreigners stand out could teach their fellow citizens to stop treating interveners like oddities – pointing at them, catcalling them, and so on. These actions are not usually meant to be cruel, but they do contribute to alienating the expatriates.

Increased socialization between interveners and local people would enable the former to build the trust, connections, and understanding indispensable to the success of their efforts. It would also help decrease the gap between the two groups and facilitate a greater reliance on the acceptance approach to safety.

- Use an Acceptance Approach to Security

Given how extensively bunkerization procedures contribute to the solidification of the boundaries between expatriates and host populations, another important step to improving relations between the two groups would be to review the security procedures that interveners follow when deployed in conflict zones, and use an approach based on acceptance by local communities whenever possible.[41]

Moving away from bunkerization would likely encounter significant resistance, given that the climate of fear prevalent among interveners often makes strict security procedures seem essential to their survival. However, looking at the positive experiences of the few organizations that already use the acceptance approach would help lessen this anxiety: As detailed in Chapter 7, such groups have faced fewer security incidents than the rest of the intervening agencies, even in the most dangerous environments. To further facilitate the transition, donors, think tanks, and high-ranking policy-makers could commission large-scale research to ensure that acceptance is indeed a more efficient and effective way to promote the interveners' safety. They could then disseminate their findings through advocacy and media campaigns. The goal would be to transform the way interveners and the public in their home countries view the attributes associated with bunkerization (such as barbed wires and armored cars). By altering perceptions so that interveners and the domestic audience view these characteristics as a factor, not of security, but of insecurity, these campaigns would reduce the pressure on security officials to automatically use such means of protecting their teams. Finally, to further ease the switch to a more integration-oriented protocol, civilian intervening agencies should stop recruiting former military personnel for security positions, since their training, experience, and professional instincts entice such interveners to rely on military methods to ensure safety.[42] Instead, peacebuilding organizations should favor civilians who would be more comfortable with acceptance methods.

Admittedly, in some contexts, expatriates are likely to be more at risk than local people – notably in places like Afghanistan, Darfur, or Somalia, where armed groups specifically target foreigners. Furthermore, until the rest of the

---

[41] See Fast, Finucane, et al. 2011 for practical guidelines on how to adopt an acceptance approach.
[42] Also Fast 2014, pp. 181–182.

reforms advocated in this chapter are implemented, potential criminals and local armed groups will continue to perceive expatriates as aloof and easy targets because they do not understand local dynamics well. If and when this perception abates, expatriates will still likely be viewed as more lucrative targets than local people. Interveners in many conflict zones will thus continue to need stricter safety precautions than host communities. In these situations, international peacebuilders could use measures that are more discreet than the standard approach and yet provide the same level of safety. Jan Egeland, Adele Harmer, and Abby Stoddard for instance explain that "using facilities set back from the road" or reinforcing the walls of an office with sandbags from the inside instead of from the outside can serve the purpose of protection without creating a militarized appearance.[43] International agencies could also decentralize the decision-making power on this issue as much as possible, so that the staff most familiar with local conditions would make final security decisions. Additionally, intervention structures could revise the overall guidelines for their security approach. Instead of the current default option of privileging more restrictions whenever they perceive a risk, the motto could be to ease the security restrictions whenever possible, adding measures only if a cost-benefit analysis suggests that the expected security benefits would be worth the potential harm to the peacebuilding efforts.

The growing reliance on the acceptance approach would further decrease the costs of international interventions, as bunkerization procedures currently consume significant financial and logistical resources. The easing of security restrictions, when combined with other measures like promoting better professional and social relationships between local people and international peacebuilders, would also facilitate the interveners' data collection efforts.

- Practice Discretion, Not Visibility

Finally, aid should become an exercise in discretion. The current standard practice of promoting visibility creates a number of problems, while the few organizations that consistently maintain a low profile have been more successful in their peacebuilding efforts (see Chapter 7). Adopting this tendency toward inconspicuousness would also bolster organizations' attempts to switch to an acceptance approach and thus reinforce the staff's security.[44]

Forgoing as much as possible the standard practice of using logos and banners to identify each foreign contribution would be relatively simple to implement. Admittedly, several agencies that have tried to adopt a low-profile approach to their work have faced extensive criticisms from donors and stakeholders. Explaining how strongly the existing practice undermines some of the results that donors and local counterparts wish to reach – and how successful the opposite approach often is – should go a long way toward addressing these issues.

---

[43] Egeland, Harmer, et al. 2011, p. 29.
[44] On low-profile approaches promoting acceptance and security, see ibid., pp. 27–28.

Facilitating Factors

Two final measures, though not indispensable, would be important to consider, as they would greatly expedite the suggested reforms:

• Acknowledge the Community

The first measure would be to recognize the existence of the community of interveners. Expatriates on the ground currently make considerable efforts to distinguish their organizations from others – so that, for instance, a civilian NGO or UN agency does not suffer from the negative perception that local people have of the nearby peacekeeping mission. This strategy has little chance of succeeding, as the experience of *Médecins Sans Frontières* (MSF) demonstrates. MSF heads of missions, project coordinators, representatives in headquarters and capitals, and lower-ranking staff members in the field strive to ensure that all their partners understand their organization's distinct identity as an impartial, non-governmental, humanitarian agency, separate from other NGOs and from UN interveners, donors, and diplomats. As I experienced when working for MSF and later confirmed through talking to other employees, this is an uphill battle. In Congo, for instance, MSF and other NGOs have spent more than ten years trying to distinguish themselves from the UN Mission in Congo (the local peacekeeping mission, long called by its French acronym MONUC), but local people still call out "MONUC, MONUC" when they see cars with MSF logos crossing through their villages. Across the board, in most conflict zones, despite coordinated efforts by humanitarian agencies to differentiate themselves from military interveners, there is still a major conflation of foreign military and civilian groups. As explained in Chapter 5, in Congo and in other areas of intervention, host populations rarely distinguish between different types of foreign interveners.

The time and effort that interveners dedicate to affirming their distinct identities is thus regularly wasted. Worse, expatriates often disparage other organizations in the process. Unfortunately, every negative statement they utter about one of their colleagues is likely to reflect back on them in the long run, as local stakeholders rarely differentiate the criticizer from the criticized.

At the most basic level, refraining from such denunciations would benefit everyone involved. A more ambitious change, however, would be for interveners to concede the fact that, whether they like it or not, host populations view all of them as part of one broad community, and they should act accordingly, including when implementing the reforms advocated here.

• Plan Interventions over the Long Term

A number of the measures to rebalance the value of thematic and local knowledge and to promote better relationships between interveners and host populations require donors to review their funding strategy for conflict and post-conflict areas, so that they can set up long-term budgets with provisions allowing the disbursement of funds directly to local organizations. Ideally, this reform would be part of a broader change, replacing the current short-term thinking with a longer-term outlook.

It is probable that longer deployments would already decrease the incentives to view peacebuilding as a short-term endeavor and to implement quick-fix programs. This is necessary but not sufficient. Another essential measure (which the development of context-specific intervention strategies would promote) would be planning international efforts over the long term – several decades if possible. It has taken Europe centuries to build sustainable domestic and regional peace, functioning states, and a certain level of economic and social prosperity; it is absurd to expect today's post-war countries to achieve similar results in a few years.[45]

Shifting to long-term programming is not impossible. The large, well-established mining companies that work in conflict zones plan their actions over the duration that they expect the mine to be profitable (which may be ten to fifty or more years). They design their corporate social responsibility programs, when they have them, over similarly long time frames – twenty to thirty years – which they then divide into shorter, five-year projects. Another, more macro-level model that donors could study would be the Marshall Plan. Implemented after World War II, it enabled the reconstruction and stabilization of Europe through a loan process that put European actors in the driver's seat, but still allowed U.S. funders to retain some control of the program.[46] Or donors could draw their inspiration from the Danish development agency DANIDA, which already offers relatively long-term funding to peacebuilding organizations.[47]

Other scholars have extensively studied how intervening organizations could switch to adopting such a long-term outlook.[48] It is beyond the scope of this book to reiterate their analyses and reprint their policy recommendations. Suffice it to say that following their advice would help alleviate some of the elements that perpetuate a number of the problematic practices and habits documented throughout this book (see Chapter 7). Planning peacebuilding efforts over a longer period would also reinforce the positive effects of the various reforms detailed in the previous sections: Long-term involvement would give interveners sufficient time to develop a good understanding of their

---

[45] Also Pritchett, Woolcock, et al. 2010.

[46] For useful studies of the Marshall Plan and the lessons we can learn from it for current post-war reconstruction efforts, see Mac Ginty 2006, pp. 149–151; and Machado 2007.

[47] Hayman 2012, p. 40. For details on DANIDA's operations, see its Web site: http://um.dk/en/danida-en/ (last accessed in December 2013).

[48] See especially Bush 1996; and Edelstein 2009, notably pp. 94–101. Other useful sources include: Fisher and Zimina 2009, p. 21; Lederach 1997, notably chapters 4 to 6; Paris and Sisk 2009, pp. 313–314; UN General Assembly 2009, notably paras. 17–20 and 52–60; and UN Peacebuilding Support Office 2012.

area of deployment and to adequately train their local counterparts. This would enable international peacebuilders to work at the pace of their host community to develop the trust, confidence, and commitment that any durable transfer of ideas and experience requires. It would also provide local staff with a sense of job security, therefore reducing the incentives to embezzle resources.

Conclusion

One and a half billion people live under the threat of violence in conflict zones around the world.[49] International interveners can critically assist host countries in building a sustainable peace. Unfortunately, the everyday, on-the-ground practice of peacebuilding regularly orients international efforts toward ineffective or counterproductive strategies.

This is exactly what I experienced when I lived in Peaceland. In my first days as an intervener, I was so concerned about fitting in that I did not stop to question what it was that I was fitting in to. I was so eager to make a difference in the lives of war-affected populations that I did not pause to reflect on the practices I followed while trying to accomplish this goal. It was not until I stepped outside of the expatriate bubble that I realized what an odd, self-contained community we interveners were. Over the course of my career, I have met incredible peacebuilders, worked alongside committed organizations, and seen firsthand the vital impact expatriates can make. Unfortunately, I have also witnessed programs to which friends, colleagues, and I had dedicated months of hard work – programs to which we had sacrificed our health and happiness – turn out to be ineffective or even counterproductive.

This frustration pushed me to search for solutions and, eventually, that search became a long-term academic inquiry. The research led me to discover the extent to which my own everyday actions had undermined my goals. It has been a humbling experience, but also an inspiring one, as I met extraordinary interveners who offer a new model of engagement in conflict zones.

These exceptional individuals actively oppose the narratives, practices, and habits that I had once so unwittingly embraced. They acquire profound understandings of the areas in which they work, become embedded in local communities, and develop strong stakes in the future of their new countries. They do everything they can to bridge the gap between expatriates and host populations. They relentlessly fight the daily intervention routines that impede international peace efforts. However, these standard ways of thinking and acting are so deeply ingrained in Peaceland that such dissenters face strong resistance from their peers. Expatriates regularly marginalize and ostracize the few among them

---

[49] Source of the statistics: World Bank's Web page on fragile and conflict-affected countries, "FCS Countries Are a Key Priority for the World Bank" (available at http://go.worldbank.org/NVS5ERWAY0, last accessed in December 2013).

who challenge the norm. As a result, change occurs very slowly, and most of the detrimental modes of action persist. This book has striven to amplify the voices of Peaceland's reformers. I hope it will advance the process of change so that, one day, international peacebuilders can fulfill their potential and truly help people affected by war claim a better future for themselves.

APPENDIX

An Ethnographic Approach

As I mentioned in the Introduction to this book, scholars of international interventions have yet to investigate thoroughly the influence of everyday practices and habits on peacebuilding effectiveness. This gap in current research, which my book aims to narrow, is due in part to the extreme difficulty in documenting factors predicated on background knowledge. Such knowledge is not easily conveyed through words because it is practical rather than representational – meaning that it is implicit and automatic rather than explicit or deliberate – and because its contents are, in essence, "unsaid and unthought."[1] Moreover, practices and habits themselves are often taken for granted to such an extent that asking their enactors to identify them is usually about as productive as "asking fish, if they could speak, to describe the water in which they swim."[2] As a result, researchers interested in this subject cannot rely solely on the most common political science methodologies like surveys, interviews, or document analyses. To understand the influence of such everyday elements, researchers must experience those elements personally and learn them through practice. Both these objectives can be achieved only through participant and field observations.[3]

Admittedly, such an approach, which is typical of ethnographic research, presents several complications for scholars of international relations. To begin with, its emphasis on direct contact requires researchers to gain privileged access to organizations that have a culture of secrecy, such as diplomatic missions or United Nations (UN) peacekeeping operations. Furthermore, researchers must reconcile international topics, which are usually macro-level subjects, with empirical methodologies that work best in "very localized fields of study."[4] Finally, the findings of such research are often so controversial that the

---

[1] Pouliot 2008, pp. 284–285. Also Higate and Henry 2009, p. 19. The rest of this paragraph draws on Pouliot 2010, chapter 2, notably pp. 28–29.

[2] Pouliot 2010, p. 51 based on Rubin and Rubin 1995, p. 20.

[3] Pouliot 2010.

[4] Abrahamsen and Williams 2011, p. 328.

"subjects" of a given study may attempt to prevent the publication of results because they feel that ethnographies "objectify" or expose them.[5] As I have experienced in the past, and as David Mosse similarly relates, publically scrutinizing informal or behind-the-scenes relationships and behaviors risks not only infuriating colleagues and supervisors, but also closing doors to future research and consulting opportunities.[6]

Scholars of war and peace face an additional challenge. Developing a "thick description" of everyday peacebuilding requires researchers to spend extended periods of time in the dangerous environments where intervention actually takes place.[7] This is often impossible for academics due to security concerns, family imperatives, and teaching obligations. As a result, although there are exceptions, most scholars of peacebuilding conduct, at best, brief trips into the field. They spend even less time outside capital cities and national headquarters. This limited access provides them with little material on the everyday dynamics of intervention on the ground. It also precludes them from gaining access to sensitive data, as the inclination toward secrecy common among diplomatic and UN missions prevents staff members from conveying such information to outsiders.

My goal in this project was to research intervention practices on the ground, so I had to find a way to overcome these challenges and embed myself in a conflict zone where peacebuilders were actually working. Thanks in large part to those I acknowledged at the beginning of the book, I was able to accomplish this goal. Thus, for more than a year, I lived and worked in eastern Congo with a specific community of interveners deployed there. Over the course of this in-depth fieldwork, I established the foundation of my analysis. Comparative research in eight other conflict zones around the world before, during, and after my deployment in Congo enabled me to develop my analysis further and assess its potential for generalization. At these various sites, I collected five kinds of data, which allowed me to generate, refine, discard, and revise various parts of my explanation. The rest of this appendix provides more details on the research process I used to gather the material at the heart of this book.

Theory Building in Congo

From June 2010 to July 2011, I researched a group of peacebuilders stationed in the Congolese province of North Kivu. The most violent area in the country at that time, North Kivu hosted an extremely diverse array of interveners, in terms of both the types of organizations they represented and the countries they came from. In addition to European and North American diplomats, peacebuilders

---

[5] Mosse 2011, p. 20; also Gross Stein 2011.

[6] Mosse 2005 (pp. viii–xiii) and 2011 (pp. 20–23). See also the analysis of these dynamics in Fechter and Hindman 2011b, p. 11.

[7] On thick descriptions, see Geertz 1973, chapter 1.

included African, Asian, and Latin American soldiers deployed in the second-largest peacekeeping mission in the world. Also present were civilian interveners and military officials who came from all over the world. They worked for humanitarian, development, and conflict-resolution agencies and represented an array of professional, political, and religious affiliations. This wide variety of backgrounds diminished the likelihood that interveners might show significant commonalities, thus providing a "tough test" for my hypothesis that they shared practices, habits, and narratives.[8]

During my thirteen months of research in Congo, my investigation focused primarily on the situation in North Kivu, but I also gathered data from the other unstable provinces, notably South Kivu, North Katanga, and Oriental Province, as well as the capital city of Kinshasa. In addition, I completed three short trips to Europe (Belgium, France, and Norway) and North America (the United States and Canada) to study the perception of Congo among interveners based in capitals and headquarters.

Thanks to my history first as an intervener and then as a researcher in the Kivus, a number of Congolese and expatriates there already knew me personally or by reputation. Some of them had also read my publications. This preexisting network greatly eased my reentry into the field, but a long-term deployment in Congo was still the only possible way to gather the material necessary for this project.

It takes time to build relationships that are strong enough to enable the exchange of sensitive information.[9] Most interveners follow a professional code of secrecy and political correctness, so they speak freely only with people they trust and consider full members of their community. Getting beyond the discourse manufactured for outsiders (usually given on record to journalists and transient researchers) required months of repeated interactions. Most useful in this regard were not only my formal interviews, but also, as detailed later in this chapter, the countless informal discussions I had after meetings, over drinks, during dinners, and at parties. It was through these interactions that I became privy to the peacebuilders' personal opinions, which often differ significantly from the official discourse and are voiced only in informal settings or after repeated formal interviews – and almost always under strict conditions of anonymity.

Furthermore, a number of interveners – notably in military, diplomatic, and peacekeeping circles – are suspicious of researchers. Many consented to meet with me only after I had been on site for several months, when they felt assured of my trustworthiness. It took even more time, along with countless formal and informal meetings, to gain permission to shadow them in their daily work, a

---

[8] On tough tests and their potential to wield generalizable findings, see Eckstein 1975; and George and Bennett 2005, pp. 120–123.

[9] For a similar claim from a well-known anthropologist of peacekeeping, see Rubinstein 2008, p. 104.

crucial development that enabled me to observe their practices in action. Only once I had secured this access could I accompany them on patrols, participate in missions and internal meetings, and sleep in their bases or compounds. Still, it was clear that my contacts remained on their best behavior during my first few visits. Over time, however, I faded into the background, and the bias created by my presence progressively decreased (although it probably never fully disappeared). Overall, building sufficiently good relationships and becoming, as one of my interviewees put it, "part of the furniture" required the better part of a year.

Long-term ethnographic research among a specific group of interveners was also essential to document the differences between peace interventions in theory (the mandate, or the instructions from headquarters and capitals) and in practice (what actually happens on the ground).[10] Although my previous experiences as an intervener gave me a solid foundation on which to build, it was only after months of research that I could fully appreciate that foreign peacebuilders on the ground belong to a loose and informal community that defines itself primarily by differentiating its members from local people. Only after these months working alongside peacebuilders could I fully grasp the undercurrent of prejudice that permeates interactions between interveners and their intended beneficiaries – a realization that inspired my analysis of how such biases impact the effectiveness of international efforts.

Consolidation and Generalization through Fieldwork in Eight Other Conflict Zones

While this in-depth ethnographic inquiry was indispensable for theory building, I needed to distinguish those collective understandings that were limited to the community of interveners in Congo from those that were shared by all peace-builders, regardless of where they are deployed. I therefore considered five other theaters of international intervention around the world: Burundi (where I did research in 2010 and 2011), Cyprus (in 2011), South Sudan (in 2011), Israel and the Palestinian Territories (in 2012), and Timor-Leste (in 2012) – see Figure 1. I conducted approximately one month of fieldwork in each country.

I selected these settings to provide variation on several dimensions that are critical for my analysis. My primary concern was to analyze both interventions usually labeled as failures (Congo) and those presented as successes (Burundi and Timor-Leste).[11] I also needed to ensure variation on those dimensions that

---

[10] Papadakis 1997, pp. 360–361, traces a similar experience during his one-year ethnographic research on the Cypriot village of Pyla. Interviewees stated the "official discourse" when he first arrived in September 1994, and then moved beyond these standard positions as time progressed.

[11] On Congo as a case of intervention failure, among many others: Autesserre 2010; Kreps 2010; International Crisis Group 2012b; Trefon 2011; and "Defining Peacekeeping Downward: The U.N. Debacle in Eastern Congo," by Jessica Hatcher and Alex Perry, *Time World*, November 26,

scholars and practitioners widely view as influencing the processes and outcomes of peacebuilding efforts. I thus researched interventions in wealthy settings (Cyprus and Israel) and in desperately poor ones (Burundi, Congo, and South Sudan); in very dangerous environments (Congo and South Sudan) and in less violent ones (Burundi, Cyprus, Israel and the Palestinian Territories, and Timor-Leste); in well-functioning states (Cyprus and Israel) and in dysfunctional ones (Congo and South Sudan); in democracies (Cyprus, Israel, and Timor-Leste) and in authoritarian settings (Burundi, Congo, and South Sudan); in some of the largest countries in the world (Congo and South Sudan) and in some of the smallest (Burundi, Cyprus, and Timor-Leste); in peace processes with a high degree of international involvement (Cyprus, Israel and the Palestinian Territories, and Timor-Leste) and with limited involvement (Burundi); in situations where the national authorities owed their existence and survival to the interventions (South Sudan and Timor-Leste) and in others where they viewed international involvement as illegitimate (Congo and Israel); in countries where interveners mostly congregate in the capital (Burundi, Cyprus, and Timor-Leste) and where they are mainly deployed away from headquarters (Congo and South Sudan); and in places with considerable cultural and social differences between interveners and local populations (Burundi, Congo, South Sudan, and Timor-Leste) and with fewer such differences (Cyprus and Israel).[12] Interviewees familiar with these places repeatedly emphasized how dissimilar they were, reinforcing my claim that the commonalities I had observed do indeed represent a transnational, worldwide phenomenon.[13] My investigation in South Sudan was also particularly useful because this country hosted a range of interveners on par with that found in Congo, thus providing further confirmation of my preliminary finding that international peacebuilders from various backgrounds share everyday practices, habits, and narratives.

It is important to note that the overrepresentation of African countries in my study reflects the fact that, currently, international peacekeeping and state

---

2012. On Timor-Leste as a success case: Dobbins 2005; Doyle and Sambanis 2006; Fortna 2008; and Howard 2008. On Burundi: Boshoff, Vrey, et al. 2010; Call 2008; Hanson 2009; Peen Rodt 2011; and Elizabeth Dickinson, "Burundi: An Unlikely International Success Story," *The Interdependant*, December 20, 2011.

[12] On the influence of the level of wealth on peacebuilding effectiveness, among others: Doyle and Sambanis 2006, pp. 335 and 337; Lund 2003, p. 15; Richmond 2011, p. 8; Yilmaz 2006, p. 36; and Zartman and Rasmussen 1997, pp. 4 and 31–32. On the level of violence: Doyle and Sambanis 2006, pp. 291, 335, and 337; Mac Ginty 2006, pp. 65–66; Rubinstein 2008, p. 6; and Stedman, Rothchild, et al. 2002, p. 664. On state capacity: Barron and Burke 2008, notably pp. 3–4; Chopra and Hohe 2004, p. 290; Diamond 2006; and Lund 2003, pp. 20 and 25. On regime type: Diamond 2006; and Doyle and Sambanis 2006, pp. 341. On the size of the country: Skjelsbaek 1990, p. 57. On the level of international involvement: ibid., p. 59; and Stedman, Rothchild, et al. 2002, pp. 664 and 666–667. On the legitimacy of international involvement: Doyle, Johnstone, et al. 1997, pp. 3–5; and Sending 2009, p. 4. On concentration in capital cities: Chambers 2006, notably pp. 8–10; and Last 2000, pp. 87–88. On cultural differences: Chopra and Hohe 2004, pp. 291–296 and 298; Duffey 2000; and Rubinstein 2008, p. 11.

[13] On the use of most dissimilar cases to yield generalizable findings, see Mill 1888, pp. 278–283.

reconstruction efforts occur mostly in Africa. Notably, 78 percent of UN peace-keepers worldwide are stationed on this continent.[14] Nevertheless, the research in Cyprus, Israel and the Palestinian Territories, and Timor-Leste enabled me to ensure that my findings were relevant outside of Africa.

On top of this material, I drew on interviews, field observations, and several years of aid work experience in Afghanistan (2002), Kosovo (2000), and Nicaragua (1998), as well as in Western capitals and headquarters (intermittently from 1999 to 2013). This material further enables me to assess the generalizability of my argument outside of Africa and also provides variation on several additional dimensions critical for the analysis. While most powerful states have only limited economic, political, and geostrategic interests in countries like Burundi, Congo, Sudan, and Timor-Leste, the cases of Kosovo and Afghanistan allow me to verify whether the dynamics I study hold for places that are prominent on the peacebuilders' agenda.[15] Looking back at my work in Afghanistan, I can also evaluate whether my findings might hold for interventions whose primary goal was not the reestablishment of peace in the host country (as the intervention there was aimed primarily at combating terrorism).

My brief research visits to Burundi, Cyprus, Israel and the Palestinian Territories, South Sudan, and Timor-Leste, and the memories of my work in Afghanistan, Kosovo, and Nicaragua, enabled me to assess the limits and the generalizability of the findings from my study of the international intervention in Congo. I continued the same line of inquiry I had followed in my Congo sites and checked whether I needed to revise, nuance, or discard my preliminary findings. In each of these countries, I strove to spend time away from capital cities and headquarters, so that I could study peacebuilding in the provinces and rural areas where it largely took place. In addition to researching in the capitals Bujumbura, Nicosia, Tel Aviv, Ramallah, Juba, and Dili, I conducted interviews and field observations in the provinces of Gitega and Ngozi (Burundi), the village of Pyla (Cyprus), the cities of Jerusalem, Bethlehem, and Hebron (Israel and the Palestinian Territories), the town of Malakal (South Sudan), and the district of Baucau (Timor-Leste).

Given the emphasis I place on the importance of sustained involvement in a field site, the reader may wonder whether I could gather useful material in places where I spent a relatively short period of time. This is particularly relevant to my work in Burundi, Cyprus, Israel and the Palestinian Territories, Sudan, and Timor-Leste, as I spent slightly less than a month in each of these places (it is less problematic for Afghanistan and Kosovo, where I worked for respectively

---

[14] Statistics calculated from the figures available on the official Web site of the UN Department for Peacekeeping Operations (http://www.un.org/en/peacekeeping/documents/bnote0813.pdf, last accessed in December 2013). Thanks to Alexandra Russo for compiling the data.

[15] On prominence of a conflict on the peacebuilders' agenda as a determinant of intervention effectiveness, see Call and Cousens 2008, pp. 11–12; Downs and Stedman 2002, pp. 48–49 and 50–52; Doyle and Sambanis 2006, notably pp. 3–5, 13–15, and 27–40; Gilligan and Stedman 2003, pp. 39 and 51; and Howard 2008, notably pp. 9, and 11–13.

three and six months). Thankfully, the fact that my research focuses on a transnational community (the interveners), which I study in different environments (Congo, Timor-Leste, etc.), makes this concern less troublesome for my project than for standard comparative research designs. Arriving in a new field site did not require me to restart my work completely, as it would have if I had studied, for instance, grassroots dynamics of violence. Instead, the research in each new location added to a larger body of data that I had begun collecting elsewhere. I was already familiar with the interveners' world, which made my inquiries quicker and more efficient. I recognized many practices, habits, and narratives from my previous field sites, which enabled me to focus on the elements that actually varied in each new place. Some people already knew me from previous work in other locations and vouched for my trustworthiness. For instance, I interviewed a peacebuilder in Congo; then I held long discussions with him in Burundi, and, by the time we met again in Sudan, we had become friends, and he went to great lengths to facilitate my research there. Others were friends of my husband, who had accompanied me to the field, and still others knew me by reputation or through common acquaintances and introduced me to their contacts as a full-fledged member of the interveners' community ("This is Séverine; she is visiting from Congo"). This established a certain level of trust, which enabled me to conduct useful interviews and to obtain some opportunities for participant observations. To mitigate further my concerns about the limitations of my briefer visits, I also sought the help of scholars who for years had researched topics related to mine in Burundi, Cyprus, and Timor-Leste, and we spent hours brainstorming on the portability and limitations of my analysis in these countries.[16]

Of course, the material from my comparative field sites is still less comprehensive than my Congo data. I had countless interviews full of "canned responses" – discourse manufactured for passing researchers and journalists. For instance, a number of contacts would repeat back to me the official descriptions of their work displayed on their organizations' Web sites or recently articulated by their public relations officers, even though the presentations were very different from what I, other researchers, and other interviewees had observed. Other interviewees would offer no specifics, answering my questions only with abstract generalities and refusing to follow up when I requested more detailed explanations. Although these discussions were not useful to document "backstage," informal practices, they enabled me to assess what my interviewees viewed as the proper way to portray themselves to an outsider they did not trust – thus providing insights into what my contacts viewed as proper, official, and noncontroversial and what they viewed as private and sensitive. I also still had enough meaningful fieldwork data from other sources to support my claim

[16] I am particularly grateful to James Scambary (independent researcher, Australian National University), Dr. Anna Powles (visiting fellow, Fragile States Project, University of New South Wales, Australia), and Dr. Meghan Lynch (assistant professor, Temple University, USA).

that the everyday practices and habits I present are not specific to peacebuilding in Congo, but are common to international interveners regardless of where they are deployed.

Five Kinds of Material

The original insights for this project, as well as some of the information on which this book draws, originated from my experience as a genuine member of the interveners' club. The memories of my work in Afghanistan, Congo, Kosovo, Nicaragua, and the United States allow me to present an insider's perspective on some of the dynamics I detail in this book. At the same time, the bulk of my material comes from later research in Congo and other areas, and therefore from the point of view of an outsider (or, at times, an outside-insider) conducting a purposeful inquiry. In each of these later research sites, I collected data through participant observations, field observations, in-depth interviews, and document analysis.

Participant observation included patrolling with military peacekeepers, implementing state reconstruction programs alongside UN officials, and attending community reconciliation projects with non-governmental organizations (NGOs). I also joined in on trainings and briefings. I witnessed dozens of coordination meetings among a variety of international interveners as well as between foreign interveners and local actors. I was fortunate enough to obtain access to settings usually closed to researchers, such as highly confidential management meetings and peacekeeping military bases. In total, I conducted 124 discrete participant observations events, totaling approximately 330 hours of formal participant observation work, all of which required countless hours of informal interactions to attain such access in the first place.

I also recorded field observations whenever I was in a conflict zone. I examined the interactions among international interveners as well as between them and local populations. In Congo, Burundi, Israel and the Palestinian Territories, and South Sudan, I rented apartments in the compounds of restaurants that were popular gathering places for international actors. Furthermore, in all of my field sites, I gained access to study peacebuilders in their daily lives. Once interveners were familiar with me and my research, and once they had accepted me into their community, they offered countless opportunities to be in their company in informal settings. Some of my most illuminating insights came from interactions in these settings – restaurants, private homes, social gatherings, and so on. They generated ideas that I could later expand upon and nuance through formal observations and interviews. Altogether, the material collected specifically for this project includes fifteen months of field observations, and I also use the data that I collected for an earlier project on peacebuilding, including another year and a half of ethnographic research in Congo (during six visits between early 2000 and mid-2007). All of these field observations provided further insights into peacebuilding practices and habits, interactions among various international actors, and relationships between them and local stakeholders.

In addition, I conducted and analyzed 295 in-depth interviews. (I also draw on 330 more interviews that I completed for my previous project on Congo.) I carried out these conversations without intermediaries, usually in French or in English, and used a translator only in the rare cases when I could not find a common language with which to communicate with my contacts. I interviewed both interveners and their intended beneficiaries. These lengthy, often multiple-hour interviews enabled me to document how interveners viewed and rationalized their daily practices, and to assess which frames and narratives were most influential in shaping peacebuilding strategies on the ground. Our discussions offered unparalleled insights into how international peacebuilders saw the ongoing situation, the roles of their particular organizations in the peace efforts, their own roles in these institutions, the constraints they faced, the contributions they made, and the improvements they thought were most necessary. These conversations also provided additional comparison points, as I asked my contacts to reflect on their experiences in their current areas of deployment and on their previous missions. Moreover, my meetings with local actors of all kinds supplied me with extensive data on the perspectives of the recipients of intervention, which are often overlooked in the research on international peacebuilding.[17] In Chapter 7, I provide a telling illustration of the importance of decoding the significance of events from both sides of the intervention: What foreign peacebuilders see as merely commonsense, indispensable security procedures, local populations often see as a form of separation that effectively transforms expatriates into "other kinds of human beings."[18]

During my field observations, participant observations, and formal interviews, I worked mainly with low- to mid-ranking interveners in order to gather material on what was happening on the ground. When I did contact those in higher ranks, I did not focus on the top-level practitioners and policy-makers, but on their advisors or close subordinates, in order to eschew preestablished, politically correct answers and instead gather genuine insights on how peacebuilding worked.

Whenever possible, I paid particular attention to new cases of intervention, such as when a new peacebuilding actor arrived, when an established actor started a project in a new place, or when the situation changed so drastically that international actors had to revise their strategy entirely. For instance, I observed closely the dynamics at work in the replacement of the UN peacekeeping mission by a new stabilization operation in Congo in 2010. I briefed various small foundations that considered expanding their operations to Congo. I participated in exploratory missions with agencies assessing whether and how

---

[17] Fortna 2008; and Pouligny 2004. In addition to these two books, exceptions include, among others, all of the authors who work on the concept of "hybridity," such as Richmond and Mitchell 2011 and Mac Ginty 2010.

[18] On the importance of decoding significance from a "local" point of view, see Chabal and Daloz 2011, p. 4.

to intervene in new rural areas. I also traveled to South Sudan immediately following the 2011 referendum that granted independence to the country, at a time when international peacebuilders were revising their strategies in response to this new geopolitical situation. By observing the moment of arrival – most likely before established rules, routines, and procedures took hold – I was able to effectively document how international interveners encounter and make sense of their environment.

In addition to this field material, I analyzed hundreds of documents of various kinds. Policy reports, agency memos, internal guidelines, and news articles provided additional points of entry into the peacebuilders' mindsets. Notably, they offered "rationalizing narratives of official strategies": formal representations of intervention efforts for donors, government officials, and other external audiences.[19] They also provided insights into the knowledge and assumptions about the physical and social world that organizations encode in their documents – what Lynn Eden terms "knowledge-laden routines."[20] Finally, I built on practitioners' reports and academic writings about various other international interventions to further enrich and refine my analysis.

Developing a Trustworthy Analysis

Generalizing or even just talking about trends often poses a challenge for ethnographers, whose attention to context-specific processes lies at odds with political scientists' ambition to produce universal claims. My approach was to aim for assertions valid only for the specific community under consideration (the peace interveners) at a specific point in time (the early 2000s to 2014), and to document the main exceptions to and contestations of these trends. It is true that even my fifteen years of direct experience in this world and the hundreds of formal and informal discussions I had in eight different conflict zones and various capitals and headquarters during that time cannot possibly cover all situations in which interveners worked during that period. Nevertheless, I used several techniques to maximize the potential that my claims could potentially apply to other settings.

To begin with, my research design fulfills important criteria of social inquiry. Notably, as explained in the second section of this appendix, the field sites I selected provided variation on all of the main dimensions that researchers and policy-makers have identified as influencing the effectiveness of international efforts. Such a qualitative research design may not enable me to provide a definitive "test" of my claims – as quantitative scholars do – but it does allow me to suggest global trends.[21]

---

[19] Mosse 2005, p. 132.
[20] Eden 2004, p. 3.
[21] This idea was inspired by (and this sentence and the preceding two paraphrase) Cooley and Ron 2002, p. 8.

In addition, I purposefully gathered information to assess whether my claims were relevant for the times and places that I had not personally observed. During my formal and informal discussions, I asked interveners, local populations, and outside observers to describe how things worked in settings outside of my field sites, and in times before those that I remembered. The enormous amount of written material that exists on conflict and peacebuilding, including the gray literature (documents written by practitioners and policy-makers and published informally), the scholarly analyses, and the numerous blogs, newspaper articles, and Web sites available, provided further information on these times and places. Thanks to these various types of information, I identified multiple converging sources that enabled me to develop plausible interpretations of trends.

Finally, I did my best to engage with a diverse selection of actors in terms of gender, national origin, organizational affiliation, professional background, religion, socioeconomic status, and occupation on the ground. I also intentionally sought out people whose voices were usually ignored or even silenced – such as local staff members of international organizations, local intellectuals, and members of foreign ministries or international and non-governmental organizations ostracized by their colleagues – in order to document contestations of the dominant understandings.

I used several other common research techniques to ensure that my analysis was trustworthy. Throughout the research process, I looked not only for data that could confirm my tentative explanation but also for material that might challenge it (for example, indications that only constraints, interests, and liberal values shape intervention strategies or that conclusions I had drawn from my fieldwork in Congo were not generalizable to other conflict zones). I eagerly sought out contradictory evidence, alternative answers to my questions, unexpected findings, conflicting perspectives, and new interpretations.

I remained aware of how my biological, sociological, and personal characteristics might orient my data collection and analysis.[22] As a woman, I had privileged access to women and to civilian men working in male-dominated environments, such as peacekeeping circles. The former seemed to enjoy interacting with one of their own; the latter acknowledged how starved they were of female company. However, my gender was an obstacle to interacting with military units that had no female members in their ranks. Hurdles ranged from the mundane, such as finding places to sleep or shower when conducting participant observations, to the serious: Several of my hosts worried that I might get sexually assaulted, or that I might wrongly accuse them and their troops of improper behavior. My gender, combined with my relatively young age – I was in my early to mid-30s during the fieldwork – also led a number of contacts to disregard me. This was both a challenge (as low status made it more

---

[22] On reflexivity and its importance to developing trustworthy analyses, see among others Hammersley and Atkinson 2007, pp. 14–18; Kunz 2013; Leander 2008, pp. 23–26; and Schwartz-Shea and Yanow 2012, chapter 6.

difficult for me to obtain perks, confidential documents, and appointments with important people) and an opportunity (as it enabled me to ask seemingly naïve questions regarding taken-for-granted practices, and contacts viewing me as a nobody seemed to feel comfortable talking and acting relatively freely in my presence).

My general appearance and mannerisms created a number of additional challenges and opportunities. It marked me as a foreigner in all countries where I researched (except maybe Cyprus), enabling me to experience things from an intervener's point of view, but not from a local one. It also meant that "non-Western" interveners viewed me as part of the "Western" clique, with all the negative connotations that it carries in peacekeeping circles – see Chapter 5. It most likely triggered distrust and rejection among interviewees for whom the term "research" is "inextricably linked to European imperialism and colonialism."[23] My socioeconomic status and my research choice to live and work as interveners do facilitated my access to international peacebuilders and further enabled me to experience the world from their perspectives but also widened the gap between me and host populations. My privileged social and educational background also put me in a position of power when I interviewed interveners and local people who were in vulnerable situations. Finally, my upbringing and personal values and beliefs made me distrustful of people in positions of authority, hostile to contacts who used, promoted, or justified violence or inequality, and (overly) sympathetic to those who viewed themselves as powerless or discriminated against.

To overcome these challenges, I intentionally sought out people who openly distrusted or rejected me, or with whom I had no affinity. I made sure that I conducted interviews and participant observations with them and that I took every possible opportunity for informal interactions. The fact that my husband accompanied me throughout most of my fieldwork helped me to overcome some of the hurdles I faced when investigating male-only environments. I used my personal history in Congo as an asset to bond with Congolese interviewees, as we regularly found out during our discussions that we had a common friend or that we had both lived through a difficult experience (such as the attack on a specific town or village). Friends and colleagues also facilitated my relationships with individuals belonging to the other circles that I could not easily access.

During the analysis and writing process, I treated all of these experiences, and the varying success of the different strategies I used to overcome the challenges mentioned above, as material illuminating the relationships among various members of the intervention community and between them and host populations. I also paid particular attention to the views of people with whom I disagreed, and I made sure that I included them in the manuscript. I remained conscious that my physical appearance, use of language, socioeconomic status,

---

[23] Smith 2012, p. 1 and throughout the book.

geographic location, personal history, and disciplinary training influenced the questions I asked, the answers I received, the conceptual and analytical categories I used, and the interpretation I developed, and I analyzed the resulting material in this light. I never ceased doubting that I might have missed part of the story, overlooked alternative viewpoints, or misconstrued telling silences and contradictions, so I ceaselessly searched for new sources of data and interpretations (in the gray and scholarly literatures and in new interviews and participant observation events).

Finally, I constantly looked for feedback on my manuscripts. Once I had a preliminary version of my analysis, I presented it not only to scholarly audiences, but also to the practitioners, policy-makers, and local actors at the heart of this book. This step aimed to ensure that I had accurately understood how their world functioned and to give them an opportunity to respond to what I had said about them – not to mention to share the knowledge that I had just produced.[24] I also sent draft papers and chapters to researchers and interveners who had expressed an interest in reading the preliminary version of my book and who had the time to comment on them. I revised the manuscript based on the feedback from all of these contacts, refining parts of the analysis, discarding statements that were inaccurate, nuancing certain sections, and developing further my explanation of several key aspects.

Conclusion

By embedding myself in an intervention setting for more than a year, I exposed myself to the significant possibility of losing my autonomous identity and critical perspective, especially as I am a former intervener. To mitigate this risk, during my field research I followed Vincent Pouliot's advice and went back and forth between theory and practice.[25] I analyzed my data as I collected it, moving constantly between the subjective assessments made by the people I studied and the generalizations necessary for political science analysis.[26] I also traveled outside of my primary field site approximately once every three months. In addition to providing me with an opportunity to take a step back from Congo and to reclaim some distance from my primary theater of observation, this travel schedule enabled me to replicate the experience of the international interveners I observed (as they have mandatory breaks outside of their area of deployment every two to three months and, for management staff, meetings abroad). These trips were also an opportunity to present my preliminary findings to policy and

---

[24] On the importance and benefits of allowing one's research participants to comment on one's preliminary findings, see among others Carpenter 2012, p. 373; Emerson and Pollner 1988; Lincoln and Guba 1985, pp. 373–378; Miles and Huberman 1994, pp. 275–278; Mosse 2005, pp. ix, x-xi, and 20; and Schwartz-Shea and Yanow 2012, pp. 106–107.

[25] Pouliot 2007.

[26] Ibid. provides a convincing demonstration of the benefits of this approach for any research on practice.

scholarly audiences, and thus to gather different perspectives on my topic. Finally, I moved outside of the intervention world to write this book in order to ensure that I had the critical distance indispensable to scholarly inquiry.

Even in these circumstances, I grew so close to a number of interveners, and I was so grateful to be granted such privileged (and, I suspect, unparalleled) access to their world, that I was in a difficult moral position whenever my writings became critical. To negotiate this hurdle, I tried to be as uncompromisingly honest as possible about my and their experiences. I strove to be truthful to their ways of seeing the world and, in appreciation for their help, I sought to offer a valuable answer to the question at the heart of our countless discussions: how to render their efforts more effective. It is my hope that all those who have devoted their lives to building peace will consider any critique this book advances to be constructive and useful, and thus worth the time and effort they dedicated to helping me with this study of Peaceland.

Bibliography

Abbott, H. Porter. 2008. *The Cambridge Introduction to Narrative*. Cambridge: Cambridge University Press.

Abrahamsen, Rita and Williams, Michael C. 2011. "Privatization in Practice: Power and Capital in the Field of Global Security," in *International Practices*, edited by Pouliot, Vincent and Adler, Emanuel (pp. 310–332). New York: Cambridge University Press.

Acharya, Amitav. 2009. *Whose Ideas Matter? Agency and Power in Asian Regionalism*. Ithaca, NY: Cornell University Press.

Adam, Hussein. 2004. "Somalia: International Versus Local Attempts at Peacebuilding," in *Durable Peace: Challenges for Peacebuilding in Africa*, edited by Taisier, Ali and Matthews, Robert O. (pp. 253–281). Toronto: University of Toronto Press.

Adam, Jeroen and Vlassenroot, Koen. 2010. "The Politics of Taxation in Eastern Congo." Paper presented at the Annual Meeting of the African Studies Association. Washington, DC.

Adebajo, Adekeye. 2011. *UN Peacekeeping in Africa: From the Suez Crisis to the Sudan Conflicts*. Boulder, CO: Lynne Rienner Publishers.

Adler, Emanuel. 2005. *Communitarian International Relations: The Epistemic Foundations of International Relations*. New York: Routledge.

African Security Review. 2011. "Book Symposium on the Trouble with the Congo." *African Security Review* 20 (2): 56–124.

Alao, Abiodun, Mackinlay, John, and Olonisakin, Funmi. 1999. *Peacekeepers, Politicians and Warlords: The Liberian Peace Process*. New York: United Nations University Press.

Alinsky, Saul David. 1989. *Rules for Radicals: A Practical Primer for Realistic Radicals*. New York: Vintage Books.

Amadae, S. M. 2003. *Rationalizing Capitalist Democracy: The Cold War Origins of Rational Choice Liberalism*. Chicago: University of Chicago Press.

Amnesty International. 2012. *Amnesty International Report 2012: The State of the World's Human Rights*. London: Amnesty International.

Andersen, Louise. 2005. *International Engagement in Failed States: Choices and Trade-Offs*. DIIS Working Paper no. 2005/20. Copenhagen: Danish Institute for International Studies.

Anderson, Mary B. 1999. *Do No Harm: How Aid Can Support Peace – or War.* Boulder, CO: Lynne Rienner Publishers.

Anderson, Mary B. 2008. "The Giving-Receiving Relationship: Inherently Unequal?" In *The Humanitarian Response Index 2008*, edited by Hidalgo, Silvia, López-Claros, Augusto, and Altinger, Laura (pp. 97–105). London; Madrid: DARA; Palgrave Macmillan.

Anderson, Mary B., Brown, Dayna, and Jean, Isabella. 2012. *Time to Listen: Hearing People on the Receiving End of International Aid.* Cambridge, MA: CDA Collaborative Learning Projects.

Anderson, Mary B. and Olson, Lara. 2003. *Confronting War: Critical Lessons for Peace Practitioners.* Cambridge, MA: The Collaborative for Development Action, Incorporated.

Aoi, Chiyuki, De Coning, Cedric, and Thakur, Ramesh Chandra. 2007. *Unintended Consequences of Peacekeeping Operations.* Tokyo: United Nations University Press.

Apthorpe, Raymond. 2005. "Postcards from Aidland." Paper presented at the Institute of Development Studies, Brighton, United Kingdom.

Apthorpe, Raymond. 2011. "Who Is International Aid? Some Personal Observations," in *Inside the Everyday Lives of Development Workers: The Challenges and Futures of Aidland*, edited by Fechter, Anne-Meike and Hindman, Heather (pp. 193–210). Sterling, VA: Kumarian Press.

Arimatsu, Louise and Mistry, Hemi. 2012. *Conflict Minerals: The Search for a Normative Framework.* London: Chatham House.

Atta-Asamoah, Andrews and Githaiga, Nyambura. 2012. *Addressing the 'Conflict Minerals' Crisis in the Great Lakes Region.* Policy Brief 35. Pretoria, South Africa: Institute for Security Studies.

Autesserre, Séverine. 2009. "Hobbes and the Congo: Frames, Local Violence, and International Intervention." *International Organization* 63 (2): 249–280.

Autesserre, Séverine. 2010. *The Trouble with the Congo: Local Violence and the Failure of International Peacebuilding.* New York: Cambridge University Press.

Autesserre, Séverine. 2011. "Construire la Paix: Conceptions Collectives de son Établissement, de son Maintien, et de sa Consolidation." *Critique Internationale* (51): 153–167. English translation, "Constructing Peace: Collective Understandings of Peace, Peacemaking, Peacekeeping, and Peacebuilding," available at www.sciencespo.fr/ceri/sites/sciencespo.fr.ceri/files/critique_add/art_sa.pdf

Autesserre, Séverine. 2012. "Dangerous Tales: Dominant Narratives on the Congo and their Unintended Consequences." *African Affairs* 111 (443): 202–222.

Autesserre, Séverine. 2015. "The Responsibility to Protect in the Congo: The Failure of Prevention," in *The Evolution of the Responsibility to Protect: Imperfect Duties?* Edited by O'Bannon, Brett and Bellamy, Alex. New York: Routledge.

Avruch, Kevin. 1998. *Culture and Conflict Resolution.* Washington, DC: United States Institute of Peace Press.

Babo-Soares, Dionisio. 2012. "Conflict and Violence in Post-Independence East Timor," in *The Peace in Between: Post-War Violence and Peacebuilding*, edited by Suhrke, Astri and Berdal, Mats (pp. 211–226). New York: Routledge.

Bakke, Kristin M. 2011. *Acceptance and Resistance to Foreign Ideas: Transnational Insurgents' Impact on the Chechen Separatists.* Working paper. Department of Political Science, University College London.

Bareebe, Gerald, Titeca, Kristof, and Verpoorten, Marijke. 2012. "Simplified Campaign Narratives on Civil War: Case Study of 'Kony 2012'," in *L'Afrique des Grands Lacs. Annuaire 2011–2012*, edited by Reyntjens, Filip, Stef, Vandeginste, and Marijke, Verpoorten (pp. 131–156). Paris: L'Harmattan.

Barkey, Karen. 2008. *Empire of Difference: The Ottomans in Comparative Perspective.* Cambridge: Cambridge University Press.

Barnett, Michael N. 2002. *Eyewitness to a Genocide: The United Nations and Rwanda.* Ithaca, NY: Cornell University Press.

Barnett, Michael N. 2006. "Building a Republican Peace: Stabilizing States after War." *International Security* 30 (4): 87–112.

Barnett, Michael N. 2011. *Empire of Humanity: A History of Humanitarianism.* Ithaca, NY: Cornell University Press.

Barnett, Michael N. 2012. "International Paternalism and Humanitarian Governance." *Global Constitutionalism* 1: 485–521.

Barnett, Michael N. and Finnemore, Martha. 2004. *Rules for the World: International Organizations in Global Politics.* Ithaca, NY: Cornell University Press.

Barnett, Michael N. and Zürcher, Christoph. 2009. "The Peacebuilder's Contract: How External Statebuilding Reinforces Weak Statehood," in *The Dilemmas of Statebuilding: Confronting the Contradictions of Postwar Peace Operations*, edited by Paris, Roland and Sisk, Timothy (pp. 23–52). London: Routledge.

Barron, Patrick and Burke, Adam. 2008. *Supporting Peace in Aceh: Development Agencies and International Involvement.* Washington, DC: East-West Center in Washington.

Bates, Robert H. 1981. *Markets and States in Tropical Africa: The Political Basis of Agricultural Policies.* Berkeley: University of California Press.

Baxi, Upendra. 1998. "The 'Ultimate Violation of Self': Reflections on Judicial Discourse on Attempted Rape." *The Practical Lawyer* 6 SCC (Jour): 1.

Bebbington, Anthony, Guggenheim, Scott, Olson, Elisabeth, and Woolcock, Michael. 2004. "Exploring Social Capital Debates at the World Bank." *Journal of Development Studies* 40 (5): 33–64.

Bebbington, Anthony, Woolcock, Michael, Guggenheim, Scott, and Olson, Elisabeth. (eds.). 2006. *The Search for Empowerment: Social Capital as Idea and Practice at the World Bank.* Bloomfield, CT: Kumarian Press.

Belloni, Roberto. 2008. "Civil Society in War-to-Democracy Transitions," in *From War to Democracy: Dilemmas of Peacebuilding*, edited by Jarstead, Anna and Sisk, Timothy (pp. 182–211). Cambridge: Cambridge University Press.

Belloni, Roberto and Jarstad, Anna K. (eds.). 2012. "Hybrid Peace Governance." Special issue of *Global Governance: A Review of Multilateralism* 18 (1): 1–132.

Ben-Ari, Eyal and Elron, Efrat. 2001. "Blue Helmets and White Armor: Multi-Nationalism and Multi-Culturalism among UN Peacekeeping Forces." *City & Society* 13 (2): 271–302.

Benner, Thorsten, Mergenthaler, Stephan, and Rotmann, Philipp. 2011. *The New World of UN Peace Operations: Learning to Build Peace?* Oxford: Oxford University Press.

Bennett, Jon, Pantuliano, Sara, Fenton, Wendy, Vaux, Anthony, Barnett, Chris, and Brusset, Emery. 2010. *Aiding the Peace: A Multi-Donor Evaluation of Support to Conflict Prevention and Peacebuilding Activities in Southern Sudan 2005–2010.* United Kingdom: ITAD Ltd.

Berdal, Mats R. 2009. *Building Peace after War*. New York: Routledge, for the International Institute for Strategic Studies.

Berger, Carol. 2009. "The Unintended Consequences of UN Peacekeeping in Post-War Southern Sudan: Why Everyone Wants a Uniform." Paper presented at the Symposium on Imperfect Duties? Humanitarian Intervention in Africa and the Responsibility to Protect in the Post-Iraq Era, March, De Pauw University, Indiana.

Berger, Peter L. and Luckmann, Thomas. 1967. *The Social Construction of Reality: A Treatise in the Sociology of Knowledge*. Garden City, NY: Doubleday.

Biklen, Douglas. 1983. *Community Organizing: Theory and Practice*. Englewood Cliffs, NJ: Prentice-Hall.

Birdsall, Nancy. 2004. *Seven Deadly Sins: Reflections on Donor Failing*. Working paper. Washington, DC: Center for Global Development working paper (50).

Blattman, Christopher and Annan, Jeannie. 2011. *Reintegrating and Employing High Risk Youth in Liberia: Lessons from a Randomized Evaluation of a Landmine Action Agricultural Training Program for Ex-Combatants*. Evidence from Randomized Evaluations of Peacebuilding in Liberia: Policy Report 2011. New Haven: Yale University.

Blattman, Christopher, Hartman, Alexandra, and Blair, Robert. 2014. "How to Promote Order and Property Rights under Weak Rule of Law? An Experiment in Changing Dispute Resolution Behavior through Community Education." *American Political Science Review* 108 (1): 100–120.

Bliesemann De Guevara, Berit. 2012. "Introduction," in *Statebuilding and State-Formation: The Political Sociology of Intervention*, edited by Bliesemann De Guevara, Berit (pp. 1–19). London: Routledge.

Bøås, Morten. 2009. "Funérailles pour un Ami: Des Luttes de Citoyenneté dans la Guerre Civile Libérienne." *Politique Africaine* (112): 36–51.

Bøås, Morten and Jennings, Kathleen. In progress. *Peacekeeping and the City: The Peacekeeping Economy in Liberia, DR Congo and South Sudan*. Unpublished manuscript. NUPI and FAFO, Oslo, Norway.

Bohns, Vanessa K. and Flynn, Francis J. 2010. "'Why Didn't You Just Ask?' Underestimating the Discomfort of Help-Seeking." *Journal of Experimental Social Psychology* 46 (2): 402–409.

Boshoff, Henri, Vrey, Waldemar, and Rautenbach, George. 2010. *The Burundi Peace Process: From Civil War to Conditional Peace*. Pretoria: Institute for Security Studies.

Bourdieu, Pierre. 1972. *Esquisse d'une Théorie de la Pratique. Précédé de Trois Études d'Ethnologie Kabyle*. Genève Paris: Droz.

Bourdieu, Pierre. 1979. *La Distinction: Critique Sociale du Jugement*. Paris: Éditions de Minuit.

Bourdieu, Pierre. 1980. "Le Capital Social." *Actes de la Recherche en Sciences Sociales* 31: 2–3.

Boutros-Ghali, Boutros. 1992. *An Agenda for Peace. Preventive Diplomacy, Peacemaking and Peace-Keeping*. New York: United Nations.

Bouvy, Alexis and Lange, Maria. 2012. *Ending the Deadlock: Towards a New Vision of Peace in Eastern DRC*. London: International Alert.

Bove, Vincenzo and Elia, Leandro. 2011. "Supplying Peace: Participation in and Troop Contribution to Peacekeeping Missions." *Journal of Peace Research* 48 (6): 699–714.

Bowles, Edith and Chopra, Tanja. 2008. "East Timor: Statebuilding Revisited," in *Building States to Build Peace*, edited by Call, Charles and Wyeth, Vanessa (pp. 271–302). Boulder: Lynne Rienner Publishers.

Branch, Adam. 2011. *Displacing Human Rights: War and Intervention in Northern Uganda*. New York: Oxford University Press.

Bratton, Michael. 2007. "Formal versus Informal Institutions in Africa." *Journal of Democracy* 18 (3): 96–110.

Brewer, Cecily. 2008. *Good Intentions: The UN's Integrated DDR Dilemmas in Southern Sudan*. Unpublished manuscript, Johns Hopkins University, on file with author.

Brint, Steven G. 1994. *In an Age of Experts: The Changing Role of Professionals in Politics and Public Life*. Princeton, NJ: Princeton University Press.

Brown, Keith. 2006. *Transacting Transition: The Micropolitics of Democracy Assistance in the Former Yugoslavia*. Bloomfield, CT: Kumarian Press.

Brunner, Dan and Nada, Garrett. 2012. *Can Foreign Aid Win 'Hearts and Minds?' Impact of USAID on Palestinian Public Opinion*. IMES Capstone Paper Series. Washington, DC: The Elliott School of International Affairs, George Washington University.

Bryman, Alan. 2006. "Paradigm Peace and the Implications for Quality." *International Journal of Social Research Methodology* 9 (2): 111–126.

Bryman, Alan. 2012. *Social Research Methods*. New York: Oxford University Press.

Burton, Robert. 2008. *On Being Certain: Believing You Are Right Even When You're Not*. New York: St. Martin's Press.

Bush, Kenneth D. 1996. "Beyond Bungee Cord Humanitarianism: Towards a Developmental Agenda for Peacebuilding." *Canadian Journal of Development Studies* 17 (4): 75–92.

Bush, Sarah Sunn. 2011. The Democracy Establishment. Ph.D. diss., Princeton University.

Cain, Kenneth, Postlewait, Heidi, and Thomson, Andrew. 2004. *Emergency Sex (and Other Desperate Measures): True Stories from a War Zone*. New York: Hyperion.

Call, Charles T. 2008. "Knowing Peace When You See It: Setting Standards for Peacebuilding Success." *Civil Wars* 10 (2): 173–194.

Call, Charles T. and Cousens, Elizabeth. 2008. "Ending Wars and Building Peace: International Responses to War-Torn Societies." *International Studies Perspectives* 9 (1): 1–21.

Campbell, Susanna. 2008. "When Process Matters: The Potential Implications of Organisational Learning for Peacebuilding Success." *Journal of Peacebuilding & Development* 4 (2): 20–32.

Campbell, Susanna. 2010. *Independent External Evaluation – Peacebuilding Fund Projects in Burundi*. New York: UN Peacebuilding Fund.

Campbell, Susanna. 2012. Organizational Barriers to Peace: Agency and Structure in International Peacebuilding. Ph.D. diss., Tufts University.

Campbell, Susanna. 2014. "Designed to Fail: Authority, Legitimacy, and Performance in International Peacebuilding." Paper presented at the Annual Meeting of the International Studies Association, Toronto.

Campbell, Susanna, Chandler, David, and Sabaratnam, Meera. (eds.). 2011. *A Liberal Peace? The Problems and Practices of Peacebuilding*. London: Zed Books.

Caritas. 2002. *Peacebuilding: A Caritas Training Manual*. Vatican City: Caritas Internationalis.

Carpenter, Charli. 2003. "'Women and Children First': Gender, Norms, and Humanitarian Evacuation in the Balkans 1991–5." *International Organization* 57 (4): 661–694.

Carpenter, Charli. 2012. "'You Talk of Terrible Things So Matter-of-Factly in This Language of Science': Constructing Human Rights in the Academy." *Perspectives on Politics* 10 (2): 363–383.

CDA Collaborative Learning Projects. 2008a. *The Listening Project Issue Paper: Presence: "Why Being There Matters."* Cambridge, MA: CDA Collaborative Learning Projects.

CDA Collaborative Learning Projects. 2008b. *The Listening Project Issue Paper: "Discuss Together, Decide Together, Work Together."* Cambridge, MA: CDA Collaborative Learning Projects.

CDA Collaborative Learning Projects. 2008c. *The Listening Project Issue Paper: The Cascading Effects of International Agendas and Priorities.* Cambridge, MA: CDA Collaborative Learning Projects.

CDA Collaborative Learning Projects. 2010a. *The Listening Project Issue Paper: Structural Relationships in the Aid System.* Cambridge, MA: CDA Collaborative Learning Projects.

CDA Collaborative Learning Projects. 2010b. *The Listening Project Issue Paper: The Role of Staffing Decisions.* Cambridge, MA: CDA Collaborative Learning Projects.

CDA Collaborative Learning Projects. 2011a. *Feedback Mechanisms in International Assistance Organizations.* Cambridge, MA: CDA Collaborative Learning Projects.

CDA Collaborative Learning Projects. 2011b. *Local Perceptions of International Engagement in Fragile States and Situations.* Cambridge, MA: CDA Collaborative Learning Projects.

CDA Collaborative Learning Projects. 2012. *"Outsider" Roles and Relationships in Cumulative Impacts.* Cambridge, MA: CDA Collaborative Learning Projects.

Chabal, Patrick and Daloz, Jean-Pascal. 1999. *Africa Works: Disorder as Political Instrument.* Bloomington; Oxford: Indiana University Press.

Chabal, Patrick and Daloz, Jean-Pascal. 2011. *Culture Troubles: Politics and the Interpretation of Meaning.* Chicago: The University of Chicago Press.

Chambers, Robert. 1983. *Rural Development: Putting the Last First.* London: Longman.

Chambers, Robert. 2006. *Poverty Unperceived: Traps, Biases and Agenda.* Brighton, UK: Institute of Development Studies.

Chandler, David. 2004. "The Responsibility to Protect? Imposing the 'Liberal Peace.'" *International Peacekeeping* 11 (1): 59–81.

Chandler, David. 2005. "Introduction: Peace without Politics." *International Peacekeeping* 12 (3): 307–321.

Chandler, David. 2006. *Empire in Denial: The Politics of State-Building.* London: Pluto.

Chandler, David. 2010. *International Statebuilding: The Rise of Post-Liberal Governance.* New York: Routledge.

Chandrasekaran, Rajiv. 2012. "Deadwood." *Foreign Policy* (June 26).

Chesterman, Simon. 2001. *Just War or Just Peace? Humanitarian Intervention and International Law.* New York: Oxford University Press.

Chesterman, Simon. 2004. *You, the People: The United Nations, Transitional Administration, and State-Building.* New York: Oxford University Press.

Chesterman, Simon. 2005. "From State Failure to State-Building: Problems and Prospects for a United Nations Peacebuilding Commission." *Journal of International Law and International Relations* 2 (1): 155–175.

Chopra, Jarat and Hohe, Tanja. 2004. "Participatory Intervention." *Global Governance* 10 (3): 289–305.

Chopra, Tanja. 2009. "When Peacebuilding Contradicts Statebuilding: Notes from the Arid Lands of Kenya." *International Peacekeeping* 16 (4): 531–545.

Chrétien, Jean-Pierre. 1995. *Les Médias du Genocide.* Paris: Karthala.

Coalition of Thirteen International and Congolese Civil Society Groups. 2012. *The Democratic Republic of Congo: Taking a Stand on Security Sector Reform*.

Coburn, Noah. 2011. *Bazaar Politics: Power and Pottery in an Afghan Market Town*. Stanford, CA: Stanford University Press.

Coetzee, J. M. 1982. *Waiting for the Barbarians*. New York: Penguin Books.

Cohen, Don and Prusak, Laurence. 2001. *In Good Company: How Social Capital Makes Organizations Work*. Boston: Harvard Business School Press.

Coles, Kimberley. 2007. *Democratic Designs. International Intervention and Electoral Practices in Postwar Bosnia-Herzegovina*. Ann Arbor: University of Michigan Press.

Collier, Paul, Elliott, V. L., Hegre, Havard, Hoeffler, Anke, Reynal-Querol, Marta, and Sambanis, Nicholas, 2003. *Breaking the Conflict Trap: Civil War and Development Policy*. New York: Oxford University Press.

Collier, Paul and Hoeffler, Anke. 2001. *Greed and Grievance in Civil War*. Oxford Economic Paper 56. Washington, DC: The World Bank.

Collins, Randall. 1979. *The Credential Society: An Historical Sociology of Education and Stratification*. New York: Academic Press.

Connorton, Ellen, Perry, Melissa J., Hemenway, David, and Miller, Matthew. 2011. "Humanitarian Relief Workers and Trauma-Related Mental Illness." *Epidemiologic Reviews* 34 (1): 145–155.

Cook, Thomas. 1997. "Lessons Learned in Evaluation over the Past 25 Years," in *Evaluation for the 21st Century: A Handbook*, edited by Chelimsky, Eleanor and Shadish, William (pp. 30–52). Thousand Oaks, CA: Sage Publications.

Cook-Huffman, Celia. 2000. "Who Do They Say We Are? Framing Social Identity and Gender in Church Conflict," in *Social Conflicts and Collective Identities*, edited by Coy, Patrick and Woehrle, Lynne (pp. 115–132). Lanham, MD: Rowman & Littlefield.

Cooley, Alexander and Ron, James. 2002. "The NGO Scramble: Organizational Insecurity and the Political Economy of Transnational Action." *International Security* 27 (1): 5–39.

Cousens, Elizabeth M., Kumar, Chetan, and Wermester, Karin. 2001. *Peacebuilding as Politics: Cultivating Peace in Fragile Societies*. Boulder, CO: Lynne Rienner.

Coyne, Christopher J. and Pellillo, Adam. 2012. "The Art of Seeing Like a State: State-Building in Afghanistan, the Congo, and Beyond." *Review of Austrian Economics* 25 (1): 35–52.

Crawford, Kerry Frances. 2013. "Defying Strategy: Non-strategic Recognition of Wartime Sexual Violence." Paper presented at the Annual Meeting of the International Studies Association, San Diego.

Cruz, Serena and Smits, Rosan. 2011. *Increasing Security in DR Congo: Gender-Responsive Strategies for Combating Sexual Violence*. The Hague: Clingendael Conflict Research Unit.

Curtis, Devon. 2001. *Politics and Humanitarian Aid: Debates, Dilemmas and Dissension*. HPG Report. London: Overseas Development Institute.

Daniel, Donald. 2008. "Why So Few Troops from among So Many?" In *Peace Operations: Trends, Progress, and Prospects*, edited by Daniel, Donald C., Taft, Patricia and Wiharta, Sharon (pp. 47–62). Washington, DC: Georgetown University Press.

Daniel, Donald, Taft, Patricia, and Wiharta, Sharon. 2008. *Peace Operations: Trends, Progress, and Prospects*. Washington, DC: Georgetown University Press.

D'Errico, Nicole, Tshibangu, Kalala, Bashige Nzigire, Louise, Maisha, Felicien, and Malemo Kalisya, Luc. 2013. "'You Say Rape, I Say Hospitals. But Whose Voice Is Louder?' Health, Aid and Decision-Making in the Democratic Republic of Congo." *Review of African Political Economy* 40 (135): 51–66.

De Fina, Anna and Georgakopoulou, Alexandra. 2008. "Analysing Narratives as Practices." *Qualitative Research* 8 (3): 379–387.

De Jong, Sara. 2011. "False Binaries: Altruism and Selfishness in NGO Work," in *Inside the Everyday Lives of Development Workers: The Challenges and Futures of Aidland*, edited by Fechter, Anne-Meike and Hindman, Heather (pp. 21–40). Sterling, VA: Kumarian Press.

De Koning, Ruben. 2011. *Conflict Minerals in the Democratic Republic of the Congo – Aligning Trade and Security Interventions*. SIPRI Policy Paper 27. Stockholm: SIPRI.

De Waal, Alexander. 1997. *Famine Crimes: Politics & the Disaster Relief Industry in Africa*. Bloomington, IN: Indiana University Press.

Debos, Marielle 2008. "Fluid Loyalties in a Regional Crisis: Chadian 'Ex-Liberators' in the Central African Republic." *African Affairs* 107 (427): 225–241.

Debrix, François. 1999. *Re-Envisioning Peacekeeping: The United Nations and the Mobilization of Ideology*. Minneapolis: University of Minnesota Press.

Demers, Christiane. 2007. *Organizational Change Theories: A Synthesis*. Thousand Oaks, CA: Sage Publications.

Demian, Sinziana (ed.). 2012. *International Rescue Committee in the Democratic Republic of Congo: Annual Report 2011*. New York: IRC.

Dennys, Christian and Zaman, Idrees. 2009. *Trends in Local Afghan Conflicts – Synthesis Paper*. Cooperation for Peace and Unity.

Des Forges, Alison. 1999. *Leave None to Tell the Story: Genocide in Rwanda*. New York: Human Rights Watch.

Desrosières, Alain. 1993. *La Politique Des Grands Nombres: Histoire De La Raison Statistique*. Paris: La Découverte.

Diamond, Larry. 2006. "Promoting Democracy in Post-Conflict and Failed States." *Taiwan Journal of Democracy* 2 (2): 93–116.

Dietze, Gabrielle. 2010. "Mythologies Blanches: Découvreurs et Sauveurs du Congo," in *Repenser L'indépendance: La RD Congo 50 Ans Plus Tard*, edited by Pole Institute (pp. 171–182). Goma, DR Congo: Pole Institute.

Dijkzeul, Dennis and Wakenge, Claude Iguma. 2010. "Doing Good, but Looking Bad? Local Perceptions of Two Humanitarian Organisations in Eastern Democratic Republic of the Congo." *Disasters* 34 (4): 1139–1170.

Dobbins, James 2005. "Nation-Building: UN Surpasses U.S. On Learning Curve." *Rand Review* 29 (1): 24–29.

Dolan, Chris. 2010. *War Is Not Yet Over – Community Perceptions of Sexual Violence and Its Underpinnings in Eastern DRC*. London: International Alert.

Domhoff, G. William. 1990. *The Power Elite and the State: How Policy Is Made in America*. New York: A. de Gruyter.

Donais, Timothy. 2009. "Empowerment or Imposition? Dilemmas of Local Ownership in Post-Conflict Peacebuilding Processes." *Peace and Change* 34 (1): 3–26.

Donald, Dominick. 2003. "Neutral Is Not Impartial: The Confusing Legacy of Traditional Peace Operations Thinking." *Armed Forces & Society* 29 (3): 415–448.

Doty, Roxanne Lynn. 1996. *Imperial Encounters: The Politics of Representation in North-South Relations*. Minneapolis: University of Minnesota Press.

Douma, Nynke and Hilhorst, Dorothea. 2012. *Fond De Commerce? Sexual Violence Assistance in the Democratic Republic of Congo*. Disaster Studies Occasional Paper 2. Wageningen, Netherlands: Wageningen University.

Downs, George W. and Rocke, David M. 1994. "Conflict, Agency, and Gambling for Resurrection: The Principal-Agent Problem Goes to War." *American Journal of Political Science* 38 (2): 362–380.

Downs, George W. and Stedman, Stephen John. 2002. "Evaluation Issues in Peace Implementation," in *Ending Civil Wars: The Implementation of Peace Agreements*, edited by Stedman, Stephen John, Rothchild, Donald and Cousens, Elizabeth M. (pp. 43–69). London: Lynne Rienner.

Doyle, Michael W. 2001. "Peacebuilding in Cambodia: Legitimacy and Power," in *Peacebuilding as Politics: Cultivating Peace in Fragile Societies*, edited by Cousens, Elizabeth M., Kumar, Chetan and Wermester, Karin (pp. 89–111). Boulder, CO: Lynne Rienner.

Doyle, Michael W., Johnstone, Ian, and Orr, Robert C. 1997. *Keeping the Peace: Multidimensional UN Operations in Cambodia and El Salvador*. New York: Cambridge University Press.

Doyle, Michael W. and Sambanis, Nicholas. 2000. "International Peacebuilding: A Theoretical and Quantitative Analysis." *American Political Science Review* 94 (4): 779–801.

Doyle, Michael W. and Sambanis, Nicholas. 2006. *Making War and Building Peace: United Nations Peace Operations*. Princeton, NJ: Princeton University Press.

Duffey, Tamara. 2000. "Cultural Issues in Contemporary Peacekeeping." *International Peacekeeping* 7 (1): 142–168.

Duffield, Mark. 2001. *Global Governance and the New Wars: The Merging of Development and Security*. New York: Zed Books.

Duffield, Mark. 2007. *Development, Security and Unending War: Governing the World of Peoples*. Cambridge: Polity Press.

Duffield, Mark. 2010. "Risk-Management and the Fortified Aid Compound: Everyday Life in Post-Interventionary Society." *Journal of Intervention and Statebuilding* 4 (5): 453–474.

Dunn, Kevin C. 2003. *Imagining the Congo: The International Relations of Identity*. New York: Palgrave Macmillan.

Easterly, William. 2002. "The Cartel of Good Intentions: The Problem of Bureaucracy in Foreign Aid." *The Journal of Policy Reform* 5 (4): 223–50.

Eastern Congo Initiative. 2011. *Landscape Analysis of Community Based Organizations: Maniema, North Kivu, Orientale and South Kivu Provinces of Democratic Republic of the Congo*. Seattle: Eastern Congo Initiative.

Eckstein, Harry. 1975. "Case Studies in Political Science," in *Handbook of Political Science, Vol. 3*, edited by Greenstein, Fred I. and Polsby, Nelson W. (pp. 79–138). Reading, MA: Addison-Wesley.

Edelstein, David. 2009. "Foreign Militaries, Sustainable Institutions, and Postwar Statebuilding," in *The Dilemmas of Statebuilding: Confronting the Contradictions of Postwar Peace Operations*, edited by Paris, Roland and Sisk, Timothy D. (pp. 81–103). London: Routledge.

Eden, Lynn. 2004. *Whole World on Fire: Organizations, Knowledge, and Nuclear Weapons Devastation*. Ithaca, NY: Cornell University Press.

Egeland, Jan, Harmer, Adele, and Stoddard, Abby. 2011. *To Stay and Deliver: Good Practice for Humanitarians in Complex Security Environments*. New York: UN Office for the Coordination of Humanitarian Affairs.

Eisenhardt, Kathleen M. 1989. "Agency Theory: An Assessment and Review." *The Academy of Management Review* 14 (1): 57–74.

Ellis, Stephen. 2002. "Cautions on Macro-Political Peacebuilding." Paper presented at the Workshop Building Democracy after War: State-of-the-Art Thinking about Governance and Peacebuilding, Tinas J. Watson Jr. Institute for International Studies, Brown University, Providence, RI.

Ellis, Stephen. 2005. "How to Rebuild Africa." *Foreign Affairs* 84 (5): 135–148.

Elmi, Afyare Abdi. 2010. *Understanding the Somali Conflagration: Identity, Islam, and Peacebuilding*. Oxford: Pluto Press.

Eltringham, Nigel. 2003. "'The Blind Men and the Elephant': The Challenge of Representing the Rwandan Genocide," in *The Ethics of Anthropology: Debates and Dilemmas*, edited by Caplan, Pat (pp. 96–112). London: Routledge.

Emerson, Robert and Pollner, Melvin. 1988. "On the Uses of Members' Responses to Researchers' Accounts." *Human Organization* 47: 189–198.

Englebert, Pierre. 2000. *State Legitimacy and Development in Africa*. Boulder, CO: Lynne Rienner Publishers.

Englebert, Pierre and Tull, Denis. 2008. "Postconflict Resolution in Africa: Flawed Ideas About Failed States." *International Security* 32 (4): 106–139.

Enloe, Cynthia H. 1993. *The Morning After: Sexual Politics at the End of the Cold War*. Berkeley: University of California Press.

Enloe, Cynthia H. 2000. *Bananas, Beaches and Bases: Making Feminist Sense of International Politics*. Berkeley: University of California Press.

Eriksson Baaz, Maria and Stern, Maria. 2009. "Why Do Soldiers Rape? Masculinity, Violence and Sexuality in the Armed Forces in the Congo." *International Studies Quarterly* 53 (2): 495–518.

Eriksson Baaz, Maria and Stern, Maria. 2010. *The Complexity of Violence: A Critical Analysis of Sexual Violence in the Democratic Republic of Congo (DRC)*. Stockholm: Sida and the Nordic Africa Institute.

Eriksson Baaz, Maria and Stern, Maria. 2013. *Sexual Violence as a Weapon of War? Perceptions, Prescriptions, Problems in the Congo and Beyond*. New York: Zed Books.

Escobar, Arturo. 1995. *Encountering Development: The Making and Unmaking of the Third World*. Princeton, NJ: Princeton University Press.

European Commission. 2010. *Communication and Visibility Manual for European Union External Actions*. Bruxelles: European Commission.

Eyben, Rosalind (ed.). 2006. *Relationships for Aid*. London: Earthscan.

Eyben, Rosalind. 2011. "The Sociality of International Aid and Policy Convergence," in *Adventures in Aidland: The Anthropology of Professionals in International Development*, edited by Mosse, David (pp. 139–160). Oxford: Berghahn Books.

Fahey, Dan. 2011. Rethinking the Resource Curse: Natural Resources and Polywar in the Ituri District, Democratic Republic of the Congo. Ph.D. diss., University of California-Berkeley.

Fama, Eugene F. and Jensen, Michael C. 1983. "Separation of Ownership and Control." *Journal of Law & Economics* 26 (2): 301–326.

Fanthorpe, Richard. 2006. "On the Limits of Liberal Peace: Chiefs and Democratic Decentralization in Post-War Sierra Leone." *African Affairs* 105 (418): 27–49.

Farah, Ahmed Yusuf 2002. *African Conflicts, their Management, Resolution and Post Conflict Reconstruction.* Unpublished manuscript, CODESRIA.

Farrell, Theo, Osinga, Frans, and Russell, James A. (eds.). 2013. *Military Adaptation in Afghanistan.* Stanford, CA: Stanford University Press.

Fassin, Didier and Pandolfi, Mariella (eds.). 2010. *Contemporary States of Emergency: The Politics of Military and Humanitarian Interventions.* New York: Zone Books.

Fast, Larissa. 2014. *Aid in Danger: The Perils and Promise of Humanitarianism.* Philadelphia: University of Pennsylvania Press.

Fast, Larissa, Finucane, Christopher, Freeman, Faith, O'Neill, Michael, and Rowley, Elizabeth. 2011. *The Acceptance Toolkit: A Practical Guide to Understanding, Assessing, and Strengthening Your Organization's Acceptance Approach to NGO Security Management.* Washington, D.C.: Save the Children Federation.

Fast, Larissa, Rowley, Elizabeth, O'Neill, Michael, and Freeman, Faith. 2011. *The Promise of Acceptance: Insights into Acceptance as a Security Management Approach from Field Research in Kenya, South Sudan, and Uganda.* Washington, DC: Save the Children Federation.

Faure, Guy Olivier and Rubin, Jeffrey Z. 1993. *Culture and Negotiations.* London: Sage Publications.

Fearon, James D., Humphreys, Macartan, and Weinstein, Jeremy M. 2009. "Can Development Aid Contribute to Social Cohesion after Civil War? Evidence from a Field Experiment in Post-Conflict Liberia." *American Economic Review: Papers and Proceedings* 99 (2): 287–291.

Fearon, James D., Humphreys, Macartan, and Weinstein, Jeremy M. 2011. *Democratic Institutions and Collective Action Capacity: Results from a Field Experiment in Post-Conflict Liberia.* Unpublished manuscript, Stanford University and Columbia University.

Fearon, James D. and Wendt, Alexander. 2002. "Rationalism versus Constructivism: A Skeptical View," in *Handbook of International Relations,* edited by Carlsnaes, Walter, Risse, Thomas and Simmons, Beth (pp. 52–72). London: Sage Publications.

Fechter, Anne-Meike and Hindman, Heather (eds.). 2011a. *Inside the Everyday Lives of Development Workers: The Challenges and Futures of Aidland.* Sterling, VA: Kumarian Press.

Fechter, Anne-Meike and Hindman, Heather. 2011b. "Introduction," in *Inside the Everyday Lives of Development Workers: The Challenges and Futures of Aidland,* edited by Fechter, Anne-Meike and Hindman, Heather (pp. 1–20). Sterling, VA: Kumarian Press.

Ferguson, James. 1990. *The Anti-Politics Machine: "Development," Depoliticization, and Bureaucratic Power in Lesotho.* New York: Cambridge University Press.

Fernandez, Sergio and Rainey, Hal G. 2006. "Managing Successful Organizational Change in the Public Sector," *Public Administration Review* 66 (2): 168–176.

Fetherston, Betts and Nordstrom, Carolyn. 1995. "Overcoming Habitus in Conflict Management: UN Peacekeeping and Warzone Ethnography." *Peace and Change* 20 (1): 94–119.

Fewer, International Alert, and Saferworld. 2004. *Conflict-Sensitive Approaches to Development, Humanitarian Assistance and Peacebuilding – A Resource Pack.* London: APFO, CECORE, CHA, FEWER, International Alert, Saferworld.

Finnemore, Martha. 1996. "Norms, Culture, and World Politics: Insights from Sociology's Institutionalism." *International Organization* 50 (2): 325–347.

Fisher, Jeffrey D., Nadler, Arie, and Whitcher-Alagna, Sheryle. 1982. "Recipient Reactions to Aid." *Psychological Bulletin* 91 (1): 27–54.

Fisher, Simon and Zimina, Lada. 2009. *Just Wasting Our Time? Provocative Thoughts for Peacebuilders*. Berlin: Berghof Research Center for Constructive Conflict Management.

Fishstein, Paul and Wilder, Andrew. 2012. *Winning Hearts and Minds? Examining the Relationship between Aid and Security in Afghanistan*. Boston, MA: Feinstein International Center, Tufts University.

Forster, E. M. 1924. *A Passage to India*. New York: Harcourt.

Fortna, Virginia Page. 2004. *Peace Time: Cease-Fire Agreements and the Durability of Peace*. Princeton, NJ: Princeton University Press.

Fortna, Virginia Page. 2008. *Does Peacekeeping Work? Shaping Belligerents' Choices after Civil War*. Princeton, NJ: Princeton University Press.

Fortna, Virginia Page and Howard, Lise Morjé. 2008. "Pitfalls and Prospects in the Peacekeeping Literature." *Annual Review of Political Science* 11: 283–301.

Foucault, Michel. 1976. *Histoire De La Sexualité*. Paris: Gallimard.

Fowler, Michael R. 2009. "Culture and Negotiations: The Pedagogical Dispute Regarding Cross-Cultural Negotiations." *International Studies Perspective* 10 (3): 341–359.

Friedman, Jeffrey. 1996. *The Rational Choice Controversy: Economic Models of Politics Reconsidered*. New Haven, CT: Yale University Press.

Fujii, Lee Ann. 2008. "The Power of Local Ties: Popular Participation in the Rwandan Genocide." *Security Studies* 17 (3): 568–597.

Fukuyama, Francis. 1995. *Trust: The Social Virtues and the Creation of Prosperity*. New York: Free Press.

Fukuyama, Francis. 2004. *State-Building: Governance and World Order in the 21st Century*. Ithaca, NY: Cornell University Press.

Gagnon, Chip. 2006. "Catholic Relief Services, USAID, and Authentic Partnership in Serbia," in *Transacting Transition: The Micropolitics of Democracy Assistance in the Former Yugoslavia*, edited by Brown, Keith (pp. 171–202). Bloomfield, CT: Kumarian Press.

Galtung, Johan. 1969. "Violence, Peace, and Peace Research." *Journal of Peace Research* 6 (3): 167–191.

Garb, Paula and Allen Nan, Susan. 2009. "The Dynamism of Shared Success in Abhkaz-Georgian Peacebuilding," in *Building Peace: Practical Reflections from the Field*, edited by Zelizer, Craig and Rubinstein, Robert A. (pp. 267–289). Sterling, VA: Kumarian Press.

Garrett, Nicholas. 2009. "Management of Mineral Resources in the DR Congo." Paper presented at the Workshop on The Post-Conflict State in the Democratic Republic of Congo, August, Johannesburg.

Garrett, Nicholas and Mitchell, Harrison. 2009. *Trading Conflict for Development: Utilising the Trade in Minerals from Eastern DR Congo for Development*. London: Resource Consulting Services.

Geertz, Clifford. 1973. *The Interpretation of Cultures*. New York: Basic Books.

George, Alexander L. and Bennett, Andrew. 2005. *Case Studies and Theory Development in the Social Sciences*. Cambridge, MA: MIT Press.

Gilbert, Andrew. 2008. Foreign Authority and the Politics of Impartiality in Postwar Bosnia-Herzegovina. Ph.D. diss., University of Chicago.

Gilligan, Michael and Sergenti, Ernest. 2008. "Do UN Interventions Cause Peace? Using Matching to Improve Causal Inference." *Quarterly Journal of Political Science* 3 (2): 89–122.

Gilligan, Michael and Stedman, Stephen John. 2003. "Where Do the Peacekeepers Go?" *The International Studies Review* 5 (4): 37–54.

Gizelis, Theodora-Ismene and Kosek, Kristin E. 2005. "Why Humanitarian Interventions Succeed or Fail: The Role of Local Participation." *International Peacekeeping* 40 (4): 363–383.

Glick, Beth and Reynolds Levy, Laina. 2009. "The Institution as Innovator: Laying the Foundation for Peaceful Change," in *Building Peace: Practical Reflections from the Field*, edited by Zelizer, Craig and Rubinstein, Robert A. (pp. 39–54). Sterling, VA: Kumarian Press.

Goetze, Catherine and Bliesemann De Guevara, Berit. 2012. "The 'Statebuilding Habitus,'" in *Statebuilding and State-Formation: The Political Sociology of Intervention*, edited by Bliesemann De Guevara, Berit (pp. 198–213). London: Routledge.

Goldman, Michael. 2001. "The Birth of a Discipline: Producing Authoritative Green Knowledge, World-Bank-Style." *Ethnography* 2 (2): 191–217.

Goldstein, Joshua. 2011. *Winning the War on War*. New York: Penguin.

Goldstein, Judith and Keohane, Robert O. (eds.). 1993. *Ideas and Foreign Policy: Beliefs, Institutions, and Political Change*. Ithaca, NY: Cornell University Press.

Green, Donald P. and Shapiro, Ian. 1994. *Pathologies of Rational Choice Theory: A Critique of Applications in Political Science*. New Haven, CT: Yale University Press.

Greenberg, Martin S. and Shapiro, Solomon P. 1971. "Indebtedness: An Adverse Aspect of Asking for and Receiving Help." *Sociometry* 34 (2): 290–301.

GRIP. 2010. *Etude sur la Prolifération des Armes Légères en République Démocratique du Congo*. Brussels.

Gross Stein, Janice. 2011. "Background Knowledge in the Foreground: Conversations About Competent Practice in 'Sacred Space'," in *International Practices*, edited by Pouliot, Vincent and Adler, Emanuel (pp. 87–107). New York: Cambridge University Press.

Guilhot, Nicolas. 2005. *The Democracy Makers: Human Rights and International Order*. New York: Columbia University Press.

Hadjipavlou, Maria and Kanol, Bülent 2008. *Cumulative Impact Case Study: The Impacts of Peacebuilding Work on the Cyprus Conflict*. Collaborative Learning Project. Reflecting on Peace Practice Project.

Hamilton, Rebecca. 2011. *Fighting for Darfur: Public Action and the Struggle to Stop Genocide*. New York: Palgrave.

Hammersley, Martyn and Atkinson, Paul. 2007. *Ethnography: Principles in Practice (Third Edition)*. London: Routledge.

Hampson, Fen Osler. 1996. *Nurturing Peace: Why Peace Settlements Succeed or Fail*. Washington, DC: United States Institute of Peace Press.

Hanson, Stephanie. 2009. *The African Union*. Backgrounder. New York: Council on Foreign Relations.

Harper, Ian. 2011. "World Health and Nepal: Producing Internationals, Healthy Citizenship and the Cosmopolitan," in *Adventures in Aidland: The Anthropology of Professionals in International Development*, edited by Mosse, David (pp. 123–138). Oxford: Berghahn Books.

Harris, Marvin and Johnson, Orna. 2000. *Cultural Anthropology*. Boston, MA: Allyn & Bacon.

Hayman, Carolyn. 2012. "Local First – A Proposal for Development in the Twenty-First Century," in *Local First: Development for the Twenty-First Century*, edited by Mcguinness, Kate (pp. 13–43). London: Peace Direct.

Heathershaw, John. 2008. "Seeing Like the International Community: How Peacebuilding Failed (and Survived) in Tajikistan." *Journal of Intervention and Statebuilding* 2 (3): 329–351.

Heathershaw, John. 2009. *Post-Conflict Tajikistan: The Politics of Peacebuilding and the Emergence of Legitimate Order*. London: Routledge.

Heiberg, Marianne. 1990. "Peacekeepers and Local Populations: Some Comments on UNIFIL," in *The United Nations and Peacekeeping*, edited by Rikhye, Indar Jit and Skjelsbaek, Kjell (pp. 147–169). Basingstoke: Macmillan.

Heiberg, Marianne and Holst, Johan Jørgen. 1986. "Peacekeeping in Lebanon: Comparing UNIFIL and the MNF." *Survival* 28 (5): 399–422.

Helfer, Laurence R. 2006. "Understanding Change in International Organizations: Globalization and Innovation in the ILO," *Vanderbilt Law Review*, 59 (3): 649–726.

Hellmüller, Sara. 2013. "The Power of Perceptions: Localizing International Peacebuilding Approaches." *International Peacekeeping* 20 (2): 219–232.

Higate, Paul and Henry, Marsha. 2009. *Insecure Spaces: Peacekeeping in Liberia, Kosovo and Haiti*. London: Zed Books.

Hindman, Heather. 2011. "The Hollowing Out of Aidland: Subcontracting and the New Development Family in Nepal," in *Inside the Everyday Lives of Development Workers: The Challenges and Futures of Aidland*, edited by Fechter, Anne-Meike and Hindman, Heather (pp. 169–191). Sterling, VA: Kumarian Press.

Hirschman, Albert O. 1981. "Morality and the Social Sciences," in *Essays in Trespassing: Economics to Politics and Beyond*, edited by Hirschman, Albert O. (pp. 294–306). New York: Cambridge University Press

Ho, Karen Zouwen. 2009. *Liquidated: An Ethnography of Wall Street*. Durham: Duke University Press.

Hoffman, Bruce. 2008. "The Myth of Grass-Roots Terrorism. Why Osama Bin Laden Still Matters." *Foreign Affairs* 87 (3): 133–138.

Hohe, Tanja. 2002. "Clash of Paradigms: International Administration and Local Political Legitimacy in East Timor." *Contemporary Southeast Asia* 24 (3): 569–589.

Holohan, Anne. 2005. *Networks of Democracy: Lessons from Kosovo for Afghanistan, Iraq, and Beyond*. Stanford, CA: Stanford University Press.

Holt, Victoria K. and Berkman, Tobias C. 2006. *The Impossible Mandate? Military Preparedness, the Responsibility to Protect and Modern Peace Operations*. Washington, DC: The Henry L. Stimson Center.

Hopf, Ted. 1998. "The Promise of Constructivism in International Relations Theory." *International Security* 23 (1): 171–200.

Hopf, Ted. 2010. "The Logic of Habit in International Relations." *European Journal of International Relations* 16 (4): 539–561.

Howard, Lise Morjé. 2008. *UN Peacekeeping in Civil Wars*. New York: Cambridge University Press.

Huang, Reyko and Harris, Joseph. 2006. "The Nuts and Bolts of Post-Conflict Capacity Building: Practicable Lessons from East Timor." *Journal of Peacebuilding and Development* 2 (3): 78–92.

Human Rights Watch. 2002. *The War within the War – Sexual Violence against Women and Girls in Eastern Congo*. Washington, DC: Human Rights Watch.

Human Rights Watch. 2012. *'You Will Not Have Peace While You Are Living': The Escalation of Political Violence in Burundi.* New York: Human Rights Watch.

Human Security Report Project. 2010. *Human Security Report 2009/2010: The Causes of Peace and the Shrinking Costs of War.* Pre-publication. Vancouver: HSRP.

Humphreys, Macartan, Sanchez De La Sierra, Raul, and Van der Windt, Peter. 2012. *Social and Economic Impacts of Tuungane: Final Report on the Effects of a Community Driven Reconstruction Program in Eastern Democratic Republic of Congo.* New York: Columbia University.

Iniguez De Heredia, Marta. 2011. "Resistance and Statebuilding: An Everyday Encounter of Political Projects in the Democratic Republic of Congo," Paper presented at the 52nd Annual Meeting of the International Studies Association, Montreal, Canada.

International Alert. 2010. *The Role of the Exploitation of Natural Resources in Fueling and Prolonging Crises in the Eastern DRC.* London: International Alert.

International Committee of the Red Cross. 2012. *International Committee of the Red Cross Annual Report 2011.* Geneva: ICRC.

International Crisis Group. 2007. *Darfur's New Security Reality.* Brussels: International Crisis Group.

International Crisis Group. 2010. *Congo: Pas de Stabilité au Kivu malgré le Rapprochement avec le Rwanda.* Brussels: International Crisis Group.

International Crisis Group. 2012a. *Burundi: Bye-Bye Arusha?* New York: International Crisis Group.

International Crisis Group. 2012b. *Eastern Congo: Why Stabilization Failed.* Nairobi: International Crisis Group.

International Rescue Committee. 2008. *Mortality in the Democratic Republic of Congo: An Ongoing Crisis.* New York: International Rescue Committee and Burnet Institute.

IRIN. 2012. *Are They Listening? Aid and Humanitarian Accountability.* Geneva: Integrated Regional Information Networks.

Irwin, Rachel. 2007. "Culture Shock: Negotiating Feelings from the Field." *Anthropology Matters* 9 (1): 1–11.

Jacobs, Alex and Wilford, Robyn. 2007. "Putting New Approaches to NGO Accountability into Action." Paper presented at the Development's Futures Conference, November, NUI Galway.

Jacobs, Alex and Wilford, Robyn. 2008. *Listen First: Practical Ways of Improving Accountability for NGOs.* Listen First project. United Kingdom: Concern and Mango.

Jacobs, Alex and Wilford, Robyn. 2010. "Listen First: A Pilot System for Managing Downward Accountability in NGOs." *Development in Practice* 20 (7): 797–811.

Jervis, Robert. 1976. *Perception and Misperception in International Politics.* Princeton, NJ: Princeton University Press.

Jervis, Robert. 2006. "Understanding Beliefs." *Political Psychology* 27 (5): 641–663.

Johnson, Dominic. 2013. *No Kivu, No Conflict? The Misguided Struggle against "Conflict Minerals" in the DRC.* Goma: Pole Institute.

Johnson, Kirsten, Scott, Jennifer, Rughita, Bigy, Kisielewski, Michael, Asher, Jana, Ong, Ricardo, and Lawry, Lynn. 2010. "Association of Sexual Violence and Human Rights with Physical and Mental Health in Territories of the Eastern Democratic Republic of the Congo." *Journal of the American Medical Association* 304 (5): 553–562.

Johnston, Patrick. 2005. "Dynamics of Post-War and Peacekeeping in Sierra Leone." Paper presented at the 49th Annual Meeting of the African Studies Association Conference, Washington, DC.

Jones, Adam. 1994. "Gender and Ethnic Conflict in Ex-Yugoslavia." *Ethnic and Racial Studies* 17 (1): 115–134.

Jones, Bruce D. 2001. *Peacemaking in Rwanda: The Dynamics of Failure.* Boulder, CO: Lynne Rienner Publishers.

Jones, David Martin and Smith, M. L. R. 2010. "Whose Hearts and Whose Minds? The Curious Case of Global Counter-Insurgency." *The Journal of Strategic Studies* 33 (1): 81–121.

Joseph, Edward. 2007. "Ownership Is Over-Rated." *SAIS Review* 27 (2): 109–123.

Juma, Monica Kathina and Suhrke, Astri. 2002. *Eroding Local Capacity: International Humanitarian Action in Africa.* Uppsala: Nordic African Institute.

Kalyvas, Stathis N. 2001. "'New' and 'Old' Civil Wars: a Valid Distinction?" *World Politics* 54 (1): 99–118.

Kalyvas, Stathis N. 2003. "The Ontology of 'Political Violence': Action and Identity in Civil Wars." *Perspectives on Politics* 1 (3): 475– 494.

Kalyvas, Stathis N. 2004. "The Urban Bias in Research on Civil Wars." *Security Studies* 13 (3): 1–31.

Kalyvas, Stathis N. 2006. *The Logic of Violence in Civil War.* New York: Cambridge University Press.

Kapoor, Ilan. 2004. "Hyper-Self-Reflexive Development? Spivak on Representing the Third World." *Third World Quarterly* 25 (4): 627–647.

Kassimir, Ronald. 2001. "Producing Local Politics: Governance, Representation, and Non-State Organizations in Africa," in *Intervention and Transnationalism in Africa: Global-Local Networks of Power*, edited by Callaghy, Thomas M., Kassimir, Ronald and Latham, Robert (pp. 93–112). New York: Cambridge University Press.

Keck, Margaret E. and Sikkink, Kathryn. 1998. *Activists Beyond Borders: Advocacy Networks in International Politics.* Ithaca, NY: Cornell University Press.

Kelly, Jocelyn. 2010. *Rape in War: Motives of Militia in DRC.* Washington, DC: United States Institute of Peace.

Keystone Accountability. 2011. *NGO Partner Survey 2010.* Keystone Performance Surveys. London: Keystone Accountability.

Keystone Accountability. 2013. *Development Partnerships Survey: Headlines for International Development.* London: Keystone Accountability.

Kim, Cheryl M. Lee and Metrikas, Mark. 1997. "Holding a Fragile Peace: The Military and Civilian Components of UNTAC," in *Keeping the Peace*, edited by Doyle, Michael W, Johnstone, Ian and Orr, Robert C. (pp. 107–133). New York: Cambridge University Press.

King, Elisabeth. 2009. "From Data Problems to Data Points: Challenges and Opportunities of Research in Postgenocide Rwanda." *African Studies Review* 52 (3): 127–148.

King, Elisabeth. 2013. *A Critical Review of Community-Driven Development Programmes in Conflict-Affected Contexts.* London: DFID and International Rescue Committee.

Kipp, Jacob, Grau, Lester, Prinslow, Karl, and Smith, Don. 2006. "The Human Terrain System: A CORDS for the 21st Century." *Military Review* (Sept-Oct): 8–15.

Klopp, Jacqueline and Kamungi, Prisca. 2007. "Violence and Elections: Will Kenya Collapse?" *World Policy Review* 24 (4): 11–18.

Klopp, Jacqueline and Zuern, Elke. 2007. "The Politics of Violence in Democratization." *Comparative Politics* 39 (2): 127–146.

Klotz, Audie and Lynch, Cecelia. 2007. *Strategies for Research in Constructivist International Relations.* Armonk, NY: M. E. Sharpe.

Kojan, David and Angelo, Dante. 2005. "Dominant Narratives, Social Violence and the Practice of Bolivian Archaeology." *Journal of Social Archaeology* 5: 383–408.

Krämer, Mario. 2006. "The Relations between Center and Periphery: Dynamics of Violence in Kwazulu-Natal, South Africa." Paper presented at the Order, Conflict, and Violence Speaker Series, Yale University.

Krämer, Mario 2007. *Violence as Routine: Transformations of Local-Level Politics and the Disjunction between Centre and Periphery in Kwazulu-Natal (South Africa)*. Köln: Rüdiger Köppe Verlag (Siegener Beiträge zur Soziologie vol. 8).

Kreps, Sarah. 2010. "Why Does Peacekeeping Succeed or Fail? Peacekeeping in the Democratic Republic of Congo and Sierra Leone," in *Modern War and the Utility of Force*, edited by Angstrom, Jan and Duyvesteyn, Isabelle (pp. 90–118). New York: Routledge.

Kunz, Rahel. 2013. "Reflexive Inquiry," in *Research Methods in Critical Security Studies: An Introduction*, edited by Salter, Mark B. and Mutlu, Can E. (pp. 63–66). New York: Routledge.

Lacan, Jacques. 1966. *Ecrits*. Paris: Éditions du Seuil.

Lambourne, Wendy. 2009. "Transitional Justice and Peacebuilding after Mass Violence." *The International Journal of Transitional Justice* 3 (1): 28–48.

Lange, Maria. 2004. *Building Institutional Capacity for Conflict-Sensitive Practice: The Case of International NGOs*. London: International Alert.

Lantis, Jeffrey S. 2002. "Strategic Culture and National Security Policy." *International Studies Review* 4 (3): 87–113.

Lanz, David. 2011. "The Globalisation of Darfur: Making Sense of a Trajectory from Forgotten Conflict to Global Cause Célèbre." Paper presented at the Annual Meeting of the International Studies Association, Montreal, Canada.

Last, David. 2000. "Organizing for Effective Peacebuilding." *International Peacekeeping* 7 (1): 80–96.

Laudati, Ann. 2013. "Beyond Minerals: Broadening 'Economies of Violence' in Eastern Democratic Republic of Congo." *Review of African Political Economy* 40 (135): 32–50.

Lave, Jean and Wenger, Etienne. 1991. *Situated Learning: Legitimate Peripheral Participation*. New York: Cambridge University Press.

Lavers, Tom. 2008. *The Politics of Bilateral Donor Assistance*. Geneva: UN Research Institute for Social Development.

Leander, Anna. 2008. "Thinking Tools," in *Qualitative Methods in International Relations: A Pluralist Guide*, edited by Klotz, Audie and Prakash, Deepa (pp. 11–27). New York: Palgrave.

Lederach, John Paul. 1995. *Preparing for Peace: Conflict Transformation across Cultures*. Syracuse, NY: Syracuse University Press.

Lederach, John Paul. 1997. *Building Peace: Sustainable Reconciliation in Divided Societies*. Washington, DC: United States Institute of Peace Press.

Lederach, John Paul. 2002. *A Handbook of International Peacebuilding: Into the Eye of the Storm*. San Francisco: Jossey-Bass.

Ledoux, Joseph. 2002. *Synaptic Self: How Our Brains Become Who We Are*. London: Penguin.

Lefranc, Sandrine. 2008. "Du Droit à la Paix. La Circulation des Techniques Internationales de Pacification par le Bas." *Actes de la Recherche en Sciences Sociales* 4 (174): 48–67.

Lehmann, Ingrid. 1999. *Peacekeeping and Public Information*. London: Frank Cass Publishers.

Lemarchand, René. 2008. *The Dynamics of Violence in Central Africa*. Philadelphia: University of Pennsylvania Press.

Leonard, David. 2013. *Piecing It Together: Post-Conflict Security in an Africa of Networked, Multilevel Governance*. IDS Bulletin 44.1. Brighton: Institute of Development Studies.

Leone, Suzanne. 1993. "Protecting Rape Victims' Identities: Balance between the Right to Privacy and the First Amendment." *New England Law Review* Spring 27 (3): 883–913.

Levin, Estelle (lead author). 2012. *Greening ICT Supply Chains – Survey on Conflict Minerals Due Diligence Initiatives*. International Telecommunication Union and The United Nations University.

Lévinas, Emmanuel. 1974. *Autrement qu'Etre ou Au-delà de l'Essence*. The Hague, Netherlands: Martinus Nijhoff.

Levy Paluk, Elizabeth and Green, Donald P. 2009. "Deference, Dissent, and Dispute Resolution: An Experimental Intervention Using Mass Media to Change Norms and Behavior in Rwanda." *American Political Science Review* 103 (4): 622–644.

Licklider, Roy E. 1993. *Stopping the Killing: How Civil Wars End*. New York: New York University Press.

Life and Peace Institute. 2011. *Au-delà des Groupes Armés: Conflits Locaux et Connexions Sous-Regionales. L'Exemple de Fizi et Uvira (Sud-Kivu, RDC)*. Kalmar, Sweden: Life and Peace Institute.

Life and Peace Institute. 2012. *Conflits Fonciers et Dynamiques de Cohabitation en Territoire de Kalehe, Sud-Kivu, Est de la DRC*. Kalmar, Sweden: Life and Peace Institute.

Lin, Nan, Cook, Karen S., and Burt, Ronald S. 2001. *Social Capital: Theory and Research*. New York: Aldine de Gruyter.

Lincoln, Yvonna S. and Guba, Egon G. 1985. *Naturalistic Inquiry*. Beverly Hills, CA: Sage Publications.

Lipsky, Michael. 1980. *Street-Level Bureaucracy: Dilemmas of the Individual in Public Services*. New York: Russell Sage Foundation.

Lipton, Michael. 1977. *Why Poor People Stay Poor: Urban Bias in World Development*. Cambridge: Harvard University Press.

Lund, Michael. 2003. *What Kind of Peace Is Being Built? Taking Stock of Post-Conflict Peacebuilding and Charting Future Directions*. Discussion paper. Ottawa: International Development Research Centre.

Lwambo, Désirée. 2011. *"Before the War, I Was a Man": Men and Masculinities in Eastern DR Congo*. Goma: HEAL Africa.

Lyall, Jason and Wilson, Isaiah. 2009. "Rage against the Machines: Explaining Outcomes in Counterinsurgency Wars." *International Organization* 63 (7): 67–106.

Lyons, Terrence. 2002. "The Role of Postsettlement Elections," in *Ending Civil Wars: The Implementation of Peace Agreements*, edited by Stedman, Stephen John, Rothchild, Donald and Cousens, Elizabeth M. (pp. 215–236). Boulder, CO: Lynne Rienner.

Lyons, Terrence. 2004. "Post-Conflict Elections and the Process of Demilitarizing Politics: The Role of Electoral Administration." *Democratization* 11 (3): 36–62.

Mac Ginty, Roger. 2006. *No War, No Peace: The Rejuvenation of Stalled Peace Processes and Peace Accords*. London: Palgrave Macmillan.

Mac Ginty, Roger. 2008. "Indigenous Peace-Making versus the Liberal Peace." *Cooperation and Conflict* 43 (2): 139–163.

Mac Ginty, Roger. 2010. "Hybrid Peace: The Interaction between Top-Down and Bottom-up Peace." *Security Dialogue* 41 (4): 391–412.

Mac Ginty, Roger. 2011. *International Peacebuilding and Local Resistance: Hybrid Forms of Peace*. London: Palgrave Macmillan.

Mac Ginty, Roger. 2012. "Routine Peace: Technocracy and Peacebuilding." *Cooperation and Conflict* 47 (3): 287–308.

Machado, Barry F. 2007. *In Search of Usable Past: The Marshall Plan and Postwar Reconstruction Today*. Lexington, VA: George C. Marshall Foundation.

Macrae, Joanna (ed.). 2002. *The New Humanitarianism: A Review of Trends in Global Humanitarian Action*. HPG Report. London: Overseas Development Institute.

Macrae, Joanna and Leader, Nicholas. 2000. *Shifting Sands: The Search for 'Coherence' between Political and Humanitarian Responses to Complex Emergencies*. HPG Report. London: Overseas Development Institute.

Macrae, Joanna and Leader, Nicholas. 2001. "Apples, Pears, and Porridge: The Origins and Impact of the Search for 'Coherence' between Humanitarian and Political Responses to Chronic Political Emergencies." *Disasters* 25 (4): 290–307.

Macrae, Joanna and Zwi, Anthony B. 1994. *War and Hunger: Rethinking International Responses to Complex Emergencies*. London: Zed Books.

Mamdani, Mahmood. 2009. *Saviors and Survivors: Darfur, Politics, and the War on Terror*. New York: Pantheon Books.

Manning, Carrie and Malbrough, Monica. 2010. "Bilateral Donors and Aid Conditionality in Post-Conflict Peacebuilding: The Case of Mozambique." *Journal of Modern African Studies* 48 (1): 143–69.

Manning, Carrie and Zürcher, Christoph. 2013. *Costly Democracy: Peacebuilding and Democraticratization after War*. Palo Alto, CA: Stanford University Press.

Marchal, Roland and Messiant, Christine. 2002. "De l'Avidité des Rebelles. L'Analyse Economique de la Guerre Civile selon Paul Collier." *Critique Internationale* (16): 58–69.

Marine Corps Intelligence Activity. 2008. *Cultural Islam in Afghanistan*. Washington, DC: United States Marine Corps.

Marriage, Zoë. 2006. *Not Breaking the Rules, Not Playing the Game: International Assistance to Countries at War*. London: Hurst.

Marston, Daniel and Malkasian, Carter (eds.). 2010. *Counterinsurgency in Modern Warfare*. Oxford: Osprey Publishing.

Marten, Kimberly Zisk. 2004. *Enforcing the Peace: Learning from the Imperial Past*. New York: Columbia University Press.

Martin, Mary and Moser, Stephanie. 2012. *Exiting Conflict, Owning the Peace: Local Ownership and Peacebuilding Relationships in the Cases of Bosnia and Kosovo*. London: London School of Economics – Friedrich Ebert Stiftung.

Martin, Sarah. 2005. *Must Boys Be Boys? Ending Sexual Exploitation and Abuse in UN Peacekeeping Missions*. Washington, DC: Refugees International.

Mason, Simon. 2009. *Insider Mediators: Exploring Their Key Role in Informal Peace Processes*. Berlin: Berghof Foundation for Peace Support.

Matsuzaki, Reo. In progress. *Imposing Authority: Colonial Taiwan, Philippines, and the Paradox of State-Building*. Unpublished manuscript, Trinity College, Hartford, CT.

Matthysen, Ken, and Montejano, Andrés Zaragoza. *"Conflict Minerals" Initiatives in DR Congo: Perceptions of Local Mining Communities*. Antwerpen: International Peace Information Service.

Mauss, Marcel. 1923–1924. "Essai sur le Don. Forme et Raison de l'Echange dans les Sociétés Archaïques." *L'Année Sociologique* nouvelle série, vol. I: 30–186.

May, Carl. 1990. "Research on Nurse-Patient Relationships: Problems of Theory, Problems of Practice." *Journal of Advanced Nursing* 15 (3): 307–315.

McDougal, Myres S. and Lasswell, Harold D. 1959. "The Identification and Appraisal of Diverse Systems of Public Order." *American Journal of International Law* 53: 1–29.

McGuinness, Kate. 2012. *Local First: Development for the Twenty-First Century*. London: Peace Direct.

McWha, Ishbel. 2011. "The Roles of, and Relationships between, Expatriates, Volunteers, and Local Development Workers." *Development in Practice* 21 (1): 29–40.

Mead, George Herbert. 1934. *Mind, Self and Society*. Chicago: University of Chicago Press.

Meharg, Sarah Jane. 2009. *Measuring What Matters in Peace Operations and Crisis Management*. Montreal: McGill-Queen's University Press.

Mehta, Uday Singh. 1999. *Liberalism and Empire: A Study in Nineteenth-Century British Liberal Thought*. Chicago: University of Chicago Press.

Menkhaus, Ken. 1997. "International Peacebuilding and the Dynamics of Local and National Reconciliation in Somalia," in *Learning from Somalia*, edited by Clarke, Walter and Herbst, Jeffrey (pp. 42–63). Boulder, CO: Westview Press.

Menkhaus, Ken. 2004. *Impact Assessment in Post-Conflict Peacebuilding*. Geneva: Interpeace.

Merry, Sally Engle. 2011. "Measuring the World: Indicators, Human Rights, and Global Governance." *Current Anthropology* 52 (3): S83–S95.

Miles, Matthew B. and Huberman, A. Michael. 1994. *Qualitative Data Analysis: An Expanded Sourcebook*. Thousand Oaks, CA: Sage Publications.

Mill, John Stuart. 1888. *A System of Logic*. New York: Harper & Row.

Millar, Gearoid. 2011. "Between Western Theory and Local Practice: Cultural Impediments to Truth-telling in Sierra Leone." *Conflict Resolution Quarterly* 29 (2): 177–199.

Millar, Gearoid. 2014. *An Ethnographic Approach to Peacebuilding: Understanding Local Experiences in Transitional States*. London: Routledge.

Miller, Derek and Rudnick, Lisa. 2010. "The Case for Situated Theory in Modern Peacebuilding Practice." *Journal of Peacebuilding and Development* 5 (2): 62–74.

Miller, Gary. 2005. "The Political Evolution of Principal-Agent Models." *Annual Review of Political Science* 8: 203–225.

Mills, C. Wright. 2000. *The Power Elite*. New York: Oxford University Press.

Minear, Larry. 2002. *The Humanitarian Enterprise: Dilemmas and Discoveries*. Bloomfield, CT: Kumarian Press.

Mitchell, Audra. 2011a. *International Communities in Nicosia*. Initial Pilot Study Report – Perceptions of 'International Communities' in Nicosia. Working document. UK: University of York.

Mitchell, Audra. 2011b. "Quality/Control: International Peace Interventions and 'the Everyday'." *Review of International Studies* 37 (4): 1623–1645.

Mitchell, Audra. 2011c. "The Field Trap: Fieldwork and the Dilemmas of Escaping the Ivory Tower for IR Scholars and Students." Paper presented at the 2011 Millennium Annual Conference, London School of Economics, October.

Mitchell, Audra. 2014. *International Intervention in a Secular Age: Re-Enchanting Humanity?* Oxon, UK: Routledge.

Mitchell, Timothy. 2002. *Rule of Experts: Egypt, Techno-Politics, Modernity*. Berkeley: University of California Press.

MONUSCO and UN Human Rights Office of the High Commissioner. 2011. *Final Report of the Fact-Finding Missions of the United Nations Joint Human Rights Office into the Mass Rapes and Other Human Rights Violations Committed by a Coalition of Armed Groups along the Kibua-Mpofi Axis in Walikale Territory, North Kivu, from 30 July to 2 August 2010*. United Nations.

MONUSCO Stabilization Support Unit. 2011. *International Security and Stabilization Support Strategy for the Democratic Republic of the Congo – Situation Assessment as at: 31 July 2011 – Draft Summary of Findings*. Goma: United Nations.

Moore, Adam. 2013. *Peacebuilding in Practice: Local Experience in Two Bosnian Towns*. Ithaca, NY: Cornell University Press.

Mosse, David. 2005. *Cultivating Development: An Ethnography of Aid Policy and Practice*. London: Pluto Press.

Mosse, David. 2008. "International Policy, Development Expertise, and Anthropology." *Focaal* 52: 119–126.

Mosse, David (ed.). 2011. *Adventures in Aidland: The Anthropology of Professionals in International Development*. Studies in Public and Applied Anthropology. Oxford: Berghahn Books.

Murphy, Alexander B. 1996. "The Sovereign State System as Political-Territorial Ideal," in *State Sovereignty as a Social Construct*, edited by Biersteker, Thomas J. and Weber, Cynthia (pp. 81–120). Cambridge: Cambridge University Press.

Mutua, Makau. 2001. "Savages, Victims, and Saviors: The Metaphor of Human Rights." *Harvard International Law Journal* 42 (1): 201–245.

Narten, Jens. 2009. "Dilemmas of Promoting 'Local Ownership': The Case of Postwar Kosovo," in *The Dilemmas of Statebuilding: Confronting the Contradictions of Postwar Peace Operations*, edited by Paris, Roland and Sisk, Timothy D. (pp. 252–285). London: Routledge.

Nathan, Laurie. 2007. *No Ownership, No Commitment: A Guide to Local Ownership of Security Sector Reform*. Birmingham, UK: University of Birmingham.

Nest, Michael, Grignon, Francois, and Kisangani, Emizet F. 2006. *The Democratic Republic of Congo: Economic Dimensions of War and Peace*. Boulder, CO: Lynne Rienner.

Neumann, Hannah. 2011. "Researching Peacebuilding as Seen from the Local Perspectives." Paper presented at the PACSA – PRIO conference on The Local in Global Understandings of War and Peacemaking, Nicosia, Cyprus.

Neumann, Hannah and Schia, Niels Nagelhus. 2012. *Contextualizing Peacebuilding Activities to Local Circumstances*. Security in Practice. Oslo: Norwegian Institute for International Affairs.

Neumann, Iver B. 2008. "Discourse Analysis," in *Qualitative Methods in International Relations: A Pluralist Guide*, edited by Klotz, Audie and Prakash, Deepa (pp. 61–77). New York: Palgrave.

Neumann, Iver B. and Sending, Ole Jacob. 2011. "Banking on Power: How Some Practices in an International Organization Anchor Others," in *International Practices*, edited by Pouliot, Vincent and Adler, Emanuel (pp. 231–254). New York: Cambridge University Press.

Newman, Edward. 2009. "'Liberal' Peacebuilding Debates," in *New Perspectives on Liberal Peacebuilding*, edited by Newman, Edward, Paris, Roland and Richmond, Oliver (pp. 26–53). New York: United Nations University Press.

Newman, Edward, Paris, Roland, and Richmond, Oliver. (eds.). 2009. *New Perspectives on Liberal Peacebuilding*. New York: United Nations University Press.

Nohria, Nitin, Groysberg, Boris, and Lee, Linda-Eling. 2008. "Employee Motivation: A Powerful New Model." *Harvard Business Review* 86 (7): 78–84.

Oberg, Kalervo. 1960. "Culture Shock: Adjustment to New Cultural Environments." *Practical Anthropology* (7): 177–182.

Onuf, Nicholas. 1998. "Constructivism: A User's Manual," in *International Relations in a Constructed World*, edited by Kubalkova, Vendulka, Onuf, Nicholas and Kowert, Paul (pp. 58–78). Armonk, NY: M. E. Sharpe.

Orford, Anne. 2003. *Reading Humanitarian Interventions*. Cambridge: Cambridge University Press.

Ottaway, Marina. 2002. "Rebuilding State Institutions in Collapsed States." *Development and Change* 33 (5): 1001–1023.

Ottaway, Marina. 2003. "Promoting Democracy after Conflict: The Difficult Choices." *International Studies Perspectives* 4 (3): 314–322.

Owen, Roger. 2004. *State, Power and Politics in the Making of the Modern Middle East*. New York: Routledge.

Oxfam. 2010. *Les Femmes et les Enfants d'Abord: Sur la Ligne de Front aux Kivus*. Oxford, UK.

Padesky, Christine. 1994. "Schema Change Processes in Cognitive Therapy." *Clinical Psychology and Psychotherapy* 1 (5): 267–278.

Paffenholz, Thania. 2010. *Civil Society and Peacebuilding: A Critical Assessment*. Boulder, CO: Lynne Rienner Publishers.

Paffenholz, Thania and Spurk, Christoph. 2006. *Civil Society, Civic Engagement, and Peacebuilding*. Social Development Paper 36. Washington, DC: World Bank.

Papadakis, Yiannis. 1997. "Pyla: A Mixed Borderline Village under UN Supervision in Cyprus." *International Journal on Minority and Group Rights* 4 (3–4): 353–372.

Paris, Roland. 2002. "International Peacebuilding and the 'Mission Civilisatrice.'" *Review of International Studies* 28 (4): 637–656.

Paris, Roland. 2003. "Peacekeeping and the Constraints of Global Culture." *European Journal of International Relations* 9 (3): 441–473.

Paris, Roland. 2004. *At War's End: Building Peace after Civil Conflict*. Cambridge: Cambridge University Press.

Paris, Roland. 2010. "Saving Liberal Peacebuilding." *Review of International Studies* 36 (2): 337–365.

Paris, Roland. 2011. "Critiques of Liberal Peace," in *A Liberal Peace? The Problems and Practices of Peacebuilding*, edited by Campbell, Susanna, Chandler, David and Sabaratnam, Meera (pp. 31–54). London: Zed Books.

Paris, Roland. 2013. "Afghanistan: What Went Wrong?" *Perspectives on Politics* 11 (2): 538–548.

Paris, Roland. In progress. *The Role of Governance Schemas in Foreign-Imposed Regime Change*. Unpublished manuscript, University of Ottawa.

Paris, Roland and Sisk, Timothy D. 2009. *The Dilemmas of Statebuilding: Confronting the Contradictions of Postwar Peace Operations*. London: Routledge.

Patterson, Molly and Monroe, Kristen Renwick. 1998. "Narrative in Political Science." *Annual Review of Political Science* 1: 315–331.

Peacekeeping Best Practices Section. 2008. *United Nations Peacekeeping Operations: Principles and Guidelines*. New York: Division of Policy, Evaluation and Training, Department of Peacekeeping Operations, UN Secretariat.

Peen Rodt, Annemarie. 2011. "The African Mission in Burundi: The Successful Management of Violent Ethno-Political Conflict." *Ethnopolitics Papers* 10, Exeter: University of Exeter.

Peou, Sorpong. 2012. "Violence in Post-War Cambodia," in *The Peace in Between: Post-War Violence and Peacebuilding*, edited by Suhrke, Astri and Berdal, Mats (pp. 192–210). New York: Routledge.

Pérouse De Montclos, Marc-Antoine. 2012. "Les ONG et la Mesure du Développement: Entre Performance et Communication." Paper presented at Colloque GEMDEV UNESCO Mesure du Développement, Paris, February 1–3.

Perrot, Sandrine. 2010. "Northern Uganda: A Forgotten Conflict, Again? The Impact of the Internationalization of the Resolution Process," in *The Lord's Resistance Army: Myth and Reality*, edited by Allen, Tim and Vlassenroot, Koen (pp. 187–204). London: Zed Books.

Peterson, Roger. 2011. *Western Intervention in the Balkans: The Strategic Use of Emotion in Conflict*. New York: Cambridge University Press.

Petraeus, David H. 2006. *Counterinsurgency*. Washington, DC: Headquarters – Department of the Army.

Pham, Phuong, Vinck, Patrick, Sokhom, Hean, and Stover, Eric. 2009. *So We Will Never Forget: A Population-Based Survey on Attitudes About Social Reconstruction and the Extraordinary Chambers in the Courts of Cambodia*. Human Rights Center, University of California, Berkeley.

Pham, Phuong, Vinck, Patrick, Wierda, Marieke, Stover, Eric, and di Giovanni, Adrian. 2005. *Forgotten Voices: A Population-Based Survey of Attitudes About Peace and Justice in Northern Uganda*. Human rights center, University of California, Berkeley / International Center for Transitional Justice.

Pisani, Elizabeth. 2008. *The Wisdom of Whores: Bureaucrats, Brothels, and the Business of AIDS*. New York: W. W. Norton & Co.

Pole Institute. 2011a. *DRC: The Mineral Curse*. Regards Croisés. Goma.

Pole Institute. 2011b. *The North Kivu Mining Sector: Report on the Reopening of the Mines*. Goma.

Polkinghorn, Brian, La Chance, Haleigh, and La Chance, Robert. 2008. "Constructing a Baseline Understanding of Developmental Trends in Graduate Conflict Resolution Programs in the United States," in *Pushing the Boundaries: New Frontiers in Conflict Resolution and Collaboration,* edited by Fleishman, Rachel, Gerard, Catherine, and O'Leary, Rosemary (pp.233–265). Bingley: Emerald Group Publishing Limited.

Porter, Sam. 1994. "New Nursing: The Road to Freedom?" *Journal of Advanced Nursing* 20 (2): 269–274.

Porter, Theodore M. 1995. *Trust in Numbers: The Pursuit of Objectivity in Science and Public Life*. Princeton, NJ: Princeton University Press.

Posner, Daniel N. 2005. *Institutions and Ethnic Politics in Africa*. New York: Cambridge University Press.

Pottier, Johan. 2002. *Re-Imagining Rwanda: Conflict, Survival and Disinformation in the Late Twentieth Century*. Cambridge: Cambridge University Press.

Pouligny, Béatrice. 1999. "Peacekeepers and Local Social Actors: The Need for Dynamic, Cross-Cultural Analysis." *Global Governance* 5 (4): 403–424.

Pouligny, Béatrice. 2004. *Ils Nous Avaient Promis la Paix: Opérations de L'ONU et Populations Locales*. Paris: Presses de la Fondation Nationale des Sciences Politiques.

Pouliot, Vincent. 2007. "'Sobjectivism': Toward a Constructivist Methodology." *International Studies Quarterly* 51 (2): 359–384.

Pouliot, Vincent. 2008. "The Logic of Practicality: A Theory of Practice of Security Communities." *International Organization* 62 (2): 257–288.

Pouliot, Vincent. 2010. *International Security in Practice: The Politics of NATO-Russia Diplomacy*. New York: Cambridge University Press.

Pouliot, Vincent and Adler, Emanuel. 2011a. "International Practices." *International Theory* 3 (1): 1–36.

Pouliot, Vincent and Adler, Emanuel (eds.). 2011b. *International Practices*. New York: Cambridge University Press.

Prendergast, John. 1996. *Frontline Diplomacy: Humanitarian Aid and Conflict in Africa*. Boulder, CO: Lynne Rienner.

Prendergast, John and Plumb, Emily. 2002. "Building Local Capacity: From Implementation to Peace Building," in *Ending Civil Wars: The Implementation of Peace Agreements*, edited by Stedman, Stephen John, Rothchild, Donald and Cousens, Elizabeth M. (pp. 237–349). London: Lynne Rienner.

Pritchett, Lant, Woolcock, Michael, and Andrews, Matt. 2010. *Capability Traps? The Mechanisms of Persistent Implementation Failure*. Washington, DC: Center for Global Development.

Prunier, Gérard. 1995. *The Rwanda Crisis: History of a Genocide*. New York: Columbia University Press.

Prunier, Gérard. 2008. *Africa's World War: Congo, the Rwandan Genocide, and the Making of a Continental Catastrophe*. Oxford: Oxford University Press.

Pugh, Michael. 2004. "Peacekeeping and Critical Theory." *International Peacekeeping* 11 (1): 39–58.

Pugh, Michael. 2005. "The Political Economy of Peacebuilding: A Critical Theory Perspective." *International Journal of Peace Studies* 10 (2): 23–42.

Rafaeli, Eshkol, Bernstein, David P., and Young, Jeffrey E. 2011. *Schema Therapy: Distinctive Features*. New York: Routledge.

Rajak, Dinah and Stirrat, Jock. 2011. "Parochial Cosmopolitanism and the Power of Nostalgia," in *Adventures in Aidland: The Anthropology of Professionals in Inter-national Development*, edited by Mosse, David (pp. 161–176). Oxford: Berghahn Books.

Rajasingham, Darani. 2005. "Sri Lanka and the Violence of Reconstruction." *Development* 48 (3): 111–120.

Rao, Vijayendra and Woolcock, Michael. 2004. "Integrating Qualitative and Quantitative Approaches in Program Evaluation," in *The Impact of Economic Policies on Poverty and Income Distribution: Evaluation Techniques and Tools*, edited by Bourguignon, Francois and Pereira Da Silva, Luiz (pp. 165–190). New York: World Bank and Oxford University Press.

Razack, Sherene. 2004. *Dark Threats and White Knights: The Somalia Affair, Peacekeeping and the New Imperialism*. Toronto: University of Toronto Press.

Rehn, Elisabeth and Johnson Sirleaf, Ellen. 2002. *Women, War and Peace: The Independent Experts' Assessment on the Impact of Armed Conflict on Women and Women's Role in Peace-Building*. Progress of the World's Women. New York: UN Women Headquarters.

Reno, William. 1998. *Warlord Politics and African States*. Boulder, CO: Lynne Rienner.

Reychler, Luc. 2006. "Challenges of Peace Research." *International Journal of Peace Studies* 11 (1): 1–16.

Reyntjens, Filip. 2009. *The Great African War: Congo and Regional Geopolitics, 1996–2006*. New York: Cambridge University Press.

Richards, Paul. 2005. "To Fight or to Farm? Agrarian Dimensions of the Mano River Conflicts (Liberia and Sierra Leone)." *African Affairs* 104 (417): 571–590.

Richmond, Oliver. 2002. *Maintaining Order, Making Peace*. New York: Palgrave.

Richmond, Oliver. 2005. *The Transformation of Peace*. New York: Palgrave Macmillan.

Richmond, Oliver. 2009. "The Romanticisation of the Local: Welfare, Culture and Peacebuilding." *The International Spectator* 44 (1): 149–169.

Richmond, Oliver. 2011. *A Post-Liberal Peace*. London: Routledge.

Richmond, Oliver. 2012. "Beyond Local Ownership in the Architecture of International Peacebuilding." *Ethnopolitics* 11 (4): 354–375.

Richmond, Oliver and Franks, Jason. 2009. *Liberal Peace Transitions: Between Statebuilding and Peacebuilding*. Edinburgh: Edinburgh University Press.

Richmond, Oliver and Mitchell, Audra. 2011. *Hybrid Forms of Peace: From Everyday Agency to Post-Liberalism*. New York: Palgrave.

Rieff, David. 1995. "The Humanitarian Trap." *World Policy Journal* 12 (4): 1–11.

Rieff, David. 2002. *A Bed for the Night: Humanitarianism in Crisis*. New York: Simon & Schuster.

Riordan, Christine M. and Griffeth, Rodger W. 1995. "The Opportunity for Friendship in the Workplace: An Underexplored Construct." *Journal of Business and Psychology* 10 (2): 141–154.

Roeder, Philip and Rothchild, Donald. 2005. *Sustainable Peace: Power and Democracy after Civil Wars*. Ithaca, NY: Cornell University Press.

Roth, Silke. 2011. "Dealing with Danger: Risk and Security in the Everyday Lives of Aid Workers," in *Inside the Everyday Lives of Development Workers: The Challenges and Futures of Aidland*, edited by Fechter, Anne-Meike and Hindman, Heather (pp. 151–158). Sterling, VA: Kumarian Press.

Rotmann, Philipp, Tohn, David, and Wharton, Jaron. 2009. *Learning under Fire: The US Military, Dissent and Organizational Learning Post-9/11*. Belfer Center Student Paper Series #09-04. Cambridge, MA: Belfer Center for Science and International Affairs, Harvard Kennedy School.

Rubin, Herbert J. and Rubin, Irene S. 1995. *Qualitative Interviewing: The Art of Hearing Data*. Thousand Oaks, CA: Sage.

Rubinstein, Robert A. 2008. *Peacekeeping under Fire: Culture and Intervention*. Boulder, CO: Paradigm Publishers.

Sageman, Marc. 2008. *Leaderless Jihad: Terror Networks in the Twenty-First Century*. Philadelphia: University of Pennsylvania Press.

Sageman, Marc and Hoffman, Bruce. 2008. "Does Osama Still Call the Shots? Debating the Containment of Al Qaeda's Leadership." *Foreign Affairs* 87 (4): 163–166.

Said, Edward W. 1978. *Orientalism*. New York: Pantheon Books.

Salem, Paul. 1997. "A Critique of Western Conflict Resolution from a Non-Western Perspective," in *Conflict Resolution in the Arab World: Selected Essays*, edited by Salem, Paul (pp. 11–24). Beirut, Lebanon: American University of Beirut.

Samset, Ingrid. 2011. "Building a Repressive Peace: The Case of Post-Genocide Rwanda." *Journal of Intervention and Statebuilding* 5 (3): 265–283.

Samset, Ingrid. 2012. "Sexual Violence: The Case of Eastern Congo," in *The Peace in Between: Post-War Violence and Peacebuilding*, edited by Suhrke, Astri and Berdal, Mats (pp. 229–247). New York: Routledge.

Sanghera, Gurchathen, Henry, Marsha, and Higate, Paul. 2008. *Peacekeepers as New Men? Security and Masculinity in the United Nations Mission in Liberia.* Working Paper No. 02–08. Bristol: Centre for Governance and International Affairs, University of Bristol.

Sappington, David E.M. 1991. "Incentives in Principal-Agent Relationships." *The Journal of Economic Perspectives* 5 (2): 45–66.

Save the Children-UK. 2006. *From Camp to Community: Liberia Study on Exploitation of Children.* Monrovia, Liberia: Save the Children-UK.

Save the Children-UK and UNHCR. 2002. *Sexual Violence & Exploitation: The Experience of Refugee Children in Guinea, Liberia and Sierra Leone.* Save the Children-UK and UNHCR.

Sawyer, Edward. 2008. "Remove or Reform? A Case for (Restructuring) Chiefdom Governance in Post-Conflict Sierra Leone." *African Affairs* 107 (418): 387–403.

Scambary, James. 2014. When the Personal Becomes Political: Informal Security Groups and the Dynamics of Communal Conflict in East Timor. Ph.D. diss., Australian National University, Canberra.

Schaefer, Christoph Daniel. 2010. "Local Practices and Normative Frameworks in Peacebuilding." *International Peacekeeping* 17 (4): 499–514.

Schatz, Edward. 2009. *Political Ethnography: What Immersion Contributes to the Study of Power.* Chicago: University of Chicago Press.

Schatzki, Theodore R., Knorr-Cetina, Karin, and von Savigny, Eike. 2001. *The Practice Turn in Contemporary Theory.* London: Routledge.

Schirch, Lisa. 2005. *Ritual and Symbol in Peacebuilding.* Bloomfield, CT: Kumarian Press.

Schwartz-Shea, Peregrine and Yanow, Dvora. 2012. *Interpretive Research Design: Concepts and Processes.* New York: Routledge.

Scott, James C. 1985. *Weapons of the Weak: Everyday Forms of Peasant Resistance.* New Haven: Yale University Press.

Scott, James C. 1998. *Seeing Like a State: How Certain Schemes to Improve the Human Condition Have Failed.* New Haven, CT: Yale University Press.

Scott, James C. 2009. *The Art of Not Being Governed: An Anarchist History of Upland Southeast Asia.* New Haven: Yale University Press.

Seay, Laura. 2011. "Whither Civil Society? Local Peace Building and the International Community." *African Security Review* 20 (2): 73–79.

Seay, Laura. 2012. *What's Wrong with Dodd-Frank 1502? Conflict Minerals, Civilian Livelihoods, and the Unintended Consequences of Western Advocacy.* Working Paper 284. Washington, DC: Center for Global Development.

Sen, Amartya. 2006. *Identity and Violence: The Illusion of Destiny.* New York: W. W. Norton & Company.

Sending, Ole Jacob. 2009. *Why Peacebuilders Fail to Secure Ownership and Be Sensitive to Context.* Security in Practice Working Paper Series 1. Oslo: NUPI.

Sending, Ole Jacob. 2010a. *Professionalization of Peace Operations: Causes, Dynamics and Effects.* Security in Practice Working Paper Series 10. Oslo: NUPI.

Sending, Ole Jacob (ed.). 2010b. *Learning to Build a Sustainable Peace: Ownership and Everyday Peacebuilding.* CMI Report R 2010:4. Bergen: Chr. Michelsen Institute.

Sending, Ole Jacob. 2011. "The Effect of Peacebuilding: Sovereignty, Patronage and Power," in *A Liberal Peace? The Problems and Practices of Peacebuilding*, edited by

Campbell, Susanna, Chandler, David and Sabaratnam, Meera (pp. 55–66). London: Zed Books.

Seybolt, Taylor. 1996. "The Myth of Neutrality." *Peace Review* 8 (4): 521–527.

Shaw, Ibrahim Seaga. 2007. "Historical Frames and the Politics of Humanitarian Intervention: From Ethiopia, Somalia to Rwanda." *Globalisation, Societies and Education* 5 (3): 351–371.

Shaw, Rosalind, Waldorf, Lars, and Hazan, Pierre. (eds.). 2010. *Localizing Transitional Justice: Interventions and Priorities after Mass Violence*. Stanford, CA: Stanford University Press.

Sherman, Jake. 2008. "Afghanistan: Nationally Led Statebuilding," in *Building States to Build Peace*, edited by Call, Charles and Wyeth, Vanessa (pp. 303–334). Boulder, CO: Lynne Rienner Publishers.

Simm, Gabrielle. 2013. *Sex in Peace Operations*. London: Cambridge University Press.

Simons, Claudia and Zanker, Franzisca. 2012. "Questioning the Local in Peacebuilding." Paper presented at the New Frontiers of Peacebuilding Conference, Manchester.

Sion, Liora. 2008. "Peacekeeping and the Gender Regime: Dutch Female Peacekeepers in Bosnia and Kosovo." *Journal of Contemporary Ethnography* 37 (5): 561–585.

Skjelsbaek, Kjell. 1990. "UN Peacekeeping: Expectations, Limitations and Results – Forty Years of Mixed Experience," in *The United Nations and Peacekeeping*, edited by Rikhye, Indar Jit and Skjelsbaek, Kjell (pp. 52–68). Basingstoke: Macmillan.

Slim, Hugo. 1996. "The Stretcher and the Drum: Civil-Military Relations in Peace Support Operations." *International Peacekeeping* 3 (2): 130–139.

Smillie, Ian. 2001. *Patronage or Partnership: Local Capacity Building in Humanitarian Crises*. Sterling, VA: Kumarian Press.

Smirl, Lisa. 2008. "Building the Other, Constructing Ourselves: Spatial Dimensions of International Humanitarian Response." *International Political Sociology* 2 (3): 236–253.

Smirl, Lisa. 2012. "The State We Are(n't) in: Liminal Subjectivity in Aid Worker Auto-Biographies," in *Statebuilding and State-Formation: The Political Sociology of Intervention*, edited by Bliesemann De Guevara, Berit (pp. 230–245). London: Routledge.

Smith, Dan. 2004. *Towards a Strategic Framework for Peacebuilding: Getting Their Act Together. Overview Report of the Joint Utstein Study of Peacebuilding*. Oslo: Royal Norwegian Ministry of Foreign Affairs.

Smith, Linda Tuhiwai. 2012. *Decolonizing Methodologies: Research and Indigenous Peoples*. London: Zed Books.

Snyder, Jack L. 2000. *From Voting to Violence: Democratization and Nationalist Conflict*. New York: Norton.

Solhjell, Randi. 2010. "Soldiers without a Cause? Explaining Violence by the FARDC in the Congo." Paper presented at the Annual Meeting of the African Studies Association Conference. Washington, DC.

Sørbø, Gunnar. 2010. "Local Violence and International Intervention in Sudan." *Review of African Political Economy* 37 (124): 173–186.

Sotomayor Velázquez, Arturo C. 2010. "Why Some States Participate in UN Peace Missions While Others Do Not: An Analysis of Civil-Military Relations and Its Effects on Latin America's Contributions to Peacekeeping Operations." *Security Studies* 19 (1): 160–195.

Stachowiak, Sarah. 2007. *Pathways for Change: 6 Theories About How Policy Change Happens*. Seattle, WA: Organizational Research Services.

Staniland, Paul. 2012. "States, Insurgents, and Wartime Political Orders." *Perspective on Politics* 10 (2): 243–264.

Stearns, Jason. 2011. *Dancing in the Glory of Monsters: The Collapse of the Congo and the Great War of Africa*. New York: PublicAffairs.

Stedman, Stephen John. 1991. *Peacemaking in Civil War: International Mediation in Zimbabwe, 1974–1980*. Boulder, CO: Lynne Rienner.

Stedman, Stephen John. 1997. "Spoiler Problems in Peace Processes." *International Security* 22 (2): 5–53.

Stedman, Stephen John. 2002. "Introduction," in *Ending Civil Wars: The Implementation of Peace Agreements*, edited by Stedman, Stephen John, Rothchild, Donald and Cousens, Elizabeth M. (pp. 1–40). London: Lynne Rienner.

Stedman, Stephen John, Rothchild, Donald S., and Cousens, Elizabeth M. 2002. *Ending Civil Wars: The Implementation of Peace Agreements*. Boulder, CO: Lynne Rienner.

Stewart, Keith G. 2006. *Mission Command: Elasticity, Equilibrium, Culture, and Intent*. Technical report. Toronto: Defence Research and Development Canada.

Stewart, Rory. 2007. *The Prince of the Marshes – and Other Occupational Hazards of a Year in Iraq*. Orlando: Harcourt, Inc.

Stiglitz, Joseph. 2003. "Democratizing the International Monetary Fund and the World Bank: Governance and Accountability." *Governance* 16 (1): 111–139.

Storr, Jim. 2003. "A Command Philosophy for the Information Age: The Continuing Relevance of Mission Command." *Defence Studies* 3 (3): 119–129.

Straus, Scott. 2006. *The Order of Genocide: Race, Power, and War in Rwanda*. Ithaca, NY: Cornell University Press.

Suhrke, Astri. 2011. *When More Is Less: The International Project in Afghanistan*. New York: Columbia University Press.

Suhrke, Astri and Samset, Ingrid 2007. "What's in a Figure? Estimating Recurrence of Civil War." *International Peacekeeping* 14 (2): 195–203.

Sundh, Lena. 2004. "Making Peace Keeping Missions More 'Prevention Aware'." Paper presented at Stockholm International Forum 2004: Preventing Genocide, Stockholm, Sweden.

Sunstein, Cass R. 1997. *Free Markets and Social Justice*. New York: Oxford University Press.

Swidler, Ann. 1986. "Culture in Action: Symbols and Strategies." *American Sociological Review* 51 (2): 273–286.

Swidler, Ann. 2001. "What Anchors Cultural Practices," in *The Practice Turn in Contemporary Theory*, edited by Schatzki, Theodore R., Knorr-Cetina, Karin and von Savigny, Eike (pp. 74–92). London: Routledge.

Système Intégré Des Nations Unies. 2010. *Stratégie Internationale de Soutien à la Sécurité et à la Stabilité de l'Est de la RDC (ISSSS) – Cadre Programmatique Intégré (IPF) 2009–2010*. Goma: United Nations.

Tadjbakhsh, Shahrbanou. 2011. *Rethinking the Liberal Peace: External Models and Local Alternatives*. London: Routledge.

Tajfel, Henry. 1974. "Social Identity and Intergroup Behaviour." *Social Science Information* 13 (2): 65–93.

Talentino, Andrea Kathryn. 2007. "Perceptions of Peacebuilding: The Dynamic of Imposer and Imposed Upon." *International Studies Perspectives* 8 (2): 152–171.

Taub, Amanda (ed.). 2012. *Beyond Kony2012: Atrocity, Awareness, and Activism in the Internet Age.* E-book: https://leanpub.com/beyondkony2012.

Terlinden, Ulf and Debiel, Tobias. 2004. "Deceptive Hope for Peace? The Horn of Africa between Crisis Diplomacy and Obstacles to Development." *Peace, Conflict and Development* (4): 1–20.

Terry, Fiona. 2002. *Condemned to Repeat? The Paradox of Humanitarian Action.* Ithaca: Cornell University Press.

The Sphere Project. 2011. *Humanitarian Charter and Minimum Standards in Humanitarian Response.* Rugby, UK: Practical Action Publishing.

Titeca, Kristof and de Herdt, Tom. 2011. "Real Governance Beyond the 'Failed State': Negotiating Education in the Democratic Republic of the Congo." *African Affairs* 110 (439): 213–231.

Tomforde, Maren. 2005. "Motivation and Self-Image among German Peacekeepers." *International Peacekeeping* 12 (4): 576–585.

Toshiya, Hoshino and Konishi, Weston S. 2012. *U.S.-Japan Peacebuilding Cooperation: Roles and Recommendations toward a Whole-of-Alliance Approach.* Joint compendium report. Tokyo: The Institute for Foreign Policy Analysis and the Osaka School of International Public Policy.

Touval, Saadia and Zartman, I. William. 1985. *International Mediation in Theory and Practice.* Boulder: Westview Press.

Transparency International. 2010. *Corruption Perceptions Index.* Berlin: Transparency International.

Trefon, Théodore. 2011. *Congo Masquerade: The Political Culture of Aid Inefficiency and Reform Failure.* London: Zed Books.

Tull, Denis and Mehler, Andreas. 2005. "The Hidden Costs of Power-Sharing: Reproducing Insurgent Violence in Africa." *African Affairs* 104 (416): 375–398.

Turner, Ralph. 1962. "Role-Taking: Process Versus Conformity," in *Human Behavior and Social Processes*, edited by Rose, Arnold (pp. 20–40). Boston: Houghton Mifflin.

Turner, Thomas. 2007. *The Congo Wars: Conflict, Myth and Reality.* New York: Palgrave Macmillan.

Tversky, Amos and Kahneman, Daniel. 1981. "The Framing of Decisions and the Psychology of Choice." *Science* 211 (4481): 453–458.

UN Democracy Fund. 2006. *United Nations Democracy Fund Project Proposal Guidelines Second Round.* New York.

UN Democracy Fund. 2007. *United Nations Democracy Fund Branding and Visibility Guidelines.* New York.

UN Department of Peacekeeping Operations – Department of Field Support. 2012. *Civil Affairs Handbook.* New York: United Nations.

UN Department of Peacekeeping Operations – Peacekeeping Best Practices Unit. 2003. *Handbook on United Nations Multidimensional Peacekeeping.* United Nations.

UN General Assembly. 2005. *Report to the UN General Assembly: A Comprehensive Strategy to Eliminate Future Sexual Exploitation and Abuse in United Nations Peacekeeping Operations.* New York: United Nations.

UN General Assembly. 2007. *Peacekeeping Best Practices: Report of the Secretary-General.* New York: United Nations.

UN General Assembly. 2009. *Report of the Secretary-General on Peacebuilding in the Immediate Aftermath of Conflict*. New York: United Nations.

UN Human Rights Council. 2011. *Third Joint Report of Seven United Nations Experts on the Situation in the Democratic Republic of the Congo*. New York: United Nations.

UN Integrated System. 2009. *International Security and Stabilization Support Strategy (I-SSSS)*. Integrated Program Framework 2009–2012, Democratic Republic of Congo. Goma: United Nations.

UN Panel of Inquiry. 2001–2003. *Reports of the Panel of Experts on the Illegal Exploitation of Natural Resources and Other Forms of Wealth of the Democratic Republic of the Congo*. New York: United Nations.

UN Peacebuilding Support Office. 2012. *United Nations Peacebuilding Support Office (PBSO) Strategy 2012–2013*. New York: United Nations.

UN Security Council. 2001. *No Exit without Strategy: Security Council Decision-Making and the Closure or Transition of United Nations Peacekeeping Operations*. New York: United Nations.

UN Security Council. 2004a. *Report of the Secretary-General on the Rule of Law and Transitional Justice in Conflict and Post-Conflict Societies*. New York: United Nations.

UN Security Council. 2004b. *Third Special Report of the Secretary-General on the United Nations Mission in the Democratic Republic of Congo*. New York: United Nations.

UN Security Council. 2010a. *Final Report of the Group of Experts Submitted through the Security Council Committee Established Pursuant to Resolution 1533 (2004) Concerning the Democratic Republic of the Congo*. New York: United Nations.

UN Security Council. 2010b. *Report of the Secretary-General on the United Nations Organization Stabilization Mission in the Democratic Republic of the Congo*. New York: United Nations.

UN Security Council. 2010c. *Resolution 1925 (2010)*. New York: United Nations.

UN Security Council. 2011. *Final Report of the Group of Experts Submitted through the Security Council Committee Established Pursuant to Resolution 1533 (2004) Concerning the Democratic Republic of the Congo*. New York: United Nations.

United States Agency for International Development – Office of United States Foreign Disaster Assistance. 2008. *Guidelines for Unsolicited Proposals and Reporting*. Washington, DC.

United States Department of State, Overseas Security Advisory Council (OSAC), Bureau of Diplomatic Security. 2012. *Burundi 2012 OSAC Crime and Safety Report*. OSAC Report. Washington, DC.

Uvin, Peter. 1998. *Aiding Violence: The Development Enterprise in Rwanda*. West Hartford, CT: Kumarian Press.

Verbruggen, Didier, Francq, Evie, and Cuvelier, Jeroen. 2011. *Guide to Current Mining Reforms Initiatives in Eastern DRC*. Antwerp: IPIS.

Verma, Ritu. 2011. "Intercultural Encounters, Colonial Continuities and Contemporary Disconnects in Rural Aid," in *Inside the Everyday Lives of Development Workers. The Challenges and Futures of Aidland*, edited by Fechter, Anne-Meike and Hindman, Heather (pp. 59–82). Sterling, VA: Kumarian Press.

Vinck, Patrick, Pham, Phuong, Baldo, Suliman, and Shigekane, Rachel. 2008. *Living with Fear: A Population-Based Survey on Attitudes about Peace, Justice, and Social Reconstruction in Eastern Democratic Republic of Congo*. Human Rights Center, University of California, Berkeley; Payson Center for International Development, Tulane University; International Center for Transitional Justice.

Vlassenroot, Koen and Raeymaekers, Timothy. 2004. *Conflict and Social Transformation in Eastern D.R. Congo.* Gent: Academia Press Scientific Publishers.

Vlassenroot, Koen, Schomerus, Mareike, and Allen, Tim. 2012. "Kony 2012 and the Prospects for Change: Examining the Viral Campaign." *Foreign Affairs* March.

Vogelaar, Ad L. W. and Kramer, Eric-Hans. 2004. "Mission Command in Dutch Peace Support Missions." *Armed Forces & Society* 30 (3): 409–431.

Walter, Barbara F. 2002. *Committing to Peace: The Successful Settlement of Civil Wars.* Princeton, NJ: Princeton University Press.

Walzer, Michael. 1977. *Just and Unjust Wars: A Moral Argument with Historical Illustrations.* New York: Basic Books.

Warters, William. 2008. "Graduate Studies in Dispute Resolution: A Delphi Study of the Field's Present and Future." *Online Journal of Peace and Conflict Resolution* 2 (2): 1–12.

Weaver, Catherine. 2008. *Hypocrisy Trap: The World Bank and the Poverty of Reform.* Princeton, NJ: Princeton University Press.

Wedel, Janine R. 1998. *Collision and Collusion: The Strange Case of Western Aid to Eastern Europe, 1989–1998.* New York: St. Martin's Press.

Wehr, Paul and Lederach, John Paul. 1991. "Mediating Conflict in Central America." *Journal of Peace Research* 28 (1): 85–98.

Weick, Karl E. 1995. *Sensemaking in Organizations.* Thousand Oaks, CA: Sage Publications.

Weinstein, Jeremy M. 2005. *Autonomous Recovery and International Intervention in Comparative Perspective.* Working Paper Number 57. Washington, DC: Center for Global Development.

Weiss, Thomas. 1999. "Principles, Politics, and Humanitarian Action." *Ethics and International Affairs* 13 (1): 1–22.

Weller, Marc. 1998. "The Relativity of Humanitarian Neutrality and Impartiality." *The Journal of Humanitarian Assistance* February 28.

Wenar, Leif. 2006. "Accountability in International Development Aid." *Ethics & International Affairs* 20 (1): 1–23.

Wendt, Alexander E. 1987. "The Agent-Structure Problem in International Relations Theory." *International Organization* 41 (3): 335–370.

Wendt, Alexander E. 1992. "Anarchy Is What States Make of It: The Social Construction of Power Politics." *International Organizations* 46 (2): 391–425.

Wendt, Alexander E. 1999. *Social Theory of International Politics.* Cambridge: Cambridge University Press.

Wenger, Etienne. 1998. *Communities of Practice: Learning, Meaning, and Identity.* Cambridge: Cambridge University Press.

Werker, Eric and Ahmed, Faisal Z. 2008. "What Do Nongovernmental Organizations Do?" *The Journal of Economic Perspectives* 22 (2): 73–92.

Wheeler, Nicholas J. 2000. *Saving Strangers: Humanitarian Intervention in International Society.* Oxford: Oxford University Press.

Whitworth, Sandra. 2004. *Men, Militarism and UN Peacekeeping: A Gendered Analysis.* Boulder, CO: Lynne Rienner.

Wilén, Nina 2009. "Capacity-Building or Capacity-Taking? Legitimizing Concepts in Peace and Development Operations." *International Peacekeeping* 16 (3): 337–351.

Wilson, Timothy D., Lindsey, Samuel, and Schooler, Tonya Y. 2000. "A Model of Dual Attitudes." *Psychological Review,* 107(1): 101–126.

Winslow, Donna. 1997. *The Canadian Airborne Regiment in Somalia: A Socio-Cultural Inquiry*. Ottawa: Commission of Inquiry into the Deployment of Canadian Forces to Somalia.

Winslow, Donna. 1998. "Misplaced Loyalties: The Role of Military Culture in the Breakdown of Discipline During Peace Operations." *Canadian Review of Sociology and Anthropology* 35 (3): 345–368.

Winslow, Donna. 2002. "Strange Bedfellows: NGOs and the Military in Humanitarian Crises." *International Journal of Peace Studies* 7 (2): 35–54.

Woodward, Susan. 1995. *Balkan Tragedy: Chaos and Dissolution after the Cold War*. Washington, DC: Brookings Institution.

Woodward, Susan. 1997. "Violence-Prone Area or International Transition? Adding the Role of Outsiders in Balkan Violence," in *Violence and Subjectivity*, edited by Veena Das, Arthur Kleinman, Mamphela Ramphele, and Pamela Reynolds. (pp. 19–45). Berkeley: University of California Press.

Woodward, Susan. 2003. "In Whose Interest Is Security Sector Reform? Lessons from the Balkans," in *Governing Insecurity: Democratic Control of Military and Security Establishments in Transitional Democracies*, edited by Cawthra, Gavin and Luckham, Robin (pp. 276–302). London: Zed Books.

Woodward, Susan. 2007. "Do the Root Causes of Civil War Matter? On Using Knowledge to Improve Peacebuilding Interventions." *Journal of Intervention and Statebuilding* 1 (2): 143–170.

Yilmaz, Muzaffer Ercan. 2006. "Resolving Internal Conflicts in the Post-Cold War Era: Is Peacekeeping Enough?" *Journal of Economic and Social Research* 8 (2): 27–43.

Young, Crawford and Turner, Thomas. 1985. *The Rise and Decline of the Zairian State*. Madison, WI: University of Wisconsin Press.

Youngs, Richard. 2004. "Democratic Institution-Building and Conflict Resolution: Emerging EU Approaches." *International Peacekeeping* 11 (3): 526–543.

Zartman, I. William. 1989. *Ripe for Resolution: Conflict and Intervention in Africa*. New York: Oxford University Press.

Zartman, I. William and Rasmussen, J. Lewis. 1997. *Peacemaking in International Conflict: Methods and Techniques*. Washington, DC: United States Institute of Peace Press.

Zartman, I. William and Touval, Saadia. 1996. "International Mediation in the Post–Cold War Era," in *Managing Global Chaos*, edited by Crocker, Chester, Hampson, Fen and Aall, Pamela (pp. 445–461). Washington, DC: United States Institute of Peace Press.

Zelizer, Craig and Rubinstein, Robert A. 2009. *Building Peace: Practical Reflections from the Field*. Sterling, VA: Kumarian Press.

Zürcher, Christoph. 2011. "Building Democracy While Building Peace." *Journal of Democracy* 22 (1): 81–95.

Index